Motivation
and Society

*A Volume in Honor
of David C. McClelland*

Abigail J. Stewart
Editor

✤ ✤ ✤

Motivation
and Society

 Jossey-Bass Publishers

San Francisco • Washington • London • 1982

MOTIVATION AND SOCIETY
A Volume in Honor of David C. McClelland
  by Abigail J. Stewart, Editor

Copyright © 1982 by: Jossey-Bass Inc., Publishers
                       433 California Street
                       San Francisco, California 94104
                                &
                       Jossey-Bass Limited
                       28 Banner Street
                       London EC1Y 8QE

Library of Congress Cataloging in Publication Data
Main entry under title:

Motivation and society.

   "Chronological bibliography of David C.
McClelland": p. 344
      Includes indexes.
      1. McClelland, David Clarence—Addresses, essays,
lectures. 2. Motivation (Psychology)—Social
aspects—Addresses, essays, lectures. 3. Motivation
(Psychology)—Testing—Addresses, essays, lectures.
I. McClelland, David Clarence. II. Stewart,
Abigail J.
BF504.M67   153.8   81-48666
ISBN 0-87589-526-3   AACR2

Manufactured in the United States of America

JACKET DESIGN BY WILLI BAUM

FIRST EDITION

Code 8213

The Jossey-Bass
Social and Behavioral Science Series

Preface

This book was written in honor of David C. McClelland. It includes several different kinds of attempts to articulate and illuminate aspects of his vision and his example. The range of topics covered by the three sections of the book—achievement, power, affiliation, intimacy and competence in individuals and social institutions—is evidence of the extraordinary breadth and vitality of David McClelland's career as scholar and teacher. Taken together, these chapters reflect the contributions to psychology and to the social sciences generally of the human motivation research tradition initiated by McClelland and continuing today to animate research and practice at many universities in many countries.

We have begun with a narrative of McClelland's career. This intellectual biography describes his research activities and identifies the enduring style and content features of his work. It is illustrated with photographs of important events and activities in his life.

These pictures were chosen with the help of Mary McClelland. We regret deeply that she did not live to see our collective product.

In the main body of the book, former students and present colleagues have written chapters examining key facets of McClelland's research approach. These chapters were written for those psychologists and students interested in research on motivation and personality, in application of research findings, and in interdisciplinary scholarship. The authors discuss important issues and lively topics in contemporary psychology. In Part One, John W. Atkinson, Richard deCharms, and Jacqueline Fleming discuss philosophical and methodological bases of scientific psychology. In Part Two, Joseph Veroff, Dan P. McAdams, Abigail J. Stewart, and Nia Lane Chester present empirical research on key social motives. In Part Three, Richard E. Boyatzis and David G. Winter discuss the role of motives in work and politics, while Elliot Aronson, Heinz Heckhausen, and Siegbert Krug discuss efforts to change motives and society. Following the main body of the book are McClelland's own reflections on his work (and that of his students) and a chronological bibliography documenting that work.

In the course of preparing this volume, former students and colleagues of McClelland were invited to recall some critical event in their association with McClelland. Eventually twenty-six "reminiscences" were generated, and they were collected by Robert Birney. A "thematic analysis" of those accounts indicated that three major themes pervaded the memories. Nearly three quarters of those writing recalled incidents in which McClelland performed feats of *intellectual daring*. His creative virtuosity, interpretive insight, and capacity for integrative synthesis were singled out and captured in anecdote more often than any other quality.

A similarly large number of raconteurs (60 percent) reported occasions when McClelland expressed and exemplified *lack of concern with orthodoxy*. This lack of concern ranged from indifference to the mainstream to vigorous iconoclasm. In any case, many recall the strength of McClelland's commitment to the truth in terms of his utter contempt for mere authority or convention.

Finally, nearly two thirds of those who wrote recalled McClelland's mentoring as *enabling their own autonomy*. Perhaps McClelland's iconoclasm and devotion to ideas are most fully reflected in his determination that his students and colleagues study motivation and society—among other things—in their own fashion.

All of the chapters in this book should be taken as intended: as homage to what was learned and valued and as original contributions to the continuing effort to understand human motivation and society.

Boston, Massachusetts   Abigail J. Stewart
March 1982

Contents

Contents

Contributors

Abigail J. Stewart is assistant professor and associate chair of psychology at Boston University. Following receipt of her A.B. degree in psychology from Wesleyan University (1971) and her M.Sc. degree in social psychology from the London School of Economics (1972), she went to Harvard University, where she worked with David McClelland on methods for assessing the efficacy of liberal arts education, on power motivation in women, and on the study of women's life patterns. After completing her Ph.D. degree in 1975, she joined the personality program at Boston University. While on leave from Boston University, she served as director of the Henry A. Murray Research Center of Radcliffe College (1978–1980). Her major research interest is the study of individual adaptation to life change and social change. She has focused especially on the consequences of personal and social changes for women.

Elliot Aronson is professor of psychology at the University of California, Santa Cruz.

John W. Atkinson is professor of psychology at the University of Michigan, Ann Arbor.

Richard E. Boyatzis is president of McBer and Company, Boston, Massachusetts.

Nia Lane Chester is a research associate in the Department of Psychology at Boston University.

Richard deCharms is professor of psychology and education at Washington University in St. Louis.

Jacqueline Fleming is a research scientist at Barnard College.

Heinz Heckhausen is professor of psychology at the Ruhr-Universität in Bochum, West Germany.

Siegbert Krug is a research scientist at the Ruhr-Universität in Bochum, West Germany.

Dan P. McAdams is assistant professor of psychology at Loyola University of Chicago.

Joseph Veroff is professor of psychology and faculty associate (Institute for Social Research) at the University of Michigan, Ann Arbor.

David G. Winter is professor of psychology at Wesleyan University.

David C. McClelland: An Intellectual Biography

 *David G. Winter*

In the spring of 1941, after only two years of doctoral level study, David C. McClelland completed his dissertation on "Studies in Serial Verbal Discrimination Learning—An Experimental Analysis of the Retention of Responses to Right and Wrong Words," and was awarded the Ph.D. in psychology by Yale University. Thus ended an energetic and rigorous training in scientific psychology that had begun six years before under the inspiration of John Alexander McGeoch at Wesleyan, continued with a Master's degree supervised by Arthur W. Melton (a McGeoch colleague) at Missouri, and culminated in the Yale research under the guidance of Carl Hovland.

Over the next two years, McClelland published his dissertation as a series of four major articles in the *Journal of Experimental Psychology* and added three other scientific publications (one that was still being anthologized twenty-five years later)—thus giving every promise of a vigorous and productive career in the quantitative, deductive, experimental psychology he had learned so well.

Within eight years, however, McClelland had moved in a completely new direction. With a group of undergraduates and Master's candidates at Wesleyan (later described by a reviewer as the "Wesleyan group"), McClelland had published several papers on measuring the achievement motive through content analysis of thematic apperception. Shortly thereafter, this research appeared as *The Achievement Motive* (McClelland, Atkinson, Clark, and Lowell, 1953), a work that, together with his 1951 text on personality (McClelland, 1951), established his enduring reputation in the field as an innovative theorist and researcher on projective methods, motivation, and personality.

Several years later, another change was apparent: David McClelland had begun to explore the social consequences of achievement motivation, as shown by his contribution to the Nebraska Symposium on Motivation (1955). Fully developed later as *The Achieving Society* (McClelland, 1961), McClelland's thesis of a relationship between *n* Achievement and economic development, documented at both the social and the individual levels, established his broader reputation in the social sciences. As well, the book is a landmark of interdisciplinary scholarship: in 438 pages of text, the reader encounters analyses of KLM air passenger mileage, the designs of ancient Peruvian ceramic pottery, statistics of coal imports at London from 1600–1833, and of course the motives and values expressed in the world's largest sample of children's readers. All of this is presented in a theoretical framework that includes Weber, Toynbee, Sorokin, Parsons, and Marx, among others.

Yet the book was not published before McClelland began to study how behavior changes—a line of research that led him to revise much of his earlier theory about the origins of human motives. As one student of applied economic development commented: "When I first met David McClelland in 1957, he told me that a person's achievement motivation was pretty well set by the time they were seven. When I met him four years later, he said that

Right: David McClelland, age 7-8 (ca. 1925). Courtesy of Mary McClelland.

Center: David McClelland (center front) and Mary McClelland (on his right), assistant directors for the American Friends' Service Committee, of the Sky Youth Hostel for Jewish refugees (Nyack, N.Y.) in 1940. Courtesy of Mary McClelland.

Bottom: John W. Atkinson, David C. McClelland, Russell A. Clark, and Edward L. Lowell at Yelping Hill, Connecticut, in the summer of 1950, working on *The Achievement Motive.* Courtesy of John W. Atkinson.

he was designing courses to raise achievement motivation in adult businessmen. What happened?" These achievement motivation development courses, in India and elsewhere, were the foundation of *Motivating Economic Achievement* (McClelland and Winter, 1969); but they also led McClelland to establish an enduring institution. The Human Resources Development Corporation, originally set up in 1963, went through many corporate trials and tribulations to emerge as McBer and Company, a Boston-based management research, training, and consulting firm. As both Chairman of the Board and an active participant in ongoing McBer work, McClelland has continued to explore the ways that psychology can be of use in practical human affairs and institutions. In recent years, this work has especially focused on the identification, measurement, and development of competence (McClelland, 1973), and on the evaluation of the effects of higher education (Winter, McClelland, and Stewart, 1981).

About a decade after the achievement motivation training had begun, however, David McClelland turned to the study of power and power motivation. Several doctoral theses on *n* Power seemed to provide the key to understanding the experience and motivational aspects of male social drinking, enabling McClelland to bring together elusive results of several previous studies in *The Drinking Man* (McClelland, Davis, Kalin, and Wanner, 1972). Yet this work was only an introduction to power. A few years later, McClelland's elucidation of the power motive in all its manifestations, combinations, and permutations provided new ways of understanding the farthest reaches of power: in men and women, in religious visions, and in historical cycles of war and peace. At the same time, the pages of *Power: The Inner Experience* (McClelland, 1975) reveal a breadth of literary style appropriate to the breadth of its conceptual focus: analytic dissection of psychoanalytic theory and religion, complex statistical analysis of experimental data, autobiographical narrative, cross-cultural and historical reflection, and a grand synthesis ending in a reasoned plea that "the divinity in all human beings . . . makes violence against them violence against God" (p. 359).

Once again, however, McClelland's studies of power motivation soon led him to change and to exciting discoveries in yet another new area—the relationship of psychogenic motives to phy-

David McClelland, serving as a subject in the Master's thesis research of Ralph Norman Haber, in Judd Hall at Wesleyan University, in the spring of 1954. Courtesy of Ralph Norman Haber.

siological functioning, especially with respect to the body's immune systems and thus sickness and health. The initial article (McClelland, 1979) demonstrated several connections between stressed power motivation and cardiovascular functioning. Several subsequent studies have illuminated intervening links involving catecholamine secretion, immunoglobin levels, white cell counts, and natural killer cell activity, as well as extending the connections to the frequency and severity of infectious illnesses.

As this volume is written, David McClelland is entering his fifth decade of extraordinary scholarly productivity, having evolved through five major (and numerous minor) traditions and styles of research. Yet what is past is also always present—much as in the Hindu teaching that we are the accumulated karma of our previous incarnations. Sometimes this is evident in David McClelland's work in a specific sense: for example, the early achievement motive arousal studies drew on prior work by McClelland and others (McClelland and Apicella, 1945, 1947; Sears, 1937) on the effects of experimentally induced failure and success. The concurrent general conception of a motive as "the redintegration by a cue of a change in an affective situation" (McClelland, Atkinson, Clark, and Lowell, 1953, p. 28) seems closely related to an earlier conception as the "reaction to a future stimulus," proposed by McClelland in 1938 in the final chapter of his Wesleyan psychology honors thesis on "Theories of Memory." In the midst of the *n* Achievement work, he also published a study of secondary reward in animals. One of his most recent studies links power motivation and physiological functioning back to verbal learning.

In a broader and more general sense, however, all these major shifts of emphasis reflect several deeper, enduring traits of personal and scientific style. Even the restless seeking of change and the commitment to broad intellectual values are obvious continuities from McClelland's earlier preprofessional life. By age 18, he had made a decisive geographic change from a small town in southern Illinois to the Boston-Philadelphia corridor, and a few years later he had converted from his inherited Methodism to become a devout Quaker. The emphasis on learning and the intellect, originally instilled by the teaching and examples of his grandfather, uncle, and father, found early expression in his first publication—an analysis of a chess problem—published in the *American Chess Bulletin* in 1932, when he was fourteen. Later he spent a year as a special student, studying languages, before entering Wesleyan, where he submitted high distinction honors theses in both psychology and sociology.

Beyond these continuities of intellect and change itself, David McClelland's four decades of research and teaching have been marked by three other enduring traits—elements that, taken together, are the hallmarks of the "McClelland style." First, the changing course of David McClelland's research shows a *keen sensitivity to his surroundings*, an ability to adapt and use ideas, research results, his own life events, and even his apparent failures. As a result, many major and minor events in McClelland's surroundings became the sources of later major changes and innovations in his thinking and research.

Like many young college faculty during World War II, David McClelland found himself assigned to teach unfamiliar subjects—in his case, personality, at Bryn Mawr College, in 1944–45. Like most professors in such situations, he kept one step ahead of the class at the time; but in characteristic McClelland fashion, he reworked and extended his notes until they had become a systematic textbook. Determined to apply his experimental training to the clarification of some key concepts of ambiguous and "connotative" personality theories, he then designed a series of experiments to "try to collect evidence in support (or contradiction) of the clues which Murray suggests should be used in diagnosing the existence of needs from projections" (McClelland and Atkinson, 1948, p. 206). These studies of the achievement motive became the first major innovation in his research.

Attempts to establish achievement motivation training courses in developing countries met with several obstacles and failures: first in 1963, when the United States Agency for International Development canceled a large-scale contract, and again in 1965, when the Ford Foundation drastically reduced the scope of training already underway in Hyderabad, India. After making alternative arrangements to salvage what was left, McClelland continued to ponder the causes of such seemingly arbitrary institutional behavior. In the final discussion of the Indian training, he turned to Parsonian theory (itself a legacy of his sabbatical year at Harvard in 1949–50) to explain these problems in terms of the clash of institutional functions (McClelland and Winter, Chapter 12). Concluding from this experience that raising achievement issues in real-life settings often aroused power issues, he then turned to the study of the power motive directly. Partly out of failure, then, McClelland began a new line of research that has continued down to the present, ranging from psychophysiology to war and peace.

A second enduring feature of David McClelland's scholarship is a *balance between simplicity and complexity*. For reasons of practicality, he had early proposed to simplify the scoring system for the Bernreuter Personality Inventory by discarding elaborate weightings and simply counting each item as -1, 0, or 1 (1944). (This decision is supported, interestingly enough, in recent discussions about the importance of weighted and unweighted regression coefficients.) Later he argued the case for simple measures in stronger and more general terms (1957b, pp. 375–376):

> It is precisely because the judge synthesizes many unknown factors in his judgment, that the estimate he makes, no matter how precise or quantitative it may be, is practically useless as

David McClelland (left) and David Berlew, with several Indian businessmen at a palmyra fiber company in Kakinada, India, in the spring of 1965. Courtesy of Mary McClelland.

David McClelland teaching a graduate seminar at Harvard, spring 1965. Courtesy of Harvard University News Office.

far as the development of basic science is concerned. . . . A simple count of frequency at least gives us an objective measure of
something which is not a hopeless mixture of a variety of
unknown cues to which the judge is responding, plus a variety
of personal and cultural factors influencing his judgment. We
accept the fact that such a measure is insensitive because it does
not represent a synthesis of cues, just as a physicist accepts the
fact that the thermometer reading is insensitive [to humidity,
etc.]. In short, personality psychology would be a lot better off if
psychologists would throw away their rating scales for intensity
of variables and would stick to classifying and counting.

The *n* Achievement scoring system was of course an extension of this principle: rather than making a complex rating of overall achievement strivings, scorers were instructed to code each of
several separate TAT stories for the mere presence or absence of
motive imagery and several subcategories, each according to carefully defined and described criteria. The simplification principle has
also been used to advantage in creating dependent variables, especially when the performances and outcomes of people in very different life situations are to be compared. In evaluating the effects of
achievement motivation training, for example, how could an unusual pay increase for one man be put on the same scale with a new

David and Mary McClelland with Manohar and Shalini Nadkarni in India.
Courtesy of Mary McClelland.

David McClelland with Daniel Goleman at Anuradhapura in
Sri Lanka. Courtesy of Mary McClelland.

Dinner at the McClellands' home with Buckminster Fuller, in 1977.
Courtesy of Mary McClelland.

business started by another who was in a very different life situation? McClelland's solution was to group different kinds of business activities into four categories of approximately comparable outcomes (1965; McClelland and Winter, 1969, pp. 81 and 211). Using a variety of sources of information (questionnaire data about economic performance, personal interviews, and information from colleagues or superiors), each individual was then placed in the appropriate category. While the four categories were labelled –1, 0, 1, and 2, in the final analyses the first three categories of this four-point "scale" were combined to yield a simple (and characteristic) "present/absent" dichotomy. McClelland later used the same approach in developing a measure of "early career success" that could be applied to college graduates in several different occupations (Winter, McClelland, and Stewart, 1981, p. 90).

While stressing simplification of measures, however, David McClelland's work also emphasizes the complexity of relationships among measures. Often this complexity results from considering the joint effects of a large number of different variables, drawn, typically, from different "levels" of personality or even different disciplines (McClelland, 1981). Sometimes this complexity mirrors highly contingent relationships among variables (McClelland, Davis, Kalin, and Wanner, 1972). Perhaps the simplicity-incomplexity aspect of McClelland's style appears most exquisitely in

David McClelland's palm being read by Jacqueline Fleming on the occasion of his birthday party at Harvard, in 1974. Courtesy of David G. Winter.

the overall integrative syntheses which (as figures or flow charts) typically conclude a major investigation—for example, of the structure of an individual personality (1951, p. 591), of the psychosocial substrate of economic development (1961, p. 438), or of the motivational dynamics underlying historical cycles of social reform and war (1975, p. 347). These figures often resemble the diagrams used to represent complex, cyclical physiological processes (such as the Krebs Cycle). Perhaps McClelland's strong interest in physiology during his college years helped to establish this feature of his later style. (His undergraduate psychology honors thesis, it should be noted, concludes with a pentagonal flow chart relating consciousness, motivation, drive, adience-avoidance, memory, retention, and direct experience all to behavior.) In many respects then, as is clear from his own account, McClelland has always taken physiology, rather than physics, as the appropriate scientific model for psychology.

The final enduring feature of the McClelland style can be described as an *earnest yet sometimes almost playful challenge to orthodoxy.* He himself has called this the "David versus Goliath" theme—an identification with the underdog and a challenge to institutional authority, all expressed in terms of advancing the dominion of the science of psychology in order to shape and improve human affairs. Often in the preface to a book, McClelland deliberately minimized his own preparation for the task ahead. Introducing his personality text, McClelland first listed some sixteen skills or experiences that "a psychologist ought to know before he ventures to speak with any authority about personality." Then he went on to add casually (1951, pp. xi–xii):

> Certainly I do not qualify as an expert in any of the fields mentioned. I have never been psychoanalyzed, never been to a Rorschach Institute, cannot properly interpret a Thematic Apperception Test [*sic!*], space "mhms" correctly in a nondirective interview, deduce a theorem from Hull's postulates, or ask a Navaho informant about his sex life. But perhaps all this is what qualifies me to write this book.

Characteristically, he began a major prescriptive essay on the methodology of personality research with the deprecating sentence, "What follows then might be described as a kind of naive description of what a scientist interested in human nature thinks and does

David McClelland working at McBer and Company, Boston, in 1980. Courtesy of Richard Boyatzis, McBer and Company.

when he is acting like a scientist" (1957b, p. 357). In preparing for "battle" with the "giants" of history and economics, he disarmingly says of himself (1961, pp. vii–viii): "I had unfortunately managed to escape all courses in history. . . . In fact, I had dropped my one course in college economics because it seemed to me such an abstract, rationalistic discipline. . . ." In the next sentence, however, the challenge becomes unmistakably clear: "So, having little formal training in economics, I did not accept so easily, as most economists do by habit, the long tradition of using index numbers and estimates of national income in fixed prices. This traditional method seemed to be so objectionable that I adopted a different approach."

Often the sense of challenge emerges from the sheer range of fields to which McClelland brings explanatory psychological methods, data, and generalizations. The new research on motives and physiological functioning, as (in part) a challenge to medical orthodoxy, is only the most recent example. In many respects, his 1964 collection of papers (*The Roots of Consciousness*) is a tour de force of this genre, for it offers motivational interpretations and explanations of Freud and Hull, economic growth, Germany, the United States, France, André Gide, psychoanalysis, religion, scientists, and women!

Finally, when fused with McClelland's enduring social concerns, the challenge is clearly stated. In 1957, for example, McClelland described himself as "determined to be tough-minded about tender-minded problems (like personality) and to bring order and measurement to the understanding of human motivation without losing all the subtleties of the phenomena" (1957a, p. 177). In discussing achievement motivation training and the power of scientific evidence to bring about self-understanding, he concluded (McClelland and Winter, 1969, pp. 377-378):

> If man's confidence in himself derived from his former conviction that he was created, looked after, and guided by an all-powerful God, where will it come from now that in popular terminology, "God is dead"? . . . Scientific knowledge is the new God, the new source of man's conviction that he has the competence to act.

His recent study of war ends with an even bolder call (1975, pp. 358-359):

> So, to prevent Armageddon, we must formally swear off violence as an instrument of collective policy. What the psychological data suggest is that on every church or temple a label should be struck that reads: "Warning: Christianity (or Judaism, Islam, Buddhism, Hinduism, or Marxism) is dangerous for children and other living things; if you enter here you must renounce violence as an instrument of collective policy."

Sensitive to events, ideas, and surroundings; simple and yet complex; disarmingly stating challenges to orthodoxies; constantly changing yet always imbued with the love of learning—how can David McClelland's intellectual life and contributions to date be summed up? Perhaps by the words of the Biblical historian about the deeds of the other David:

> Saul made havoc among thousands
> but David among tens of thousands. (I Samuel 18: 7-8)

References

McClelland, D. C. "Simplified Scoring of the Bernreuter Personality Inventory." *Journal of Applied Psychology*, 1944, *28*, 414–419.

McClelland, D. C. *Personality*. New York: William Sloane Associates, 1951.

McClelland, D. C. "Some Social Consequences of Achievement Motivation." In M. R. Jones (Ed.), *Nebraska Symposium on Motivation: 1955*. Lincoln: University of Nebraska Press, 1955.

McClelland, D. C. "Conscience and the Will Rediscovered." Review of *Wille und Leistung*, by K. Mierke. *Contemporary Psychology*, 1957a, *2*, 177–179.

McClelland, D. C. "Toward a Science of Personality Psychology." In H. P. David and H. von Bracken (Eds.), *Perspectives in Personality Theory*. New York: Basic Books, 1957b.

McClelland, D. C. *The Achieving Society*. New York: Van Nostrand, 1961.

McClelland, D. C. *The Roots of Consciousness*. New York: Van Nostrand, 1964.

McClelland, D. C. "Toward a Theory of Motive Acquisition." *American Psychologist*, 1965, *20*, 321–333.

McClelland, D. C. "Testing for Competence Rather than for 'Intelligence.'" *American Psychologist*, 1973, *28*, 1–14.

McClelland, D. C. *Power: The Inner Experience*. New York: Irvington, 1975.

McClelland, D. C. "Inhibited Power Motivation and High Blood Pressure in Men." *Journal of Abnormal Psychology*, 1979, *88*, 182–190.

McClelland, D. C. "Is Personality Consistent?" In A. I. Rubin, J. Aronoff, A. M. Barclay, and R. A. Zucker (Eds.), *Further Explorations in Personality*. New York: Wiley, 1981.

McClelland, D. C., and Apicella, F. S. "A Functional Classification of Verbal Reactions to Experimentally Induced Failure." *Journal of Abnormal and Social Psychology*, 1945, *40*, 376–390.

McClelland, D. C., and Apicella, F. S. "Reminiscence Following Experimentally Induced Failure." *Journal of Experimental Psychology*, 1947, *37*, 159–169.

McClelland, D. C., and Atkinson, J. W. "The Projective Expression of Needs. I: The Effect of Different Intensities of the Hunger Drive on Perception." *Journal of Psychology,* 1948, *25,* 205-222.

McClelland, D. C., Atkinson, J. W., Clark, R. A., and Lowell, E. L. *The Achievement Motive.* New York: Appleton-Century-Crofts, 1953.

McClelland, D. C., Davis, W. N., Kalin, R., and Wanner, E. *The Drinking Man: Alcohol and Human Motivation.* New York: Free Press, 1972.

McClelland, D. C., and Winter, D. G. *Motivating Economic Achievement.* New York: Free Press, 1969.

Sears, R. R. "Initiation of the Repression Sequence by Experienced Failure." *Journal of Experimental Psychology,* 1937, *20,* 570-580.

Winter, D. G., McClelland, D. C., and Stewart, A. J. *A New Case for the Liberal Arts: Assessing Institutional Goals and Student Development.* San Francisco: Jossey-Bass, 1981.

Motivation
and Society

*A Volume in Honor
of David C. McClelland*

Part I
Measuring Motives in Individuals

The approach to measuring motives introduced by McClelland has stimulated a great deal of empirical research over the past thirty years. It has also stimulated a number of important critiques. These three chapters present different approaches to conceptualizing and resolving the problems involved in the measurement of motives. Each chapter develops and elaborates aspects of McClelland's basic approach—collecting and coding "thought samples." Atkinson discusses the implications of the "theory of action" and computer simulation for understanding observed psychometric properties of TAT-based motive scores. DeCharms spells out the conceptual importance and implications of McCllelland's approach to measurement. Fleming proposes some practical convergences between McClelland's projective approach and traditional psychometric

1

approaches to measuring motives. Taken together, the three chapters provide some perspective on the meaning of McClelland's original choices of a measurement strategy, some rationale for continued commitment to that strategy, and some solutions to the problems associated with it.

Motivational Determinants of Thematic Apperception

1

   *John W. Atkinson*

Thematic apperceptive measurement of motivation now has a solid conceptual foundation, something it lacked when David McClelland led the vanguard in establishing its validity (McClelland, Atkinson, Clark, and Lowell, 1953). A new theory of motivation (Atkinson and Birch, 1970, 1974, 1978) has overcome the conceptual limitations of both statistical test theory and traditional motivational theories by emphasizing the temporal continuity of behavior and its underlying motivational structure. I will show how old puzzles about thematic apperception have been resolved and the old vision of its promise reawakened by reconsidering the method within the new theoretical framework.

This chapter was written during my term as a visiting fellow at the Educational Research Center of the University of Leyden, in 1980. My sincere thanks are extended to its director, Hans Crombag, for making it possible for me to study and to interact with others in a context so close to my present theoretical interests.

Skepticism about the scientific worth of this projective method has been sustained by two arguments. One is the criticism that the Thematic Apperception Test (TAT) n Achievement (need for achievement) score lacks acceptable reliability when one considers the lack of internal consistency among scores obtained from one story and the next in the set from which an individual's total n Achievement score is obtained (Entwisle, 1972). Reliability is considered the sine qua non of validity according to the presumptions of test theory. The other argument derives from the inherent complexity of the relationship between the strength of a motive and its behavioral expression, something about which we became very much aware in the course of developing the theory of achievement motivation (Atkinson and Feather, 1966; Atkinson and Raynor, 1974, 1978). To observers not committed to resolving the puzzle of the motivation of behavior, the symptoms of the complexity of the problem are mistakenly treated as no more than a bewildering set of inconsistencies that violate an unquestioned presumption. One should expect consistency in different behavioral expressions of anything considered a stable personality trait. Given our present theoretical perspective, we can see that the first issue is really an instance of the second. So in focusing on the critical issue of test reliability in the discussion that follows, I speak to both.

According to the logic of traditional test theory, each behavioral incident (such as the successive stories in a Thematic Apperception Test) is treated as a discrete and independent incident in the life of an individual. It is gratuitously presumed that individual differences in some temporally stable and transituational personality trait (for example, the achievement motive) imply comparable temporal and transituational consistencies in behavior. All this can be summed up in the simple expression, obtained score = true score ± random error, where the true score (or expected behavior) corresponding to a particular strength of motive is presumed to be constant in each of the successive stories of a Thematic Apperception Test. Substantial variability in the obtained scores is then attributed to substantial random error of measurement.

In contrast, the principles of the dynamics of action, to which we shortly turn, were introduced to explain variable behavior, a simple change from one activity to another even in a constant environment (Atkinson and Birch, 1970). When applied to the question of what is expected in the successive stories of a Thematic Apperception Test, the new theory of motivation specifies how a *stable* personality disposition, strength of achievement motive, is expected to be expressed behaviorally in systematically *variable* amounts of time thinking and/or writing about achievement in successive stories even before consideration of the question of random error in measurement. That, simply put, is why the new motivational principles have provided a coherent explanation of how it is possible for the test as a whole to have construct validity without reliability as traditionally defined. Computer simulations of thematic apperceptive measurement of achievement motivation based on the new principles have shown that the expected amount of time an individual spends imagining achieving during the whole temporal period of a four- to six-story test can provide a valid measure of the strength of the motive being expressed without test reliability as it is conventionally defined (Atkinson, Bongort, and Price, 1977). The more important outcome of this work has been to expose flaws in the foundation of classical test theory, long taken for granted as something akin to a settled creed (Atkinson, 1981).

The point of computer simulation of a motivational problem is simple enough. It is to apply the relatively simple principles of the theory of motivation to antecedent conditions that are too complex to think about without the deductive capacity of the computer. Thus, for example, we may ask the question: How much time should these thirty individuals who differ in strength of achievement motive spend thinking about achievement in response to each picture in this set of six pictures? The program applies the principles of the dynamics of action to deduce the systematic changes in the motivational state of each hypothetical subject and, in so doing, to spell out precise behavioral implications for each subject. The results may then be treated as equivalent to data collected using a perfectly reliable measuring instrument. This spells out the theoretically expected result prior to consideration of the error of measurement that one normally confronts in empirical research. In the case of computer simulations of thematic apperceptive measurement of motivation, we use the simulated results (given an advanced motivational psychology) to comprehend and interpret the results of many earlier empirical investigations.

The Dynamics of Action and Thematic Apperception

The basic concepts of the new dynamics of action (see, for example, Atkinson and Birch, 1978) can be conveyed as easily in reference to the stream of imaginative thought and behavior as to the stream of overt action. Both are characterized by continuity rather than by the discreteness of the episodes of traditional reactive psychology, and both are characterized by change.

The *kind* of activity (or *content* of the stream) changes from one to another and still another, even when a person's immediate environment is constant for a substantial period of time, as on a rainy Saturday morning at home or a sunny Sunday afternoon at the beach (Atkinson and Birch, 1978, pp. 24–26). This variability is an essential characteristic of operant or voluntary behavior. It is *emitted*, as Skinner has always argued, rather than *elicited* as a reaction to a given environment or stimulus situation. The dynamics of action is a theory of operant behavior. It *explains* the otherwise mysterious behavior-controlling influence of the immediate environment (the discriminative stimuli) in Skinner's radically empirical behaviorism.

So also does the *content* of thought change in what is otherwise a continuous stream of thought, even when the person is continuously exposed to the same immediate environment or stimulus situation. McClelland (1973) called attention to the operant character of imaginative behavior in his continuing effort to get personologists to distinguish the potential value of imaginative (operant) behavior from that of explicitly self-descriptive (respondent) behavior in measuring motives (McClelland, 1958a, 1980). In a recent scanning of William James's *Principles of Psychology* (1890), I was amazed to see how thoroughly and eloquently he had anticipated the "new" view, which stresses continuity in behavior and in the underlying structure of the motivational state, in his introspective analysis of the stream of consciousness. James wrote:*"Within each personal consciousness thought is sensibly continuous. . . .* Consciousness . . . does not appear to itself chopped up in bits. Such words as 'chain' or 'train' do not describe it fitly as it presents itself in the first instance. It is nothing jointed; it flows. A 'river' or a 'stream' are the metaphors by which it is most naturally described.

In talking of it hereafter let us call it the stream of thought, of consciousness, or of subjective life" (pp. 237–239).

But what of the "sudden *contrasts* in the quality of successive segments of the stream of thought" that James acknowledged. His reply: "The things [*contents*] are discrete and discontinuous; they do pass before us in a train or chain, making often explosive appearances and rending each other in twain. But their comings and goings and contrasts no more break the flow of the thought that thinks them than they break the time and the space in which they lie. . . . The transition between the thought of one object and the thought of another is no more a break in *thought* than a joint in a bamboo is a break in the wood" (p. 240).

The kind of stream of behavior (or of thought) that we have been generating, employing a computer program for the dynamics of action while holding both personal and situational (or environmental) influences constant, is shown in the continuous line with the various segments *x*, *y* and *z* along the top of Figure 1. This could be the observable stream of operant imaginative behavior produced in a given setting by a particular person when presented a particular picture in a Thematic Apperception Test.

Figure 1. An Example of a Stream of Overt Action or Imaginative Behavior and the Systematic Change in the Strength of Tendencies That Produced It (see text). (Adapted and extended from Seltzer, 1973)

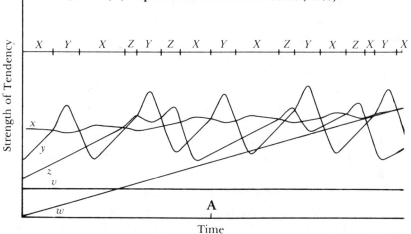

Below the observable stream of behavior, to which we apply our method of motivational content analysis, is the continuous yet systematically changing motivational state of the individual. It is composed, in this simple case, of increases and/or decreases (or mere persistence) in the strength of separate tendencies to do (or to imagine) the different hypothetical behaviors v, w, x, y, and z. The strongest among the competing tendencies is expressed in the content of the stream of behavior.

We have confidence in employing computer simulations to comprehend what is happening from moment to moment in thematic apperception because we know that the principles of the dynamics of action adequately encompass what is known about (1) the behavioral effects of previous reward and punishment in animal research and (2) the experimental facts concerning individual differences in achievement-oriented behavior (Atkinson and Birch, 1970, 1974, 1978). Furthermore, computer simulation has already been used effectively to analyze other problems: how the content of thought can motivate overt action (Birch, Atkinson, and Bongort, 1974); why the preference of persons motivated to achieve has always peaked when subjective probability of success is somewhat less than .50 rather than exactly .50 (Revelle and Michaels, 1976; Kuhl and Blankenship, 1979); the relationship between both consummatory value of success and substitution to task difficulty (Blankenship, 1979); the motivational determinants of decision time as it is influenced by the way content of thought may be implicated in deciding (Kuhl and Atkinson, 1979); and most important of all for our present discussion, the motivational determinants of allocation of time among competing alternatives in operant behavior (Atkinson and Birch, 1978, pp. 306–312, 362–366) as described in the Matching Law of de Villiers and Herrnstein (1976). In other words, the new theory and its computer program (Seltzer, 1973; Seltzer and Sawusch, 1974; Bongort, 1975) were not especially constructed to explain thematic apperceptive measurement of motivation.

The key to understanding the discussion that follows is to recognize the most fundamental difference between traditional conceptions of motivation, which define what we have called "the episodic paradigm," and the new "stream of behavior paradigm" (Atkinson and Birch, 1978, p. 375). Since the early theory of achievement motivation (Atkinson, 1957; Atkinson and Feather, 1966) was simply an application of the more general cognitive theories of Tolman, Lewin and the decision theorists to the domain of achievement-related activity, we shall refer to it to make our points. According to that theory the strength of the tendency to achieve success in a particular activity (T_s) was considered the product of the strength of motive to achieve (M_S), the strength of expectancy or subjective probability of succeeding in a given activity (P_s), and the incentive value of success of that activity (I_s), that is, $T_s = M_S \times P_s \times I_s$.

Call to mind the ring toss game. The individual is confronted with a stimulus situation defining alternative activities that differ in difficulty (P_s). The "traditional" conception said, in effect, that as soon as the individual was exposed to the ring toss game there would be elicited, *instantaneously*, a number of competing tendencies whose different strengths would remain static (as defined by the product of the three determinants) except for the kind of *random* moment-to-moment oscillations proposed by Cartwright and Festinger (1943). These "wobbling" effective tendencies would determine the individual's moment-by-moment preferences. The tendency that was expected to be strongest in its static level, according to the product of its three determinants, would probably, but not necessarily, win out in the competition for behavioral expression because of the random oscillations. The role of random oscillation both in this cognitive theory and in traditional *S-R* behavior theory (Hull, 1943) is comparable to the role of random error of measurement in classical test theory, as expressed in the simple equation, obtained score = true score ± error (de Groot, 1969). What is observed in behavior is not always quite what was expected to happen.

In the new conception, the dynamics of action, the interaction of personality (M_S) and immediate environment ($P_s \times I_s$)—a specification of what Lewin had summarized as the product of personality (P) and environment (E) in his classic equation for predicting behavior, $B = f(P,E)$—determines *the arousability* of the tendency (T_s), and not its initial and static strength. The arousability, or rate of arousal of a tendency, is represented by the different initial slopes of the curves for tendencies y, z, v, and w in Figure 1. Stable individual differences in personality (a motive) and/or the effects of the immediate environment, given previous learning experiences in that environment (as in operant conditioning), are now coordinated with the arousability of the inclination to engage in a certain kind of activity, not its expected static strength in a given setting.

Our notion is that the magnitude of *instigating force* (*F*) for a particular activity accounts for how rapidly a tendency to engage in that activity (*T*) is aroused and strengthened on a given occasion. One is *exposed* to the instigating forces of a particular situation. The other important factor is time, the duration of exposure to the instigating force (*t*). Thus, in the dynamics of action, the old idea $T_s = M_S \times P_s \times I_s$ is replaced by a new idea, $F_s = M_S \times P_s \times I_s$, for the simplest case.

Returning to Figure 1, we see that when a tendency becomes dominant (that is, becomes the strongest among simultaneously aroused and competing tendencies) it is expressed in behavior. This expression of a tendency in behavior, as in catharsis, is what reduces its strength. The *consummatory force* (*C*) of the activity depends, we think, on two factors: the nature of the activity and the strength of the tendency being expressed in that activity. We speak of the *consummatory value* of a particular activity (*c*), having in mind that the tendency to eat is reduced more rapidly by one kind of food than by eating some other kind, that succeeding reduces the tendency to achieve more than failing, and so on. We generalize this idea and presume that all activities have some consummatory value (*c*). They differ only in degree. So-called goal activities presumably have more consummatory value than so-called instrumental or preparatory activities. And, as mentioned already, we consider the strength of the tendency being expressed in the activity as the other important determinant of the consummatory force (*C*) of an activity, that is, $C = c \times T$. The instigating force (*F*) and the consummatory force (*C*) produce changes in the strength of a particular tendency (*T*).

The newest thing we have learned from empirical research guided by computer simulation is that the consummatory value of success (c_s) is greater when one succeeds at an easy task than when one succeeds at a difficult task (Blankenship, 1979). In everyday terms, this means that tendencies to achieving activities are more "turned off" or satisfied by a success when P_s at the task is .70 than when P_s at the task is .30. According to the theory of achievement motivation, the instigating forces for these two tasks—easy and difficult—are equivalent.

Given our conception that the change in the strength of a tendency depends on these two forces, one representing the effect of the stimulus situation and the other the effect of the occurrence of the activity itself, that is, $dT/dt = F - C$, and continuing to refer to Figure 1 as if it represented the stream of imaginative activity instigated by a particular picture in a Thematic Apperception Test, we have the following three implications. When $F > C$, the strength of a tendency (T) will increase. This is the case at the outset for T_y, T_z, and T_w in Figure 1. They are instigated by cues of the picture to which the individual is exposed but are not, as yet, being expressed in imaginative behavior, so $C = 0$ for each of them. When $C > F$, the strength of a tendency (T) will decrease. This is shown most clearly for T_y, shortly after activity y is initiated. Finally, when $F = C$, the strength of the tendency (T) will tend to become stable. This is the case for T_x, which is being expressed in activity x at the beginning of our interval of observation.

Given these implications, combined with our notion that $C = c \times T$, we should expect that in a given situation a particular tendency expressed in behavior will rise or fall in strength, but that sooner or later, if the activity continues, the strength of the tendency will become stable. Why? Because if $F > C$ at the outset and T increases, then C will also increase (because $C = c \times T$). Or if $C > F$ and T decreases as a result, then C will also decrease. In both cases, sooner or later $F = C$ and at a level equivalent to F/c for that activity. (The expression $C = F$ may be written $c \times T = F$, which is equivalent to $T = F/c$. A tendency, T, will increase rapidly and ultimately become stable at a high level when F is strong but will increase less rapidly and become stable at a lower level when F is weak.) This guarantees variability of behavior in a constant environment without any need to introduce the concept of random oscillation as in the traditional, episodic theories. Sooner or later some other initially subordinate tendency will become dominant, unless no other activity is instigated in a particular situation—a very unlikely prospect.

In fact, the conceptual analysis of a simple change from one activity to another *in a constant environment* is what suggested the new conception of the functional significance of exposure to "a stimulus" (that it controls the rate of arousal of a tendency and not its static level) and of the functional significance of "the response" of traditional psychology (that it influences the rate of diminution of a tendency). The logic of the principle of a simple change in activity can be simply stated in reference to the several logical possibilities shown in Figure 2 (Atkinson and Birch, 1970, Ch. 1).

A living individual is always doing something when an observer takes note. The dominant tendency (in Skinnerian terms, "inclination") is expressed in behavior. That activity A is already in progress implies that initially

$$T_{A_i} > T_{B_i},$$

where B is the next activity to occur. When, at some point in time, activity A ceases and B is finally initiated,

$$T_{B_f} > T_{A_f}.$$

Figure 2. Ways in Which a Change in the Relative Strength of Two Tendencies Can Come About During an Interval of Time in a Constant (see text). (From Atkinson and Birch, 1970, 1974, 1978)

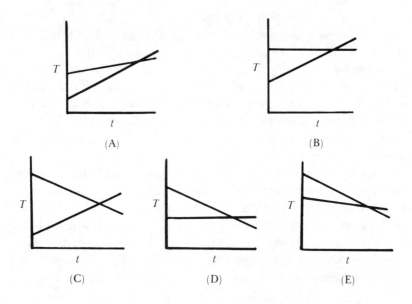

In every instance shown in Figure 2, the time (t) to change from A to B (which represents a measure of persistence of A and latency of B) is given by the simple equation

$$t = T_{A_f} - T_{B_i}/F_B.$$

All measurable aspects of behavior that reduce to the questions *which activity* will occur and *when* can be deduced from the principle of a change in activity (Birch, 1972): initiation of an activity, persistence of an activity, and choice among alternatives (as shown in the *initial* preference for y instead of z in Figure 1). To get beyond a single change in activity and to generate a stream of operant behavior, one must assume that there are temporal lags in the initiation and cessation of the full consummatory force of an activity. In addition, one is more continuously exposed to cues producing the instigating force for the dominant tendency that is motivating the ongoing activity than to cues instigating other activities instead. Being exposed to an instigating force for something less than 100 percent of the time when another activity is occurring is equivalent to being exposed continuously to an instigating force having a somewhat lower average magnitude, as shown in Figure 1. These last two concepts, consummatory lags and selective attention, allow us to deduce the additional behavioral measures that can be taken from the molar stream of operant behavior: relative frequency, operant level (or rate) of an activity, and most important for our discussion, the allocation of time among various activities—that is, the percentage of time spent expressing one tendency (as in a TAT story) instead of others.

The principle of a change in activity specifies both how variations in persisting strength of an already aroused tendency and how the rate of its arousal, attributable to direct exposure to some stimulus, jointly influence the expression of the tendency in imaginative behavior. Look again at Figure 1, and compare the fate of T_z, having greater initial strength, and T_w for an explanation of why experimental arousal of a tendency prior to a Thematic Apperception Test, as in the earliest validation studies, should then immediately influence the content of imaginative thought in response to pictures. And while considering the figure again, notice that a comparison of the slopes of T_y and of T_z provides a model for thinking about the well-documented effects of strongly cued versus weakly cued pictures on thematic content (McClelland, Atkinson, Clark, and Lowell, 1953; Atkinson, 1958a).

There is more to the dynamics of activity. Changes in activity can occur for negative as well as positive reasons. So far, in focusing on the tendency to perform an activity or *action tendency* (*T*), we have attended either to the motivational implications of prior reinforcement for some activity in a given situation or to the effect of being exposed to stimulation for some activity that has been intrinsically enjoyable in the past. But prior punishment, frustration, rejection, failure—any negative outcome of an activity in a given setting—can be the antecedent of subsequent *inhibitory force* (*I*). This would cause the arousal of a tendency *not* to do the activity, a *negaction* tendency (*N*), which would produce resistance to the activity by opposing and dampening the resultant action tendency ($\bar{T}$), which is what ultimately gets expressed in behavior. The resultant action tendency is simply represented as $\bar{T} = T - N$. One may recall the conflict between tendency to achieve (T_s) and to avoid failure (T_f) in the early theory of achievement motivation ($T_{res} = T_s - T_f$).

The conception of resistance has some interesting new implications for thematic apperception. But I will put off discussing resistance in order to simplify my discussion of why we may have validity without reliability in thematic apperception and the meaning of the *n* Achievement score. In what follows I shall refer often to Figure 1. Consider Figure 1 an illustration of what might be expected in the stream of imaginative behavior "emitted" by an individual having a stable achievement motive (M_Y) of given strength. It will be a determinant of F_y, the rate of arousal of T_y, as would any other determinant of the instigating force to achieve, for example, future orientation (Raynor, 1969, 1974). The imaginative activity *y* in the figure represents the kind of concern about competition with standards of excellence that we tried to identify and code with the manual for TAT *n* Achievement (McClelland, Atkinson, Clark, and Lowell, 1953, Ch. 4; Atkinson, 1958a, Ch. 12).

To begin with, note that T_x, T_y, T_z, and T_v are assumed already to be aroused even before individual subjects are exposed to the first picture. Here is the very basic initial premise of the dynamics taken from Freud—the wish (tendency) once aroused will persist long after the source of its instigation is gone. So our subjects are already active in two senses when we turn our attention to them. They are engaged in some activity and also actively aroused and motivated to do many other things (in this case only three) even before exposure to the first picture of our TAT. Only T_w, which begins at zero strength, reminds us of the traditional presumption that the organism is at rest, awaiting a stimulus to goad it to react. Note that T_v persists unchanged in strength throughout the whole duration of exposure to the first picture and the writing of the first imaginative story. (This particular tendency is not instigated directly during exposure and writing, nor are many others we might have introduced but at the cost of complication. Nor is T_v increased indirectly by *displacement*, or decreased indirectly by *substitution*. These are important topics we shall take up later.)

Notice that T_y is not expressed in imaginative behavior continuously. It shares the stage with other concerns, x and z, which come up from time to time. The total amount of time expressing T_y (concern over achievement) is represented by a summation of the line segments y. The percentage of time spent thinking about achievement is represented by this total time thinking about y divided by the total time spent thinking about x, y, and z, all the other activities that occurred during the interval of the first four-minute story.

In this case, the person with a certain strength of motive, considered a stable characteristic of personality (M_Y), is expected to spend about 37 percent of the total time expressing achievement-related concern in the stream of imaginative behavior. Were the index we obtain using our present scoring system equivalent to a perfect clock, the obtained n Achievement score would be proportional to this 37 percent. But put aside the possible question of inadequacies in our present technology; that is an issue, but not the vitally important issue. We have a theoretical basis for expecting the person with a stable M_Y (which is identified in the graph with F_y, the slope of the curve for T_y) to express achievement-related concern 37 percent of the time. One can imagine that if the motive (M_Y) were weaker, then the slope of the curve corresponding to F_y would be less steep than the one in the figure (more like that of z), the initial expression of y in the stream of thought would be delayed, and each occurrence would be of shorter duration and less frequent. In other words, the percentage of time thinking about achievement (y) would be less. In contrast, we can visualize the effect of a stronger motive (M_Y). The initial slope of T_y would be steeper, describing a more rapid arousal of the tendency. The latency of the initial achievement-related activity would be shorter than shown here. The absolute level of T_y when expressed would be higher, implying deeper involvement in the subject. The number of separate occurrences of y would be greater and the average duration longer. In sum, our subject with the stronger motive would spend more time thinking about achievement.

Now look again at the initial and final strengths of the competing action tendencies at the extreme left and right sides of Figure 1, respectively. At the end of the first story, and therefore at the very beginning of the second story, whatever the incentive characteristics of the second picture, T_x is stronger than it was at the beginning of the first story. So are T_z, T_y, and especially T_w. The rank order of the strengths of tendencies was T_x, T_y, T_z, T_v, T_w at the outset of the first story. But it is $T_x = T_w$, T_z, T_y, T_v when the picture for the second story is presented. So even if that second picture were *exactly equivalent* to the first one in its motivational properties (that is, if its effect were the same on the various instigating forces for v, w, x, y, z as the first picture), the content of the stream of imaginative behavior would nevertheless be different. Probably the most noticeable difference would be the early and repeated expressions of activity w, which didn't occur at all in the first story because there had been no persistent carryover from previous experiences to give T_w some initial strength for the first story.

In this hypothetical example, both determinants of the instigating forces—personal (motives) and environmental (incentives)—are presumed constant. Yet the expected imaginative behavior would be different. In other words, the assumption of stability in personality throughout the temporal interval of two successive imaginative stories does not imply an equivalent constancy in the expected behavior even if the picture stimuli were identical. This expected behavior corresponds to the *true score* in the equation of traditional test theory: obtained score (what you see and measure) = true score (what you expected to see)+random error. According to the conventional logic, individual differences in stable dispositions of personality (P) imply comparably stable and consistent differences in the expected behavior (true score). This would be observed in successive samples of behavior (tests) were it not for random error. Each test, subpart of a larger test, or item on a test, is assumed to be a discrete and independent episode in the life of a person. The variations in behavior from moment to moment are attributable to error of measurement. It is assumed to be independent from one test to the next, normally distributed, with mean zero.

The fundamental flaw in this logic is the unjustified leap from stable differences in personality to the expectation of comparably stable differences in behavior.

The very same point is easily made if one divides Figure 1 in half at point A on the abscissa, as if this point corresponded to the end of the first story and the beginning of a second story responding to an equivalent picture stimulus. The time spent thinking about y (achievement) is here *expected to be* 40 percent greater in the second story than in the first story though the personality disposition (M_Y) and the pictures influencing F_y (the arousal of T_y) have both remained constant.

Here, then, is the basis for the main theoretical conclusion from twenty-five computer simulations of thematic apperceptive measurements of individual differences in strength of motive under varied conditions: The construct validity of the total score does not require internal consistency (reliability). The computer input consisted of individual differences in strength of achievement motive for samples of eighteen to thirty hypothetical subjects for whom other determinants of the stream of imaginative behavior were held constant. Hypothetical subjects differed in strength of achievement motive, but were assumed equivalent in strength of competing motives or in the sum of the strengths of all motives. The incentive characteristics of pictures in a set of five to twelve differed, but were the same for all subjects in a given study. Certain parameters, such as selective attention, the consummatory lags at initiation and cessation of activities, and the relative magnitude of achievement versus other incentives in the pictures, were varied from one study to another so as to sample a range of conditions.

The simulated time spent thinking about achievement in each of a set of stories was treated as the n Achievement score for that story. The expected test reliability, as measured by coefficient alpha taken as an estimate of the average of all corrected split-half reliabilities for a given test (Cronbach, 1951), was computed using the simulated behaviors the way one would use the actually obtained scores in empirical research. The expected construct validity of the total time spent thinking about achievement in all the stories (the theoretically deduced n Achievement score for each hypothetical subject) was computed by correlating this simulated measure with the individual differences in strength of motive fed into the computer as input for the simulation. The expected internal consistency reliability could be as low as .07, .08, or .09 (with an errorless measuring instrument) and the construct validity of the conventional measure of individual differences in strength of motive could be as high as .90, .85, or .85, respectively. Table 1 shows why.

Table 1 shows the theoretically deduced or expected time spent expressing "concern over achievement" in response to each of five pictures for hypothetical subjects who are strong, moderate, and weak in strength of achievement motive (as defined by the computer input). These data come from one of our earliest simulations, which had produced an alpha of .08 (internal consistency reliability) and a construct validity of .85 as defined above. The personalities of the three hypothetical subjects are constant, but the expected behavior in successive stories (the true scores of traditional test theory)

Table 1. Expected Time Spent Expressing Tendency to Achieve According to Computer Simulation

Subject	Motive strength	Computer Time Units per Picture Minutes					Total
		A	B	C	D	E	
4	High (1.5)	12	8	11	24	25	80
16	Medium (1.0)	2	19	16	9	19	65
24	Low (0.5)	15	9	9	14	10	57

Source: From Atkinson, Bongort, and Price (1977, p. 13).

obviously are not. Our conclusion, succinctly stated, was this:

> The theory of motivation specifies how a *stable* personality disposition, strength of motive, will be expressed behaviorally in *variable* amounts of time spent thinking and/or writing about achievement. It tells us specifically how, under various conditions, the "truly expected" time spent expressing the tendency to achieve will vary in a sequence of consecutive incidents. . . .
>
> Basic theory about the underlying psychological process is logically prior to any application of traditional test theory. One must, in other words, have some sound theoretical basis for expecting a certain "true score" on a given test before one introduces the whole logic of test theory, which has to do with the implications of random error in the effort to measure accurately. With thematic apperception, it has been a mistake to assume that the "true score" (some [expected] behavioral manifestation) should be constant just because the strength of the underlying trait (motive) is presumed constant. One needs a theory to get from personality to something measurable, viz., behavior [Atkinson, Bongort, and Price, 1977, p. 24].

The fundamental fallacy in the application of classical test theory to the assessment of individual differences in personality is the unstated presumption that the central problem of motivation—explaining how personality is expressed in behavior—had already been solved and that the solution was a simple one. I had implicitly accepted that presumption in an early display of interest in test reliability (Atkinson, 1950) and in an earlier effort to view thematic apperceptive measurement of motives within the context of a theory of motivation (1958b). It is this long-taken-for-granted but mistaken presumption about what one should expect to observe that has sustained the argument that there are no stable, transituational differences in personality because the correlations among various behavioral manifestations of the same trait are so low (Mischel, 1968). We have tried to challenge that argument by showing how modest the *expected* correlations are among such behaviors as risk preference in a ring toss game, arithmetic performance alone in a room, a Thematic Apperception Test, and so forth in computer simulations of how individual differences in achievement motive should be expressed in a variety of behaviors and settings (Atkinson, 1980; Reuman, Atkinson, and Gallop, 1981). The essence of that argument is apparent in the expected variability from story to story in Table 1.

The point at issue in this confrontation between the "statistical" framework of traditional test theory and the "psychological" conception of motivation is to define the proper relation between the two. Are they to be viewed as alternative theories of motivation between which we must choose to move the science ahead? Or does the dynamics of action, which purports to be a general theory about the basic process of motivation, provide a basis for defining conditions under which the premises of traditional test theory should and should not hold? We have pointed out, both here and elsewhere (Atkinson, Bongort, and Price, 1977; Atkinson and Birch, 1978, p. 378), that if an individual engages in a particular activity, such as solving arithmetic problems or describing one's behavior on the typical personality inventory, for a sustained period, the strength of the tendency sustaining that kind of activity will become stable. Under these conditions, assuming constancy in the relevant personality traits, such as arithmetic ability or one's conception of self, the assumption of equivalent constancy in the expected behavioral expressions of the trait (the true scores on successive subtests) is justified. It obviously is not justified in reference to a constantly changing stream of operant behavior.

It is in the context of sustained performance of mental tests and self-descriptive tests of personality that high internal consistency is typically achieved. And in reference to thematic apperception, where there may often be very little internal consistency in the content of the stream of imaginative thought, we have found that alpha based on the number of words per story is .96. This measure refers to imaginative-verbal productivity in each of eight stories over a period of 32 minutes when the actually obtained alpha for the empirical n Achievement in those eight stories was .57 (Atkinson, Bongort, and Price, 1977, p. 25).

The Meaning of the Total TAT n Achievement Score

The most important generalization to come from the new dynamics of action supports its claim of being a theory of operant behavior. It has to do with allocation of time among competing activities in a given setting. Initially developed mathematically in reference to the simple case of two competing activities (Atkinson and Birch, 1970, pp. 101–107), it was extended to the case of multiple alternatives (Sawusch, 1974) and has since been supported by the results of computer simulations under varying conditions (Atkinson, Bongort, and Price, 1977, p. 177; Atkinson and Birch, 1978, pp. 145–146, 364–366). The generalization is stated:

$$\% \text{ time spent in activity } A = \frac{F_A/c_A}{F_A/c_A + F_B/c_B + \dots F_N/c_N}$$

where F_A, F_B, ... F_N refer to magnitudes of the instigating forces for activities A, B ... N; c_A, c_B ... c_N refer to the consummatory values of those activities, and the ratio F/c in each case refers to the asymptotic strength of the tendency T_A, T_B ... T_N, in a given setting. The latter is the level at which the strength of the tendency would become stable if the activity were to continue uninterrupted for a sustained period of time.

This theoretical generalization corresponds in form to the Matching Law in operant behavior (de Villiers and Herrnstein, 1976) according to which the relative strength of a particular response (when there are multiple alternatives) equals or matches its relative frequency of reinforcement. The consummatory values of activities in animal studies of operant conditioning, such as pressing a bar or pecking at a spot, are so similar that we assume they would cancel out in the time allocation generalization. What is left, then, is the implication that in operant behavior the magnitude of instigating force for an activity depends upon the frequency of prior reinforcement of that activity. We had already presumed this in showing how the new dynamics of action is related to the long historical development concerning the law of effect (Atkinson and Birch, 1970, Ch. 5).

The same principle applies to allocation of time among competing alternatives in the stream of operant imaginative behavior. As we proceed, recall that the earlier theory of achievement motivation (Atkinson and Feather, 1966) and its more recent elaboration by Raynor (1969, 1974) to include "future orientation" is now taken to be an hypothesis about the components or determinants of instigating force ($F_s = M_S \cdot P_s \cdot I_s$ in the simplest case). For the moment let us presume that the consummatory values of different kinds of imaginative activity (achievement, affiliation, power, and so forth) are reasonably equivalent. Assuming this, the time allocation rule may be simplified to read:

$$\% \text{ time spent in activity } A = \frac{F_A}{F_A + F_B + \ldots F_N}.$$

If we suppose that F_A represents the instigating force to achieve, F_B the instigating force for affiliation, and so on, we can consider the meaning of the thematic apperceptive n Achievement score (that is, the percentage of time spent in activity A) in a new light.

Consider an experiment in which the average strength of achievement and affiliation motives can be considered equal in two random samples of college students. Now suppose that the same Thematic Apperception Test is administered to each subject in one group in the context of working alone in a room providing only a strong incentive to achieve and to each subject in the other group in the context of working to achieve but in the presence of an audience that, presumably, provides an additional incentive for approval.

Intuition suggests that the average n Achievement score should be rather high and constant across conditions, but that the average n Affiliation score (often taken as a measure of the need for social approval in achievement settings) should increase in the audience condition. The principle of time allocation (above), which takes into account the influence of the strength of instigating force for achievement or affiliation (in the numerator) *relative to* the influence of the sum of all instigating forces produced by incentives in the situation (in the denominator) implies something different. The effect of the audience should be to increase time spent thinking about social approval (n Affiliation) but to decrease time spent thinking about achievement (n Achievement) in comparison with the alone condition. Kawamura-Reynolds (1977), employing this logic, found that the average n Achievement score decreased from 4.83 (alone) to 3.86 (audience), while the n Affiliation score increased from 2.75 (alone) to 3.36 (audience). Neither trend by itself was statistically significant, but the combined effect of both was (see also Atkinson and Birch, 1978, p. 345).

These results help to begin to concretize the interpretive problem spelled out in the principle concerning allocation of time among competing alternative activities. Time, like money, cannot be spent twice. And if the amount to spend is limited, twenty minutes for a sample of thematic apperception and twenty-four hours in a day, an increase in time allocated to one kind of activity must be accompanied by a compensatory decrease in time allotted to others.

One may consider the interpretive problem faced by Veroff, Depner, Kulka, and Douvan (1980) when confronting trends in thematic apperceptive n Achievement, n Affiliation, and n Power scores obtained from national samples in 1957 and 1976. In addition to teasing apart the personal (motive) and situational (incentive) determinants of the motivational state at a particular time, we must now be aware that time spent thinking about achievement, for example, depends also on the number and strength of competing alternatives. This conception should apply as well to "thought samples" obtained from literature in societal studies (for example, McClelland, 1955, 1958b, 1961). The new idea does not solve the problem of what to make of an increase or decrease in n Achievement for an individual, or a society, over a period of years; perhaps, by identifying the determinants, it will at least clarify the nature of the interpretive problem.

If one were to assume for simplicity that other determinants of tendencies to achieve, affiliate, gain power, and so forth produced by the test situation and pictures are reasonably equivalent among subjects engaged in thematic apperception, one might rewrite the generalization about allocation of time so that it refers only to the systematic effect of the strength of motives as determinants of differences among people in the magnitude of the various instigating forces:

$$\% \text{ time spent in activity } A = \frac{M_A}{M_A + M_B + \dots M_N}.$$

These are obviously very strong and unwarranted assumptions given the number of variables known to influence the magnitude of an instigating force (for instance, probability of obtaining the goal, incentive value of the goal, future orientation). They are made here to simplify the discussion of the new insight about the meaning of the *n* Achievement score (taken as an indicator of time spent thinking about achievement).

In the past we have rather glibly taken individual differences in *n* Achievement score to mean individual differences in absolute strength of motive to achieve. Now we can see that we are dealing with the problem of a hierarchy of motives suggested by Murray (1938) and McClelland (1951) and popularized by Maslow (1954). The measure obtained from thematic apperception should always provide a useful basis for predicting other differences in behavior that also depend upon the *relative* strength of achievement motive within an individual (initiation and persistence of achievement activities, preference for them over other kinds of activity, time spent achieving in everyday life, and so forth) but not necessarily differences in behavior that depend upon differences in *absolute* strength of motive, such as choice among achievement tasks that differ in difficulty (Hamilton, 1974; Schneider, 1978) or level of performance in an achievement task engaged in constantly for a period of time (Atkinson and Reitman, 1956). Individuals who differ greatly in absolute strength of achievement motive (in the numerator in the above equation) might, nevertheless, obtain the same thematic apperceptive *n* Achievement score if they also differed in a certain way in number and/or strength of competing motives (in the denominator). For example, the ratio $1/1+1+1$ is equivalent to $3/3+2+1+3$ is equivalent to $2/2+1+1+1+1$. All equal $1/3$ and imply spending the same percentage of time (that is, having the same *n* Achievement score for) thinking about and engaging in achievement-related activities. Yet the strengths of achievement motives are 1, 3, 2. In light of this, it is important to note that some of the repeatedly obtained empirical results (for instance, those concerning TAT *n* Achievement and risk preference or performance level) imply that variations among individuals in strength of achievement motive (numerator) must not be as highly correlated with the sum of the strengths of all of their competing motives (denominator) as suggested in the examples above.

Here is a new problem to engage the interest of psychometricians: to specify the conditions under which variations in time spent imagining achievement or engaging in achievement-related behavior can unambiguously be attributed to individual differences in the strength of that motive, or at least to the overdetermined numerator, the instigating force, in the time allocation ratio.

In the first simulation of time spent in an activity as a function of the strength of tendency to do it (the numerator, ranging randomly from 1 to 9) versus the sum of the strengths of *other* competing tendencies (ranging randomly from 3 to 27 to comprise a major part of the denominator), Sawusch (1974, p. 436) found time spent correlated .69 with strength of tendency for that activity and –.57 with the sum of the strengths of *other* competing tendencies. The correlation between these two normally distributed components of personality ($N=80$) was by design not significant, .08. In some of the computer simulations of thematic apperception described earlier, the sum of all competing tendencies *including* the tendency to achieve was held constant among the hypothetical subjects so that individual differences in strength of achievement motive would be the only possible source of variation in time spent thinking about achievement. To the extent that individuals vary substantially in the sum total of the strengths of their competing tendencies, represented in the denominator of the time allocation principle, it would seem that correlations between the strength of a particular tendency (numerator) and percentage of time expressing it in behavior should be lower. Dato de Gruijter (1980) has analyzed the problem mathematically. Assuming that the mean and variance of the strengths of several motives in a sample of persons is the same and that they are independent, the numerator in the time allocation ratio becomes more highly correlated with the overall ratio itself, as the number of the subjects' other competing motives increases. Under the assumed conditions, his analysis showed that strength of motive to achieve (M_A) in the numerator would be expected to correlate .70 with percentage of time doing A if there were only one competing motive, .82 if there were two competing motives, .86 if there were three, and around .90 or higher if there were four or more. This corroborates one result of a preliminary exploration by Virginia Blankenship (reported in Atkinson, 1980) for the special case of four independent motives, all equal in mean strength and variance. Her results also showed that strength of achievement motive (M_A) and the idealized thematic apperceptive n Achievement score, as defined by the time allocation ratio, increased to .92 when its strength was correlated −1.00 with one of the other motives. In this case, the strength of that other motive would be correlated −.92 with the idealized n Achievement score. And the correlation of M_A and idealized n Achievement score dropped to .82 when M_A was correlated +1.00 with one of the alternatives.

These early explorations, referring to very special and often idealized conditions, open up a line of inquiry that must be followed if we are to have an adequate psychometrics of measures obtained from the stream of operant imaginative behavior.

The Effect of Resistance

The theory of achievement motivation (Atkinson and Feather, 1966; Raynor, 1969, 1974) presumes that the challenge to achieve is always accompanied by the threat of failure, the other possible outcome in a test of one's competence. So let us again use the model of achievement motivation to introduce the new conception of resistance in the dynamics of action and to see how it might influence thematic apperception. I say *might* because I mean to confine this preliminary discussion to one of at least two plausible possibilities. It is the possibility that the effect of arousal of a tendency to avoid failure on the content of imaginative thought is analogous to its effect on the stream of overt instrumental achievement-related action. That is, the avoidance tendency always functions to dampen or suppress expression of the positive tendency. The other possibility, and one that is perhaps more consistent with Heckhausen's (1967) success in obtaining measures of both "hope of success" and "fear of failure" from the manifest content of thematic apperception, is that *thoughts* about succeeding and failing both are positively instigated (as in the discussion to this point), but the content of the thoughts, success versus failure, have exactly opposite motivational implications for overt action. This second possibility requires the more elaborate kind of analysis we have already undertaken, but in reference to simpler problems: cognitive control of action (Birch, Atkinson, and Bongort, 1974) and motivational determinants of decision time (Kuhl and Atkinson, 1979).

The discussion of the first alternative will provide a model that might be applied more generally to suppression of manifest sexual content in imaginative behavior (as in Clark, 1952), or of aggression, or of achievement-related content in the stories of conflicted women (see Lesser, Krawitz, and Packard, 1963; Horner, 1974).

The treatment of the arousal and expression of a tendency to avoid failure in the dynamics of action is analogous to the treatment of arousal and expression of a tendency to achieve. Corresponding to arousal of an action tendency (T) by exposure to an instigating force (F) is the arousal of a tendency not to engage in an activity, a *negaction tendency* (N), when the consequences of the activity in that situation have been negative in the past. This is attributable to exposure to an inhibitory force (I). The tendency not to do something (N), a disinclination to act, will produce resistance to the activity. It opposes, blocks, dampens; that is, it subtracts from the action tendency to determine the *resultant action tendency* $(\bar{T} = T - N)$. It is the resultant action tendency that competes with the resultant action tendencies for other, incompatible activities for expression. And now we may add a refinement to what was said earlier. It is the resultant action tendency $(\bar{T})$ that influences the consummatory force of the activity in which it is expressed, that is, $C = c \times \bar{T}$. Similarly, the resistance to an action tendency, produced by the opposition of a negaction tendency (as represented in $\bar{T} = T - N$), constitutes an analogous *force of resistance* (R), which diminishes in a comparable way the strength of the negaction tendency.

The argument by analogy, which is developed more fully elsewhere (Atkinson and Birch, 1970, 1974, 1978), explains why the suppressive negaction tendency (N) increases but eventually becomes stable in strength. In Figure 3 we see what happens when the immediate environment, and/or the picture stimulus in thematic apperception, produces both instigating and inhibitory forces for the same activity, B, to succeed $(F_{B,s})$ and to avoid failure $(I_{B,f})$. A hatched line shows arousal and linear growth of the action tendency, $T_{B,s}$ (as in the earlier Figure 2, which had ignored the problem of resistance).

Figure 3. The Dynamics of a Simple Change from an Affiliative Activity to an Achievement-Related Activity. Resistance attributable to a tendency to avoid failure (N_f) will, in time, be overcome by the tendency to achieve success (T_s) when an individual is exposed to instigating force to achieve success (F_s) and inhibitory force to avoid failure (I_f) (see text). (From Atkinson and Birch, 1978, p. 132)

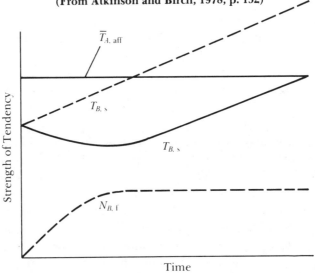

Time

Simultaneously, below, another hatched line shows the trend in the growth of the tendency *not* to engage in activity B, the negation tendency, $N_{B,f}$. As soon as N_B is aroused, it resists T_B to determine the strength of the resultant action tendency ($\bar{T}_B = T_B - N_B$) as depicted in the solid curve, $\bar{T}_B$. This process of blocking the expression of T_B—resistance—produces a force of resistance (R) analogous to the consummatory force (C) that occurs when an action tendency is expressed in action. So N_B will increase as long as $I_B > R_B$, but as N_B becomes strong and produces more resistance, R_B becomes stronger. The initial difference between I_B and R_B favoring growth of N_B diminishes. In time $R_B = I_B$, so N_B becomes stable, as shown in Figure 3.

The effect of the resistance attributable to a negation tendency is always a temporary suppression of the action tendency. It delays the initiation of activity B for a period of time. The duration of the delay, or suppression, is the amount of time the action tendency T_B would require (given the magnitude of F_B) to become strong enough to compensate for the maximum strength of N_B. This continued growth in the strength of T_B is shown in the figure. Quite obviously the "temporary delay" or suppression of activity B will be relatively short or long depending upon the magnitude of the inhibitory force, I_B, which defines the level at which the disinclination to act will stabilize.

In reference to overt achievement-related action, the dynamics of action recovers the conflict between tendencies to succeed and to avoid failure, but does not view it as static. Viewing the product of motive to avoid failure (M_F), subjective probability of failure, and incentive value of failure as now determining the magnitude of the inhibitory force to avoid failure (I_F), which defines the arousability of the negation tendency (N_F) and ultimately the level at which its strength will become stable, we have this important new implication: No matter how strong the motive to avoid failure relative to the strength of achievement motive (i.e., $M_F > M_S$), the resultant tendency to achieve success ($\bar{T}_s = T_s - N_F$) will sooner or later become dominant and be expressed in the stream of behavior.

Let us apply this idea that the negative tendency temporarily suppresses the positive tendency to the stream of imaginative behavior in thematic apperception. It implies that the conflicted person should inhibit expression of achievement-related content during the early period of a sustained stream of imaginative behavior but should begin to express it later when he has overcome the resistance. This would mean that the typical short four-story Thematic Apperception Test of n Achievement may be yielding a measure that is sensitive to individual differences in the relative strengths of motive to achieve (M_S) and motive to avoid failure (M_F) rather than only to individual differences in M_S.

To excite interest in the task of studying the various logical possibilities and complexities by the method of computer simulation, I refer to one of the intriguing results from one of our very earliest explorations of how the combination of an instigating force (F_X) and an inhibitory force (I_X) for the same activity X would influence the way subjects allocate time to that activity. The effect of an inhibitory force was to increase the latency of activity X, that is, to delay the initial occurrence of activity X in the stream of operant behavior but to increase both its frequency and the time spent in activity X once the activity had been initiated the first time in the face of resistance. The effect was most pronounced when the inhibitory force was very strong relative to the instigating force (Atkinson and Birch, 1974, 1978, pp. 64–67).

These two possible effects of an inhibitory force might combine to produce certain trends in a long Thematic Apperception Test. In the early stories of a longer set, the time spent expressing concern over achievement would favor those in whom the achievement motive was clearly dominant, $M_S > M_F$. Expression of this concern would be suppressed among those in whom $M_F > M_S$. But then as the sequence of stories continued, the previously bottled-up expression of tendency to achieve in the latter would begin, and if the test were sufficiently long, those expressing this concern latest in the test would be those who were literally most inhibited, most conflicted about it. One might therefore expect the following: the n Achievement score obtained from stories early in the test will correlate positively with some other behavioral manifestation of achievement motivation; the n Achievement scores obtained from stories in the middle of the test will not correlate with this behavioral criterion at all; and the n Achievement scores obtained from stories very late in the test will correlate negatively with this behavioral criterion.

This may explain why Reitman and Atkinson (1958) found that n Achievement scores obtained from the first four of eight stories were positively related to fourteen minutes of arithmetic performance alone in a room but scores from the last four of eight stories were not. And the effect described may explain why clinical psychologists have argued that the more significant material (given their special interest) emerges late rather than early in the standard Thematic Apperception Test.

Displacement and Substitution

Two other important motivational concepts deserve comment. Lazarus's (1961) critical arguments concerning our early use of thematic apperception helped to keep our thinking focused on the importance of the basic psychoanalytic concepts of displacement and substitution.

Displacement refers to the possibility that the arousal of one impulse might have a general effect and indirectly cause arousal of another related impulse. Substitution refers to the possibility of the same kind of interaction among tendencies but in reference to the process of consummation or diminution in the strength of a tendency. In the context of the principles of the dynamics of action, these concepts provide a theoretical basis for use of more general terms such as "achievement motive" and "tendency to achieve" in description and discussion of individual differences in personality.

In retrospect it is clear that our earliest use of the terms "achievement motive," "affiliative motive," "power motive," and the like was based on the presumption of a *basic personality structure* acquired early in life, and in part describable in terms of a limited number of general motivational dispositions that could be attributed to common life problems that arise for everyone, everywhere, in early childhood (McClelland, 1951, pp. 341–352). Later, in the initial statement of a theory of achievement motivation (Atkinson, 1957), the motive to achieve (M_S) was conceived as a relatively general and stable disposition that would (as in a ring toss game) influence the strength of a number of separate tendencies to succeed (T_s), a *family* of functionally related tendencies each member of which might vary in strength depending upon the subjective probability of success (P_s) and incentive value of success (I_s). The latter variables were considered relatively transient situational determinants of motivation. The basic idea was that a family of functionally related tendencies would generally be stronger in one person than another. It was convenient to use the family name, such as "motive to achieve" and "tendency to achieve," in describing individual differences in personality and motivational state. In a sense the concept of a general motive was a convenient fiction. Now, however, we can find more theoretical justification for the concept of a family of functionally related tendencies in the concepts of displacement and substitution. Let us begin with the latter.

Among the different ways in which a simple change from one activity to another can come about, as shown earlier in Figure 2, one in particular, graph (E), deserves our attention. Here, the initially dominant tendency is becoming weaker as the initial activity continues because, presumably, the consummatory force of that activity is greater than the instigating force of the stimulus situation. But why is there also a declining trend for the initially subordinate tendency? It is not being expressed in behavior. We might presume that it would persist at its initial strength, as in graph (D), if there were no instigating stimulus in the immediate environment or that it would increase in strength when there was an instigating stimulus, as in the other graphs. The last pattern (E) would seem impossible unless certain tendencies, or the activities they motivate, were functionally related so that what happened to one directly might have a similar but indirect effect on the other. We know from common observation that the aroma of a steak broiling over a charcoal fire increases not only the tendency to eat the steak but to eat other foods as well; and we know that eating the steak reduces not only the tendency to eat more steak but tendencies to eat other foods as well.

We refer to the capacity of one activity to reduce the tendency for another activity as its *substitute value* for the other. The indirect reduction in the strength of a tendency for one activity, T_y, by the behavioral expression of another, T_x, that is, the degree of substitution, will depend upon the magnitude of the consummatory force of the activity that is occurring (C_x) and the degree of relationship between the two activities. In a more detailed and technical discussion of this (Atkinson and Birch, 1970, Ch. 2), we have supposed that the closeness of the relationship between two activities can depend upon their association in the person's history; their symbolic equivalence (both proposed by Freud); their being two instances of essentially the same kind of consummatory activity; or their being alternative means to the same or similar goals or effects. Whatever the cause of the functional equivalence of the two activities, we represent the magnitude of the indirect or substitute consummatory force on T_y that is attributable to behavioral expression of T_x this way: $C_{xy} = C_x \cdot \gamma_{xy}$.

The magnitude of the indirect or substitute force C_{xy} depends upon the magnitude of the direct consummatory force C_x and the degree of relationship (0 to 1.00), γ_{xy}, between the two activities. Since C_x depends upon the consummatory value of activity x (c_x) and the strength of resultant tendency $(\bar{T}_x)$ being expressed at the time, that is, $C_x = c_x \cdot \bar{T}_x$, the *substitute consummatory value* of one activity for another is given by the expression $c_{xy} = c_x \cdot \gamma_{xy}$. Thus, for example, success in one activity may provide an indirect or *substitutive* effect on the tendency to succeed in another activity, as Blankenship (1979) has recently demonstrated: Success at a difficult task has the indirect effect of also reducing the tendency to succeed at easier tasks.

How substitution might influence the stream of overt or imaginative operant behavior is shown in Figure 4. Consider the lower curve as T_y; it has been aroused previously. At the outset there

Figure 4. Effect of Substitution. The occurrence of activity x indirectly reduces T_y, Which persists from an earlier setting, because the degree of relationship between activities x and y is .20. Once a strong instigating force for activity y is introduced, and activity y is initiated, then T_x is reduced by substitution, and it never again attains dominance (see text). (Based on Atkinson and Birch, 1978, p. 69)

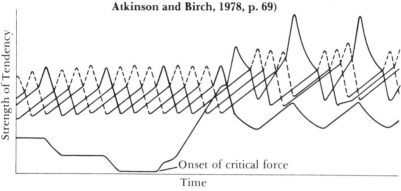

is no instigating stimulus for y in the immediate environment. The occurrences of activity x in the stream of behavior reduce the strength of T_y because it is here assumed that γ_{xy}, the degree of relationship between the two activities, is .20. At a certain point in time the instigating stimulus for activity y is introduced. It produces a strong F_y, and so T_y begins to increase rapidly, though one can still see the substitutive effect of activity x on T_y before activity y is initiated for the first time. Then this more strongly instigated of the two alternatives ($F_y > F_x$) begins to produce a strong, indirect substitute force C_{yx}, which reduces T_x. Activity y replaces activity x in the stream. To use a concrete example, one might think of eating potato chips until the host brings on the peanuts, which are preferred.

Here, in Figure 4, we provide a formal conceptual foundation for the argument about the importance of "alternative behavioral manifestations" of the same motive that was introduced by Frenkel-Brunswik (1942) and emphasized by McClelland (1958a, 1980). One must not, as Wittenborn (1955) also argued, expect too much from simple correlational analysis at the phenotypic surface of behavior. Displacement, the indirect instigation of an activity, is treated in a comparable way. Displacement depends upon the magnitude of the instigating force that is directly attributable to exposure to an instigating stimulus in the environment and the degree of relationship between the two activities. Thus the indirect or displaced force, F_{xy}, should depend upon the magnitude of the force that is directly instigated, F_x, and the degree of relationship between the two activities (0 to 1.00) as represented in δ_{xy}. That is, $F_{xy} = F_x \cdot \delta_{xy}$. We represent the degree of relationship between two activities with different symbols in reference to instigation (δ_{xy}) and consummation (γ_{xy}) in order not to beg the question, are tendencies organized into families in the same way in reference to their arousal and their reduction? That point is illustrated in Figure 5. Here we have a stream of

Figure 5. Displacement and Substitution. Three activities are directly instigated by forces in the immediate environment; one of these, activity x, is functionally related to both y and z; the tendencies for these activities are increased by displacement and diminished by substitution (see text). (Figure contributed by Virginia Blankenship; from Atkinson and Birch, 1978, p. 68)

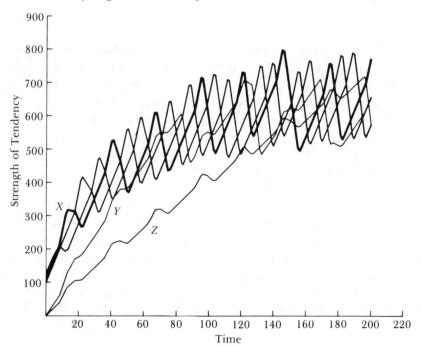

behavior in a constant environment producing three different instigating forces, among them F_x. It is assumed, concerning instigation,
that the degree of relationship between activity x and activity y (for
which there is no stimulus in the environment) is .60, and that the
degree of relationship between activity x and activity z (also without
a stimulus) is .40. Neither activity is directly instigated, but there is
nevertheless continuous exposure to indirect or displaced instigating force equal to .60 F_x for activity y and .40 F_x for activity z. With
respect to substitution, a .20 degree of relationship is assumed
between x and each of the other activities y and z. This means that
whenever activity x occurs, there are indirect consummatory forces
equal to .20 C_x influencing (that is, reducing) the strength of both T_y
and T_z. One observes the arousal of T_y and T_z by displacement, the
occasional reductions attributable to substitution, and the initial
expression of T_x at about 80 on the time scale and of T_z at about 170
on the time scale.

Thus broadened to include these more general and indirect
effects, we systematically embrace the concept of *a family of functionally related tendencies* that will ordinarily tend to increase and
decrease together in strength relative to other families of tendencies.
The members of the same family will, in other words, tend to have a
common fate. It can simplify our discussion of effects to use the
family name, a class term, such as "tendency to eat," "tendency to
achieve," or "tendency for power," that embraces all the specific
action tendencies affected by displacement and substitution, rather
than trying to list exhaustively and in precise detail (which is probably impossible) what happens to the strength of each specific
action tendency. This means that when we say the tendency to
achieve is aroused by administering a test of ability in a given situation, we mean, specifically, that the effect of the direct instigation to
achieve on the test spreads (that is, is displaced) and thus indirectly
influences the strength of a whole family of functionally related
action tendencies. When the cues of a particular picture in a Thematic Apperception Test presented immediately afterward produce a
direct instigating force that arouses a very specific achievement-
related concern, we need only combine the notions of a previously
aroused and persisting family of tendencies and instigating force of
the immediate stimulus to understand what we learned very early

about the combined effects of prior situational arousal of motivation and picture cues on thematic content (McClelland, Atkinson, Clark, and Lowell, 1953, Ch. 1; Atkinson, 1958b; Haber and Alpert, 1958). The more general terms "motive to achieve," "motive for power," and so forth are used in reference to the corresponding family of instigating forces. Individual differences in strength of achievement motive are differences among individuals in the arousability of the tendency to achieve. The concepts of displacement and substitution take us from the specifics of particular life situations to description of the more general motivational implications for an individual and the convenience of using more general terms in descriptions of personality.

A new conception of the problem of motivation (namely, to explain the stream of operant behavior) and its solution (the dynamics of action) have provided a theoretical foundation for response to critics of thematic apperceptive measurement of motivation. I hope that the new conception outlined here will provide the systematic guide needed to suggest new and better ways of realizing the promise of content analysis of imaginative thought for understanding motivation and personality.

References

Atkinson, J. W. "Studies in Projective Measurement of Achievement Motivation." Unpublished doctoral dissertation, University of Michigan, 1950.

Atkinson, J. W. "Motivational Determinants of Risk-Taking Behavior." *Psychological Review*, 1957, *47*, 359–372.

Atkinson, J. W. (Ed.). *Motives in Fantasy, Action, and Society.* New York: Van Nostrand, 1958a.

Atkinson, J. W. "Thematic Apperceptive Measurement of Motives Within the Context of a Theory of Motivation." In J. W. Atkinson (Ed.), *Motives in Fantasy, Action, and Society.* New York: Van Nostrand, 1958b.

Atkinson, J. W. "Thematic Apperceptive Measurement of Motivation in 1950 and 1980." In G. d'Ydewalle and W. Lens (Eds.), *Cognition in Human Motivation and Learning.* Hillsdale, N.J.: Erlbaum, 1980.

Atkinson, J. W., "Studying Personality in the Context of an Advanced Motivational Psychology." *American Psychologist,* 1981, *36,* 117-128.

Atkinson, J. W., and Birch, D. *The Dynamics of Action.* New York: Wiley, 1970.

Atkinson, J. W., and Birch, D. "The Dynamics of Achievement-Oriented Activity." In J. W. Atkinson and J. O. Raynor (Eds.), *Motivation and Achievement.* Washington, D.C.: Winston, 1974.

Atkinson, J. W., and Birch, D. *An Introduction to Motivation.* (Rev. ed.) New York: D. Van Nostrand, 1978.

Atkinson, J. W., Bongort, K., and Price, L. H. "Explorations Using Computer Simulation to Comprehend TAT Measurement of Motivation." *Motivation and Emotion,* 1977, *1,* 1-27.

Atkinson, J. W., and Feather, N. T. (Eds.). *A Theory of Achievement Motivation.* New York: Wiley, 1966.

Atkinson, J. W., and Raynor, J. O. (Eds.). *Motivation and Achievement.* Washington, D.C.: Winston (Halsted Press/Wiley), 1974.

Atkinson, J. W., and Raynor, J. O. *Personality, Motivation, and Achievement.* Washington, D.C.: Hemisphere (Halsted Press/ Wiley), 1978.

Atkinson, J. W., and Reitman, W. R. "Performance as a Function of Motive Strength and Expectancy of Goal Attainment." *Journal of Abnormal and Social Psychology,* 1956, *53,* 361-366.

Birch, D. *Measuring the Stream of Activity.* Michigan Mathematical Psychology Publication, No. MMPP 72-2. Ann Arbor: University of Michigan, 1972.

Birch, D., Atkinson, J. W., and Bongort, K. "Cognitive Control of Action." In B. Weiner (Ed.), *Cognitive Views of Human Motivation.* New York: Academic Press, 1974.

Blankenship, V. "Consummatory Value of Success and Substitution in Relation to Task Difficulty." Unpublished doctoral dissertation, University of Michigan, 1979.

Bongort, K. "Revision of Program by Seltzer and Sawusch: Computer Program Written to Simulate the Dynamics of Action." Unpublished program, University of Michigan, Sept. 4, 1975.

Cartwright, D., and Festinger, L. "A Quantitive Theory of Decision." *Psychological Review,* 1943, *50,* 595-621.

Clark, R. A. "The Projective Measurement of Experimentally

Induced Levels of Sexual Motivation." *Journal of Experimental Psychology*, 1952, *44*, 391–399.

Cronbach, L. J. "Coefficient Alpha and the Internal Structure of Tests." *Psychometrika*, 1951, *16*, 297–334.

de Groot, A. D. *Methodology: Foundations of Inference and Research in the Behavioral Sciences.* The Hague: Mouton, 1969.

de Gruijter, D. "A Note on the Correlation between Strength of a Motive and Time Spent Expressing It in Thematic Apperception." Unpublished manuscript, University of Leyden, 1980.

de Villiers, P. A., and Herrnstein, R. J. "Toward a Law of Response Strength." *Psychological Bulletin*, 1976, *83*, 1131–1153.

Entwisle, D. R. "To Dispel Fantasies About Fantasy-Based Measures of Achievement Motivation." *Psychological Bulletin*, 1972, *77*, 377–391.

Frenkel-Brunswik, E. "Motivation and Behavior." *Genetic Psychology Monographs*, 1942, *26*, 121–265.

Haber, R. N., and Alpert, R. "The Role of Situation and Picture Cues in Projective Measurement of the Achievement Motive." In J. W. Atkinson (Ed.), *Motives in Fantasy, Action, and Society.* New York: Van Nostrand, 1958.

Hamilton, J. O. "Motivation and Risk-Taking Behavior: A Test of Atkinson's Theory." *Journal of Personality and Social Psychology*, 1974, *29*, 856–864.

Heckhausen, H. *The Anatomy of Achievement Motivation.* New York: Academic Press, 1967.

Horner, M. S. "The Measurement and Behavioral Implications of Fear of Success in Women." In J. W. Atkinson and J. O. Raynor (Eds.), *Motivation and Achievement.* Washington, D.C.: Winston, 1974.

Hull, C. L. *Principles of Behavior.* New York: Appleton-Century-Crofts, 1943.

James, W. *The Principles of Psychology.* Vol. 1. New York: Holt, 1890.

Kawamura-Reynolds, M. "Motivational Effects of an Audience in the Content of Imaginative Thought." *Journal of Personality and Social Psychology*, 1977, *35*, 912–919.

Kuhl, J., and Atkinson, J. W. "Motivational Determinants of Decision Time: An Application of the Dynamics of Action." Unpublished manuscript, University of Michigan, 1979.

Kuhl, J., and Blankenship, V. "The Dynamic Theory of Achievement Motivation: From Episodic to Dynamic Thinking." *Psychological Review*, 1979, *86*, 141-151.

Lazarus, R. S. "A Substitutive Defensive Conception of Apperceptive Fantasy." In J. Kagan and G. S. Lesser (Eds.), *Contemporary Issues in Thematic Apperceptive Methods.* Springfield, Ill.: Charles C. Thomas, 1961.

Lesser, G. S., Krawitz, R. N., and Packard, R. "Experimental Arousal of Achievement Motivation in Adolescent Girls." *Journal of Abnormal and Social Psychology*, 1963, *66*, 59-66.

McClelland, D. C. *Personality.* New York: William Sloane, 1951.

McClelland, D. C. "The Psychology of Mental Content Reconsidered." *Psychological Review*, 1955, *62*, 297-302.

McClelland, D. C. "Methods of Measuring Human Motivation." In J. W. Atkinson (Ed.), *Motives in Fantasy, Action, and Society.* New York: Van Nostrand, 1958a.

McClelland, D. C. "The Use of Measures of Human Motivation in the Study of Society." In J. W. Atkinson (Ed.), *Motives in Fantasy, Action, and Society.* New York: Van Nostrand, 1958b.

McClelland, D. C. *The Achieving Society.* New York: Van Nostrand, 1961.

McClelland, D. C. "Testing for Competence Rather Than for 'Intelligence'." *American Psychologist*, 1973, *28*, 1-14.

McClelland, D. C. "Motive Dispositions: The Merits of Operant and Respondent Measures." In L. Wheeler (Ed.), *Review of Personality and Social Psychology.* Beverly Hills, Calif.: Sage, 1980.

McClelland, D. C., Atkinson, J. W., Clark, R. A., and Lowell, E. L. *The Achievement Motive.* New York: Appleton-Century-Crofts, 1953.

Maslow, A. H. *Motivation and Personality.* New York: Harper & Row, 1954.

Mischel, W. *Personality and Assessment.* New York: Wiley, 1968.

Murray, H. A. *Explorations in Personality.* New York: Oxford University Press, 1938.

Raynor, J. O. "Future Orientation and Motivation of Immediate Activity: An Elaboration of the Theory of Achievement Motivation." *Psychological Review*, 1969, *76*, 606-610.

Raynor, J. O. "Future Orientation in the Study of Achievement Motivation." In J. W. Atkinson and J. O. Raynor (Eds.), *Motiva-*

tion and Achievement. Washington, D.C.: Winston (Halsted Press/Wiley), 1974.

Reitman, W. R., and Atkinson, J. W. "Some Methodological Problems in the Use of Thematic Apperceptive Measures of Human Motives." In J. W. Atkinson (Ed.), *Motives in Fantasy, Action, and Society.* New York: D. Van Nostrand, 1958.

Reuman, D., Atkinson, J. W., and Gallop, G. "Computer Simulation of Behavioral Expressions of Four Independent Personality Traits." Unpublished manuscript, University of Michigan, 1981.

Revelle, W., and Michaels, E. J. "The Theory of Achievement Motivation Revisited: The Implications of Inertial Tendencies." *Psychological Review,* 1976, *83,* 394–404.

Sawusch, J. R. "Computer Simulation of the Influence of Ability and Motivation on Test Performance and Cumulative Achievement and the Relation Between Them." In J. W. Atkinson and J. O. Raynor (Eds.), *Motivation and Achievement.* Washington, D.C.: Winston (Halstead Press/Wiley), 1974.

Schneider, K. "Atkinson's 'Risk Preference' Model: Should it be Revised?" *Motivation and Emotion,* 1978, *2,* 333–344.

Seltzer, R. A. "Simulation of the Dynamics of Action." *Psychological Reports,* 1973, *32,* 859–872.

Seltzer, R. A., and Sawusch, J. R. "A Program for Computer Simulation of the Dynamics of Action." In J. W. Atkinson and J. O. Raynor (Eds.), *Motivation and Achievement.* Washington, D.C.: Winston (Halstead Press/Wiley), 1974.

Veroff, J., Depner, C., Kulka, R., and Douvan, E. "Comparison of American Motives: 1957 Versus 1976." *Journal of Personality and Social Psychology,* 1980, *39,* 1249–1262.

Wittenborn, J. R. "The Study of Alternative Responses by Means of the Correlation Coefficient." *Psychological Review,* 1955, *62,* 451–460.

That's Not Psychology!   2

Some Implications
of McClelland's Approach
to Motivation

 *Richard deCharms*

"The field of social motivation appears excessively fragmented, theoretically incoherent, and isolated from other specialties within psychology" (Brody, 1980, p. 165). Thus ends a recent review article. The reasons given for this state of affairs are as follows: (a) there is no "comprehensive theoretical framework," (b) "current work is devoid of biological reference," and (c) current work does not deal with the traditional problem of the influence of motivation on the performance of cognitive tasks. This situation may reflect the state of psychology more than the state of the field of social motivation. Psychology and Western scientific thought demand a comprehensive theoretical framework, grounded in biological data, that assumes an antecedent link between motivation and cognitive tasks. But perhaps asking these criteria of social motivation is like asking why a teacup does not have a firing pin (to use Peter Ossorio's 1966 example). Perhaps social motivation is not an area that can be reduced to biology, or that can be captured cognitively in a comprehensive theoretical framework. It may not lend itself to the causal analysis implied by looking for the influence of motivation on cognitive tasks. Perhaps social motivation is not scientific in this narrow sense of the term.

In the mid-1950s, David McClelland presented a colloquium before a large audience of psychologists. His thesis was that human social motives affect the level of economic development of nations. His data, in part, were samples of literature from men long dead (for example, funeral orations from Ancient Greece), location and carbon dating of ceramic pots documenting the extent of Greek trade in the Mediterranean Sea, and graphic analyses of the decorations on the pots (the "doodles" measure, Aronson, 1958). Using these techniques, he claimed to have demonstrated the relationship between the intensification and the subsequent decrease of achievement motivation and the rise and subsequent decline of the economy of Ancient Greece. When he had completed his presentation, one experimental psychologist was heard to say, "That's not psychology!" Such a reaction may have been prophetic. Ultimately, the study of social motivation may have little resemblance to current practice in psychology.

Unique in its position between the causes of behavior and the reasons for action, the ambiguous term "motive" raises problems that cannot be solved simply. Ignoring half of the common sense meaning of the term, a consistent and currently persuasive position can be reached by the reduction of motivation to needs and drives, with the concomitant assumption that only such physical events can be the object of scientific study.

It is the thesis of this chapter, however, that an adequate understanding of human motivation demands a conception of human beings that can encompass the everyday feeling of volition, of deliberate, intentional action—the experience of personal causation. Underlying this thesis is the proposition that human action is free, in the sense that a person can, by choice, influence the future. Action is therefore not determined by physical events. Human action is not *just* human behavior, because behavior *is* determined by and reducible to physical or biological events.

This thesis has many implications. First, two levels of discourse are being confused. At the biological level, we talk of *stimuli, needs, drives,* and *behavior.* At the experiential level, we use words like *goals, purposive behavior, desires,* and *intentional action.* We must avoid confusing the two levels just as we would avoid writing a mathematical formula mixing algebraic and geometric symbols. Probably the most ambiguous term, ignoring for the moment "motive" itself, is "behavior." As a technical term describing some physical act, behavior is well established. To avoid confusion, I shall use "behavior" when speaking at the physical-biological level and "action," with its implication of psychological intention, when speaking at the experiential level.

If psychology is defined as the study of behavior, then psychology is only the groundwork for the study of human action since action is *not* behavior (Mischel, 1969; White, 1968; Macmurray, 1957). Just as the whole (gestalt) is not *more than* but *different from* the sum of the parts, so action is not more than but different from behavior. Action must conform to what we know about behavior, but it is not reducible to that alone. Wittgenstein asked, "What is left over when I subtract the fact that (a) my arm goes up, from the fact that (b) I raise my arm?" If the answer is the intention to raise the arm, then action contains within it the implication of intention. But the action (raising) is not *just* behavior (arm going up) plus intention. The action is different from behavior, raising is different from going up. The difference is that when we use phrase "a" (go up) we assume one set of circumstances and use one level of discourse. When we use phrase "b" (raise) we assume a different set of circumstances and use another level of discourse.

The thesis stated above has implications for the measurement of motives, research methodology, the goals of research, and the morality of research. Sections devoted to each of these four areas constitute the "data" of this paper, all of them deriving from the research career of David McClelland. The study of social motivation has confronted McClelland with all four of the above issues and in each case he has had to innovate and break the rules of traditional psychology. (1) In *The Achievement Motive* (1953) he and his colleagues tried to develop a theory based on biological drives that could undergird the technique for measuring achievement motivation. The measurement techniques are no longer dependent on this theory. (2) In *The Achieving Society* (1961) McClelland found that the methods of science could be augmented by what Hexter (1971) might call the rhetoric of history. Unhesitatingly, McClelland moved forward to historical analysis. (3) In *Motivating Economic Achievement* (1969) he and Winter found that mere experimentation and observation were inadequate and that attempts to *change* motivation were necessary for understanding social motivation. (4) Finally, in *Power: The Inner Experience* (1975) McClelland confronted the time-honored distinction between facts and values, commingling values with the interpretation of scientific fact out of concern for the betterment of human beings. From this we will draw the conclusion (unstated by McClelland) that research, in social motivation at least, must be seen as a moral act.

In each of our four selected areas, there is confusion between the two levels of discourse: behavior and action. (1) The measurement of motives is often thought to consist solely of physiological measures or self-reports of sense-data, yet McClelland has used personal documents to infer organizing principles of thought. The underlying confusion is between conceiving of motives as based only in the sense-data of impressions and conceiving of them as recognizable in cognitive thought. (2) Research methodology suffers from the confusion between the natural science goal of general-law-type explanations and historical descriptions of human actions (Hexter, 1971). (3) Those who discuss the goals of research tend to vacillate between theoretical and applicable research, creating a division between theory and practice. (4) Finally, when practical implications are considered, the realms of objective science and values seem to clash. At the very least one would hope that some clarification of these confusions could be gained through examination of them. In every case, however, traditional experimental psychology has accepted the first of each of the four dual aspects as scientific psychology and, with the recent exception of cognitive thought, has not considered the second aspect within its scope.

Measurement Problems

Understanding what moves people to act is a radically different enterprise from pursuing the causes of behavior. The word "motive" comes from a Latin root involving both the idea "to move" and the idea "to cause." Some of the most puzzling problems in the psychology of motivation come from mystification in our use of words—from long-standing ambiguities in the use of words like motive, cause, and even the innocent-looking "idea" and "experience."

A "motive' is often thought to be a cause of behavior. In order to have the characteristics of something that can cause a physical event like behavior, a motive must itself be a physical event like a stimulus or a noxious sensation. Using this form of the logic of physicalism, motivation theorists have developed all the classic paraphernalia for reducing a motive to a physical state. A motive was first a need, then a drive, then a drive stimulus, then a stimulus that impelled action.

To relate the stimulus concept of motive as drive to behavior, people like Hull, Mowrer, Young, and Berlyne developed variations on propositions that drive stimuli are unique in that they are affective stimuli, that is, they are (or cause) positive or negative feelings. These feelings in turn get associated with other stimuli and responses by the principles of learning. This was the basis of McClelland's theory of motivation as stated in *The Achievement Motive*. A motive was an affective response to a stimulus ("the redintegration by a cue of a state of affect"). The logical way to measure a motive so defined would be to measure affect. Concisely, there are three basic assumptions: motives are antecedent to behavior; they cause, force, or impel behavior; and they themselves are sensations, that is, primary sense-data.

These assumptions base the study of human motivation solidly on the foundations of psychology as a natural biological science, assuming the logical-positivist tenets of reductionism and physicalism, and using the building blocks of observation sentences.

This was the program for the understanding of human motivation implicit in Chapter 2 of *The Achievement Motive*. Ralph Haber's (1958) study of adaptation levels was intended to show the direct link between external stimulus conditions, sensations relative to the adaptive state of the organism, and positive or negative affect (self-report of the subject).

One might ask, then, in what way is the basic technique used to measure motives such as achievement, power, and affiliation related to this conception? As is well known, the basic tool is a group-administered form of the Thematic Apperception Test (Murray, 1943); stories written by subjects (thought samples) are coded for imagery relevant to the motive of interest to the experimenter. The early researchers were at pains to demonstrate that objectively manipulable physiological needs like hunger (number of hours of food deprivation) were reflected in the subjects' stories (Atkinson and McClelland, 1948). The assumption was that the "drive stimulus" of hunger formed the antecedent of a social motive such as achievement motivation.

To this day there remains a basic ambiguity, however, concerning exactly what the thought samples are measuring. There are at least two possibilities. Perhaps, as the biological level of discourse implies, they are tapping basic sensations of affect that are the stimulus roots of motivation. Or perhaps they are measuring something more general. Perhaps they measure organizing principles, deriving from human understanding of others, that the psychologist and the subject have in common. The subject's thoughts are organized by these principles; and the psychologist, being human, can recognize them in the thoughts. As in the case of a motive "moving" a person to do his duty rather than causing a person to behave, so in the case of motive as sensation or motive as organizing principle, the two conceptions are radically different.

A bit of philosophical history may shed light on this ambiguity. (Much of this history comes from Watling, 1964.) The word "idea" as used by Descartes in his theory of human understanding had a similar ambiguity to that of motive. As a thoroughgoing rationalist, Descartes accepted the premise that all knowledge resulted from deduction from first principles. As a trained mathematician who learned to describe geometrical figures with algebraic equations, he thought of knowledge as being produced by applying forms of implication (like algebra) to basic propositions. Assuming that Euclidean geometry was *the* valid picture of the physical world, he conceived of ideas as concepts, like "circle," "triangle," and so on. As long as such elements remained mental concepts, his rationalistic stand was secure, but to be consistent, he had to explain how one "understands" the concept "triangle." Here he resorted to *"mental images"* or mental objects, which could be *clearly* and *distinctly* imagined (I almost said perceived). He explicitly used the visual analogy and yet seemed to say that the mental object (idea) existed in the mind's eye. In one sense, "idea" was a kind of nonempirically based image-less thought, yet at the same time, the "idea" directly represented or "pictured" objects in the world. It was but a short step to ideas as empirical sense-data. And, of course, that is exactly the way that the empiricist Locke used the term "idea" as the basic sense-data elements inscribed from birth on the *tabula rasa*.

Is it just coincidence that Descartes' term "idea" (as mental concept without empirical base, yet at the same time representative of physical objects) is ambiguous in much the same way as the term "motive," which can be thought of as a concept that organizes thought and action or as a stimulus of primary sense-data?

With the philosophies of Locke and especially Hume, the "motive"-"cause" ambiguity became compounded with the concept-sensation ambiguity. Hume showed that there was no empirical, sensation-based evidence for the concept "cause" in the sense of a necessary connection between two events. In a little known derivation from what he thought was strict empiricism, Maine deBiran (see Moore, 1970 and Hallie, 1959 for a discussion of his work) deduced that we learn our concept of cause empirically from causing things ourselves. The experience of causing something, then, could be reduced to the raw sense-data that came to be referred to as the "feeling of innervation"—the raw feeling of causing. Of course, no one has ever identified through the hard labor of introspection the sense-datum "cause," but still motive-cause and concept-sensation remain ambiguities.

Skipping a century or so, we find the Logical Positivists puzzling over the relationship between propositions and observations. Drawing on Russell's "logical atomism" (see Turner, 1967), Wittgenstein ([1922], 1961) assumed a picture theory of representation of the world. About this time philosophers stopped talking about concepts directly and started talking about the language we use to communicate our concepts and observations. Thus Logical Positivists talked about observation sentences (protocol sentences) as the basic building blocks of science. Russell assumed that everyday langauge was imprecise in describing natural phenomena. Members of the Vienna Circle (Logical Positivists) at first accepted the philosophical task as one of outlining the formal structure of an adequately precise scientific language. "At one time Carnap supposed that it was a factual question whether observation sentences . . . refer to the simplest sensations and feelings, or to the Gestalts of single sensory fields, or to material objects. Later, however, he came to hold the view that this is not a factual, but a linguistic question, the answer to which depends entirely upon our choice of a form of language for reporting our observations." Watling reports that it was Neurath who first rejected Wittgenstein's statement that "Reality is compared with the proposition." Neurath came to believe that "a fact is not something independent of language. Sentences are to be compared with sentences, not with 'experience,' not with a 'world,' nor with anything else" (Watling, 1964, pp. 500-501). To conceive of observation sentences as descriptions (pictures) of a person's world would only lead to solipsism. The only recourse was to reduce observation sentences to statements about physical relationships—the famous "thesis of physicalism."

Whether or not reductionism and physicalism solve the problem of statements concerning observations of the physical world, they certainly do not help when observation statements concern personal states of motivation. We do not, in fact, always experience or report "thrills, twinges, pangs, throbs, wrenches, itches, prickings, chills, glows, loads, qualms, hankerings, curdlings, sinkings, tensions, gnawings, and shocks" (Ryle, 1949, pp. 83-84) when we are motivated.

To return to McClelland's measurement of motivation, it seems that he set out to ground the measure in sensations of affect. Yet the primacy of affect did not clearly emerge from the validating data reported (McClelland and others, 1953). To measure the motive, eleven categories are coded in written stories. Two of the categories are positive and negative affect and two are anticipatory affect. The rest derive from a schematic diagram of an adjustive behavioral sequence and do not directly imply affect (McClelland and others, 1953, p. 109). Two things may be noted about this behavioral sequence analysis of a written story. First, in analyzing the potency of each individual category, the affectively laden categories did not stand out from the others. Second, what seemed to make the scoring valid was the whole schema with its related parts—the total form or gestalt that appeared in the story. And what indicated high motivation was more in the style of telling the story than in its actual content.

The evidence seems to suggest that the reason the measure was related to behavior could be explained less well in molecular, Lockean, sensationalist terms (affect) than in terms of tapping a molar concept. The molar tradition of Gestalt psychology (Köhler, 1947) has been a perceptual, conceptual psychology that conceived of mental images much the way Descartes did. The paradox is that, with the exception of Kurt Lewin, the original Gestalt psychologists have almost completely ignored motivation and affective states. In fact, when Lewin and later Gestalt-derived cognitive theorists took up the problem of motives, they translated them into interactions between perceptual-cognitive states (see, for example, Heider's balance theory or Festinger's cognitive dissonance).

There is again a resemblance between this evolution of the use of thought samples and the evolution of philosophical writings that seems more than coincidence. In their analysis of Wittgenstein's "second thoughts" after writing the *Tractatus Logico-Philosophicus*, Janik and Toulmin (1973) argue that Wittgenstein moved steadily away from a picture theory of knowledge to conceiving of knowledge as inextricable from language. "The early logical positivists believed that, in principle, at any rate, all the abstract terms of a meaningful theory have their 'physical meaning' conferred on them through their association with appropriate collections of sensations. . . . This was once again a return to Hume, with 'sensations,' 'sense-data,' and/or Protokollsätze standing in for 'impressions' and statements recording 'impressions.' Wittgenstein had no use for any such doctrine" (p. 217). "So, from now on, Wittgenstein focused his attention instead on *language as behavior*: concentrating his analysis on the pragmatic *rules* that govern the uses of different expressions, on the *language games* within which those rules are operative, and on the broader forms of life which ultimately give those language games their significance" (p. 223).

This fragment of Janik and Toulmin's analysis gives only the flavor, yet even this suggests that concepts like "language games" and "forms of life" may hold promise in explaining the use of thought sampling in motivation measurement. Could it be that McClelland has hit upon a type of "language sampling" that reveals "forms of life," including motives, in the "language games" people use?

Two further parallels between McClelland and Wittgenstein make this seem a bit more plausible. First, McClelland has always stressed the importance of early childhood experiences in the development of motives (McClelland, 1951), and early childhood is clearly when "language games" are developed. Wittgenstein "found himself, at fifty, urging his hearers to reflect more carefully on the ways in which children do, in fact, learn . . . the standard patterns of behavior within which our language has a practical function" (Janik and Toulmin, 1973, p. 224).

Second, McClelland has urged a type of characterology in a unique way to study the relationships of motives to national character types and economic development. His analysis of German, French, and Indian characteristics (McClelland, 1964, 1976) have been more or less successfully ignored in psychology, yet they reveal different "forms of life" in relation to motives and behavior and avoid the central tautology of most characterologists.

Conceiving of the Thematic Apperception Test as a "language sample" that taps the "forms of life" implicit in "language games" learned by human beings is a far cry from the original conception of a measure of affect. It is also a far cry from any psychophysical theory of measurement. It suggests just how far off base criticisms of fantasy measures from the traditional measurement perspective may be (Entwisle, 1972; see also McClelland, 1980). Yet it goes a long way in explaining both the successes in measuring long-term styles of life (McClelland, 1965) and the failures to predict specific behaviors of McClelland's motive measures; and it further explains McClelland's operant-respondent distinction (McClelland, 1980). In the right hands, it might suggest a new and unique set of standards for developing and evaluating "measures" of the "springs of action" and the "roots of consciousness" (McClelland, 1964) in human beings.

On Doing History Versus Doing Science

The basic distinction between scientific research and the rhetoric of history is the distinction between the two levels of discourse mentioned earlier. "There is an irreducible divergence between the rhetoric of history and the rhetoric of science. . . . In the rhetoric of history itself there are embedded assumptions about the nature of knowing, understanding, meaning, and truth and about the means of augmenting them that are not completely congruent with the corresponding assumptions in the sciences, at least insofar as the philosophy of science has succeeded in identifying them" (Hexter, 1971, pp. 68-69).

Further, underlying the scientific-historical distinction is the age-old distinction in logic between *universal* statements and *particular* statements. Universal statements are "all" statements like "all behavior is motivated." Particular statements are about specific cases, for example, "In the first half of the eighteenth century, high achievement motivation in England was followed by increased economic growth."

Recently Gergen (1973) has characterized social psychology as history, and McClelland in 1961 (p. viii) said that " The general methodological approach of the book *[The Achieving Society]* . . . is in the tradition of comparative history, comparative economics, or a psychology interested in generalizations that apply to all or most of the human species." McClelland was not interested in history for its own sake. He was interested in human motivation. The nature of the topic forced him out of the pure rhetoric of science and into the rhetoric of history. Although he sought generalizations that applied to all human beings, he did not seek to predict specific behaviors (for example, skill in arithmetic) in all humans. Nor, on the other hand, did he seek the keys to the whole meaning of life in history as philosophers of history (metahistorians) such as Hegel, Marx, or Toynbee might have done. He sought instances of connections between very general cultural motivational trends and indices of cultural behavioral trends. Natural experiments found in history were used to count positive and negative instances. Two examples of this unique method will suffice here—one relating achievement motivation to economic conditions and one relating motivation patterns to war.

In *The Achieving Society* McClelland set out to test the hypothesized connection between achievement motivation and economic growth in societies of the past. He cites in detail six cases from various periods and cultures. Case 1 was Ancient Greece. Samples from six types of Greek literature, such as poetry and funeral orations, were collected from three different periods: the "growth period," from 900 B.C. to 475 B.C.; "climax," from 475 B.C. to 362 B.C.; and "decline," from 362 B.C. to 100 B.C. Achievement motivation scores from these three periods showed that the highest mean score was in the growth period and the lowest in the period of decline—a linear decline. Economic rise and fall were indexed by the area of Greek trade around the Mediterranean Sea, as determined by the location of unearthed vases in which olive oil and wine, the chief exports, were transported. Here the peak of exports occurred in the climax period as predicted. As a check on the achievement motivation scores from literature, Aronson's (1958) graphic "doodle" measure was applied to the vases. The data confirmed the high level of motivation in the growth period, followed by steady decline.

Case 2 spanned the period A.D. 1200 to A.D. 1730 in Spain— the period that saw the flourishing of exploration, including the discovery of America, and the beginning of the decline with the defeat of the Armada (1588).

Cases 3 and 4 derive from an analysis of literature and imports of coal for industrial use in England over the period 1500 to 1800. Here two waves of motivation and economic rise and fall were shown, and the second one coincided with the rise of Protestantism, in accordance with Weber's ([1904], 1930) hypothesis.

Case 5 traces achievement motivation and economic growth in the United States from 1800 to 1950 using children's readers and an index of number of patents issued. Here the wave peaked about 1900 (deCharms and Moeller, 1962).

Finally, Case 6 was an excursion into archaeology, showing a similar pattern of motivation and economic growth in pre-Incan Peru, a civilization that left us no written history. As in Case 1, vases were used to determine achievement motivation. A quantitative estimate of cultural growth was determined using the volume of public buildings constructed. Again the data conform to the hypothesis.

The second example of deriving generalizations about motivation and cultural trends is presented in *Power: The Inner Experience* (1975). Here McClelland set out to demonstrate the relationship between certain configurations of motives and violence or war. "A combination of high *n* Power and low *n* Affiliation is associated with or may lead to violence or warfare, as it did around 1550, 1650, and to a lesser extent 1750 in England" (McClelland, 1961, p. 324). Tracing changing motive patterns in the United States, McClelland found the predicted configuration before the War of 1812, the Mexican War, the Civil War, World Wars I and II, and the Vietnam War; only the Spanish-American and Korean Wars were exceptions.

These are only two of many examples where McClelland sought generalizations about relations between human motivation and action in historical data. No longer content to study the behavior of the college sophomore in the laboratory, he confronted the reasons for action as it occurred naturally in the history of cultures. As Macmurray has pointed out (1957, p. 24), "Action is inherently particular; and therefore questions of the form 'What shall I do?' have a historic reference. They cannot be answered without regard to the circumstances in which we have to act."

Research for Practical Purposes

The psychology of the first half of the present century was dominated by the desire to develop grand theories. Probably the best known theories were theories of learning, and of course Hull's learning theory was one of the most influential. Simply put, the impetus behind this movement was the idea that once we had developed adequate theories in psychology, then someone could go about applying them to the problems of the "real world."

Implicit in this thinking was a critical gap—the gap between theory and practice (Habermas, 1973). The grand theories are generally considered now to have failed in their objective. Setting their sights a bit lower, many psychologists in the 1960s were hoping for mini-theories that might sometime in the future combine into an adequate larger theory that could then be applied. Even in the 1970s few would deny that the ultimate goal was to be able to develop theory for practical purposes (Miller, 1969).

The epistemological goal of theorists is knowledge. The basic question is 'How do I know what I know?" The methods are methods of verification (Logical Positivism) or of falsification (Popper, 1959). Experimental methods and statistical techniques used in psychology are all ultimately based on this derivative of the Cartesian "Method of Doubt." Although twentieth-century psychology has thrown off the yoke of philosophy, we still base much of what we do on a theory of knowledge with direct roots in that philosophy.

"Knowing" based on "I think" does not lead easily to "knowing what to do." The most carefully derived hypothetico-deductive theories (Hull-Spence is a good example) have rarely led to great insights into what to do with people's problems. In fact, many of the most practical techniques claimed by psychologists were not deduced from grand theory; they resulted more often from trying one thing and stumbling over a result. The classic example is described by Skinner (1959), who, working under the theory that behavior (learning) is a direct function of amount of reinforcement, stumbled onto the notion of partial reinforcement when the reinforcing appartus broke down. A case can be made that some of the most useful ideas about how to use rewards in education have come from psychologists who eschewed theory and simply manipulated educational settings to see what they could do (O'Leary and O'Leary, 1972).

Such efforts derive from an "I do" orientation that makes knowledge of what to do primary and produces practical results without having to cross that yawning gap from theory to application. At the same time, contained within the practical knowledge of what to do is basic theoretical knowledge. Making theoretical knowledge primary gives us no assurance of ever knowing how to do anything practical.

The separation between thinking and doing or between theory and practice is hard to achieve when you pursue social motivation. To understand the reasons for human action, you cannot simply observe and communicate your findings verbally. In the nature of things, you are *doing*, no matter how hard you try not to: You are affecting and influencing your subjects. You are therefore confronted with the "new" problem of your responsibility to your subjects. This is not a simple matter of the rights of human subjects. Responsibility is at the heart of the phenomenon that you set out to study—motives and reasons for action. As Macmurray (1961,

p. 129) observes, "If I am watching a hive of bees . . . I may form a theory of the principles which are at work. . . . My theory may be true or false, adequate or inadequate, but in any case, it makes no difference to the bees. . . . But if I form theories about human society in the same fashion, this is not the case. For I am not just a spectator of human activity, but a participant." In fact, Macmurray (p. 131) suggests that the motive for making theoretical pursuits primary "is the desire to know the truth without having to live by the truth. It is the secret wish to escape from moral commitment, from responsibility."

Steeped in the Hullian theory-building tradition, McClelland early moved beyond it. Without self-consciously espousing the philosophical foundations of an action psychology, he gave up traditional theory building and moved more and more toward answering the question he posed for himself: "so the scientist cannot help wondering whether what he has learned can be put to some practical use" (McClelland, 1961, p. 392). Having observed a relationship between achievement motivation and economic development, McClelland proceeded to action. He tried to stimulate economic development in the small city of Kakinada, India, and to compare it with a neighboring city, Rajahmundry. The stimulant was training most of the prominent businessmen of Kakinada to increase their achievement motivation. As described in *Motivating Economic Achievement* (McClelland and Winter, 1969), this was an enormous undertaking. Twelve educational inputs were designed based on twelve motivational propositions (see McClelland, 1965). The propositions and inputs fell into four main divisions: the achievement syndrome (learning to think and act like a person with high achievement motivation), self-study (especially with regard to career), goal setting (committing oneself to an achievement goal and devising a work plan), and interpersonal supports. The residential courses ran for seven to ten days of intensive experiences and planning. Once the courses were over, follow-up contacts were made both to remind participants of their involvement and to collect data on the effects of the course.

Statistical data on seventy-six trained and seventy-three untrained businessmen are reported, showing such changes in the trained men as greater business activity, longer working hours, starting more new businesses, making more investments in productive capital, and employing more workers. "Thus by measures of all the basic aspects of entrepreneurial function, they have become improved entrepreneurs" (McClelland and Winter, 1969, p. 231). Descriptions of individual cases flesh out the statistics by showing the effects of increased achievement motivation on individual lives.

The evidence is clear—the intervention of achievement motivation training changed individuals' lives and did stimulate economic growth in the little town of Kakinada.

Inevitably actions of one person or group that affect another's life raise the moral question of responsibility. McClelland and Winter (p. 26) ask, "Is it morally right to change people?" and answer, "The offering of personality change or increased *n* Achievement to a person can be made compatible with preserving his freedom, dignity, and self-respect." Is it enough just to make research compatible with human values?

Research as a Moral Act

Making knowledge ("I know so and so") the goal of research leads to the primacy of verification, for knowledge is the capacity to discriminate between true and false thoughts. Making practical action ("I can do so and so") the goal of research ultimately leads to the primacy of moral justification, for reason (as in reasonable action) is the capacity to discriminate between right and wrong actions.

Science, including scientific psychology, was once thought to be of supreme value and therefore above value judgments, since it attained the ultimate in objectivity. This state of immaculateness derived from the intellectualists' striving for objective verification. It was therefore necessary to separate science from values completely. The idea is ironically captured in Tom Lehrer's couplet,

> "Once the rockets are up, who cares where they come down?
> That's not my department," says Wernher von Braun.

The events of the 1960s, particularly the Vietnam War and Watergate, forced the questioning even of science. It is now reasonable to ask about the values of science and even to propose the study of the science of values.

The intrusion of values into the science of psychology can be seen at three levels. The rights of human subjects, at the first level, have been debated in psychology. Despite all the controversy, however, subjects' rights are merely the negative side of a much broader issue. It is negative in that it merely asks how human beings can be assured of their rights while the scientist continues to pursue the truth through objectivity.

At a much more comprehensive second level, when one sets out to do something practical, something for the good of someone, one cannot avoid the intrusion of values. Long ago Kant raised this issue in the *Critique of Practical Reason.* "But since, in Kant's view, the exercise of the will (as distinct from the operation of mere inclinations or desires) is an exercise of reason—'practical reason'—it follows that in exercising his will, man is not merely part of the order of nature, and hence in this field there is no conflict with natural causation" (Warnock, 1964, p. 309). "The distinctive feature of Kant's moral philosophy could be said to be its unbending rationalism" (p. 307). As pointed out by Macmurray (1957), Kant therefore asked the intellectualist question, "How do we *know* what is right and wrong?" rather than the actionist question, "How can we know what we *should do?*"

The third level of intrusion of values in psychology confronts the moral issue directly by asking what the psychologist *should do?* It suggests that the psychologist should conceive of research itself *as a moral act*—that psychology be conceived, in Shotter's (1975) terms, as the "moral science."

The psychological study of human motivation is perhaps unique (compared to other areas of psychological research such as learning, perception, and even cognitive processes) in that ultimately the distinction between caused behavior and intentional action comes up. As long as one stays on the "safe" ground of reducing motives to drives, needs, and so on, one can assume that they are merely "part of nature" and a product of "natural causation." Inevitably, by engaging in research as an intentional act to change another's motives, the motivation researcher is confronted with the problem of doing good rather than bad. The end of this chain of reasoning is accepting research in general as a human act and asking whether particular research is a moral act.

The evidence that McClelland is concerned about the use of psychology, at least at the second level of the intrusion of values on research, is increasingly abundant in his more recent writings. An early finding that may, in retrospect, have been critical is a possible starting point for a development of some of his more recent concerns. One of the more or less incidental findings of the attempt to relate motives to cultural trends was the following. When children's readers from forty or so countries were coded for power motivation and affiliation motivation, it turned out that countries with a high power motive score and a low affiliation motive score in a 1929 sample later showed a tendency toward totalitarianism that was greater than chance. This finding led McClelland to speculate about motive patterns and *this* one in particular that seemed to be associated with "ruthlessness." The importance of power motivation in political affairs became of more and more interest to McClelland. He had tried (in 1970) to distinguish between two faces of power—selfish, ruthless, personalized power motivation, and more altruistic, mature socialized power. Later, he refined the relationship between high power and low affiliation motivation and ruthlessness into a characterization of a type of leadership; and, more important, gathered impressive evidence for the relationship between motivation patterns and political violence.

Ultimately McClelland (1975) concludes with a discussion of the causes of war. He sees a cycle in history that could lead to Armageddon. Characteristically, he asks, "What can we do?" His answer states that "psychological regularities . . . are not like physical laws in the sense that they 'have to' occur. . . . There is no *necessary* linkage between the events, just a probabilistic one" (McClelland, 1976, p. 356). "So to prevent Armageddon, we must formally swear off violence as an instrument of collective policy" (p. 358). Pacifism, then, as practiced by the Quakers, must accompany religious fervor. "Whatever the justification for their beliefs, they [Quakers] have hit on a formula that holds promise for the future of mankind" (p. 359).

Conclusion

By now it should be evident that what McClelland has done is not traditional psychology. Yet it is not presented as a revolution in psychology. In fact, McClelland sees himself as carrying on the traditions of psychology. Early on he says, "I have wanted to deal with Freudian psychodynamics in the rigorous quantitative way characteristic of a modern behavorial scientist like Hull" (McClelland, 1964, p. 1). In confronting the thorny problems of social motivation in unconventional ways, McClelland has come far from that goal and may have outlined a critical transition in psychological thought about human action.

Transitions in the history of knowledge are often initiated by people trying to work within the traditional mode, understating the uniqueness of their work, but finding traditional modes and methods inadequate when confronting the boundaries of knowledge. In pushing beyond what is known, they must invent new modes and methods, yet they may be dismayed when their work is criticized by more traditional colleagues. Janik and Toulmin (1973) point out that early in this century, Vienna was the center for the critique and communication of ideas in many fields of thought, yet most often "the men of the first generation, came to appear in retrospect to consist of highly reluctant revolutionaries." They cite a recent study of Arnold Schonberg, for instance, that explicitly called him "the conservative revolutionary" (p. 250). Perhaps McClelland is more like Mahler than Schönberg, however, as captured in Janik and Toulmin's phrase—a "contemporary of the future."

It has been the thesis of this paper that in at least four areas—measurement of motives, psychology as history, researcher as agent, and research as a moral act—McClelland has broken ground that has yet to be understood and appreciated. Examined according to the traditional principles of psychology, what he has done and is doing is, in fact, not scientific psychology as a biological science.

Be it psychology or not, some such innovations are necessary to unravel the mysteries of causes, motives, and intentions. We may have to give up the simplifying notion that they can all be reduced to one level. We may have to realize (with Macmurray, 1957) that causes are physical, cause movement, and partake of the "form of the physical" that may be captured in the logic of mathematics and the physical sciences. Motives are biological, motivate habitual behavior, and partake of the "form of the organic" that may be captured in the logic of dialectics or homeostasis of the biological sciences. Intentions are personal, are contained within and inseparable from action, and partake of the "form of the personal" that may be captured in the logic of language games and forms of life. Objects are moved by causes, organisms behave from motives, and persons act with intention. The catch is that persons are at the same time organisms and objects. Our lack of understanding of the "form of the personal" is for Macmurray the crisis of philosophy. The corresponding problem for psychology is to produce evidence for the distinction between motives and intentions by distinguishing between behavior and action.

References

Aronson, E. "The Need for Achievement as Measured by Graphic Expression." In J. W. Atkinson (Ed.), *Motives in Fantasy, Action, and Society.* New York: Van Nostrand, 1958.

Atkinson, J. W., and McClelland, D. C. "The Projective Expression of Needs. II: The Effect of Different Intensities of the Hunger Drive on Thematic Apperception." *Journal of Experimental Psychology,* 1948, *38,* 643-658.

Brody, N. "Social Motivation." *Annual Review of Psychology,* 1980, *31,* 143-168.

deCharms, R., and Moeller, G. H. "Values Expressed in American Children's Readers, 1800-1950." *Journal of Abnormal and Social Psychology,* 1962, *64,* 136-142.

Entwisle, D. R. "To Dispel Fantasies About Fantasy-Based Measures of Achievement Motivation." *Psychological Bulletin,* 1972, *77,* 377-391.

Gergen, K. J. "Social Psychology as History." *Journal of Personality and Social Psychology,* 1973, *26,* 309-320.

Haber, R. N. "Discrepancy from Adaptation Level as a Source of Affect." *Journal of Experimental Psychology,* 1958, *56,* 370-375.

Habermas, J. *Theory and Practice.* Boston: Beacon Press, 1973.

Hallie, P. P. *Maine de Biran: Reformer of Empiricism, 1766-1824.* Cambridge, Mass.: Harvard University Press, 1970.

Hexter, J. H. *Doing History.* Bloomington: Indiana University Press, 1971.

Janik, A., and Toulmin, S. *Wittgenstein's Vienna*. New York: Simon & Schuster, 1973.

Köhler, W. *Gestalt Psychology*. New York: Liveright, 1947.

McClelland, D. C. *Personality*. New York: William Sloane, 1951.

McClelland, D. C. *The Achieving Society*. New York: Van Nostrand, 1961.

McClelland, D. C. *The Roots of Consciousness*. New York: Van Nostrand, 1964.

McClelland, D. C. "Toward a Theory of Motive Acquisition." *American Psychologist*, 1965, *20*, 321-333.

McClelland, D. C. "The Two Faces of Power." *Journal of International Affairs*, 1970, *24*, 29-47.

McClelland, D. C. *Power: The Inner Experience*. New York: Irvington, 1975.

McClelland, D. C. "Motive Dispositions: The Merits of Operant and Respondent Measures." In L. Wheeler (Ed.), *Review of Personality and Social Psychology*. Vol. 1. Beverly Hills, Calif.: Sage, 1980.

McClelland, D. C., Atkinson, J. W., Clark, R. A., and Lowell, E. L. *The Achievement Motive*. New York: Appleton-Century-Crofts, 1953.

McClelland, D. C., and others. *The Achievement Motive*. New York: Halsted Press, 1976.

McClelland, D. C., and Winter, D. G. *Motivating Economic Achievement*. New York: Free Press, 1969.

Macmurray, J. *The Self as Agent*. London: Faber & Faber, 1957.

Macmurray, J. *Persons in Relation*. London: Faber & Faber, 1961.

Miller, G. "Psychology as Means of Promoting Human Welfare." *American Psychologist*, 1969, *24*, 1063–1075.

Mischel, T. (Ed.), *Human Action*. New York: Academic Press, 1969.

Moore, F.C.T. *The Psychology of Maine de Biran*. Oxford: Clarendon Press, 1970.

Murray, H. A. *Thematic Apperception Test Manual*. Cambridge, Mass.: Harvard University Press, 1943.

O'Leary, K. D., and O'Leary, S. G. *Classroom Management*. Elmsford, N.Y.: Pergamon Press, 1972.

Ossorio, P. G. *Persons*. Boulder, Colo.: Linguistic Research Institute, 1966.

Popper, K. *The Logic of Scientific Discovery*. New York: Basic Books, 1959.

Ryle, G. *The Concept of Mind*. New York: Barnes & Noble, 1949.

Shotter, J. *Images of Man in Psychological Research*. London: Methuen, 1975.

Skinner, B. F. *Cumulative Record*. New York: Appleton-Century-Crofts, 1959.

Toulmin, S. *Human Understanding*. Princeton, N.J.: Princeton University Press, 1972.

Turner, M. B. *Philosophy and the Science of Behavior*. New York: Appleton-Century-Crofts, 1967.

Warnock, G. J. "Kant." In D. J. O'Connor (Ed.), *A Critical History of Western Philosophy*. New York: Free Press, 1964.

Watling, J. L. "Descartes." In D. J. O'Connor (Ed.), *A Critical History of Western Philosophy*. New York: Free Press, 1964.

Weber, M. *The Protestant Ethic and the Spirit of Capitalism*. New York: Scribner's, 1930. (Originally published 1904.)

White, A. R. (Ed.). *The Philosophy of Action*. New York: Oxford University Press, 1968.

Wittgenstein, L. *Tractatus Logico-Philosophicus*. D. F. Pears and B. F. McGuinness (trans.). London: Routledge & Kegan Paul, 1961. (Originally published 1922.)

Projective and Psychometric Approaches to Measurement

3

The Case of Fear of Success

 *Jacqueline Fleming*

When the motive to avoid success was first presented to the psychological public (Horner, 1969), it aroused intense enthusiasm because it promised to shed light on the murky psychology of women, enable the male-oriented theory of achievement motivation to finally become relevant to female subjects, and heighten general awareness of the irrational motivational forces that play an active part in human psychology. Yet over ten years after its introduction, the promise of the provocative concept remains unrealized. The concept of fear of success has been unmercifully assailed because it did not consistently predict impaired competitive performance against

males, because it did not show the expected relationship to academic
performance, and because the level and content of fear-of-success
imagery did not show reliable trends over time (Tresemer, 1974,
1976, 1977; Zuckerman and Allison, 1976). The confusion produced
by the motive's inconsistent performance in the literature has led to
a search for reliable methods of measurement exemplified by objective, rather than projective, tests that yield reassuringly consistent
estimates of reliability (Zuckerman and Allison, 1976; Tresemer,
1977; Canavaan-Gumpert, Garner, and Gumpert, 1978; Sadd,
Lenauer, Shaver and Dunivant, 1978). The concept has reached a
methodological impasse.

While fear of success is the newest achievement-related motivation, the events in its history have a familiar ring. Indeed, these
events remind us that the study of personality in general and motivation in particular has long been split into projective and psychometric methods of measurement, with a history of mutual animosity
between the two camps dating from the 1920s (Lanyon and Goodstein, 1971). Far from advancing the art of personality research, the
split in the field may actually have acted to retard our understanding
of individual differences by requiring an allegiance to one camp or
the other. At a time when the usefulness of personality research itself
has been called into question (see Mischel, 1968), it would seem that
the assumptions on which the dispersal of research energies are
based need to be reexamined.

Despite the seemingly impassable roadblocks raised by
researchers with psychometric leanings (for example, Klinger, 1966;
Entwisle, 1972; Tresemer, 1976; Mischel, 1968), nothing generates
interest, enthusiasm, and excitement like the subject of motivation,
and fear of success has been no exception. Fear of success, like
achievement motivation in the 1950s, had an uncanny personal relevance to many and struck a powerful, intuitive chord. Admittedly, it
has been hard to prove that an internalized fear of success exists in
women, much less in men, and it may well be, as Condry and Dyer
(1976) contend, that the phenomenon resides in society rather than
in the individual and will disappear when institutional barriers to
success weaken. Nonetheless, a good working hypothesis is that
where there's smoke, there's fire, and that the excitement generated
by the concept of fear of success betrays something real, tangible,

and discoverable. Thus, this chapter explores possible theoretical and statistical solutions that fall between projective and psychometric approaches to personality measurement in order to find ways of reintegrating the concept of fear of success.

Examining solutions to problems of measurement may not seem a straightforward way of honoring David McClelland. Yet he teaches us that our everyday understanding of phenomena—including methodological problems—only scratches the surface of things, because the real sources lie in the roots of consiousness. Moreover, he has demonstrated that societal problems are surface manifestations of motivational forces. The problems of measurement faced by the community of psychologists may prove no exception to this principle.

Fear-of-Success Theory

The Problem of Methodological Inconsistency. The familiar methodological saga that runs through the history of motivation research was perhaps destined to be repeated with fear of success. The fear-of-success hypothesis met with a most enthusiastic response, especially on the part of female psychologists. After scores of studies had appeared in the literature, researchers with psychometric leanings began to point out inconsistencies of every conceivable kind (for example, Tresemer, 1974, 1976; Zuckerman and Wheeler, 1975). With the methodological problems evident, the fast flow of research came to a near halt in the confusion over whether or not the phenomenon really existed, whether it was more prominent in women than in men, and whether the measure tapped motivation at all (Tresemer, 1974, 1976, 1977; Feather and Simon, 1973; Zuckerman and Wheeler, 1975; Condry and Dyer, 1976).

Horner's (1968) first experimental measure of fear of success, based on responses to the cue "After first term finals, Anne (John) is at the top of her medical school class," was in fact discredited because of the empirical inconsistencies that it yielded. First, the fact that sex differences in fear-of-success imagery were not uniformly found across studies was considered a problem. While the signifiant sex differences in favor of women found by Horner were upheld in several studies (Horner, 1972; Hoffman, 1974), a number of others found no sex differences or even a higher percentage of negative imagery in males (see Horner, 1972; Tresemer, 1974). Second, the level of fear of success in both sexes was interpreted as unstable from study to study, in that it ranged from 20 percent to 88 percent among females and from 9 percent to 76 percent among males (Zuckerman and Wheeler, 1975). Third, changes in the content of fear-of-success imagery cast doubt on the stability of an implicated motivational disposition, a cause of concern because the first themes identified by Horner failed to appear in later studies. Fourth, according to often-cited reviews of the performance data, this measure of fear of success yielded few consistent results. While a number of studies obtained performance decrements among women in the presence of men, as many other studies were unsuccessful in unearthing this pattern, and several actually found significant reversals of the expected effect for example, Feather and Simon, 1973; Karabenick and Marshall, 1974; Heilbrun, Kleemeier, and Piccola, 1974). Zuckerman and Wheeler (1975, p. 943) thus conclude that "for the most part, various experimental manipulations such as masculine versus feminine tasks, male versus female competition, alone versus competitive situations, and feedback of success versus feedback of failure have not shown consistent interactions with fear of success." In the face of inconsistent findings with measures of academic performance that yielded either positive correlations, negative correlations, or no correlation, Tresemer flatly states (considering these studies together) that fear of success has shown no relationship to ability. Finally, a less discussed issue is the problem of frequent methodo-logical flaws and noncomparable study designs that make serious consideration of this literature seem almost pointless (Tresemer, 1976; Fleming, 1977). Nowhere in the literature was the suggestion entertained that behavioral inconsistency might reflect a meaning-ful aspect of the fear-of-success conflict.

There were, in fact, far better grounds on which to discard the one-stimulus measure of fear-of-success imagery than inconsistent results, for example, the inappropriateness of using one stimulus and one level of ambiguity in measuring motivation (Kenny, 1964; Murstein, 1965), the lack of independent validation of the instru-ment, and lack of proof of uniqueness (McClelland, 1958). Accord-ing to a review by Fleming, Beldner, and Esposito (1980), this first measure of fear of success failed to meet most of the major criteria for a measure of motivation.

Development of a New Projective Measure. Aware of the first measure's difficulties from the start, Horner (1973) abandoned the a priori measure and tried to follow the traditional method of developing scoring systems for approach motives by: (1) leading an experimental group of women to believe that they had been successful in direct competition with a male of similar ability; (2) comparing Thematic Apperception Test (TAT) stories written under arousal conditions with those written by a control group of women under non-arousal conditions; and (3) incorporating the observed differences in TAT content into a scoring system (see McClelland, Atkinson, Clark, and Lowell, 1953; Atkinson, 1958). The six categories resulting from the analysis accounted for 44 percent of the variance in change in performance on a verbal task when going from a neutral to a competitive situation. In a second study, the same categories accounted for 36 percent of the variance in performance change, from a condition in which subjects worked alone to a condition in which subjects worked in the presence of males (see Fleming, 1977).

Of the six projective scoring categories that were isolated, three have to do with permutations of instrumental activity in a given story: complete suppression of instrumental action (Absence of Instrumental Activity), inhibition of personal responsibility for goal attainment (Relief), and channeling of action toward an affiliative goal (Interpersonal Engagement). Two categories involve the negative consequences of action (Noncontingent Negative Consequences; Contingent-Negative Consequences). The final category concerns mentioning people in the story (Absence of Others)—important, perhaps, in triggering the whole chain of associations. Thus, the scoring system suggests a reinterpretation of fear of success in that the underlying phenomenon is not avoidance of success per se, but the *problematic* expression of instrumental activity.

The new scoring system represents an improvement over the first effort at measurement in many respects, and Fleming, Beldner, and Esposito (1980) find that with the increase in stimuli and levels of ambiguity, the presence of an experimental validation, and convincing evidence of improved validity, the instrument promises far more precise measurement.

While Horner was quietly developing a sound projective measure of fear of success, other researchers were searching for more reliable "objective" methods of assessment. At least six questionnaire instruments have been developed (Pappo, 1972; Good and Good, 1973; Cohen, 1974; Zuckerman and Allison, 1976; Canavaan-Gumpert, Garner, and Gumpert, 1978; Tec, 1976), yet few have a large enough body of associated empirical research to allow assessment of their validity. Thus, energies in the field have been spread thin over many methods of measurement, and the resulting confusion now presents a stumbling block to students and researchers who are not sure what theory to follow or what method to use. In short, the confusion produced by inconsistent results has led to a splitting of research energies, the result being lack of progress in the field.

A Theory of Inconsistency. In the expectancy-value approach to motivation, motives are personality dispositions that remain latent until called into play by certain "releasing stimuli" in the immediate environment. The temporarily aroused state, called motivation, actually refers to the interaction of stable motives and immediate situational influences such that motives influence behavior only under certain conditions—when there is an aroused expectation that the current situation offers the opportunity to satisfy an incentive. Thus the *need* for achievement does not influence behavior under just any conditions on any routine task, but only when the situation offers a personal challenge (that is, with 50-50 subjective probability of success). Even where researchers try to design situations of such subjective probability, the subject is the final judge of whether the situation activates his own sense of what constitutes a personal challenge. To the insensitive observer, this critical difference in what situations mean to subjects can create the impression of inconsistent performance (as in Klinger, 1966).

In the case of avoidance motives, the anxiety surrounding the attainment of an incentive is aroused and acts to inhibit or redirect a motive. Of course, the conditions under which maximum inhibition occurs can also be specified mathematically in terms of the subjective probability of success. The task is not to require a motive to influence behavior across all situations in a specified way, but to understand why it predicts when it does and why it does not when it does not (see McClelland, 1966). Once a measure of motivation passes certain tests of construct validity (see Fleming, Beldner, and Esposito, 1980, on the new measure of fear of success), the test for validity then becomes whether or not a theoretically meaningful network of relationships appears to exist (McClelland, 1958; Loevinger, 1957).

Since fear of success is an approach-avoidance conflict, it might be expected that individuals who fear success both approach and avoid achievement-related situations under certain conditions, and that the potential for expressions of both tendencies may certainly appear to be inconsistent. Indeed, early psychoanalytic conceptions of the phenomenon recognized its now-you-see-it-now-you-don't aspects as paradoxical, but interpretable. Freud ([1915], 1959) tells us that certain individuals fall ill on the verge of recognizing a success, but that the wish for success is harmless as long as the wish does not become a conscious reality. In this event a person can even work fervently toward a goal that remains distant. For Sullivan (1953), fear of success is the inhibition or redirection of attempts at growth and mastery, owing to a parent's interference in the process that originates in a child's need to change itself to restore a positive state in an anxious, unpredictable, and possibly inconsistent parent. According to Horney (1936), the stage is set for the development of fear of success in a home and in a society which acts to convey the message that it is important to succeed and important not to fail, but risky to carry success too far. Thus, on the verge of success, individuals who fear success belittle themselves; on the verge of failure they substitute grand ambition for attainable goals. Thus, it is central to clinical fear-of-success theory that inhibition of achievement drives may occur under certain conditions, but that even the opposite may occur under other conditions.

Enough studies have appeared using Horner's new fear-of-success scoring system to allow some systematic determination of when fear-of-success motivation is operative. Results from the eight performance studies that have appeared (see Fleming, Beldner, and Esposito, 1980), show that individuals high in fear of success suppress achievement desires in some situations but not others. Among women, fear of success is negatively correlated with performance criteria in a number of experimental situations involving the presence of males (Shinn, 1973; Fleming, 1974, 1977), but not in situations where women competed against other women (Jackaway, 1974; Beldner, 1979). While performance impairment was found among women who scored high on the measure in three basic study paradigms requiring performance in test-like situations, with or without direct competition against a male (Shinn, 1973; Karabenick, 1977; Beldner, 1979), no performance impairment was found when a concerted effort was made to create a relaxed, nontest condition (Horner, 1973; see Fleming and Watson, 1980). In one study by Karabenick (1977), competitive performance was impaired among women on supposedly easy lists of anagrams sex-typed as masculine, but not on those sex-typed as feminine.

In studies of career aspirations, the aspirations of success-avoidant women were generally depressed downward, particularly with regard to careers requiring assertiveness or instrumentality (Esposito, 1976, 1977; Beldner, 1979; Jenkins, 1979). At the same time these women showed a preference for careers perceived as less threatening or more feminine (such as traditionally feminine occupations and homemaking), even if such low threat careers were incongruent with their real interests. As might have been expected, in two of the three studies of achievement-oriented women that used college grade point averages (Fleming, 1976; Beldner, 1979; Kripke, 1980), fear of success showed no relationship to grades; but Beldner found fear of success to be negatively correlated to grades in a subsample of relatively traditional women in the School of Education. Thus, the selective situation- and group-specific aspects of fear of success prediction are clearly apparent.

The pattern of selective prediction suggests that the instrumental energy of women high in fear of success is withdrawn from goals perceived as competitive, masculine, or challenging and thus imbued with the threat of negative consequences, but is directed toward less challenging goals perceived as more feminine, for which there is societal support. But what is seen as challenging by one sample may well be seen as "easy" by the next.

Selective inhibition and preference of this kind signals an underlying conflict that is also empirically evident in choosing careers that are incompatible with real interests (Esposito, 1977; Jenkins, 1979); feeling conflict over the feminine role; and denying the effort women expend (Jenkins, 1979). Difficulties in resolving conflicts have a way of expressing themselves in behavioral paralysis, which also appears in the literature as indecision over career choices (Fleming, 1978), paralysis in the face of a crisis (Stewart, 1975), and perhaps worse, the waste of admirable energy in pursuing unimportant goals (Jenkins, 1979).

The new scoring system for fear of success specifically indicates that the phenomenon concerns the problematic expression of instrumental action, and the problematic aspects of life for fear-of-success individuals come through in the data. It is unfortunate that so few of the available studies concern developmental antecedents of the motive, from which we might be able to fathom the sources of this problematic orientation to the world. However, a study using a method of subliminal stimulation (Cherry, 1977) found that fear-of-success scores were aroused in both men and women by cues related to separation and castration anxieties. The fact that these seemingly inconsistent anxieties have been linked to rejecting and seductive mothers respectively (Stolorow and Lachman, 1980) now has a familiar ring. It may prove to be the case that inconsistent behaviors on the part of parents is the development problem facing individuals charaterized by fear of success.

As if the data for women were not hard enough to interpret, the results for men add another twist. In accordance with expectancy-value theory, there are two possible theoretical resolutions of avoidance motivation—inhibition or redirection of achievement drives. While the results for women more closely resemble a redirection of achievement energy away from high-threat to low-threat goals, the results for men suggest only inhibition of achievement motivation. When substantial trends have been found in the performance studies using male subjects, the motive shows weak positive correlations with achievement striving for males (Fleming, 1974; Karabenick, 1977). The different directions in which the motive predicts behavior for men and women are clearer in the studies of occupational aspirations, where among males significant but modest positive correlations were found with level of aspiration (Esposito, 1976, 1977). Furthermore, there tend to be no sex differences in fear-of-success scores when the TAT is given under neutral testing conditions, but significant sex differences when it is given under arousal conditions—with females producing the higher scores (Shinn, 1973; Jackaway, 1974; Esposito, 1976, 1977). The sex differences in aroused scores suggest a more intense arousal of the conflict in women that seems compatible with the performance results which indicate a weak positive correlation among males, but strong negative correlations with achievement behaviors in most samples of women. For males, then, the direction of the findings suggests that they, like women, inhibit the desire for instrumentality, but do not redirect it from the achievement arena.

It may well be that the theory of fear of success should be a theory of people who behave inconsistently because they have good developmental reasons for doing so. However, it may also be, as suggested by psychoanalytic theory, that such people are unaware of their own inconsistency and put themselves in situations where they can avoid the feeling of successful mastery that precipitates behavioral or affective lapses. At this point, of course, it is quite interesting that the very characteristic of the first projective measure of fear of success that elicited the most criticism now, with a precise measure, appears to be a meaningful aspect of the phenomenon.

Separate Domains of Projective and Psychometric Theories

The first projective measure of fear of success failed largely because of inconsistency in the behavioral results. While the new measure meets the projective criteria for a measure of motivation (for example, McClelland, 1958) and lets us see the "inconsistency" in behavioral manifestations as a meaningful aspect of the approach-avoidance conflict, it has already run into difficulty on charges of failure to meet psychometric standards of reliability (Zuckerman and Wheeler, 1975; Karabenick, 1977).

As a measure of the degree of accuracy of a test, and thus its potential effectiveness (its actual effectiveness depending upon its validity), reliability has always occupied a prominent place in psychometric theory. Of the three specific reliability issues confronting the TAT (that is, intercoder reliability, test-retest reliability, and internal consistency reliability), the less problematic issue of intercoder reliability has largely been solved by the presence of TAT scoring manuals and the requirement of .85 scoring reliability.

Unlike the first projective measure of fear of success, the second is accompanied by a detailed scoring manual with practice sets and explicit instructions on how to attain expert-level scoring reliability (Horner and Fleming, 1977). However, satisfaction of criteria for test-retest and internal consistency reliability promise to be tough issues that psychometricians consistently raise, issues that projective proponents find it more comfortable to avoid. This situation thus renews a long-standing argument between the two camps of theorists.

Historically, projective techniques have developed outside the traditions of psychological measurement (Atkinson, 1958; Kenny, 1964). According to Lanyon and Goodstein (1971), it was an accident of history that two separate lines of inquiry concerning the personality developed into the clinical assessment of psychopathology and the academic study of individual differences. The important point to note is that the followers of each tradition are known for their strong negative emotional bias toward one another—a bias apparent by 1920—and their refusal to take the other camp's assumptions seriously. Thus, each approach to personality measurement adheres to a different set of assumptions on the reliability issues.

Assumptions of the Psychometric Approach: The Homogeneity Model. The academic study of individual differences has been exemplified by paper-and-pencil instruments and has emphasized the atheoretical study of discrete traits and the use of statistical procedures for establishing norms and measures of reliability (Lanyon and Goodstein, 1971). With questionnaires—the psychometrician's tool par excellence—high reliabilities are a routine possibility. Since reliability estimates are assumed to set the upper limit on validity, low reliability essentially signals that there is no point in pursuing the issue of validity (Guilford, 1954; Nunnally, 1967). The first step in attaining good validity is attaining high intercoder reliability; with questionnaires the problem of scoring error virtually disappears. Test-retest reliability (the self-correlation of a test on different administrations) provides an index of how stable a set of measurements is over time—an important consideration for a test that presumes to reflect enduring aspects of the personality. Good retest reliability coefficients are found with questionnaires between same and alternate forms of the test, confirming that a stable trait is being assessed. The internal consistency of a test refers to the intercorrelation of equivalent forms of the test or of test items; it provides a kind of information different from retest reliability, since the parts or items of a test might intercorrelate zero in the face of high retest coefficients (Guilford, 1954). With questionnaires, the high internal consistency estimates that are routinely produced suggest that all items measure the same phenomenon and can be treated additively, such that the higher the score the stronger the disposition in question. Thus, the questionnaire methods of the psychometrician claim impressive reliability achievements, and the adherence to statistical standards against which to judge personality measures comes out of the conviction that powerful mathematical methods are needed to advance the state of the science (Guilford, 1954).

The reliability assumptions and methods of the psychometric school of thought derive from a random-sampling or homogeneity model of human behavior (see Loevinger, 1957; Lundy, 1980). There is assumed to be a large pool of relatively similar items that appropriately measure a concept, from which some are randomly sampled (Entwisle, 1972; Lundy, 1980). According to Lundy the traditional practice is to use a homogeneous set of predictors that define a narrow construct with great accuracy, and the test itself becomes the operational definition of the construct. Cronbach's (1951) alpha is justified as an unbiased assessment of reliability only for the limiting case of perfect domain homogeneity. A negative alpha is theoretically not possible. Not only are homogeneity of items and the responses to them expected, but homogeneity in expression of the traits, that is, cross-situational consistency, has also become a theoretical expectation. The logic of the homogeneity model clearly justifies the use of reliability statistics requiring consistency, and reliability has become the central concept in test construction.

Despite their logical coherence, the psychometric arguments have been assailed for betraying inherent flaws. Lundy (1980) and Loevinger (1957), for example, point out that the assumption of perfect domain homogeneity for Cronbach's alpha is never met, and that the best items rather than a random sample are chosen. The items actually sampled from the homogeneous domain tend to measure superficial and obvious aspects of behavior subject to distortion. It is not, therefore, surprising that self-report instruments notoriously arouse many kinds of defensiveness by requiring subjects to report on needs or defense mechanisms of which they may be unaware (Morgan and Murray, 1935; Lanyon and Goodstein, 1971).

Loevinger notes that test constructors have had to struggle with the massive distortions produced by questionnaires that aim for direct personality measurement (rather than indirect measurement). Questionnaire measures indeed turn out to be good at predicting themselves (that is, the same or alternate forms of the test) rather than real behavior, and while self-descriptions seem stable over time, the behaviors to which they refer do not (Mischel, 1968). The lack of attention given to issues of validity in establishing reliability criteria (Loevinger, 1957) makes it no surprise that the magnitude of prediction obtained with questionnaires is not impressive, hovering around 9 percent of the variance. Perhaps the hardest blow of all is that the assumption of homogeneity in items across situations has been seriously questioned as little more than our own human need to see consistency in behavior(Mischel, 1968).

Assumptions of the Projective Approach: The Multiple Regression Model. If one accepts the reliability criterion of the psychometric approach and evaluates TAT measures of motivation accordingly, the apparent problems of reliability for a measure like fear of success appear to be enormous. Although the issue of interscorer reliability is largely solved with research versions of TAT scoring systems that require a minimum of .85 intercoder reliability, the retest reliabilities in the TAT literature range from.03 to .59 with a mean of .28 (Entwisle, 1972; Winter and Stewart, 1977); these coefficients are much less than acceptable by psychometric standards and indicate measurement instability. Internal consistency reliabilities for the TAT are so low as to suggest the scores from different pictures represent random unrelated events that provide no basis for prediction from one story to another and cannot be regarded in an additive way (Entwisle, 1972).

Projective theorists, of course, do not accept the rules of the psychometric approach to personality measurement. As the legacy of the clinical approach to behavior, projective techniques have traditionally emphasized global, rather than discrete, aspects of personality and have assumed that the important aspects of behavior were buried deep in the unconscious. There has thus been a preoccupation with studying the hidden aspects of personality, rather than the obvious. Because ambiguous stimuli are used in the projective tradition, the subject is not aware that in creating a TAT story, he is revealing his deepest needs. Through this disguise the defenses are relaxed and a deeper level of consciousness can be penetrated (Morgan and Murray, 1935). Such methods are said to tap the pattern of internal organization without disturbing the personality itself (Jensen, 1959). Projective measures are typically derived from and associated with sophisticated psychodynamic theories of behavior that attempt to order findings to understand the underlying world view. In the study of human motivations, need states can be manipulated independently of the measuring instruments derived from the experimental inductions (see McClelland, 1958). Furthermore, theories of human motivation do not posit consistency in behavior across situations, but rather posit dispositions that remain latent until called into play by the cues of relevant situations. The situations that arouse motives may look inconsistent to the eye of an objective observer, but are actually found to be guided by an internal logic or world view. Thus, with a different logic of personality dynamics and the legitimacy given to presumed behavioral inconsistency, it is little wonder that psychometric reliability measures seem irrelevant to projective proponents.

In defense of low retest coefficients, failure in reliability is attributed to: (1) the retest being a psychologically different experience such that taking it once renders it unsuitable for future use and may spoil the subject for a retest (McClelland, 1958; Loevinger, 1957; Jensen, 1959); (2) a "self-destruct" quality of the associative refractory phase where making a certain associative response tends to introduce resistance to giving it again (Telford, 1931; McClelland, 1958); (3) memory for initial responses that contaminates the test such that retesting may be a matter of recall and not reliability (Jensen, 1959; Winter and Stewart, 1977). Thus, researchers using the TAT believe its "true" reliability to be higher than estimates would indicate.

As for low estimates of internal consistency, there is widespread belief that split-half or internal consistency reliability is impossible, incorrect, or meaningless in the case of the TAT because (1) projective tests use a limited number of stimulus items, making the construction of split halves unfeasible (Jensen, 1959); and (2) the stimuli are not selected to resemble each other in obvious ways or in statistical properties, but to explore a unique aspect of the personality unduplicated by other stimuli (Ainsworth, 1954; Frank, 1965). Moreover, the associative refractory phase and the tendency it exerts to inhibit similar responses also poses a problem for this kind of reliability (McClelland, 1958). McClelland, Atkinson, Clark, and Lowell (1953) have shown that with a special set of pictures, high internal consistency (over .70) can be achieved. However, inter-item similarity is not seen as desirable at the expense of inter-item redundancy.

Clearly projective theorists do not subscribe to the same set of assumptions as their psychometric counterparts. Yet is is also clear that projective assumptions have not been proposed systematically, with special statistical procedures, but largely in response to psychometric criticisms. In commenting on this state of affairs, Lundy (1980) finds that the projective theory approach is guided by a set of intuitive and informal assumptions that, when viewed systematically, actually parallel a multiple regression model. Lundy explains that instead of sampling randomly from a supposedly homogeneous set of items, the projective researcher depends on a limited number of stimuli; consequently items must be selected that maximize the test's correlation with a criterion. Rather than dictating a high intercorrelation among a set of predictors, the regression model assumes that an ideal set of predictors will have inter-item correlations of zero since a nonzero correlation between any two items represents wasteful redundancy of information. Rather than assuming a homogeneous domain of items that theoretically have equal ability to reflect the disposition in question, the multiple regression model assumes that items have differential ability to reflect an underlying motive. This motive may or may not be expressed in response to all scenes, depending on early experiences with the situations depicted in the stimuli. It is logical then to add together scores from a broad domain, provided that the criterion for the test itself is heterogeneous. Rather than using the test as the operational definition of the construct, projective researchers work with constructs having broad implications for behavior; they are defined more imprecisely, but with the aid of independent validation techniques, such as the intuitive arousal (see McClelland, 1958).

In sum, the problems for TAT measures of motivation are not only the failure to hold up well against psychometric standards of reliability, but also the failure to propose a systematic, alternative set of rules and procedures that might better fit the dynamic assumptions. Lundy's explication of the multiple regression model is a first step in this direction. While such measures also do not posit cross-situational consistency in behavior, there has been no convincing demonstration that similar genotypic dispositions have different inconsistent phenotypic expressions in behavior (see Mischel, 1968). Like psychometric instruments, TAT measures are also guilty of achieving only modest degrees of success in prediction, with magnitudes of prediction rarely exceeding 9 percent of the variance. Thus, despite the psychodynamic sophistication associated with the TAT, its poor methodological status renders its promise unrealized (Lanyon and Goodstein, 1971).

The Status of Personality Research. The projective and psychometric approaches, then, are at odds on a number of issues in personality measurement. The psychometrician is content to rely on subjective reports of what are often superficial aspects of behavior, and the questionnaire acts as the definition of the construct with no independent source of validation of a given construct. Yet construct validity, according to McClelland (1958), is a separate criterion that must be met in addition to validating the measuring instrument. For the projective theorist, more ingenious techniques indirectly assessing the state of the unconscious mind are used with measurements that rely on experimental validations as part of the evidence for their accuracy. Reliability, of course, is the emotional issue on which the two sides are divided. There has been uncritical acceptance of psychometric rules demanding consistency of test items and behavior that may or may not reflect the way behavior really is. Yet projective theorists have been reluctant to propose alternative statistical solutions that defend the assumption that heterogeneous items can tap a construct for a given person.

The curious part of the quarrel is that neither objective nor projective methods have been able to predict behavior terribly well.

Despite the inspiring fact that objective mathematical rigor is the name of the game for psychometrics, the measures still do not account for more than 9 percent of the variance on the average. And despite the powerful indirect methods and theoretical sophistication of projective theories, TAT measures rarely obtain better prediction than questionnaires. With this track record, the whole field of individual differences has been called into question and Mischel argues that while personality may be "interesting" there is no point spending time studying it. There can be little doubt that the split in the personality field, with each side ignoring the strong points of the other, has contributed to the poor status of personality measurement. It could even be that the split in points of view, with the accompanying rigidity and diffusion of methodological energies, is *responsible* for the poor status of personality research.

Reliability and Prediction

If there is any possible truth to the suspicion that the existence of separate camps in personality research has impeded our progress in predicting behavior, some effort should be expended in exploring the practical statistical convergence of the two points of view. The question of interest thus becomes, What would happen in the TAT measurement of motivation if projective theorists were to take psychometric assumptions seriously? This section will review some recent attempts to test the quarrels between the two camps.

Test-Retest Reliability. At least in the case of fear of success, the complete absence of test-retest reliability data illustrates just how wide the gap between psychometric and projective thinking can be. Although at least four researchers using the new measure have administered TATs to the same subjects twice (Shinn, 1973; Horner, 1973; Jackaway, 1974; Fleming, 1978), only one of them considered it important to report the correlation of fear-of-success scores between Time 1 and Time 2 administrations. Shinn (1973) found fear-of-success scores to be well correlated from Time 1 to Time 2 for women ($r = .51$, $p < .001$), but not for men ($r = .02$), which suggested to her that the motive appears to be a stable personality disposition among women, but not among men. Her interpretation, however, is complicated by the fact that the testing conditions were not similar

in both time periods; Time 1 involved testing in single sex classrooms that were merged into one coed institution just before the
Time 2 classroom testing. The change in sex composition of the
classrooms clearly constituted an arousal situation for high fear-of-
success women, whose performance on achievement tasks deterio-
rated in the coed setting. The point is that all of the available fear-of-
success studies sampled behavior in *different* situations for each
administration. Having once given the TAT under standard neutral
conditions that provide the best reflection of individual differences
(McClelland and Clark, 1956), the next logical step is to find situations that arouse the motive in question and pull for its expression
in observable behavior. It seems not to occur easily to researchers
working with measures of motivation that it is a meaningful use of
time and energy to administer the TAT under the *same* conditions
twice, as it would to a psychometrician concerned with homogeneity.
Behind the projective intuition that prediction is the critical concern
is the knowledge that TATs given under neutral conditions predict
behavior best when the relevant behaviors are sampled under
arousal conditions (see Klinger, 1966; Lundy, 1981).

Admittedly, fear of success is a very young motive, especially
if its age is dated from the new scoring system, and this accounts for
the lack of retest studies. Since the scoring system has already been
judged to be as good (or bad) as other TAT measures of motivation
(Karabenick, 1977), reminders of its reliability failures will undoubtedly generate forthcoming reliability studies. Note, however,
that this likely trend repeats the history of other motivation studies:
namely, reliability studies testing homogeneity as an afterthought in
response to vehement criticism, with no convincing defense of the
original position guided by implicit but unspoken heterogeneity
assumptions. It appears that with psychometricians always on the
offensive, projective proponents remain on the defensive.

Nevertheless, investigations that have played by the psychometric rules with motive other than fear of success have proved
encouraging for the future of projective techniques.

Recall that the failure in test-retest reliability is attributed by
projective theorists to the retest being a psychologically different
experience, such that taking the test once spoils the subject for a
retest. Furthermore there is said to be a self-destruct quality of the

associative-refractory phase, such that making a certain associative response introduces resistance to making it again. Finally, memory for initial responses allegedly contaminates the retest, such that retesting becomes a matter of recall and not reliability. In a test of differential recall, Winter and Stewart (1977) tried to control differential self-instruction by leaving the subject to himself to write the same stories or different stories upon retest. In their study seventy Wesleyan University students, about half male and half female, wrote TAT stories about four pictures and then returned for one of the three retest conditions. In the same-story condition, subjects were asked to put themselves in the same frame of mind they were in during the first administration and to try to write the same story they wrote at that time. In the different-story condition, they were asked to try to write stories as different as possible from the ones they had written before. In the no-instruction condition, subjects were asked not to worry about whether their stories were the same or different, and to write whatever stories they wished.

The results showed that in the same-story condition the reliability was high; the coefficient was .61, and a gamma test for high-low placement for above or below the mean was .60. These figures are, of course, higher than any of those reported for TAT measures of motivation so far. In the no-instruction condition, reliability was almost as high, with a coefficient of .58 and a gamma of .60. In the different condition, the reliability drops to chance levels on the low side of the retest reliability range, with a coefficient of .27 and a gamma of −.23.

Winter and Stewart conclude that one of the greatest problems in retest reliability is substantially resolved either by telling the subjects not to worry about whether their stories are the same as or different from the first administration or by asking them to write the same story. They believe that the drop in reliability in the different-story condition occurs because the subject responds by giving a story lower in the motive hierarchy, that is, one of lower regnancy. Thus, the generally low reliabilities for TAT measures may occur because some subjects are instructing themselves to write the same stories, while others are instructing themselves to write different stories. Indeed, averaging the reliabilities from the same and different conditions produces the usual reliabilities found in TAT research! By bringing this factor under experimental control, reliabilities now approach those found by objective personality tests. So, low reliability seems to be largely a function of the instructional set peculiar to the TAT, such that it requires special instruction to undo that factor.

Lundy (1980) repeated the Winter and Stewart procedure for need affiliation and need intimacy after one year. With the appropriate instructions, good retest correlations were found in the range of other objective personality tests ($.43 < r < .61$), but Lundy also demonstrates that these correlations were the highest ever obtained over a comparable time span for a TAT measured motive. He further demonstrates the negligible effects of recall on retest coefficients. Most important, the study showed that contrary to the psychometric assumption that alpha sets the upper limit on other kinds of reliability estimates, retest coefficients were substantially higher than alpha coefficients.

As Winter and Stewart (1977) point out, there is great divergence even in the instructional set required by objective and projective tests. According to them, objective tests typically instruct participants, explicitly or implicitly, to be consistent or to give the same response on retest, so that there is an effective pull for consistency (or reliability) as part of the normal or "helpful" way of responding on the second administration. Typical TAT instructions, on the other hand, stress imagination, creativity, variability—in other words, unreliability. Yet the vastly different views taken of retest reliability need not continue to divide students of personality. If, as Loevinger (1957) advises, validity considerations become part of the process of establishing reliability criteria, one then becomes concerned not with how well correlated two sets of tests are over time, but how well each test predicts some important criterion, or how well it predicts a *pattern* of behavior reflecting personality organization. Clearly the issue would take on a new and more relevant focus for personality research. If magnitude of prediction becomes the final arbiter of our disagreement, it may be harder to find ways of prolonging the quarrel.

Internal Consistency Reliability. For the motive to avoid success, it is possible to report concrete progress on the issue of internal consistency and success in prediction. Remember that from the psychometric point of view, good intercorrelation of test items is necessary if the items are to be combined additively, and low internal consistency means that the items are random, unrelated events, not measuring the same phenomenon. From the projective point of view, stimuli are chosen for the information they reveal about the personality, and not being well correlated means that items are not redundant and truly tap different aspects of the psychological process.

Only one published study has investigated the homogeneity of TAT test items with the new scoring system (Marshall and Karabenick, 1977). Although no alpha coefficient was reported, low positive intercorrelations were found among three cues similar to those used in Horner's validation study, suggesting a level of internal consistency similar to that obtained with other projective measures of motivation. However, more evidence of test homogeneity was found for females than for males. It appears that while scores to each cue were consistently negatively related to performance among females, the prediction obtained with the first cue (sunset; see below) was greater than that with a summary score using all three cues. Monotonic decreases in the magnitude of the correlations by cue suggested order effects, but the degree to which each cue contributed to prediction was not investigated.

In a reanalysis of data from Horner's (1973) validation study of the fear-of-success scoring system, Fleming and Watson (1980) determined the intercorrelations of the six scoring categories: Contingent Negative Consequences, Noncontingent Negative Consequences, Interpersonal Engagement, Relief, Absence of Instrumental Activity, and Absence of Others. While some of the correlations were substantial (up to .68), most range from low positive to low negative with an alpha of only .29. Intercorrelations were also found for the five stories used:

1. Carol is looking through the telescope.
2. Joan seems to be particularly pleased.
3. Diane has just received word that she is one of the three students in the state to get a perfect score on the LSAT (Law School Admission Test).
4. Linda is looking out at the sunset.
5. Barbara is in the midst of a heated argument.

Note, however, that to avoid the problem of defensive imagery only the three "neutral" cues (excluding the success and power cues) were used to develop the scoring system (see Kenny, 1964; Epstein, 1966). Thus the intercorrelations of all five range only from low positive to low negative with an alpha of -.15. The alpha for the three neutral cues is worse, -.69, with all cues being negatively related. Clearly, internal inconsistency estimates for fear-of-success scoring categories and test battery items have produced the lowest internal consistency estimates on record. Furthermore, the negative alphas produced are, according to the psychometrician, a theoretical impossibility.

Despite this poor showing against psychometric standards, Horner was able to show that when the scoring categories (summed across the three neutral stimuli) were entered into a regression equation, they accounted for an impressive 46 percent of the variance in performance change in women from a neutral testing setting to successful competition against a male competitor. Scoring categories, however, can be derived from many different stimuli, all of which have different properties and a different significance to the subject. Thus, when fear-of-success scores from all five cues were put into a regression equation, they accounted for 40 percent of the variance in performance change, with a multiple correlation of -.70 ($p < .001$). In another regression equation, the three neutral cues alone accounted for 39 percent of the variance ($R = -.62$, $p < .001$). Needless to say, the magnitude of prediction in these regression results is unusually high for motivation research.

But what of the consequences for prediction when cue scores for fear of success are combined additively across stimuli? The single best predictor of female performance was the "pleased" cue, accounting for 24 percent of the variance ($R = -.49$, $p < .005$). In combination with fear-of-success scores from the "telescope" cue, the second best predictor of performance, maximum prediction is obtained with 37 percent of the variance ($R = .61$, $p < .001$). But thereafter, adding cue scores reduces the magnitude of prediction. To wit, the summary measure of the three neutral cues accounts for 24 percent of the variance ($R = -.40$, $p < .005$), and using all five cues in summary, only 12 percent of the variance can be accounted for ($R = -.34$, $p < .10$), a level of prediction similar to that found in most motivation research. Note that the prediction achieved with the two best cues is similar to the optimal level obtained in a regression equation with the scoring categories, even though these two best cues are *negatively* correlated ($r = -.18$).

It would seem, then, that high internal consistency is not necessary for maximum prediction. This kind of reliability is clearly no requirement when cue scores can be entered into a regression equation, and even the best summative combinations of projective items seem in no way to depend on strong intercorrelations. Yet, it is also clear that indiscriminately adding scores across cues that are not well intercorrelated results in substantial losses in predictive power. Only certain combinations of item scores rivaled the magnitude of prediction achieved in a regression equation. The critical point is that motivation research relies on the indiscriminate summation of cue scores, but here this procedure resulted in dramatic losses in predictive power, from 49 percent to 12 percent of the variance when compared to the results from a regression analysis, and from 37 percent to 12 percent of the variance when compared to the two cues providing maximum predictive power. The clear implication is that the magnitude of the findings in the literature could be severe underestimates of true relationships.

In any case it seems that low internal consistency for TATs is a methodological issue that can be resolved, but there are a number of snags to get free of before clear methodological guidelines for obtaining maximum prediction can be set forth. For example, the scores to all cues do not predict in the same direction. The "pleased" and "telescope" cues are negatively correlated with performance change ($r = -.49$, $r = -.29$, respectively); the "argument" and "sunset" cues produce low positive correlations ($r = .11$, $r = .15$, respectively); and the "success" cue is unequivocally correlated in a positive direction ($r = .31$).

The positive correlation with the success cue is clearly the most problematic. Yet the highly specific and drive-relevant nature of this cue is expected to arouse defensiveness that would reduce its validity (see Kenny, 1964; Epstein, 1966; Lundy, 1981). Lundy finds that defensiveness-arousing cues result in stereotypic imagery less reflective of true individual differences. Epstein found that approach-avoidance conflict can be detected with stimulus dimensions (that is, stimuli ranked according to drive relevance) by the simultaneous occurrence of overresponding at the low end of the dimension and underresponding at the high end, or by inverted V-shaped curves that shift with intensity of conflict. Indeed, the pattern shown by mean levels of fear-of-success responses to Horner's stimuli were found to conform to the first pattern, that is, with the highest mean scores to (affect) cues of low drive relevance (i.e., pleased) and the lowest means to cues of high drive relevance (i.e., success). This pattern of mean scores and differential prediction may mean that some defensive blocking occurs to anxiety-provoking cues of high achievement relevance.

Indeed, there is even further evidence in this study that mean scores decrease from neutral conditions to the competitive arousal condition, but also that scores to affect cues (pleased, smile) increased under arousal while those to other cues, regardless of achievement relevance, decreased. Since several other studies have found increases in mean scores under arousal (for example, Shinn, 1973; Jackaway, 1974), more knowledge of the conditions under which approach-avoidance motive scores fluctuate is required. At the very least, the findings indicate that success-specific or high-drive relevant cues are the least useful for prediction. However, it may well be, as Epstein suggests, that their usefulness depends on the intensity of the conflict in varying subject populations. The research question then becomes, In which populations (for example, male versus female) and under what conditions (neutral versus arousal) are cues of high achievement relevance poor predictors?

It is important to note that no additive combination of cue scores provided as good a prediction as was observed in the regression analyses, where contributions of all cue variances could be taken into account. Clearly the use of regression analysis is best suited to the purpose of obtaining maximum prediction and should be used far more than it is to demonstrate the power of projective stimuli. Yet the cumbersomeness of the procedure, especially in instances of more than one dependent variable, necessitates the development of TAT batteries that can provide close to the same level of prediction. Consideration of items that are highly internally consistent is one alternative, but it may be that the price of inter-item redundance will be paid in reduced magnitude of prediction. In the data reported here, contiguous cues of low and moderate achievement relevance provided maximum prediction. Considerable research will have to be done to determine which batteries provide optimal predictive power and in which populations they are most suitable.

One guideline for the research to be done is that fear-of-success scores (motive scores in general) are actually samples of thoughts produced to a variety of situations, such that when summed across five cues one is left with potential success-avoidance in the *average* situation (see McClelland, 1966). It is probably no accident that the level of prediction produced from summing five cue scores is the same as that obtained from objective personality inventories that ask subjects to respond in the usual or the average way. The advantage of the TAT is that it provides not a report on the average response, but a piece of fantasy behavior in response to a specific situation. Wise use of this behavior could reveal a great deal about human motiation and guide us toward better predictive validity.

Implications for Measurement of Motives. This exploration into a practical convergence of statistical solutions that heed aspects of both psychometric and projective approaches has revealed two important points. First, it seems clear that psychometricians adhere to a rigid consistency model of personality item selection that has culminated in a consistency model of human behavior. On the other hand, projective theory more aptly fits a heterogeneity model of item selection and human behavior that is best illustrated by a multiple regression model. Second, psychometricians have been vehement in their demand for conformity to rules of consistency, even when inappropriate, while proponents of projective methods have adhered to an intuitive model of behavior that recognizes inconsistency as meaningful, but have never proposed or defended the underlying assumptions. With the field split into two extreme positions, poor predictive validity seems to be the consequence.

Yet the few empirical tests of both positions promise to point the way toward bridging the gap. For retest reliability the projective theorists were found to be right in suspecting that something about the first test administration spoils the subject for retest. But by taking the psychometric question seriously, it is now clear that a large part of that problem is due to differential self-instruction to write the same or different stories. Also, alpha does not appear to set the upper limit on the magnitude of retest reliabilities. For internal consistency reliability, the projective theorists were right in assuming that these cues tap different, nonredundant (that is, unrelated) aspects of the personality and that nonredundancy is achieved at the expense of internal consistency reliability. The psychometric theorists, however, were also partly right in saying that items not internally consistent cannot be added. Indeed, the evidence indicated that while indiscriminate addition resulted in dramatic losses in predictive power, items need not be internally consistent in order to produce maximum prediction. For magnitude of prediction, it is certainly true that motive measures characteristically yield low levels of intercorrelation, yet there were dramatic gains in predictive power either when all cue variances could be used in a regression analysis or when cue scores were not summed indiscriminately.

If it is actually possible for the two competing views to converge, achieving impressive predictive validity and eliminating false assumptions, why have the two camps been so vehemently split for so long despite attempts to readjust the unproductive assumptions (for example, Loevinger, 1957; McClelland, 1958)? Also, why have the two sets of arguments been carried out, as Lundy notes, on a purely theoretical plane, with few actual tests of their relative merits? And why, after just a few preliminary attempts to test competing assumptions does future research in this area seem so promising? It looks as though the split in the field of personality served as little more than a smoke screen—but for what?

Bridging the Gap

In the short space of an essay, decent progress has been made toward bridging the gap between psychometric and projective points of view by asking the right statistical questions. Once the quarrels between the two camps were put to a test, the evidence presented showed only that reliability was enhanced, prediction was improved, and the future promises a better understanding of the motives in question. Despite the statistical inconvenience of motive scores, the projective medium was not too sloppy, murky, or incomprehensible to yield good or meaningful prediction. While serious attention to psychometric matters proved important, many of the psychometric assumptions were found to be inaccurate and to betray faulty assumptions about statistical and human behavior.

On the surface it appears as though the dualism in personality assessment was an accident of history. If so, it is one that served no useful purpose, since convergence in the viewpoints promises to further the science. Furthermore, it has served as a smokescreen that shielded both the defensible position of projective theory and the psychometric abhorrence of the inconsistency that exists in much of human behavior. This accident, then, seemed responsible for an inaccurate picture of human personality, just as inappropriate methods for measuring personality erected a barrier to progress in the study of personality. It makes one wonder if erecting barriers to progress in personality was not the unwitting purpose of the dualism. If the suggestion that the split was more than an accident seems ludicrous, consider the following.

Research in the psychometric tradition has produced a body of research following a homogeneity model that demands consistency in instrumentation and behavior even when it is inappropriate, resulting in a body of research reflecting not true personality but (perhaps) the need of psychologists to see consistency in behavior, even where it does not exist. The making of statistical rules of procedure that rely too heavily on techniques that require consistency completes an approach that cannot penetrate the defenses of subjects, perhaps because it serves the defenses of psychologists. Thus, behind the rigid demand for consistency lie assumptions that blind one to the realities of much of human behavior. This view could be described as rational, cognitive, self-serving in its defensiveness, and wrong in many instances.

On the other hand, projective theorists have stubbornly refused to have their beloved fantasy world subjected to rigorous scrutiny and have avoided the important reality of the psychometrician. Although intuitively following an implicit heterogeneity model of behavior, they have failed to explicate rules or statistical models, and refused to defend a defensible position. This view could be described as infantile in its avoidance of reality testing.

Consider also that the opposition between the two camps has generated more confusion than understanding and threatens to result in the lack of credibility of personality as a worthy discipline. The competition has come at the expense of predictive validity, as if the two warring sides to personality research, one catering to ego defense and the other to infantile impulse, were more intent on the fight than on progress in the field. Does this not suggest that a purpose, albeit an irrational one, has been served by the dualism? As with splits in the abnormal personality that arise from attempts to defend against a double bind, reintegrating the parts is the only true road to health and progress.

Fear of success provides an excellent illustration of how the competing views act jointly to obscure understanding of a behavioral pattern. The fear-of-success phenomenon has faced more obstacles than the laws of probability would allow. Although the first projective measure was found to pull defensive reactions to success rather than motivation (for example, Feather and Raphelson, 1974), the body of literature produced by it was so full of methodological errors that reviewers have had to comment on the difficulty of assessing true results (Tresemer, 1976; Fleming, 1977). Researchers have also refused to control for story length or ability, and have given inappropriate tasks as well as inappropriate instructions (Fleming, 1977). In the pioneering efforts of McClelland, Atkinson and Winter, there was sufficient direction given to avoid all of these mistakes, but that direction was ignored. Although the psychological public eagerly seized upon an obviously unreliable measure of motivation, the new measure cannot get the attention it deserves. The old measure met its demise because of inconsistent results and evaluations by social psychologists using psychometric yardsticks, yet the new projective measure shows inconsistency to be a meaningful aspect of the behavioral phenomenon. The new scoring system, however, is under attack for "unreliability." The retreat from projective methods of measurement into more objective but less diagnostic methods adds to a state of confusion too overwhelming for most interested students to tackle. The situation adds up to a collective attempt at internal and external sabotage—internal sabotage by those unable to defend the concept soon enough or well enough, and external sabotage by the greater credibility of misleading reliability standards.

Why has there been such a loud response both by those interested in the phenomenon and by those who feel it is not worthy of study? Perhaps in the case of fear of success, the best current illustration of a general problem, an understanding of the phenomenon might be too threatening, even for people who are doing research in the area. We all wonder if we fear success at some time or other, but we rationalize the thought away because we are, after all, successful psychologists. Perhaps the threat potential issues from the fact that fear of success is linked to Oedipal conflicts surrounding envy and hostility from the same-sex parent that results in the punishment of striving for competence—a phenomenon aptly captured in the projective scoring system (see Freud, 1959; Horney, 1936). It is far from trivial to suggest that researchers who study fear of success unknowingly sabotage their own effort, perhaps to avoid understanding their own painful Oedipal dilemmas. Indeed, the related research tells us that fear of success is one solution to exposure to inconsistent parents who first encourage, but then interfere with, competence striving, so that the individual learns to fall ill on the verge of mastery—the projective proponents' position (see Fleming, 1981). The same exposure to inconsistent parents, however, can lead to other behavioral solutions as well, such as a rigid denial of the inconsistency and/or identification with the parent—the psychometric position (see Shapiro, 1965). Perhaps the root issue behind fear of success strikes home to more than women psychologists; it may be too close to home for those who would prefer to deny difficult childhoods even though it may have drawn them to the study of personality. But the issue is open to empirical testing by anyone willing to pursue it.

Even without accepting this explanation for the unwarranted schism between projective and psychometric approaches to measuring personality, the important message of this essay is that a practical convergence between these two points of view holds promise for better research.

References

Ainsworth, M. "Problems of Validation." In B. Klopfer and others (Eds.), *Developments in the Rorschach Technique*. Vol. 1: *Technique and Theory*. New York: World Book, 1954.

Atkinson, J. W. (Ed.). *Motives in Fantasy, Action, and Society*. New York: Van Nostrand, 1958.

Beldner, J. "Fear of Success and Achievement-Related Behavior in College Women." Paper presented at annual meeting of the Eastern Psychological Association, Philadelphia, 1979.

Canavaan-Gumpert, D., Garner, K., and Gumpert, P. *The Success-Fearing Personality*. Lexington, Mass.: Lexington Books, 1978.

Cherry, E. F. "On Success Avoidance in Women: A Comparative Study of Psychoanalytic Theories." Unpublished doctoral dissertation, Adelphi University, 1977.

Cohen, N. E. "Explorations in the Fear of Success." Unpublished doctoral dissertation, Columbia University, 1974.

Condry, J., and Dyer, S. "Fear of Success: Attribution of Cause to the Victim." *Journal of Social Issues*, 1976, *32*, 63-83.

Cronbach, L. J. "Coefficient Alpha and the Internal Structure of Tests." *Psychometrika*, 1951, *16*, 297-334.

Entwisle, D. R. "To Dispel Fantasies About Fantasy-Based Measure of Achievement Motivation." *Psychological Bulletin*, 1972, *77*, 377-391.

Epstein, S. "Some Theoretical Considerations on the Nature of Ambiguity and the Use of Stimulus Dimensions in Projective Techniques." *Journal of Consulting Psychology*, 1966, *30*, 183-192.

Esposito, R. P. *The Relationship Between Fear of Success Imagery and Vocational Choice by Sex and Grade Level*. Final Report to the Spencer Foundation, New York University, 1976.

Esposito, R. P. "The Relationship Between the Motive to Avoid Success and Vocational Choice." *Journal of Vocational Behavior*, 1977, *10*, 347-357.

Feather, N. T., and Raphelson, A. C. "Fear of Success in Australian and American Student Groups: Motive or Sex-Role Stereotype." *Journal of Personality*, 1974, *42*, 190-201.

Feather, N. T., and Simon, J. G. "Fear of Success and Causal Attribution for Outcome." *Journal of Personality*, 1973, *41*, 525-542.

Fleming, J. "Approach and Avoidance Motivation in Interpersonal Competition." Unpublished doctoral dissertation, Harvard University, 1974.

Fleming, J. "Significance of Fear of Success Imagery Among Black

Male and Female Students." Unpublished manuscript, Radcliffe Institute, 1976.

Fleming, J. "Comment on David Tresemer's 'Do Women Fear Success?'" *Signs: Journal of Women in Culture and Society*, 1977, *2*, 706-717.

Fleming, J. "Fear of Success: Achievement-Related Motives and Behavior in Black College Women." *Journal of Personality*, 1978, *46*, 694-716.

Fleming, J. "Special Needs of Blacks and Other Minorities." In A. W. Chickering and others (Eds.). *The Modern American College: Responding to the New Realities of Diverse Students and a Changing Society*. San Francisco: Jossey-Bass, 1981.

Fleming, J., Beldner, J., and Esposito, R. "On the Projective Measurement of Fear of Success." Barnard College, 1980, in review.

Fleming, J., and Watson, R. I. "Examination of the New Empirically Derived Scoring System for the Motive to Avoid Success." Unpublished manuscript, Barnard College, 1980.

Frank, L. "Projective Methods for the Study of Personality." In B. I. Murstein (Ed.), *Handbook of Projective Techniques*. New York: Basic Books, 1965.

Freud, S. "Some Character-Types Met with in Psychoanalytic Work." In E. Jones (Ed.), *Sigmund Freud: Collected Papers*. Vol. IV. New York: Basic Books, 1959. (Originally published 1915.)

Good, L. R., and Good, K. C. "An Objective Measure of the Motive to Avoid Success." *Psychological Reports*, 1973, *33*, 1009-1010.

Guilford, J. P. *Psychometric Methods*. New York: McGraw-Hill, 1954.

Heilbrun, A. B., Kleemeier, C., and Piccola, G. "Developmental and Situational Correlates of Achievement Behavior in College Females." *Journal of Personality*, 1974, *42*, 420-436.

Hoffman, L. W. "Fear of Success in Males and Females: 1965 and 1971." *Journal of Consulting and Clinical Psychology*, 1974, *42*, 353-358.

Horner, M. S. "Sex Differences in Achievement Motivation and Performance in Competitive and Noncompetitive Situations." Unpublished doctoral dissertation, University of Michigan, 1968.

Horner, M. S. "Fail: Bright Women." *Psychology Today*, Nov. 1969.

Horner, M. S. "Toward an Understanding of Achievement-Related

Conflicts in Women." *Journal of Social Issues*, 1972, *28*, 157-176.

Horner, M. S. *Success Avoidant Motivation and Behavior: Its Development, Correlates, and Situational Determinants*. Final report, Office of Education. Grant OEG-1-71-0104 (508), 1973.

Horner, M. S., and Fleming, J. "Revised Scoring Manual for an Empirically Derived Scoring System for the Motive to Avoid Success." Unpublished manuscript, 1977.

Horney, K. "Culture and Neurosis." *American Sociological Review*, 1936, *1*, 221-230.

Jackaway, R. "Sex Differences in Achievement Motivation, Behavior, and Attributions About Success and Failure." Unpublished doctoral dissertation, State University of New York at Albany, 1974.

Jenkins, S. R. "Fear of Success, Sex Roles, and Personal Success Goals." Paper presented at annual meeting of the American Psychological Association, New York City, 1979.

Jensen, A. R. "The Reliability of Projective Techniques: Review of the Literature." *Acta Psychologica*, 1959, *16*, 108-136.

Karabenick, S. A. "Fear of Success, Achievement, and Affiliative Dispositions, and the Performance of Men and Women Under Individual and Competitive Situations." *Journal of Personality*, 1977, *45*, 117-149.

Karabenick, S. A., and Marshall, J. M. "Performance of Females as a Function of Fear of Success, Fear of Failure, Type of Opponent, and Performance—Contingent Feedback." *Journal of Personality*, 1974, *42*, 220-237.

Kenny, D. T. "Stimulus Functions in Projective Techniques." In B. A. Maher (Ed.), *Progress in Experimental Personality Research*. Vol. 1. New York: Academic Press, 1964.

Klinger, E. "Fantasy Need Achievement as a Motivational Construct." *Psychological Bulletin*, 1966, *66*, 291-308.

Kripke, C. F. "The Motive to Avoid Success and Its Impact on Vocational Choices of Senior College Women." Unpublished doctoral dissertation, Boston University, 1980.

Lanyon, R. I., and Goodstein, L. D. *Personality Assessment*. New York: Wiley, 1971.

Loevinger, J. "Objective Tests as Instruments of Psychological Theory." *Psychological Reports*, 1957, Monograph Supplement 9.

Lundy, A. "The Reliability of the Thematic Apperception Test." Manuscript submitted for publication, 1980.

Lundy, A. "Situationally-Evoked Schemata Sets in TAT-Based Research: An Explanation for Differential TAT Validity." Thesis prospectus, Harvard University, 1981.

McClelland, D. C. "Methods of Measuring Human Motivation." In J. W. Atkinson (Ed.), *Motives in Fantasy, Action, and Society.* New York: Van Nostrand, 1958.

McClelland, D. C. "Longitudinal Trends in the Relation of Thought to Action." *Journal of Consulting Psychology,* 1966 *30*(6), 479-483.

McClelland, D. C., Atkinson, J. W., Clark, R. A., and Lowell, E. L. *The Achievement Motive.* New York: Appleton-Century-Crofts, 1953.

McClelland, D. C., and Clark, R. A. "A Factor Analytic Integration of Imaginative and Performance Measures of the Need for Achievement." *Journal of General Psychology,* 1956, *55*, 73-83.

Marshall, J. M., and Karabenick, S. A. "Validity of an Empirically Derived Measure of Fear of Success." *Journal of Consulting and Clinical Psychology,* 1977, *45*, 564-574.

Mischel, W. *Personality and Assessment.* New York: Wiley, 1968.

Morgan, C. D., and Murray, H. A. "A Method for Investigating Fantasies: The Thematic Apperception Test." Archives of Neurology and Psychiatry, 1935, *34*, 289-306.

Murstein, B. I. "The Stimulus." In B. I. Murstein (Ed.), *Handbook of Projective Techniques.* New York: Basic Books, 1965.

Nunnally, J. D. *Psychometric Theory.* New York: McGraw-Hill, 1967.

Pappo, M. "Fear of Success: A Theoretical Analysis and the Construction and Validation of a Measuring Instrument." Unpublished doctoral dissertation, Columbia University, 1972.

Sadd, S., Lenauer, M., Shaver, P., and Dunivant, N. "Objective Measurement of Fear of Success and Fears of Failure: A Factor Analytical Approach." *Journal of Consulting and Clinical Psychology,* 1978, *46*, 405-416.

Shapiro, D. *Neurotic Styles.* New York: Basic Books, 1965.

Shinn, M. "Secondary School Coeducation and the Fears of Success and Failure." Unpublished doctoral dissertation, Harvard University, 1973.

Stewart, A. J. "Longitudinal Prediction from Personality to Life Outcomes Among College-Educated Women." Unpublished doctoral dissertation, Harvard University, 1975.

Stolorow, R. D., and Lachman, F. M. *The Psychoanalysis of Developmental Arrest.* New York: International Universities Press, 1980.

Sullivan, H. S. *The Interpersonal Theory of Psychiatry.* New York: Norton, 1953.

Tec, L. *Fear of Success.* New York: Signet Books, 1976.

Telford, C. W. "The Refractory Phase of Voluntary and Associative Processes." *Journal of Experimental Psychology,* 1931, *14,* 1-36.

Tresemer, D. "Fear of Success: Popular but Unproven." *Psychology Today,* 1974, 7, 82-85.

Tresemer, D. "The Cumulative Record of Research on 'Fear of Success.'" *Sex Roles,* 1976, 2, 217-236.

Tresemer, D. *Fear of Success.* New York: Plenum Press, 1977.

Winter, D. G. and Stewart, A. J. "Power Motive Reliability as a Function of Retest Instructions." *Journal of Consulting and Clinical Psychology,* 1977, *45,* 436-440.

Zuckerman, M., and Allison, S. N. "An Objective Measure of Fear of Success: Construction and Validation." *Journal of Personality Assessment,* 1976, *40,* 522-530.

Zuckerman, M., and Wheeler, L. "To Dispel Fantasies About the Fantasy-Based Means of Fear of Success." *Psychological Bulletin,* 1975, *82,* 932-946.

Part II

Exploring Fundamental Social Motives

Much of McClelland's own career has been devoted to empirical examination of the behavioral consequences of fundamental human motives. The three chapters in this section describe basic research aimed at establishing a secure definition of motivational constructs based on evidence. Veroff draws on data from a national survey to delineate the differences between achievement and power motivation. McAdams describes a number of studies that together provide a definitional framework for the study of intimacy motivation. Stewart and Chester review thirty years of research on sex differences in achievement, affiliation, and power motivation. In short, all three chapters are concerned with the problems encountered in establishing the construct validity of important social motives.

Assertive Motivations

4

Achievement Versus Power

Joseph Veroff

To my mind, David McClelland's two most exciting contributions to psychology are *The Achieving Society* (1961) and *Power: The Inner Experience* (1975). Separated by more than a decade, these studies elaborate in rich detail the effects of complex personal motivational systems both on people's strivings and on resultant social-historical phenomena. *The Achieving Society* brilliantly and persuasively documents the extent to which the strength of the personal achievement motive in a society accounts for task strivings underlying the economic activity of that society. The thrust of *Power: The Inner Experience* is equally convincing in detailing the effect of personal power motivation on the way people organize their social life, especially if you also account for their level of ego maturity. McClel-

The research reported in this chapter was supported by grants from the National Institute of Mental Health. The author wishes to acknowledge the assistance of David Reuman and Elyse Sutherland in the analyses for this report.

land's work constitutes a strong argument for distinct differences in the two motivational systems, and yet, from our everyday understanding of the motives for achievement and power as well as from more integrated theories of social motivation (Ansbacher and Ansbacher, 1956; Bakan, 1966; Maslow, 1954; Veroff and Veroff, 1980), we can very well find it hard to distinguish them. Achievement brings power; and power brings achievement recognition. Both are assertive concerns; both require consideration of one's impact. How should we differentiate them as motivations? That will be the focal problem of this chapter.

I think an important impetus to McClelland's original interest in studying the power motive was his wish to understand great movers in organizations. He had been working within programs whose goal was to foster economic development by enhancing achievement motivation in businessmen (McClelland and Winter, 1969) when he observed that the achievement-motivated person, while critical to keeping an organization going and making technical progress, did not seem so critical to making highly creative changes for the organization. It was the power-oriented person who was often indispensible for dramatic innovations.

The small bit of research contrasting the relationships of these two motives with behaviors and attitudes (for example, McClelland, 1971; Mueller, 1975; Veroff and Feld, 1970), and the thinking that emerged from McClelland's observations about organizations, leads to the following general thesis: Achievement motivation directs people to meeting socialized standards of excellent performance and thus to highly efficient task-centered strivings, whereas power motivation directs people to doing whatever draws most attention to their own effect on the world. For the power-motivated person, the social world is omnipresent as a reactive contingency for satisfaction. For the achievement-motivated person, by contrast, the social world makes itself felt only in the original learning of or ongoing adaptation to norms of excellence. The two motives seem to be fused in instances where the standard of excellence is to win in a social competitive activity or to solve a problem that will be given a great deal of recognition. There are many achievement settings, however, where such results are not forthcoming. Such settings will discourage a power-motivated individual but still motivate an achievement-oriented person. And there are many settings where having personal impact will not involve meeting a standard of excellence. These settings will be of considrable interest to the power-motivated person, but will certainly be uninteresting to the person high in achievement motivation.

This thesis will be the guiding framework for this chapter. Though it undoubtedly will require much qualification, it can serve as the launching platform for our study of these motives in people's lives. In writing in David McClelland's honor, I will be presenting some data from a national study of motives conducted in 1976, a rich array of results about American men and women. I have not yet shared these data with McClelland, but judging from his past performances I know he will integrate them in an exciting way. And I hope he and others do. I am using these data explicitly to amplify distinctions that I think need to be drawn between two contrasting assertive motivations—achievement and power. Although my formulations are tentative, the data will stand on their own.

The 1976 National Study of Motives

In 1976, Elizabeth Douvan, Richard Kulka, and I had the opportunity to replicate the essential parts of a 1957 study of the American population. The basic information on the study is located in three sources. The first describes the subjective mental health of American people—how they feel about their lives, their roles, their self-perceptions, their symptoms of distress, as well as how they handle personal problems that arise (Gurin, Veroff, and Feld, 1960). The second lays out in considerable detail the methodology involved in obtaining reliable measures of achievement, affiliation, and power motives—and how these motives are distributed in various social groups (Veroff, Atkinson, Feld, and Gurin, 1960). The third examines complex interactions of the measures of motives and subjective reactions to marriage, parenthood, and work (Veroff and Feld, 1970).

The 1976 replication, like the 1957 study, used a national sample of adults living in residential households in the coterminous United States. The replicated assessment of subjective mental health and how it compares to the 1957 sample has been published (Veroff,

Douvan, and Kulka, 1981). We have also done a similar analysis of motives from 1957 to 1976 (Veroff, Depner, Kulka, and Douvan, 1980). This chapter will be the first presentation of how the assessments of motives in 1976 are related to other aspects of people's lives.

For complete details of our method for assessing motives in the national studies it will be necessary to see other resources (Veroff, Atkinson, Feld, and Gurin, 1960). Briefly, each respondent was shown six pictures and asked to tell a story about them as a way of seeing how people "feel about life situations in daily experience." Using procedures outlined by Atkinson (1958), the stories were coded for achievement, affiliation, and power motives, the power motive being primarily an assessment reflecting fear of weakness (see Veroff and Veroff, 1972). The stories were also coded for power using a method developed by Winter (1973) that reflects the more positive component of power motivation. Since the measure of power motives in the 1957 stories had been based on my earlier work (Veroff, 1957), the 1957 stories were coded for the Winter system so that year comparisons in that measure could be made. To avoid confusion the original assessment of power motivation based on the system outlined in Atkinson's book will be called fear of weakness; the newer assessment based on Winter's system will be called hope of power. It should be noted, however, that in "hope of power" I am referring to the entire Winter scoring of the power motive and not just the partial component that has been isolated in his research to distinguish hope of power from fear of power. Reliability of coding was relatively high for the four motives assessed. Comparable coding in 1976 and 1957 was guaranteed by training the 1976 coders to the conventions used by the 1957 coders. Corrections for score correlation with story length were made. Subjects with inadequate protocols for coding were eliminated.

In this chapter I will present different types of data that can be used to assess the potential differential meaning of power and achievement motivations in adult life. First, having scores on motives from a national sample for two widely separated years, we can assess year, age, education, and cohort effects. Second, using only 1976 data, we can make a very extensive appraisal of how motives relate to a wide array of subjective phenomena assessed in that survey, as well as assessments of reported behaviors about people's own lives. Third, we can see how people from different backgrounds differ in their motives. (These analyses will ignore many other possible analyses that we intend to do in later reports. For the current chapter we will limit ourselves to the straightforward correlations of motives to other measures.)

Year, Age, Education, and Cohort Differences in Motives

Because in any one sample there is no adequate control for historical setting, we have in a generational comparison of motives the possibility of looking for effects of age or education or year or cohort independent of other effects. This becomes particularly important in comparing 1957 to 1976, because over that period there has been a distinct shift in the nation's level of education as well as in the age distribution of the population. People in 1976 are clearly much better educated than people in 1957, and they are more likely to be young or old, but not middle-aged. By comparing 1957 and 1976 and simultaneously controlling for age, education, and year effects, we can be more confident about effects that may be attributable to any single variable. We used a log-linear hierarchical analysis that enabled us to look for significant effects of each variable and its interactions (Goodman, 1978). Thus, any year differences we discuss are more clearly a function of change in generation, and any education or age effects are those that transcend the particular year of measurement. Thus we will be more confident about discussing developmental changes in motives as well as status effects on achievement and power motives.

Year Effects. Significant year differences in motives are very clearly apparent in the data. Among men, the achievement motive has remained constant and both kinds of power motives have increased. Among women, the achievement motive and fear of weakness have increased, while the hope of power motive has remained stable. The interpretation of these results will begin to establish the differences in the meaning of achievement and power.

What do the changes in men's scores imply? Our basic interpretation is that with the erosion of men's dominant authority in the family, coupled with disillusionment about achievement in the work place, men have significantly turned to power rather than achievement as a self-assertive orientation. We have argued that this change has particularly occurred in the work setting. For men, having personal impact through work has become a more central motivational incentive than being excellent at a particular task performed on the job. Our study of the nature of work in both 1957 and 1976 (Veroff, Douvan, and Kulka, 1981) and trends in the Quality of Employment Surveys (Quinn and Staines, 1979) suggest that between 1957 and 1976 work as an avenue for social integration in our society has been openly questioned. Work's binding powers have come unglued. In 1976, men have an increased individuated orientation to satisfaction in the work place, but that orientation is more with regard to personal impact than with regard to task accomplishment. One consequence of this pressure to feel individual gratification from achievement at work is that men are more discontented with the social fabric of the work setting.

For women something different went on over the generation. While men's authority in the family was fiercely shaken, women did not have much authority to begin with. The consciousness raising of the women's movement in the 1960s and the 1970s highlighted women's sense of weakness, mostly vis-à-vis men. Work became a means to overcome weakness. Women turned to jobs and individual task performance (achievement) as a vehicle for self-differentiation, particularly for use in the direct struggle that women anticipated in establishing their power vis-à-vis men.

The basic changes in motive strength can be interpreted as a greater motivation in 1976 to overcome a sense of weakness. For women the achievement motive has become an ancillary expression of that struggle, while for men it has been translated directly into interpersonal power, because the route to power via achievement was seriously questioned by men in the 1960s and 1970s. For women, therefore, we see a much greater fusion of power and achievement in 1976 than for men. In fact, in 1976 there is a significant ($p < .05$) albeit slight correlation between the achievement motive and hope of power (.08), where there was none (-.05) in 1957, nor any for men in either year (.00 in 1957; .03 in 1976).

In this regard it is important to point out that there was a remarkable decrease in the affiliation motive for men from 1957 to 1976, but not for women. Again a look at the pattern of intercorrelations of motives helps interpret the findings. These correlations will be small but meaningful. For men the affiliation motive, while slightly correlated with the achievement motive (-.07 in 1957; -.09 in 1976), is somewhat more reliably related to fear of weakness (-.11 in 1957; -.13 in 1976). For women, by contrast, the affiliation motive, while negatively related to fear of weakness (-.07 in 1957; -.14 in 1976), is positively related to the achievement motive (.10, $p < .01$, in 1976; but only .03 in 1957). Thus the affiliative motive is supporting the achievement orientation of women, which may be why they are able to use achievement as a vehicle for power. Women have recognized achievement as a socialized way of asserting power in an attempt to establish their equality with men. It is interesting to note that they do not now share men's apparent disillusionment with achievement-through-work as a means of successful assertion. Perhaps their different job experience accounts for this.

Age Effects. Studying two representative cross sections of the American population over nineteen years was particularly informative about the meaning of age effects on motives. If such effects are consistent across the generation we feel more confident about attributing developmental meaning to age differences in motives. If not, if there is no consistency in age differences across the generation, then we would have to argue that the particular age effects obtained were bound to the social-historical period in which young, middle-aged, and old people existed.

There were no consistent age effects in achievement motivation for men, whereas there were for women. For these analyses we used year-specific motive scores in order to control for year effects and to allow for the greatest amount of variance attributed to age differences. A peak in achievement motivation for men aged forty to forty-nine was found in 1957, but that peak was thirty to thirty-nine in 1976. (There very well may be a cohort effect but we had no measure of the thirty- to thirty-nine-year-olds of 1976 in 1957, and so we cannot say that as a group they have a high achievement motive socialized early that they carried with them to their middle-age.) In both years the peak in achievement motivation for women was twenty-one to twenty-nine, and in both years the low point in achievement motivation for women was sixty-five and older. These results are significant from our log-linear analyses controlling for status differences as well.

The opposite was true about power motives. There were no consistent age effects for women, but there were for men. Middle-aged men, especially forty- to forty-nine-year-olds, show a peak in the hope-of-power motive in both years, while older men show a peak in fear of weakness (sixty to sixty-four for high-school-educated men; sixty-five and older for college-educated).

How can these results help us distinguish achievement from power? The men's achievement results suggest that peaking of achievement interest occurs much earlier now than a generation ago—perhaps because work, which still may be men's dominant mode of achievement expression, peaks in its potential for gratification much earlier than it once did. There are few jobs where men "come into their own" after fifty. The increasing technocratic emphasis of our society determines that it is the younger people who are better trained, who know the latest ways of handling organizational shifts coordinated with technological change, and that these younger, more up-to-date professionals are often the ones most sought after and rewarded.

If we assume that men's achievement *motive* peaks a decade before their actual *performance*, we can suggest that the 1957 generation looked to the ages fifty to sixty for gathering in the rewards of their achievement, while the 1976 generation looked to the ages forty to fifty. If a man's long-term understanding of a job is that his goals come to fruition most dramatically at an earlier rather than a later age, we would expect that a future-oriented achievement motivation would also peak earlier. It is in such a vein that we interpret the shift of the peak achievement motive scores in men from the years forty to forty-nine in 1957 to the years thirty to thirty-nine in 1976. This analysis highlights what Raynor (1969) has emphasized about achievement motivation—its future orientation. Achievement motivation is a concern about mastery that takes account of the future, allows a person to think of present accomplishment as means to future ends, and thus orients a person to efficient use of present time to accomplish future goals. This future perspective may differentiate achievement from power motivation; the sense of personal impact may have to be more immediate in the power-motivated person than in the achievement-motivated person.

Education Effects. For both men and women we find a distinct correlation between higher education and level of achievement motivation. College-educated men and women are significantly higher in achievement orientation than are the less educated adults in our society. These results are not surprising and are important to keep in mind as we think of the nature of achievement motivation. We can interpret the results to mean that as men and women go farther with formal education, they become imbued with the social orientation to doing well that we have defined as achieving. To further their success throughout their years in school, men and women pick up the standards society sets for efficiency and persistence (Atkinson and Raynor, 1974) and for promotion to the next higher rung on the ladder. Their achievement orientation thus accounts for their educational accomplishment. Another interpretation of the correlation is possible. As men and women are channeled into the highest levels of education by whatever means, they pick up the achievement orientations of colleges and universities. In these institutions standards of excellence are not only applied explicitly to course work but are applied subtly to expectations about performance in many arenas of life for which college is expected to prepare students. Thus we can reason both that people with higher levels of achievement motive attend institutions of higher education and that people who are socialized by higher education institutions end up with higher levels of achievement motive.

Surprisingly, we found no distinct relationship between power orientations and level of education. Indeed, the only effect found was that college-educated men had distinctly *lower* fear of weakness than other men. Otherwise there was no clear-cut correlation between educational status and power motivation. These are important results to bear in mind since they are so different from the results on achievement orientation. We had previously argued that men with less than college education in our society learn to be concerned about weakness (Veroff and others, 1960). I still prefer to interpret the results in that way rather than to conclude that college education lowers people's power orientations, although the latter is also plausible. While I would argue that as men find themselves in less prestigious occupations in our society because of lack of education, their lack of status vis-à-vis other people will promote a concern about weakness, it is possible to focus on a different effect underlying these data. As men progress through college and have access to more prestigious jobs, their fear of weakness may diminish.

Why does the same pattern not appear for women? One could suggest that it is because considerable ambivalence is associated with the meaning of college education for women, despite the great number of women who go to college. It is a status that may increase women's competence and sense of effectiveness, and yet it may subtly decrease their sense of femininity within our society's stereotyped sex roles.

Our interpretation of these results foreshadows a major distinction that will be drawn between achievement and power. Achievement motivation is thought to affect and be responsive to people's overt strivings. Power motivation is thought to affect and be responsive to people's status. Achievement seems to be performance-centered; power seems to be position-centered.

Cohort Effects. Certain patterns emerged from our analyses of year, age, and educational differences in achievement and power motives, patterns indicating that particular birth cohorts had developed a distinctly high or low level of achievement or power motives that they maintained across the generation we were examining. Because some age-year interactions were apparent in our analyses, we analyzed the data for cohorts.

We divided the men and women in both 1957 and 1976 into five birth cohorts: Cohort 1 (twenty to twenty-nine in 1957; forty to forty-nine in 1976); Cohort 2 (thirty to thirty-nine in 1957; fifty to fifty-nine in 1976); Cohort 3 (forty to forty-nine in 1957; sixty to sixty-nine in 1976); Cohort 4 (fifty to fifty-nine in 1957; seventy to seventy-nine in 1976); Cohort 5 (sixty to sixty-nine in 1957; eighty and above in 1976). Since we were dealing with representative samples we felt we could consider these a cross section of each birth cohort in the population. We were surprised by the total absence of any clear cohort effects for men on either achievement or power motives. Nothing in the data for men indicates that men attain a certain level of achievement or power motive at some point during their early development and maintain that level throughout life. For men we thus have considerable evidence to suggest that adult motivation shifts as men proceed through the life cycle. The exigencies of the different points of the life cycle have an impact on the level of achievement or power motives in men. This is not to say that there are no groups of men whose level of achievement or power motives remains constant because their life situations tend to maintain their original level of motives. Nor is it to say that one's level of achievement motive as a young adult has no bearing on what one is like as an older adult. Indeed, the level of motivation is probably predictive of the kinds of life situations that people attain in early adulthood, which then in turn have effects on their later life, including changes in level of motivation.

We have some evidence of cohort effects on women's achievement motives but, as with men, no evidence of cohort effects on power motives. Women of Cohort 1, those who were twenty to twenty-nine in 1957, maintained their high level of achievement motive in 1976. These levels were very high in the early time period and they continued to be very high at middle-age. In a similar way, women in Cohort 5, those who were sixty to sixty-nine in 1957 and over eighty in 1976, were very low in the achievement motive. The latter result is hard to interpret totally as a cohort effect, since we have found older people to be particularly low in achievement motives. With that cohort we may be picking up a developmental result more clearly than a cohort result. But the Cohort 1 results are important, since they suggest that young women who had high achievement motives in 1957 continued to have high achievement motives in 1976. This cohort was the group that was both most oriented to the "feminine mystique" in the 1950s and most susceptible to the demystification in the 1970s. These were the women who were returning to work as a source of gratification once their children had grown up. Betty Friedan particularly directed her concern about women's submersion in suburban life to this cohort. And indeed it seems to consist of women who have maintained a high orientation to achievement, in contrast to the general tendency for women to decrease their achievement orientation as they proceed through the life cycle. Stewart has aptly pointed out that these women may have maintained their orientation to achievement because as adolescents during World War II many of them must have experienced the model of a working mother. This is important because it suggests that women's achievement orientation can be increased or maintained through the life cycle if there is enough political and historical pressure *on women* to be concerned about their competence in relation to men. Combined with the results for age, one would have to say that whether or not middle-aged women maintain an achievement value for their performance depends on the historical circumstances of the society.

Despite this result for women, we can be impressed with the absence of cohort results in most of our data. And, indeed, there were no results suggesting cohort effects with the other motive for which we had data—the affiliation motive. These results are important because they underscore the fact that situational factors in men and women's adult lives can have important consequences for their level of motives as they make transitions with age. We must conclude that this is true for both the achievement and the power motive.

Correlates of the Assertive Motives

Many facets of life experience were measured in the 1976 national survey. To assess their experiences, we asked people to evaluate their subjective mental health either generally or in specific life roles in eight areas: general well-being, behavior, background, and five life settings.

General Well-Being. Well-being was defined as people's feelings of happiness, depression, or zest in life (Zung, 1965), general self-esteem (Rosenberg, 1965) and satisfaction (Campbell, Converse, and Rodgers, 1976), and efficacy. We used people's reports of how they experience their ongoing lives; these assessments make no reference to specific behaviors. For example, the measure of zest was derived from the Zung scale of depression, which asked people to judge whether they found life in general interesting and worthwhile.

Behavior. This measure asked about aspects of participation in leisure time activities and organizational life, attendance at church, whether or not the person drinks or takes drugs to relieve tension, and other activities, rather than feelings. In the case of drugs the question directed these respondents largely to prescribed medicines, such as tranquilizers. Since these are self-reports it is not strictly accurate to say that they are behaviors, but they are closer to the actual content of the activities than to feelings about life circumstances.

Background. A few items asked people to describe their life situation while growing up. From these questions we had measures of the father's type of occupation, whether or not the person's family life was disrupted by death or divorce, and the order of the person's birth in his family.

Leisure. This measure asked people whether or not they were satisfied with their leisure time, whether they felt challenged by doing things in their leisure time, and whether leisure fulfilled their life values.

Marriage. This measure asked people about the following facets of marriage: satisfaction, happiness, problems (frequency of irritation), general interaction or harmony (frequency of chatting and being physically affectionate), and sense of adequacy as a spouse. As with measures of leisure, there were assessments of persons' value fulfillment through marriage, and how much married life validated their self-image. In addition, some questions were intended to make distinctions in people's conceptions of marriage as a relationship of interdependence (seeing marriage as being a "couple") or individuation ("two separate people").

Parenthood. This measure assessed people's sense of well-being with regard to parenthood. It was hard to get people to talk about negative feelings about children in general, but a number of questions were asked about difficulties in raising children.

The Housewife Role. Three questions were directed to housewives: whether they had ever wanted a career, how satisfied they were as housewives, and whether they were planning to do paid work in the future.

Work. We asked many questions about people's satisfactions and dissatisfactions with work and their feelings of confidence and adequacy in their work life. Some were parallel to reactions to other roles (for example, how much value fulfillment or self-image validation occurs through work); others were directed specifically at achievement-power issues at work (making decisions, finding work interesting and challenging, getting a chance to do one's best and talk to others); and others asked about the degree of supervising and supervision that the person experiences at work and the general prestige of the occupation. For the last mentioned, ratings in the *Dictionary of Occupation Titles* (Temme, 1975) were used.

Analyses

Clearly some of the above questions were closed ended and some were open ended. The open-ended questions required qualitative analyses of people's responses; when people were asked what it was that they liked and disliked about their work, for example, we coded the specific content of their responses.

Our analysis of these measures is very straightforward. Controls are applied to correlations but are not directly assessed in statistical descriptions. For correlations (Pearson rs), interval scales are needed. For some of our measurements, such scaling is appropriate. The motive scores, for example, are standardized regression scores based on the regression analysis of each motive for each sex on story length. For others, however, the interval scale assumption is crudely applied, especially to those better considered as rank orders. For two of the assessments—birth order and respondent's father's occupation—we retained nominal scaling and performed one-way analyses of variance in place of correlations, but introduced no control for respondents' age or education.

Since age and education might condition the results, we not only ran correlations of motives with the eight other measures separately for men and women, but we ran them separately for four subgroups: cross-classifications by two levels of age (young—twenty-one to thirty-nine; older—over forty) and two levels of education (less than college; some college or more). Sometimes these controls destroyed an overall significant pattern and sometimes they just weakened it. Sometimes a significant finding emerged for one group distinctly. Since there are so many data to present, we simplified our integrative task by adopting two decision rules to avoid both Type I and Type II errors. First, we consider an overall result significant and withstanding controls when its p value is $< .10$, but its pattern is consistent in all four subgroups. Second, we consider a general correlation significant when its p value is $< .05$ and its pattern is consistent in three out of four of the groups. If an overall result is not significant, a result for a specific subgroup is considered significant if its p value is $< .05$. In most instances we are citing correlations that are beyond chance occurrence. The wide array of results at which we are looking certainly contains a number that may occur by chance alone; therefore in instances where we thought we were capitalizing on such chance results because the finding seemed so discrepant from other results, we did not include the results in the summary tables. We may still be guilty of Type I errors, but from our perspective the results to follow present a consistent pattern. I will not highlight results separately for each control group but will highlight only the *general* correlational patterns.

When should we expect significant general correlations of motives to other measures? As I have discussed elsewhere (Veroff and Feld, 1970; Veroff and Veroff, 1980), motives sensitize people to the dimensions of ambiguous settings; consequently they can have general meanings across a variety of settings. But motives may also show a general pattern of correlations with attitudes and reactions about explicitly different settings. Men and women may have common motivational expectations about the nature of leisure, marriage, parenthood, and work, simply because they share a common cultural and historical interpretation of the meaning of these settings. These universal interpretations will then have differential impacts on people whose motives are different, regardless of the specific work they are doing, the particular significant others in their lives, their age, or their social position. Highly achievement-motivated persons are likely to react differently from less motivated persons to the expectation that their competence is being or will be evaluated by others who do the same work—whether they are professors or bricklayers, whether they are twenty-two or sixty-three. We should then expect correlations between the achievement motive and work regardless of the age of the person or the type of work he is doing.

Let me now turn to the correlates of the achievement motive found in men and women in the 1976 study. I will then proceed to the correlates of the two power motives, from which we can begin a data-based integration that distinguishes among assertive motivational systems.

Correlates of the Achievement Motive

The significant correlates of the achievement motive with the selected assessments of subjective mental health available from the 1976 national survey are listed in Table 1. They appear to show that

Table 1. Significant Correlates of the Achievement Motive with Selected
Assessments in Subjective Mental Health (by sex)

Area of Assessment	Men (N = 508)	Women (N = 700)
General Well-Being	Low on symptoms of ill health High feelings of efficacy High overall happiness Satisfaction with life (college-educated only)	Many experiences of zest
Behavior	Participation in organizations Frequent church attendance Not taking drugs to relieve tension	High family income
Background		Being oldest child in family[a] Being a daughter of a manager[a]
Leisure		Participation in challenging leisure activities Seeing leisure as fulfilling major life value and as being very satisfying (older, college-educated only)
Marriage	Seeing marriage as fulfilling major life value High marital satisfaction Perceiving own marriage as a couple (rather than two separate people)	High marital interaction Perceiving own marriage as two separate people (rather than couple)
Parenthood	Less involved with own image as good father (young only)	Admits to feeling inadequate as mother at times Seeing children as interfering with use of time
Work	Job satisfaction Seeing work as fulfilling major life value Preferring work to leisure Evaluating job as interesting, place to do best, place to talk to people Not seeing work as inter-	

Table 1 (continued)

Area of Assessment	Men (N = 508)	Women (N = 700)
	fering with family Holding job that is super- vised Holding a prestigious job	
Housework	————b	

Note: Overall correlation (r) is either (1) significant at .05 level with at least 3/4 subgroups cross-classified by two age levels (twenty-one to thirty-nine; over forty) and two educational levels (high school graduate or less; some college or more) showing same pattern or (2) significant at .10 level with all subgroups showing same pattern. Any correlation reported for just one major subgroup is significant at least at .05 level.

N shown is potential total. Correlations are based on smaller numbers where data are missing because measures were non-ascertained or inappropriate (for example, marriage assessments for unmarried people).
a Based on analyses of variance of mean scores rather than correlations.
b No appropriate questions asked of men.
Source: National Sample Survey, 1976.

men and women with high achievement motivation are highly socialized people, adults who have adopted idealized societal prescriptions for the conduct of their lives and as a consequence feel comfortable and adjusted.

Why do we come to that conclusion? It is clear from Table 1 that men with high achievement motivation are highly oriented toward the work role. They are satisfied with their jobs, see work as fulfilling major life values, prefer work to leisure, evaluate their jobs as interesting, do not see work as interfering with their family, and generally speaking, hold prestigious jobs. Indeed, that array of findings would suggest that the achievement motive is highly facilitative of work adjustment for men.

An interesting result also found in the 1957 study is that men who have high achievement motives are more likely to be in jobs that are supervised than in jobs that permit them to be autonomous. On the face of it, this seemed like a surprising result. With deeper reflection, one can suggest that men whose achievement orientations are high enjoy being in jobs that give them feedback about their performance. McClelland (1961) long ago saw feedback for performance as being critical to maintaining an achievement orientation in the work setting.

The one very interesting finding about work and achievement motivation for men is that in 1976 job satisfaction and achievement motivation are positively correlated (even when we instituted controls for a host of dimensions of type of work), whereas in the 1957 study the correlation was reversed: Men with high motives in 1957 tended to be more dissatisfied with work. This change is highly provocative, suggesting either that the achievement motive has changed in its meaning (making people more generally accommodating to their performance setting), or that the nature of work in American society has shifted somewhat. I am more inclined to the latter view. An attenuation in men's time perspective about work has developed. The future orientation to achievement goals has become foreshortened. I have already suggested that peaking in most men's achievement motivation in the work setting occurs much earlier in their lives than it did in 1957. Men in the 1970s are much more present-oriented about the nature of work and its relationship to motivation than in times past. Whereas in the 1950s men with high achievement orientation could be dissatisfied with their work and could simultaneously expect that the future would give them higher rewards with regard to their competition with standards of excellence, men in the 1970s are in jobs which have little future perspective guaranteed. They thus are much more present-oriented in their achievement satisfactions from work, and because they are task-oriented, they are successful, rewarded, and satisfied.

The achievement motive and its importance to work for the adjustment of men in our society is the factor that weaves together many of the other results in Table 1. I would argue that this work orientation produces positive effects for men; they feel generally well off, have no symptoms of ill health, high feelings of efficacy, high overall happiness, and satisfaction with life. They also report high marital satisfaction and see marriage as fulfilling their life values. They are not, however, particularly involved with their own image of being a good father. Parenthood is not the domain in which achievement gratification occurs; the domain of importance for achievement is work, which in turn has reverberating benefits for their feelings about their marriages. Efficient participation in work and adjustment to the work organizations in our society, I would argue, also have implications for the more general adjustments that we find in the behavior of highly achievement-motivated men. These men are more likely to participate in civic organizations and to attend church often. Their "adjusted" work orientation thus seems to generalize to adjustment to other norms that the society holds for their participation in the civic community. Men with high achievement motives do not take drugs to relieve tension, a form of behavior that is distinctly frowned on by majority norms, more so than drinking alcohol to relieve tension, a behavior that bore no relationship to the achievement motive.

Altogether, the 1976 study revealed a clear pattern of relationships concerning high achievement motivation for men in American society: it is a core motivational orientation to a successful adjustment to social norms. We get no sense of the turbulence or tense competition sometimes assumed to exist in the achievement-motivated person. Rather, we get an impression of men who willingly adopt a standard of excellence proposed to them, perform tasks efficiently to meet that standard, and are rewarded in their interpersonal life as well. Most of these results survive controls for age and education, and therefore we see the positive consequences of achievement motivation as fairly general for men in all walks of life.

The interpretation of the achievement motive as one based on the internalization of idealized norms is less immediately apparent in the results for women, but it can nevertheless be used to integrate the data. Most striking in Table 1 is the absence of *any* relationship between the motive and work or job assessments for women. We will find, however, that these variables are significantly correlated with women's power motives. Evidently a work orientation meshes better with women's power interests than with their achievement incentives. We find, by contrast, that women's achievement motives are relevant to roles separate from work. Women's achievement motives are relevant to their leisure time activities and to their performance as wives and parents. The higher their achievement motive, the more they participate in challenging leisure activities, the more they see leisure as fulfilling major life values and very satisfying. The higher their achievement motive, the more likely they are to talk of high marital interaction (spending a lot of time chatting and being affectionate with their spouse) and the more likely they are to see their own marriages as a bond of two separate people rather than an interdependent couple. (This latter result is interesting because the opposite relationships occurred for men, for whom higher achievement motive meant that they were more likely to see themselves as a couple. We would interpret this difference as indicating that highly achievement-oriented men see marriage as tangential to their general orientation to work. Performance in work is critical in maintaining the bond in marriage. Men, however, do not see themselves as operating as a special person "performing" in the marital interaction itself. They see their relationship to their spouse as an alliance of a couple working together on an agreed upon separation of work for the man and more interpersonal aspects for the woman.) Women with high achievement motives clearly make a distinction between their own performance in marriage and their husband's. They are aware of themselves as individuals performing in the marital interaction, meeting challenges, and preserving the alliance. Their contributions to their marriages may be vicarious identification with their husbands and that identification may underlie the fact that women with high achievement motives have high family incomes. They make marriage a performance arena.

The same seems to be true for women's reactions to parenthood. The results in Table 1 suggest that a high achievement motive underlies women's setting high standards of excellence for motherhood. More often than those with low achievement motives they feel some inadequacies as mothers, as well as seeing their children as interfering with their use of time. Women with high achievement motives are apparently devoting more time to the care of children than perhaps they want to because they see it as a role requirement that reflects on their competence. Thus we find women with high achievement motivation to be involved in several roles, *but not the work role.*

Evidently achievement-motivated women are especially apt to adopt prevailing role expectations as their own standards of excellence. The fact that they report having many experiences of zest in life—finding life very interesting and finding themselves very useful—suggests that they not only adjust to the normative standards that are imposed on them but they enjoy it.

Some other pieces of data confirm the view that women who have high achievement motives have learned them in connection with idealized conceptions of women's responsibility to the family or to the social order. These women tend to have been the oldest child in their family, a position that induces considerable responsibility for both sons and daughters but especially for daughters. Furthermore, there is an interesting family background correlate of the achievement motive in women. Women who are daughters of managers (executives or businessmen) tend to have higher achievement motives than other women. One could speculate that women who grew up in a bureaucratic environment may be more susceptible to the values for responsibility, which may be translated into meeting standard role requirements for women, that is, being concerned about family and civic role performances, but not careers.

It is important to realize that these results are based on a sample of women raised well before the current women's movement had much impact. That these highly achievement-motivated women largely confine their activities and involvement to traditional socially valued routes to excellence is thus not surprising. When social standards of excellence for women change and encompass career orientations, as they seem to be doing, perhaps the correlates of the achievement motive in women will also change.

If I am right about my interpretation of these correlates of the achievement motive, it helps explain why there has been so much difficulty in establishing the relationship of achievement motivation to performance and to career orientations in women in our research. For many years now we have been searching for a valid way of measuring women's achievement motives that could predict the kinds of performance that are seen as critical to achievement in the work setting. It may be that achievement motivation in women is not generally related to the work role at all, but to the performance of responsible stereotypically female behaviors in civic and family roles. The clearest validity for the achievement measure occurs in studies that also account for women's sex role orientation, for example, French and Lesser, 1964; Lesser, Kravitz, and Packard, 1963; Lipinski, 1965. Most of them show clearest validity with performance in stereotypical female roles. As we shall see in later sections, power motivation rather than achievement motivation seems to be critical to an orientation to the work role for women.

For both men and women there emerges a picture of the achievement motive as a measure of *socialized* assertive motivation for fulfilling expected roles. Adjustment to these external standards of excellence seems to be quite critical. People with high achievement motives seem not only to have assumed these standards, but in trying to fulfill them work out a satisfying pattern of life adjustment. If achievement motivation also underlies people's understanding of doing a task efficiently, then the tasks involved for men and women are quite different. For men they are clearly relegated to the work setting, and for women to family roles and to civic life.

Correlates of Fear of Weakness

Turning now to Table 2, which reports the significant subjective mental health correlates of fear of weakness, we find a very different picture of concern about assertion. This concern seems to contribute to considerable distress in men and to some dysfunctional feelings among women. It is more obvious that fear of weakness is a negative motivation for men than it is for women. Nevertheless, underlying the pattern of results for men and women there seems to be a common concern, one not directly apparent in the results but one that I will argue is the latent psychological question that men and women with high fear of weakness ask of themselves: Am I an adequate male or female? Fear of weakness seems to be the underlying motivation of men and women who are concerned about their sexual identity. Let us look at Table 2 as a way to corroborate this general interpretation of this concern about assertion in American society.

How does the pattern of results for men in Table 2 add up to a concern about sexual identity? The pattern more prevalent in men with high fear of weakness indicates low self-esteem along with lowered zest (for the young college-educated), an orientation to drinking and to taking drugs, and being in less prestigious occupations. These results add up to a negative set of feelings about one's life experience. Men with high fear of weakness do, however, report

Table 2. Significant Correlates of Fear of Weakness with Selected
Assessments of Subjective Mental Health (by sex)

Area of Assessment	Men (N = 508)	Women (N = 700)
General Well-Being	Low self-esteem (young college-educated only) Few experiences of zest (young college-educated only)	High self-esteem
Behavior	Drinking problem causing family trouble Taking drugs to relieve tension High income Low church attendance (less educated only) Being in unprestigious occupation	Low reliance on informal support for crises
Background	Being a son of blue collar worker[a]	
Leisure		Leisure not very satisfying
Marriage	High marital interaction	
Parenthood	Seeing fatherhood as fulfilling major value	Seeing children as drawing couple apart (older, less educated only)
Work	Perceiving work as not interesting Feeling good about work competence Preferring power potential from work to affiliation Not mentioning affiliation satisfactions of job Not seeing opportunity to talk at work	Mentioning ego satisfactions from work Preferring work to leisure Job satisfaction
Housework	————[b]	Low satisfaction with housework Seeing housework as not fulfilling major value

Table 2 (continued)

Note: Overall correlation (*r*) is either (1) significant at .05 level with at least 3/4 subgroups cross-classified by two age levels (twenty-one to thirty-nine; over forty) and two educational levels (high school graduate or less; some college or more) showing same pattern or (2) significant at .10 level with all subgroups showing same pattern. Any correlation reported for just one major subgroup is significant at least at .05 level.

N shown is potential total. Correlations are based on smaller numbers where data are missing because measures were non-ascertained or inappropriate (for example, marriage assessments for unmarried people).

[a]Based on analyses of variance of mean scores rather than correlations.
[b]No appropriate questions asked of men.
Source: National Sample Survey, 1976.

high marital harmony (a measure that asks how often they interact affectionately with their wives and thus comes close to asking about their sexual activity), see fatherhood as fulfilling major life values, and feel especially good about their work competence. This trio of findings—reporting high marital harmony, seeing fatherhood as important, and feeling good about their own work competence— suggests a protest about masculinity among men with high fear of weakness. I propose this interpretation because these men demonstrate an absence of both the general feelings of well-being and behaviors that usually go along with a positive involvement with marriage, parenthood, and work. I would thus suggest that men are protesting too much about their masculine competence. They are extreme in reporting work competence. In addition they see fatherhood as important, perhaps because it is a concrete demonstration of their masculinity, and they report harmonious marriages, perhaps because it enhances their feelings of sexual adequacy.

Let us look at some other results that may corroborate this interpretation of the fear of weakness. Having drinking problems, taking drugs, more common among men with high fear of weakness, can be seen as ways of guaranteeing power, as McClelland and his associates (1972) have suggested. These may be seen as masculine compensatory devices for general feelings of lack of assertiveness in their lives. Another interesting result in Table 2 finds less educated men not attending church very often if they have high fear of weakness compared to men with less education who have low fear of weakness. Men's reluctance to attend church may be seen as a way of protecting their independence from women's influence. Finally, we find that sons of blue collar workers have especially high fear of weakness. Perhaps their own father's concerns about lack of status in the society have generalized to their own concerns about adequacy. We thus see all of these findings as fitting into the general syndrome: Fear of weakness is a concern about sexual identity.

Let us now turn to results for women. What evidence is there in the pattern of results in Table 2 to suggest that high fear of weakness may also reflect women's concern about their sexual identity? Presumably, if a woman herself feels competent in dealing with the arenas of life that are usually assigned to men, she may be concerned about her own sexual identity. It is in this way that we interpret the results in Table 2, which shows that women with high fear of weakness have higher self-esteem, are much less likely to rely on other people for support during crises (that is, are more autonomous), are not strongly oriented toward leisure, do not find much in the marital role that relates to their concerns, and are much more likely to turn to the work role as a way to find satisfaction than women with low fear of weakness. They are more likely to be satisfied with jobs, to mention the ego satisfactions from work, and to prefer work to leisure. They are also less likely to be satisfied with housework and more likely to say that housework does not fulfill their major life values. Furthermore, they see their children as drawing their husbands and themselves apart (for the less educated, older women only). These results all point to the highly power-motivated woman (fear of weakness) as being a competent, work-oriented woman who may feel comfortable about her own autonomy, but in turn may be concerned about her image. This concern does not, however, seem to be a highly anxious one; quite the opposite. It is more *cognitive* than is men's concern about sexual identity. Indeed I sense a conscious fear of success from a woman high in fear of weakness.

I might argue that women's concern about sexual identity is a late developing syndrome, one that women experience as they become successful in the job world. It is likely that the fear of weakness we are assessing in women did not arise in early childhood but evolved as women achieved. Indeed, we have no relationships between the fear of weakness measure in women and any background factors. A slightly different interpretation of how adult fear of weakness evolves in women might be the following: women, in relationship to men, might become politically and personally concerned about their fear of weakness, and, as a result, turn to the job arena as a way of enacting their competitive struggle with men. Indeed, we use such an explanation of why scores on the fear-of-weakness measure have increased so much in women between 1957 and 1976. Such an explanation, however, could be wrong, and we could suggest that the fear of weakness measure has increased because entering the labor force precipitates some concerns about sexual identity.

In any case, as a measure of assertive concerns, fear of weakness taps motivations that reflect people's lack of adjustment to the dominant norms of the society. These less adjusted people may be men and women struggling with their own uniqueness. In these struggles they perhaps find conformity to the more *socialized* norms for assertion burdensome. In heightened fear of weakness, we may also pick up the personalized struggles that men and women have with each other, as they strive to demonstrate their own adequacy with each other and their own sense of separateness. Nevertheless, it is this investment in more personalized assertion, whether with the opposite sex or with other people in general, that spearheads the goals of this motive. People with high fear of weakness are very closely attuned to how they are interacting with particular people in their environment and whether they have influence over them. For both men and women such motivation is part and parcel of their stake in their sexual identities.

Correlates of Hope of Power

In Table 3, which presents the significant subjective mental health correlates of the hope-of-power motive, we see one obvious pattern: Many results occur for men and women who have hope of power *across all age and education groups*. The control for age and education makes a big difference in how the hope-of-power motive relates to assessments of subjective mental health. This is clearest in one set of results for women's assessments of general well-being: For older college-educated women, those with high hope of power are more likely to have high feelings of efficacy, whereas for older less

Table 3. Significant Correlates of the Hope of Power Motive with Selected
Assessments of Subjective Mental Health (by sex)

Area of Assessment	Men (N = 508)	Women (N = 700)
General Well-Being	Lack of satisfaction with life	Satisfaction with life (older, college-educated only) High feelings of efficacy (older, college-educated only) Low feelings of efficacy (older, less educated only)
Behavior	Drinking problems creating family troubles Drug-taking to relieve tension (older, college-educated only) Drinking to relieve tension (younger, less educated only) Participation in organizations (older, college-educated only)	Drinking problems creating family troubles (older only) Drinking to relieve tension (older, college-educated only) Drug-taking to relieve tension (young, college-educated only)
Background	Having an older sibling[a] Having a parent who died while person was young	
Leisure	Not perceiving leisure as fulfilling major life value Leisure not satisfying (older only)	
Marriage	No feelings of inadequacy as a husband Seeing self as getting more out of marriage than spouse (young, college-educated only) Perceiving marriage as fulfilling major life value	Involvement with image of self as good wife Seeing self as getting more out of marriage than spouse Seeing marriage as fulfilling major life value
Parenthood	Perceiving children as not interfering with use of time (older, less educated only)	Feeling inadequate as a mother at times Seeing parenthood as fulfilling major life value
Work	Not wanting to work if money not needed	Not wanting to work if money not needed (older,

Table 3 (continued)

Area of Assessment	Men (N = 508)	Women (N = 700)
	Finds work uninteresting (young, less educated only) Mentions social dissatisfaction with work	less educated only) Preferring work to leisure (young, college-educated only)
Housework	————ᵇ	Housework not satisfying Seeing housework as not fulfilling major life value (young, college-educated only)

Note: Overall correlation (*r*) is either (1) significant at .05 level with at least 3/4 subgroups cross-classified by two age levels (twenty-one to thirty-nine; over forty) and two educational levels (high school graduate or less; some college or more) showing same pattern or (2) significant at .10 level with all subgroups showing same pattern. Any correlation reported for just one major subgroup is significant at least at .05 level.

N shown is potential total. Correlations are based on smaller numbers where data are missing because measures were non-ascertained or inappropriate (for example, marriages assessments for unmarried people).

ᵃ Based on analyses of variance of mean scores rather than correlations.
ᵇ No appropriate questions asked of men.
Source: National Sample Survey, 1976.

educated women the opposite is true. I would interpret this pattern of results and the pattern from the whole table as indicating that the hope-of-power motive is very responsive to the *specific situational pressures* on people. One's age or one's general social status in the community has a clear bearing on the type of reactions elicited from power-motivated people. That phenomenon, the situational boundedness of the power motive, leads us to suggest the following about the nature of hope of power: This assertive motive reflects people's concerns about having impact on their environment, about causing change. In many ways I think of this motive as a concern about boredom, reflecting a need for excitement in life. Having impact or producing change in the environment is a way of vesting interest in a world that if left unchanged might be uninteresting and even cause anxiety. McClelland's description of the power-motivated man as liking extreme risk (McClelland and Watson, 1973) is another way of looking at this orientation to excitement or change. As a motivational interest in change, a hope of power alerts a person to the specific nature of an ongoing situation. And it is on this basis that the controls for age and education are critical in attaining correlations between the hope-of-power motive and measures of other reactions.

We can also conclude that the dominant characteristic of the hope-of-power motive is an orientation to excitement in the following data about men from Table 3: Men with high hope-of-power motives are likely to be dissatisfied with life, to be oriented toward drinking and drug taking as a way to reduce tension, to find leisure unsatisfying, and to see leisure as not fulfilling major life values. They also find work uninteresting or at least are dissatisfied with the social aspects of work and would not work if they did not need the money. Highly power-motivated men seem less oriented toward work and more oriented toward the interpersonal roles of marriage and parenthood. They see themselves as getting more out of marriage than their spouse, see marriage as fulfilling their major life values, and do not see children as interfering with their use of time. It is as if these men find in interpersonal roles the possibility for constant stimulation and change in their lives. One might suggest that they have more immediate control over their primary group and less immediate control over the social life in their work setting. Among older college-educated men hope of power orients them to participation in organizations, which suggests that power-motivated men can turn to the less intimate interpersonal life to enact power, but possibly only when their power is ensured by the status associated with their age and education.

For women, there seems to be a more complicated pattern, although some of the same correlates of the high hope of power emerge for them as for men. Women with high hope of power are also oriented toward drinking and drug taking, are also involved with marriage and parenthood as arenas for expressing hope of power, and like men, would not work if they did not need the money. Only among college-educated younger women do we find any evidence that power-motivated people prefer work to leisure. They certainly do not like housework or find it satisfying or feel that it fulfills their values. Indeed they distinctly do not orient themselves toward housework. Thus, it is within the interpersonal roles that women with high power motivation find their excitement.

It is interesting to see that both men and women with high power motivation see themselves as getting more out of marriage than their spouse. It is as if such people see the marriage as an arena for battles of equity, comparative evaluation deciding who gets more out of it and who gets less. This orientation to marriage among the people who have high hope of power instills excitement. With it, marriage is not taken for granted. Everyday life is a battleground. I am reminded of the image of marriage that Albee drew in "Who's Afraid of Virginia Woolf?"—a constant reiteration of struggle for the sake of symbiotic excitement.

What can we make of the fact that older college-educated women seem particularly satisfied with life and have high feelings of efficacy, if they have high power motivation? One can only suggest that at this stage of life, higher status women are given the accoutrements of power that allow them to exercise power not only in the marital relationship but in the world at large. The low feelings of efficacy among less educated older women who have high power motivation supports the notion that credentials of status among older women may be critical to their finding satisfaction.

How would we contrast the fear-of-weakness measure of power motivation with hope of power? These two measures of motivation are positively correlated in the 1976 sample, both for men (+.42) and for women (+.32). How then are they different? I have suggested that the fear-of-weakness measure reflects more concern about identity, and the hope-of-power measure reflects concern about inducing change. These two are not entirely unrelated. One can argue that affirming one's sexual adequacy reflects more compelling anxiety than effecting change, although each requires impact on other persons as a demonstration of goal attainment. Each of these assertive motivations is much less socialized to the idealized norms of society than the achievement orientation; consequently neither can easily be gratified by a social definition of success. We could therefore suspect that people with an assertive motivation concerning either sexual identity or orientation to change are more likely to experience stress in their ongoing lives. It

is perhaps for these reasons that McClelland (1979) found that people with high power orientations are more likely to have physical
symptoms correlated with the stress they experience. The demonstration of assertion through power perhaps needs constant reaffir-
mation; the demonstration of assertion through achievement is
constantly socially validated.

Conclusion

Starting with a guiding framework that differentiated
achievement motivation from power motivation as an assertive concern focused on performance, and power from achievement as an
assertive concern focused on personal impact, I have reviewed data
from a 1976 national survey of motives and have refined this
formulation considerably. Critical to this refinement are three major
ideas: (1) Achievement assertiveness occurs in meeting *socialized*
norms, whereas power assertiveness occurs mostly in the expression
of *uniqueness*. (2) Achievement concerns arise out of resolved feelings of sex role competence, whereas power concerns arise out of
feelings of sex role inadequacy. (3) Achievement motivation is more
oriented to *future goal attainment*, whereas power motivation is
more oriented to *present fulfillment*.

There may be a fairly direct connection between the first two
refinements. If a person is comfortable with socialized norms for
assertion, he may be likely to feel comfortable with his sex role
competence. It less directly follows, however, that if a person is
uncomfortable about sex role adequacy, he may be oriented toward
uniqueness in assertive strivings.

The difference in time orientation of the two assertive motivations noted in the third refinement encapsulates a number of other
facets about achievement and power that have been highlighted in
the analyses presented here. The future orientation to achievement
accounts for the moderate risk taking of achievement-motivated
people, their successful efficiency, and their interest in feedback.
The present orientation to power motivation accounts for the
extreme risk taking of power-motivated people and their refined
orientation to the cues of their immediate social situation, including
its potential for change and excitement.

While I have been highlighting the differences between these two motivational systems, we have detected almost as many differences between a fear-of-weakness orientation to power and a hope of power as we have between achievement and power motivation generally. In his own research McClelland (1975) has focused on various typologies of power, distinctions that account for many differences among people. My colleagues and I have done a similar analysis of types of achievement motivations (Veroff, McClelland, and Ruhland, 1975). Nevertheless, there is a commonality found in types of power motivation as well as in types of achievement orientation that I have highlighted in this chapter. Further distinctions both between power and achievement motivations and among types of power and achievement orientations need explication in the future.

References

Ansbacher, H. L., and Ansbacher, R. *The Individual Psychology of Alfred Adler*. New York: Basic Books, 1956.

Atkinson, J. W. (Ed.). *Motives in Fantasy, Action, and Society*. New York: Van Nostrand, 1958.

Atkinson, J. W., and Raynor, J. O. *Motivation and Achievement*. New York: Winston (Wiley), 1974.

Bakan, D. *The Duality of Human Existence*. Chicago: Rand McNally, 1966.

Campbell, A., Converse, P. E., and Rodgers, W. L. *The Quality of American Life*. New York: Russell Sage Foundation, 1976.

French, E. G., and Lesser, G. S. "Some Characteristics of the Achievement Motive in Women." *Journal of Abnormal and Social Psychology*, 1964, *68*, 119-128.

Goodman, L. A. *Analyzing Qualitative Categorical Data: Log-Linear Models and Latent Structure Analysis*. Cambridge, Mass.: Abt, 1978.

Gurin, G., and others. *Americans View Their Mental Health*. New York: Basic Books, 1960.

Horner, M. S. "Toward an Understanding of Achievement-Related Conflict in Women." *Journal of Social Issues*, 1972, *28*, 157-175.

Lesser, G. S., Krawitz, R. N., and Packard, P. "Experimental Arousal of Achievement Motivation in Adolescent Girls." *Journal of Abnormal and Social Psychology*, 1963, *66*, 59-66.

Lipinski, B. G. "Sex Role Conflict and Achievement Motivation in College Women." Unpublished doctoral dissertation, University of Cincinnati, 1965.

McClelland, D. C. *The Achieving Society.* New York: Van Nostrand, 1961.

McClelland, D. C. *Motivational Trends in Society.* Morristown, N.J.: General Learning Press, 1971.

McClelland, D. C. *Power: The Inner Experience.* New York: Irvington, 1975.

McClelland, D. C. "Inhibited Power Motivation and High Blood Pressure in Men." *Journal of Abnormal Psychology*, 1979, *88*, 182-190.

McClelland, D. C., Davis, W. N., Kalin, R., and Wanner, E. *The Drinking Man: Alcohol and Human Motivation.* New York: Free Press, 1972.

McClelland, D. C., and Locke, S. "Power Motivation, Stress, Psychosomatic Symptoms, and Immunocompetence." Unpublished manuscript, 1978.

McClelland, D. C., and Watson, R. I., Jr. "Power Motivation and Risk-Taking Behavior." *Journal of Personality*, 1973, *41*, 121-139.

McClelland, D. C., and Winter, D. C. *Motivating Economic Achievement.* New York: Free Press, 1969.

Maslow, A. H. *Motivation and Personality.* New York: Harper & Row, 1954.

Mueller, S. "Motivation and Reactions to the Work Role Among Female Performers and Music Teachers." Unpublished doctoral dissertation, University of Michigan, 1975.

Quinn, R. P., and Staines, G. L. *The 1977 Quality of Employment Survey: Descriptive Statistics, with Comparison Data from the 1969-1970 and 1972-1973 Surveys.* Ann Arbor: Survey Research Center, Institute for Social Research, University of Michigan, 1979.

Raynor, J. O. "Future Orientation and Motivation of Immediate Activity: An Elaboration of the Theory of Achievement Motivation." *Psychological Review*, 1969, *66*, 606-610.

Rosenberg, M. *Society and Adolescent Self-Image*. Princeton, N.J.: Princeton University Press, 1965.

Temme, L. V. *Occupation: Meanings and Measures*. Washington, D.C.: Bureau of Social Science Research, Inc., 1975.

Veroff, J. "Development and Validation of a Projective Measure of Power Motivation." *Journal of Abnormal and Social Psychology*, 1957, *54*, 1-8.

Veroff, J., Atkinson, J. W., Feld, S. C., and Gurin, G. "The Use of Thematic Apperception to Assess Motivation in a Nationwide Interview Study."*Psychological Monographs*, 1960, *74*, 12 (whole number 499).

Veroff, J., Depner, C., Kulka, R., and Douvan, E. "Comparison of American Motives: 1957 Versus 1976." *Journal of Personality and Social Psychology*, 1980, *39*, 1249-1262.

Veroff, J., Douvan, E., and Kulka, R. *The American Experience*. New York: Basic Books, 1981.

Veroff, J., and Feld, S. C. *Marriage and Work in America*. New York: Van Nostrand Reinhold, 1970).

Veroff, J., McClelland, L., and Ruhland, D. "Varieties of Achievement Motivation." In M. Mednick, S. Tangri, and L. Hoffman (Eds.), *Women and Achievement*. Washington, D.C.: Hemisphere, 1975.

Veroff, J., and Veroff, J. B. "Reconsideration of a Measure of Power Motivation." *Psychological Bulletin*, 1972, *48*, 211-219.

Veroff, J., and Veroff, J. B. *Social Incentives: A Life Span Developmental Approach*. New York: Academic Press, 1980.

Winter, D. G. *The Power Motive*. New York: Free Press, 1973.

Zung, W. W. "A Self-Rating Depression Scale." *Archives of General Psychology*, 1965, *12*, 63-70.

Intimacy Motivation

5

 *Dan P. McAdams*

"It is private life that holds out the mirror to infinity; personal intercourse, and that alone, that ever hints at a personality beyond our daily vision." When the English novelist E. M. Forster thus exalts the private life in *Howard's End* (1910, p. 78), his prose surely resonates with the behavior and experience of many people, but certainly not all. If we were to view human lives as books lending themselves to various interpretations, close interpersonal relations would be the central motif of many texts, but in others it would be obscure, perhaps hidden in some chapters and even absent in others. Philosophers and poets who have extolled the benefits and virtues of warmth and closeness among human beings have generally recognized that individuals differ markedly with regard to a proclivity for this quality of experience (read Auden, 1971; Buber, 1965; or Marcel, 1964). Yet most personality psychologists studying individual differences have not developed a sensitive measure of this human tendency to be intimate. Their failures have been documented in some detail elsewhere (see Boyatzis, 1973; McAdams, 1979).

Recently, however, a new thematic measure of intimacy motivation has been derived and cross-validated in a number of experiments. Initial evidence bolstering the construct validity of the measure promises a theoretically and empirically fertile next decade in the scientific investigation of motivation and relationships. Employing the Thematic Apperception Test (TAT) methodology popularized by David McClelland, I have delineated ten themes, readily detectable in narrative responses elicited by picture cues, that comprise a coding system for intimacy motivation. The system is designed to assess an individual's *preference* or *readiness* for experiences of closeness, warmth, and communication, and it is assumed to do this through an analysis of the quality of the interpersonal relationships manifested by characters in imaginative stories written by the individual. Although the intimacy motive has been operationalized in a context of scientific research, its theoretical origins lie in philosophy, humanistic psychology, and psychiatry. Before the measure itself, then, is described, the theoretical roots of intimacy motivation will be unearthed in the writings of David Bakan, Abraham Maslow, Martin Buber, and Harry Stack Sullivan.

Theoretical Origins of Intimacy Motivation

In his interdisciplinary inquiry into the "duality of human existence," the philosopher-psychologist David Bakan (1966) defines two fundamental modalities of living forms. The first, *agency*, refers to the existence of a living organism as an individual, implying those internal characteristics that distinguish the organism from its surrounding context. Therefore, agency manifests itself in the formation of separations between individual and other, in tendencies toward self-protection, self-expansion, self-assertion, isolation, alienation, and aloneness. To be an agent is to assert one's self without regard to the integrity of the surroundings and in so doing to master one's environment and make it his or her own. In the animal kingdom, Bakan points to the cancer cell as the paradigmatic case of "unmitigated agency." The cancer cell continues to divide and multiply without regard to limits or boundaries. Eventually it completely dominates its embedding context, but in so doing destroys the context, kills the host, and itself dies.

What mitigates agency, according to Bakan, is the second fundamental modality, *communion*. Whereas agency represents the existence of an organism as an individual, communion refers to the "participation of the individual in some larger organism of which the individual is a part" (p. 15). The individual organism is embedded in a larger context, conceived by Bakan as a structured "organism" in itself, and an identity (a definition or function) is conferred on the individual by the context in terms of *relatedness*. Whereas agency indicates separation and mastery, communion manifests itself in contact, openness, union, cooperation, and a sense of being at one with other organisms. Healthy human adaptation presupposes a dynamic tension between the agentic and the communal, Bakan maintains, and yet individual differences in personality can be understood in part according to which of the two central tendencies is given priority in behavior and experience (Maddi, 1976). The organism tending toward communion appears highly sensitized to opportunities for blurring the boundaries of self in the process of relating. He or she is open to the interpersonal surroundings, ready for merger. This communal pose, however, is one of attentive waiting, not active striving. And the merger—the interaction with another as it spontaneously unfolds—is not conditional nor is it a means to another end.

The humanistic psychologist Abraham Maslow (1954, 1968) docments this unconditional and noninstrumental merger with another by reported experiences of *Being-Love (B-Love)*. Instead of an active striving to attain friends and friendship, B-Love is characterized by a welcoming of the other into a mutually enjoyed, reciprocal, egalitarian union. The tone of the interaction is "gentle, delicate, unintruding, undemanding, able to fit itself passively to the nature of things as water gently soaks into crevices" (1968, p. 41). The emphasis upon "being" differentiates B-Love from *D-Love (Deficiency-Love)* in which "doing" (striving) is predominant; D-Love is characterized by striving to fill a void, to satisfy a lack in the individual's interpersonal world. According to Maslow, D-Love operates on a negative feedback principle such that an unsatisfying interpersonal condition feeds information back, impelling the organism to alter its response patterns to regain a satisfying equilibrium. B-Love, on the other hand, is not so constrained: "It [B-Love] can never be sated; it may be enjoyed without end. It usually grows greater rather than disappearing. It is intrinsically enjoyable. It is ends rather than means" (1968, p. 42). Moreover, Maslow insists that B-Love can enhance psychological growth for all individuals involved, providing experiences profoundly therapeutic in times of distress.

Although he explicitly denies that he is writing about love or intimacy per se, Martin Buber (1965, 1970) has been a lyrical spokesman for a philosophy that undergirds the present approach to intimacy motivation. Buber is concerned with dialogue or communication between people. The *I-Thou* relation is characterized by a special and rare form of dialogue in which each partner is completely absorbed in what the other has to offer, and yet each remains unique and separate. The dialogue is what Sullivan (1953) has termed *syntactic* experience at its best, an exchange of information in which all symbols and signals are fully comprehended by both partners. Of course, such a happening is an ideal that is only approached in the most reciprocal and egalitarian exchanges. Buber maintains that these exchanges or encounters present themselves in a myriad of situations in everyday life, and as a theologian Buber (1970, p. 59) points to them as opportunities for making the mundane sacred: "When I confront a human being as my Thou and speak the basic word I-Thou to him, then he is no thing among things nor does he consist of things. He is no longer He or She, limited by other Hes and Shes, a dot in the world grid of space and time, nor a condition that can be experienced and described, a loose bundle of named qualities. Neighborless and seamless, he is Thou and fills the firmament. Not as if there were nothing but he; but everything else lives in *his* light."

The I-Thou is a momentary vignette in people's lives in which each person focuses unswervingly on the other. It is not a long-term relationship in the sense that a marriage, siblingship, or love affair is. Rather, episodes of intimate exchange are possible between all kinds of people, and at virtually any time.

The psychiatrist Harry Stack Sullivan offers a developmental perspective on the capacity to engage in intimate exchange. According to Sullivan, the *need for interpersonal intimacy* first arises in the human life cycle during the brief but crucial stage of preadolescence. At this time, the appearance in the child's life of the same-sex "chum" may mark a critical transition in the development of the individual's understanding of interpersonal relations: "But if you look very closely at one of your children when he finally finds a chum—

somewhere between eight-and-a-half and ten—you will discover something very different in the relationship—namely, that your child begins to develop a real sensitivity to what matters to another person. And this is not in the sense of "what should I do to get what I want," but instead "what should I do to contribute to the happiness or to support the prestige and feeling of worthwhileness of my chum." So far as I have ever been able to discover, nothing remotely like this appears before the age of, say, eight-and-a-half, and sometimes it appears decidedly later" (Sullivan, 1953, pp. 245–246).

The chumship catalyzes the emergence of a developmentally unprecedented preoccupation with the well-being of another. This emergence precedes puberty and what Sullivan terms the awakening of the "lust dynamism." Hence, the need for interpersonal intimacy is somewhat independent of genital sexuality, although the two must be successfully integrated in the mature heterosexual union between adults.

Concomitant with the emergence of the need for intimacy are the first experiences of loneliness, the vexing condition of living outside an intimate relation. Sullivan remarks that "loneliness, as an experience which has been so terrible that it practically baffles clear recall, is a phenomenon ordinarily encountered only in preadolescence and afterward" (p. 261). The opposite pole of loneliness is intimacy—the collaborative relation with another, first encountered, for many, in the chumship. The capacities to experience these two phenomena—loneliness and intimacy—develop in tandem.

In sum, the writings of Bakan, Maslow, Buber, and Sullivan converge upon a particular quality of interpersonal experience. The experience can be described as an egalitarian exchange between or among persons characterized by the following themes:

1. joy and mutual delight (Maslow)
2. reciprocal dialogue (Buber, Sullivan)
3. openness, contact, union, receptivity (Bakan, Maslow)
4. perceived harmony (Buber, Sullivan)
5. concern for the well-being of the other (Sullivan)
6. surrender of manipulative control and the desire to master in relating to the other (Bakan, Buber, Maslow)

7. being, in an encounter which is perceived as an end in itself,
rather than doing, or striving to attain either a relationship or
some extrinsic reward (Bakan, Buber, Maslow, Sullivan).

A guiding assumption of work in intimacy motivation is that
the recurrent conscious and/or unconscious preference for intimate
experience characterized by many or all of the above seven themes is
not the same for all people. The thematic coding system for intimacy motivation is designed to be sensitive to differences in this
recurrent preference. What follows is a cursory description of the
development of the intimacy motivation coding system and a review
of recent studies speaking to the validity of the measure. Two related
questions are thereby addressed: How does one derive such a measure? And how can one test the measure, once derived, as a measure
of individual differences in personality? With regard to the second
question, the studies to be reviewed here have aimed at assessing to
what extent the experiential preference in intimacy motivation can
be shown to *energize, direct,* and *select* behavior in certain situations.
To the extent that the measured preference can be shown to exert an
energizing, directing, and selecting effect upon behavior, it can justi-
fiably be considered a significant social motive in human lives
(McClelland, 1971).

Derivation of the Coding System

Arousal Experiments. The derivation of the intimacy motive
coding categories for interpreting TAT stories and other imaginative productions (McAdams, 1980b) closely follows the general
model of developing a scoring system for a social motive originally
outlined by McClelland and his coworkers (McClelland, Clark,
Roby, and Atkinson, 1949; McClelland, Atkinson, Clark, and
Lowell, 1953). The first step in the process is to find or create the
experience of interest, in this case the intimacy experience described
by the seven themes named above. Once the researcher is successful
in finding persons engaged in something akin to the relevant experience, the second step is to obtain, as inobtrusively as possible,
samples of their imaginative thought. Hence, the TAT is administered in situations of high intimacy arousal, and the stories written

by the aroused subjects serve as discrete thought samples that in some way may mirror the subjects' contemporaneous experience. The third step is to determine precisely in what way these thought samples mirror the experience of intimacy; therefore they are compared to thought samples obtained from similar subjects who are presumed *not*, as a rule, to be experiencing intimacy. This second group of people constitutes the control group, who are administered the TAT under neutral (nonarousal) conditions (for example, in a classroom setting).

Once two sets of stories have been obtained (the arousal stories and the control stories), the researcher begins the fourth and crucial step of content analysis, in which an attempt is made to delineate the consistent differences between the two sets of stories in terms of content motifs. These thematic differences comprise a rudimentary first scoring system for intimacy motivation, which is then cross-validated (the fifth step) through blind scoring of another sample of arousal and control stories. To the extent that the scoring system can differentiate between the two sets of stories on this second, cross-validational sample, it reveals itself to be a sensitive measure of *group* differences in motive *states*. The evaluation of the coding system as a sensitive measure of consistent *individual* differences in motive *dispositions* awaits the final sixth step of further construct validation, which is detailed below under "Evidence for Construct Validity."

In deriving the intimacy motivation coding system, four separate arousal experiments were designed, three taking advantage of naturally occurring events and one creating experiences of intimacy in the laboratory. In all four, a control group also took the TAT. Although suggestions of each of the seven experiential themes enumerated above can be found in one or more of the four experiments, the first three themes of delight (more generally, positive affect), reciprocal dialogue, and openness-contact-receptivity are paramount and are most clearly discernible in the arousal conditions employed.

In Experiment 1, six TAT pictures were administered according to the standard group administration format (Atkinson, 1958) to a group of twenty-one college men attending a fraternity initiation ceremony and twenty-one college women attending a sorority initiation ceremony at a small, private midwestern university. Forty-two fraternity and sorority members (twenty-one male, twenty-one female) matched with arousal subjects for graduating class (freshman, sophomore, junior, senior) and fraternity/sorority status (initiate or member) were administered the same TAT pictures under neutral classroom conditions and thus constituted the control group. The fraternity and sorority initiation ceremonies were chosen as intimacy arousal conditions because of the reported feelings of good cheer and "brotherhood" or "sisterhood" engendered at these annual celebrations. In each, the old members of the two organizations enact a ceremony welcoming the initiates into the group. According to the fraternity and sorority members, the one- to two-hour ceremonies are perennially successful in facilitating an atmosphere of warmth, closeness, and conviviality among all the participants. At the end of the fraternity ceremony, the TATs were administered by the author (a former member of the same fraternity). A female experimenter (a former member of the sorority) administered the TAT to sorority members immediately after their ceremony. Through the use of familiar experimenters and carefully detailed briefing sessions conducted before and after the ceremonies, the intrusiveness of the TAT intervention was significantly minimized.

In Experiment 2, the same set of TAT pictures was administered to thirty-eight students (nineteen male, nineteen female) attending a dancing party at the same midwestern university. All participants in the party arousal group were volunteers who reported that (a) they were having a good time and (b) they had had no more than two alcoholic drinks in the course of the evening and were not feeling the effects of the alcohol. The participants were told that the study was investigating the use of imagination in story writing under party conditions. The control group used in Experiment 1 was used for Experiment 2 as well.

In Experiment 3, data from ninety-two college students (forty-six male, forty-six female) were used. The data for the arousal group were made up of forty-six sets of TAT protocols collected in 1973 from members of heterosexual couples (described in Peplau, Rubin, and Hill, 1976) who both scored extremely high on the Rubin (1973) questionnaire, the Love Scale, indicating high intensity of love reported mutually. The emotional state of being in love, as assessed by the Love Scale, was seen as the intimacy motivation arousal condition per se. The control group consisted of forty-six students (twenty-three male, twenty-three female) attending a private university who were administered the same set of TAT pictures in 1978. The subjects in the control group were not chosen as couples, and few reported that they were in love with anybody at the time of testing. The two groups of subjects were matched for age (mean ages were 21.3 and 21.4 years for arousals and controls respectively).

Finally, Experiment 4 employed a within-group design in which forty-three students at an eastern university (twenty-three male, twenty female) were first administered the TAT in a neutral setting and then administered a comparable version of the TAT after an experimentally induced arousal session. In the arousal sessions, groups of eight or nine students engaged in a structured sequence of activities, games, discussions, and role playing (derived from standard practices used in psychodrama; Moreno, 1946) designed to promote spontaneity, sharing, warmth, and occasional frivolity. A male psychodrama instructor directed the two-and-a-half hour arousal events (which are described in more detail below, under "Interpersonal Behavior in a Psychodrama," and in McAdams and Powers, 1981).

In developing the intimacy motive scoring categories, a small subsample of TAT protocols from arousal and control conditions in Experiments 1 and 2 was selected as a "derivation sample" from which to derive thematic categories differentiating between stories written under arousal and control conditions. The author first derived nine major themes, most bearing upon the quality of the relationships manifested among the characters in the stories. These somewhat crudely defined categories were used to score (blind) the remaining TAT protocols in Experiments 1 and 2 (termed the "cross validation sample"). In this cross validation effort, six of the nine categories significantly differentiated between stories written under arousal and control conditions.

The six themes that survived the cross validation for Experiments 1 and 2 were slightly modified in a new content analysis of a small derivation sample from Experiment 3 (the "in-love" arousal).

Five new thematic categories were also derived from this subsample. Upon blind scoring of the remaining protocols in Experiment 3, three of the five new categories significantly differentiated between arousal stories and control stories. This cross validation effort suggested further modifications of the original six themes derived and cross-validated for Experiments 1 and 2. The six were expanded to seven, and when combined with the three themes surviving cross validation for Experiment 3, came to be included in a ten-category scoring system.

The ten intimacy themes were refined a final time through a content analysis of a derivation subsample from Experiment 4. All cross validation samples (excluding the derivation subsamples) from all four experiments were then rescored (blind) for intimacy motivation, using the ten themes that make up the present scoring system. Seven categories differentiated significantly between stories written by the arousal subjects and those written by corresponding controls in three of the four arousal experiments; two reached significance in two of four experiments; and one was significant in one of the four experiments. *Total* intimacy motive scores (the sum of all category scores for a given story) differentiated between arousal and control subjects $p < .001$ in Experiments 1, 2, and 4, and $p < .005$ in Experiment 3. The results were highly comparable between the sexes.

It should be noted that the process of developing a useful thematic coding system requires a careful blend of theoretical and empirical considerations. Although all the scoring categories for the intimacy motive were empirically derived and cross-validated, theoretical predilections heavily influenced what the author in fact looked for in deriving the original themes. Myriad thematic categories were tested and discarded for each derivation subsample. The resultant ten categories that ultimately met the empirical requirements, however, were generally the ones that seemed to have the most theoretical backing as well.

The Scoring System. The scoring system is made up of ten thematic categories, whose presence (score +1) or absence (score 0) is assessed in a given story. The two broadest and most prevalent thematic categories are deemed prime tests of intimacy imagery (referred to as Intimacy Imagery categories), and the other eight are termed subcategories. Each category can be scored +1 only once per story. The presence of at least one of the two Intimacy Imagery categories is a thematic prerequisite for scoring the eight subsequent subcategories in a given story. Scores on a given story range from 0 (neither Intimacy Imagery category present) to 10 (all ten themes present). A subject's total intimacy motive score, thus, is the sum of the scores for each story written, generally corrected for story length.

The thematic categories that make up the intimacy motivation scoring system are briefly described below.

+A: Relationship produces positive affect (Intimacy Imagery 1). An interpersonal encounter precipitates, facilitates, or is decidedly connected with a positive affective experience on the part of at least one of the characters. Positive affect must fall under one of five rubrics: love, friendship, happiness, peace, or tender behavior connoting positive affect. A special case for mourning or sadness associated with the separation from or loss of another person may also score for +A. *Examples:* "The two lovers . . . "; "They're just sitting there enjoying being together."

Dlg: Dialogue (Intimacy Imagery 2). Dialogue is defined as a verbal or nonverbal exchange of information between (among) characters that meets at least one of three criteria: (a) reciprocal, noninstrumental communication, (b) discussion of an interpersonal relationship, (c) conversation for the purpose of helping another person in distress. *Examples:* "The old farmers are swapping stories"; "They are discussing their future together as a couple"; "He tries to cheer he up as she listens."

The following eight categories, termed "subcategories," can only be scored if either Intimacy Imagery 1 or Intimacy Imagery 2 is present in a given story.

Psy: Psychological growth and coping. An interpersonal encounter is demonstrably instrumental in facilitating or promoting psychological growth, self-fulfillment, adjustment, coping with problems, identity formation, the search for self-knowledge, spiritual salvation, creative inspiration, maturity, or the like. *Example:* "Bev is continually becoming better adjusted to everyday life because of Harry."

CC: Commitment or concern. A character feels a sense of commitment to or concern for another (others) that is not rooted in guilt or grudging duty. Commitment includes feelings of loyalty to and responsibility for another. Concern generally indicates a felt responsibility for another's welfare usually leading to some kind of helping or humanitarian behavior, and sometimes personal sacrifice. *Example*: "He feels responsible for their well-being, and therefore he will not quit the boring job."

TS: Time-Space. Two or more characters are engaged in a relationship that transcends the usual limitations of time and/or space. This includes explicit references made to the enduring quality of a relationship over an extended period of time and in the face of physical separation. *Examples*: "They have a kind of rapport that spans time and generations"; "These very old friends. . . ."

U: Union. The writer explicitly refers to the physical or figurative coming together of people who have at one time or another been apart. *Example*: "After years apart, she came back to Switzerland to be with her grandfather."

H: Harmony. Characters find that they are in harmony with one another. They are "on the same wavelength," their actions are "in synchrony," one "truly understands" another, they find "something in common," they share similar views, and so on. *Example*: "They found that they had much in common."

Sr: Surrender. A character finds that interpersonal relations are subject to control that is in some way beyond him or her. He or she surrenders to this outside control. *Example*: "It was fated: They fell helplessly in love."

Esc: Escape to intimacy. Characters actively or mentally escape from a particular situation or state to another situation or state that affords the experiencing of happiness, peace, liberation, fulfillment, or meaning in the context of interpersonal relations. *Example*: "The two people were tired of being cooped up in the apartment so they decided to take a walk on the beach together."

COW: Connection with the outside world. A story manifests an explicit example of a connection between one of the characters and the outside world. The connection must be manifested by the writer as either a direct interaction between a character and the outside world or a metaphoric parallel between the outside world and a character or a relationship. *Example*: "They love the way the air feels on their skins."

The intimacy motive scoring system can be characterized as an attribute scoring system, as opposed to an activity scoring system like that used for scoring achievement motivation (McClelland, Atkinson, Clark, and Lowell, 1953). In intimacy thematic content, the characters in the story need not be doing anything in particular; rather the quality of the interaction between them is assessed by reference to a number of attributes that may characterize intimate interpersonal encounters. Hence, it is the task of the scorer to characterize and categorize the attributes of the characters' interpersonal encounters as manifested by the writer of the story.

A detailed scoring manual designed to teach the researcher to score reliably with numerous practice stories has been completed (McAdams, 1980a). High interscorer agreement has been obtained between the expert scoring in the manual and trained scorers. The category agreement (see Winter, 1973) for the two Intimacy Imagery categories has ranged from 91 percent to 95 percent, and the rank-order correlation between total intimacy motive story score as assessed by trained scorers and the intimacy motive story score according to the manual has ranged from $\rho = +.86$ to $+.92$.

With respect to test-retest reliability, Lundy (1980) has reported a correlation of $r = .48$ between intimacy motive scores of high school students who were administered the TAT in their junior year and then again a year later as seniors. In the second testing session, the students were given the Winter and Stewart (1977) TAT instructions, which suggest that the subjects may write stories similar to ones written in previous TAT administrations.

McAdams and Powers (1981) have provided data on the internal consistency of the individual scoring categories and individual picture cues for intimacy motivation. In a sample of forty-three undergraduates, all the intimacy motive scoring categories with the exception of Union were positively correlated with each other to a moderate extent. A factor analysis of the eight intimacy subcategories revealed that seven of the eight (Union again is the exception) load highly to moderately on a factor of General Intimacy. Intercorrelations of intimacy motive scores of stories written to five separate picture cues were generally moderate and positive, and moderately low α (Ebel, 1965) of .32 was calculated as a summary estimate of consistency among the five picture cues used to assess intimacy motivation. The reader with a special interest in the psychometric issues of test-retest reliability and internal consistency vis-à-vis the TAT are referred to Atkinson (1981), McClelland (1980), and McAdams and Powers (1981), who have cautioned against the indiscriminate extension of traditional test theory into the realm of operant thought-sampling techniques such as the TAT.

Finally, it should be mentioned that intimacy motivation has been derived, cross-validated, and investigated as a measure of individual differences using a limited set of TAT pictures that has proven especially appropriate for the thematic content involved. The most useful pictures are relatively ambiguous and thus able to elicit a wide variety of thematic content in narrative responses. Typically, a set of five or six pictures is administered, including some which may typically cue intimacy stories and some which may cue one or two of the other motives of interest to the investigator, such as power or achievement. Pictures for which some norms are available (McAdams, unpublished manuscript) include (a) two figures sitting on a park bench, (b) a man sitting at a desk upon which sits a photograph of a family, (c) a man and woman on a trapeze, (d) a silhouette of a man and woman on a rooftop, (e) a man, a woman, and a dog walking through a field with horses, (f) a solitary figure walking down a street, (g) two women scientists in a laboratory, (h) a ship captain and a reporter (both men), (i) a man and woman at a nightclub, and (j) a boy, a girl, an old man, and a dog on a river bank. Pictures a and b can be found in McClelland and Steele (1972); c, g, h, and i are in McClelland (1975).

Evidence for Construct Validity

Peer Ratings. The first evidence for the construct validity of the intimacy motive scoring system as a measure of individual differences in a relatively stable motivational disposition comes from a study of peer ratings (McAdams, 1980b). Adjective checklists, containing twenty-four adjectives selected to include ten items hypothetically related to the intimacy motive and fourteen unrelated, were mailed to ten upperclassmen each in the fraternity and the sorority used in arousal Experiment 1. Each of these twenty individuals was (a) well acquainted with all twenty-one of the *control* subjects in arousal Experiment 1 from his or her organization and (b) not a subject in the study. The upperclassmen were asked to circle the eight to twelve adjectives from the list that best described each of the subjects in the control group. Thus, each upperclassman judge completed twenty-one adjective checklists, one for each control subject from his or her organization. Strict confidentiality was observed.

The results of the peer ratings showed that both male and female subjects scoring high in intimacy motivation (under relatively neutral conditions) were perceived by their ten same-sex peers who completed the checklists as significantly more "natural," "warm," "sincere," "appreciative," and "loving" than subjects scoring lower on the motive. Correlations between motive scores and number of judges (maximum = 10; minimum = 0) endorsing each of the adjectives to describe the subject ranged from $r = +.59$ ($p < .001$) for "natural" to $r = +.34$ ($p < .05$) for "loving." Subjects high in intimacy motivation were also seen as *less* "dominant" ($r = -.43$, $p < .01$, *less* "outspoken" ($r = -.41$, $p < .01$), and *less* "self-centered" ($r = -.40$, $p < .01$). Of the ten predictions made about relationships between the intimacy motive and adjectives, eight were confirmed at significant levels, whereas only two of the fourteen correlations between motive and adjective not predicted to be signifiant reached statistical significance.

In a second study with forty-three Eastern university students (McAdams and Powers, 1981), subjects scoring high in intimacy motivation (under neutral conditions) were rated by their peers as significantly more "sincere," "likeable," "loving," and "natural" and significantly less "dominant" than subjects scoring lower on the motive. Interestingly enough, self-ratings on the same adjective checklists failed to correlate significantly with intimacy motivaton for all adjectives used. It appears that college students scoring high on the TAT intimacy motive measure are perceived by *others* as consistently more sincere and warm in interpersonal relationships and consistently less dominant than their peers scoring lower, suggesting the kind of gentle "being" orientation described by Maslow. When asked to rate themselves, however, on dimensions of warmth and dominance, these same high-intimacy subjects fail to ascribe adjectives denoting warmth and lack of dominance to themselves, or at least they do so no more often or less often than their counterparts scoring low on intimacy motivation.

Interpersonal Behavior in a Psychodrama. McAdams and Powers (1981) undertook an unusual study in which forty-three col-

lege students, previously administered the TAT under neutral conditions, were asked to act out psychodramas that were videotaped and
later coded for intimacy behavior. These were the same subjects
whose post-psychodrama TATs were used as arousal data in arousal
Experiment 4 described above. The technique of psychodrama was
pioneered by Moreno (1946) as a therapeutic tool. Traditionally,
psychodrama has been used in group therapy as a method for acting
out psychosocial problems and effecting emotional resolutions
through action. In a classic psychodrama, one group member (the
protagonist) is designated the main character in his or her own
action drama. The drama is enacted in the space available (the
stage), and other members of the group may serve as either actors/ac-
tresses or audience; the psychodrama director (the therapist) moni-
tors and interprets the proceedings. To alleviate anxiety and
promote openness and spontaneity among the group members, the
psychodrama director may preface the drama with a warm-up by
leading the group in games, role playing, and opportunities for
discussion and sharing. In the McAdams and Powers study, groups
of eight or nine subjects each were first led through a series of such
warm-up exercises, and then each subject in turn was asked to structure a mini-psychodrama (five to ten minutes long) using the group
and the room to illustrate any issue or theme he or she deemed
appropriate. The psychodrama scenarios did not generally touch on
profoundly personal issues, as they might in traditional clinical
settings, and they were not elaborated into therapeutic explorations.
Rather, the scenarios served as fairly innocuous interpersonal
vignettes in which each subject in turn sculpted a personal action
episode hypothesized to provide the researchers with a window into
his or her style of relating to others and the particular interpersonal
motifs he or she considered significant enough to warrant expression in a brief personalized drama.

The videotaped scenarios were coded by independent raters
who had no knowledge of the subjects' motive scores as assessed via
the TAT. Behavioral coding was conducted at two levels of analysis:
discrete behaviors and behavioral themes. Borrowing in part from
the work of Hall (1959) and Mehrabian (1972) on verbal and nonverbal expressions of interpersonal intimacy, the researchers delineated
seven simple coding systems for discrete behaviors hypothesized to

be associated with the protagonists' intimacy motive scores: (1) physical proximity to other group members, (2) amount of time giving instructions to others relative to amount of time acting out the scenarios, (3) number of commands delivered to others, (4) number of references to self, (5) number of references to "we" or "us," designating the group, (6) number of outbursts of laughter by group members (assumed to indicate joy or some kind of positive affect in the scenario), and (7) order of volunteering to be protagonist (from first to last). Subjects scoring high in intimacy motivation were found to spend less time introducing their scenarios to the group and more time acting out the drama, to make more references to "we" or "us" when referring to themselves and the group, to issue fewer commands to their peers, to stimulate more frequent outbursts of laughter from the group, and to position themselves in closer proximity to other group members, than subjects scoring lower on the motive.

When the psychodrama tapes were coded for behavioral themes in a fashion analogous to coding TAT stories for themes manifested in narrative, very high correlations between intimacy motivation on the TAT and intimacy behavior in the scenarios were obtained. With the help of David McClelland and Richard Boyatzis, McAdams and Powers devised a set of behavioral themes applicable to the psychodrama scenarios that (1) could be reliably coded by independent judges viewing the tapes and (2) would reflect patterns in the protagonists' behavior theoretically related to the superordinate theme of the intimacy motive—experiencing warm, close, and communicative exchange with others. Blind to the motive scores of the subjects, the researchers initially viewed nine of the forty-three taped scenarios and rated them in terms of intimacy value. By contrasting scenarios rated as high and low in intimacy, the researchers then tried to codify the major differences in terms of a few well-defined themes. Five such themes were ultimately delineated:

1. Positive affect: Score +1 if scenario manifests consistent expression of happiness, mirth, surprise, joy, or tenderness. Score 0 if scenario manifests only sporadic positive affect, mixed affect, or no affect. Score –1 if scenario manifests consistent negative affect such as anger, boredom, grief, anxiety, shame, or disgust.

2. Reciprocal dialogue: Score +1 if scenario manifests mutual dialogue and/or exchange (not necessarily verbal) that is not argumentative, competitive, or hostile. Score 0 if no such dialogue is present.

3. Surrender of control: Score +1 if protagonist surrenders control of the scenario by giving participants considerable leeway to structure their own roles and behaviors in the context of the protagonist's drama. Score 0 if protagonist controls the scenario.

4. Personal meaning: Score +1 if protagonist remarks that scenario is personally meaningful to him or her. Score 0 if no such remark is made.

5. Nature: Score +1 if scenario manifests heightened sensory imagery with reference to the natural world, fantasies of interaction between participants and nature. Score 0 if no such nature theme is present. (This theme is related to the COW subcategory of the intimacy motive scoring system for TATs. It designates a relationship established between a person and the external world in which there is openness, receptivity, and union.)

The total intimacy behavior index score was simply the sum of the scores for the five behavioral themes. When the two independent coders did not agree exactly on a given subject's total score, then the mean of the two scores was used in the data analysis. The scores ranged hypothetically from –1 to +5. In this sample they ranged from –1 to +4 with a mean of 1.5.

A sixth behavioral theme of nonthreatening touching was also coded, but because of technical difficulties in two of the five tapes this theme could be coded reliably in only twenty-eight of forty-three scenarios. Scores for this theme were either 0 to +1. It was not included in the intimacy behavior index.

The results of the behavioral theme analysis showed that subjects who scored high in intimacy motivation tended to structure behavioral scenarios in which themes of positive affect, mutual dialogue, and surrender of control in an interpersonal encounter were central. To a lesser extent, these scenarios manifested behavioral themes on nonthreatening touching, interaction with nature, and personal meaningfulness (indicating a willingness to share personal experiences with the group). When the five behavioral themes (excluding nonthreatening touching) were combined to form the total intimacy behavior index, the correlation between the two summary indices of intimacy in thought and behavior—that is, the intimacy motive score on the TAT and the intimacy behavior index—was quite striking, r (41) = +.70, $p < .001$.

The results of the psychodrama study suggest that subjects high in intimacy motivation show behavior commensurate with the preferred experience of the motive—warm, close, and communicative exchange, when given an opportunity to interact with others in a warm and supportive milieu. These subjects try to promote a communal and egalitarian spirit among their peers by structuring scenarios in which they refuse to become the sociometric centers of attraction and instead surrender centrality and control to the group. They issue few commands, make more references to "we" or "us," and tacitly endorse the individuality of other participants by allowing them to create their own roles. As a result, the psychodrama scenarios produced and enacted by these subjects high in intimacy motivation appear somewhat undirected, even chaotic at times. Nonetheless, they are almost always very warm. These dramas may not be well controlled, but they unfailingly are genuine community events. At best the protagonists appear open and involved in the group; at worst they may be seen as overly passive and self-effacing.

Information Processing. A series of studies has been conducted investigating the relationship between intimacy motivation and perceptual/cognitive processing of intimacy-relevant information. The studies have explored perception of faces, free recall of simple stimulus lists, story memory, and autobiographical memory.

One experiment (McAdams, 1979) tentatively supports the hypothesis that people high in intimacy motivation are more sensitive to facial nuance, that is, more likely to perceive changes in facial configurations and thereby to attribute more variable adjective ratings to faces differing only slightly in makeup. Among fifty-three college students, subjects scoring high in intimacy motivation showed more variance in judgments of nine schematic faces (from Brunswik and Reiter, 1938) drawn with subtle variations in eye width, nose length, height of mouth, and height of forehead than subjects scoring lower in intimacy motivation. The results indicate either (a) that subjects high in intimacy motivation are more likely to *perceive* the differences in the faces or (b) that all subjects perceive the differences equally but high-intimacy subjects are more likely to base judgments on these perceptions. Although neither conclusion can be eliminated at this point, the first is in keeping with a burgeoning literature on the relationship between eye contact and facial behavior on the one hand and interpersonal intimacy on the other. Research into mother-infant attachment (Blehar, Lieberman, and Ainsworth, 1977; Rheingold, 1961; Stern, 1979) and nonverbal communication among adults (Argyle and Cook, 1976; Exline and Winters, 1966; Mehrabian, 1972) affirms the notion that face-to-face, eye-to-eye contact may signal closeness and intimacy in a relationship, although such behavior certainly serves other functions as well. Patterson (1976) has described an arousal model of interpersonal intimacy, in which eye contact in an interpersonal exchange signals arousal that is evaluated as positive or negative depending upon contextual cues. In this light it might be expected that people high in intimacy motivation, who manifest a receptivity to intimate exchange, will generally be attuned to cues in the environment that seem to signal opportunities for such exchange. The face is unsurpassed as a stimulus configuration laden with such cues.

Leaving perception, McAdams (1979) has studied the relationship between intimacy motivation and free recall of simple stimuli differing in interpersonal value. Forty-six college students were shown a series of thirty picture-word combinations, each flashed for a few seconds on a screen, and then asked, immediately thereafter, to remember as many of the words as possible. The subjects were given two minutes to write down the words in the order in which they remembered them. The picture-word stimuli fell into three categories: relational cues (for example, lover, sister, companion), moving vehicles (submarine, motorcycle), and occupations (artist, accountant). Using a measure of clustering devised by Bousfield (1953), a moderately significant relationship was found between intimacy motivation and a tendency to cluster more relational cues in recall. The clustering measure determines the number of adjacent pairs of stimuli recalled in which both are members of the same category. This relationship between intimacy motivation and clustering, however, has proven to be quite weak in two replications of the experiment. At this point, therefore, the influence of intimacy motivation upon immediate free recall of simple interpersonal stimuli such as pictures and words does not appear to be marked or consistent.

A more powerful influence, however, has been documented in studies of memory for stimulus events that are more complex, contextual, and personally meaningful. In two unpublished studies of story memory, McAdams and McClelland demonstrated strong support for the selective effect of the intimacy motive on information processing. In the first study, an experimenter read two stories to a group of fifty-five undergraduates, each in response to a TAT picture shown on a screen. The first story (the intimacy story) was replete with intimacy themes centering around a hunting vacation in which three old friends gather for a reunion. The second story (neutral story) contained no intimacy themes. The stories were approximately the same length, and each contained thirty-three facts. After the stories were read, the subjects engaged in a variety of tasks until, about an hour later, they were shown the two TAT pictures again and asked to recall and write down the plots of the two stories they had heard. Whereas a highly significant correlation was found between intimacy motivation and number of facts recalled from the intimacy story ($r = +.56$, $p < .001$), no relationship was found between intimacy motive score and recall of facts in the neutral story ($r = +.14$, not significant).

Drawing on a sample of eighty-four males, McAdams and McClelland obtained similar results after reading a long, single story containing an equal number of intimacy and power facts, as well as a number of neutral facts. Subjects high in intimacy motivation and low to moderate in power motivation (Winter, 1973) remembered significantly more facts concerned with warmth, closeness, and communication of characters in the story, whereas subjects high in TAT power motivation and low to moderate in intimacy motivation remembered more facts concerned with characters having impact on each other.

McAdams (1982) has extended the inquiry into the joint effects of power and intimacy motivations on processing complex and contextual information into the domain of autobiographical memory. Subjects in two samples of college students (one with fifty-six subjects, one with eighty-six) were asked to recall particular personal experiences from their pasts and to describe the experiences in some detail. In the first sample, the subjects were asked to describe in four or five sentences a "peak experience" (defined as a "moment or episode in a person's life in which he or she feels a sense of transcendence, uplift, or joy and peace") and then at similar length a "great learning experience." In the second sample, the subjects described peak experiences, satisfying experiences, neutral experiences, and unpleasant experiences. In all of the memory descriptions, the subjects were asked to be as specific as possible, detailing exactly what happened, who was there, how it felt, and how (if at all) the experience changed the subject.

The memory protocols were then coded for themes of intimacy and power by independent coders blind to the motive scores of the subjects. Significant positive correlations were found between intimacy motivation assessed via the TAT and number of themes of interpersonal intimacy in recollections of peak experiences for both samples, r (54) = +.44, $p < .001$ and r (84) = +.49, $p < .001$. These intimacy themes, which tended to appear in the memories of peak experiences reported by subjects high in intimacy motivation, included "love or friendship," "communication or sharing," "helping others or being helped," and "tender interpersonal touching." A highly significant relationship between intimacy motivation and intimacy themes in great learning experiences was also obtained, $r = +.56$, $p < .001$ for a sample of 54, whereas a moderate but significant correlation was found between intimacy motivation and intimacy themes in Satisfying Experiences, $r = +.26$, $p < .05$ for a sample of 83. For memories of experiences seen as less personally meaningful (neutral experiences and unpleasant experiences), no relationship between intimacy motivation and intimacy themes revealed itself. A similar, although not identical, pattern of results was discovered for power motivation and themes of power (vigorous action, having impact, feeling strong).

The results of the autobiographical memory study suggest that intimacy motivation may exert a powerful selective effect upon the processing of autobiographical information seen by the person as particularly meaningful or salient. It appears that subjects scoring high in intimacy motivation find warm, close, and communicative exchange to be particularly rewarding and that memories of such exchange have a privileged status in the hierarchy of specific personal experiences that can be readily remembered. Thus, the intimacy motive appears to confer upon particular classes of experience a special meaning or salience that may facilitate the relatively efficient processing and ready retrieval of such information in a setting in which the subject is asked to recall a particularly meaningful event of the past. The setting is especially important. The subject high in intimacy motivation is not constantly aware of memories of friendship and love and will not recall and report such memories in response to any random cue or question. By contrast, for experiences seen as less personally meaningful, the selective effect of the intimacy motive upon autobiographical recollection is shown to be relatively weak (satisfying experiences) or nonexistent (unpleasant and neutral experiences).

Taken together, a small body of empirical studies has provided some confirmatory evidence of selective effects of intimacy motivation upon human information processing. The most marked influence of the motive has been demonstrated in cases using relatively complex stimulus events, such as stories and autobiographical experiences, and demand characteristics calling for material the subject sees as personally meaningful or obvious. Thus, with the advent in psychology of modern information processing models assigning central mediating roles to control processes and organizing schemata (Mandler, 1975; Neisser, 1976) and with the rekindling of scientific interest in story, person, and autobiographical memory (Hastie and Kumar, 1979; Markus, 1977; Robinson, 1976), personality and cognitive psychology are presently nurturing an atmosphere of newfound cooperation that should welcome investigations into the selective effects of personality variables upon the processing of certain classes of information in certain settings.

Intimacy and Psychosocial Adaptation. Two recent studies have investigated psychosocial adaptation and its relationship to intimacy motivation. The first, adopting an Eriksonian framework, addresses the role of intimacy in the development of religious identity among young adults at a private religiously affiliated college. The second, a longitudinal inquiry, documents a relationship between intimacy motivation assessed at age thirty and psychosocial adaptation determined seventeen years later in a cohort of prominent men.

Erik Erikson (1950, 1968), among others, has argued persuasively that many American teenagers and young adults are preoccupied with the questions "Who am I?" and "How do I fit in to my occupational/ideological/interpersonal world?" Identity versus role confusion has been posited as the central developmental puzzle at this time in the life cycle, and the resolution of it has been considered a developmental prerequisite for attaining the meaningful intimate relationships of Erikson's next psychosocial phase: intimacy versus isolation. Given the dearth of knowledge about the interaction of developing social motives and identity formation in adolescence and adulthood, McAdams, Booth, and Selvik (unpublished paper) undertook an investigation of social motives, ego stage, and the development of religious identity among young adults at a private midwestern college.

Drawing upon Erikson's writings (1950, 1968) and the empirical work on identity formation by Marcia and his associates (Marcia, 1980; Orlofsky, Marcia, and Lesser, 1973), the researchers collected lengthy descriptions of recent crises in religious identity from fifty-six male and female undergraduates who considered religion a central component of their lives. The protocols were classified in terms of the degree of questioning of religious belief shown (what Marcia has termed *crisis*) and the degree of resolution of the questioning eventually evidenced (what Marcia has termed *commitment*). The responses fell into four categories ranging from least to most mature with respect to identity formation: Foreclosure (no crisis shown), Restabilization (pseudocrises followed by retreat to "easy answers"), Moratorium (definite crisis described as fundamental questioning; no commitment yet), and Personalized Identity (crisis followed by well-articulated commitment). Descriptions of "particularly meaningful religious experiences" that were instrumental in forming religious identity were also collected. In addition, the TAT and Loevinger's (1976) sentence-completion measure of ego development were administered to all of the subjects.

The major developmental finding was a highly significant relationship between ego stage and maturity of religious identity formation. Also correlated with increased maturity in religious identity, however, was intimacy motivation. Although intimacy motivation was not nearly as robust a developmental predictor as ego stage, subjects scoring in the categories of Personalized Identity or Moratorium showed higher intimacy motive scores than subjects at the lower identity statuses Foreclosure and Restabilization. Intimacy motivation was also positively correlated with ego stage. Furthermore, both intimacy motivation and the power motive were shown to be related thematically to the quality of religious experiences reported by the subjects to be particularly important in their religious development. Subjects high in intimacy motivation described meaningful religious experiences laden with themes of love, communication, touching, and a perception of God as a "companion." Subjects high in power motivation, on the other hand, reported experiences of personal impact, feeling the power of God directly, heightened perceptual or cognitive abilities, and a paradoxical surrendering of one's own power in order to receive strength from beyond. These reports of power and intimacy experiences in religion provide an interesting parallel to the words of William James, who, in his classic treatise on the varieties of religious experience, distinguished the two central "psychological characteristics" of the "religious life": [1] "A new zest which adds itself like a gift to life, and takes the form either of lyrical enchantment or of appeal to *earnestness and heroism.*" [2] "An assurance of safety and a temper of peace, and, in relation to others, a *preponderance of loving affections*" (James [1902], 1958, p. 367, Italics mine).

The relationship between intimacy motivation on the one hand and ego stage and indices of religious identity development on the other suggests a developmental dynamic in intimacy motivation that is as yet not well understood. The obtained relationships are nonetheless consistent with both Erikson's notion of identity formation and Loevinger's model of ego development. According to Erikson, a well-articulated sense of identity provides a "continuity and sameness" (1950, p. 261) in an individual's life that facilitates the formation of lasting intimate relationships with significant others. Although the intimacy motive theoretically measures a recurrent preference for a particular kind of experience that need not be extended in time beyond the briefest of human encounters (Buber's momentary I-Thou), the construct may tap, in certain populations, a readiness for a long-term intimate relationship—the kind that Erikson claims so compellingly beckons the young adult who, having addressed issues of identity, stands on the threshold of intimacy versus isolation. Although religious identity is only one part of a complex occupational/ideological/interpersonal matrix that comprises an individual's total identity (Erikson, 1968; Marcia, 1966), it is certainly a central part of that matrix for the subjects in the present study, and thus the concerted reappraisal of religious value and belief evidenced in the Moratorium and Personalized Identity subjects may presage a readiness for intimacy that is reflected in part through the intimacy motive. In Loevinger's model of ego development, higher ego stages serve as frameworks of meaning entailing attendant understandings of interpersonal relations in terms of mutuality, concern for communication, respect for autonomy, and appreciation of the balance between individuality and interdependence (Hauser, 1976; Loevinger, 1976). Emancipated from the impulsive, self-protective, and conformist frameworks of meaning at the lower ego stages, the more mature ego is receptive to the egalitarian merger with another that designates the preferred experience in intimacy motivation.

The second study of intimacy and psychosocial adaptation embodying a developmental theme was conducted by McAdams and Vaillant (submitted for publication). They recoded longitudinal data to investigate the relationship between social motives and psychosocial adaptation in a cohort of middle-aged men described in Vaillant (1977). TAT stories told by fifty-seven of the men (in response to original Murray, 1943, cards), when they were about thirty years old, were scored for various social motives, corrected for story length, and standardized. Power, intimacy, achievement, and affiliation (Heyns, Veroff, and Atkinson, 1958) motivation were all scored and correlated with summary indices of psychosocial adaptation compiled by psychiatrists and mental health workers in the seventeen years that followed the administration of the TAT. An overall adult adjustment index was calculated as a sum of ratings on nine dimensions: income level, occupational advancement, recreational activities, vacations, enjoyment of job, psychiatric visits, drug or alcohol misuse, days of sick leave, and marital enjoyment. Intimacy motivation was the only one of the four measured TAT motives to predict subsequent psychosocial adaptation at a significant level. High intimacy motivation was associated with relatively high adjustment scores obtained seventeen years after the TAT, $t = 3.05$, $p < .01$, for a sample of 55; a nonsignificant trend was found for the achievement motive ($t = 1.90$, $p < .10$, for a sample of 50); and affiliation and power showed no trends.

The results showing a positive association between intimacy motivation assessed at age thirty and psychosocial adaptation at forty-seven are in keeping with the theoretical and clinical statements which have suggested that a capacity to engage in intimate relationships with others is a sine qua non of psychosocial adaptation in the adult years (see Erikson, 1950; Fairbairn, 1952; Levinson and others, 1978; Sullivan, 1953). Given the size and other limitations—sex, age, socioeconomic status, ethnic background, and so on—of the present sample, broad generalizations concerning intimacy motivation and psychological health are certainly not warranted. Yet the findings surely enhance the construct validity of the measure and may portend future applications of intimacy-motive analysis in the twin contexts of clinical psychology and adult development.

Intimacy versus Affiliation. At a number of junctures in the studies reviewed above, intimacy motivation has been compared explicitly to the older alternative TAT measure concerned with close relationships, that is, the need for affiliation (Heyns, Atkinson, and Veroff, 1958). In all the studies reviewed except one (McAdams, Booth, and Selvik on religious identity), TATs were scored for both intimacy and affiliation motivation. Because the same protocols can be scored for both motives, these comparisons are both natural and expeditious. Further, since the original impetus for the development of the intimacy motive coding system was the rather weak and inconsistent performance of the older measure in over twenty years of TAT research (see Boyatzis, 1973; McAdams, 1979), I have tried to delineate the differences between the two motive systems. Although the present understanding of the differences is not too clear, two tentative conclusions can be offered, based on data gathered up to now: (1) When the two motives are hypothesized to predict the same results, intimacy generally appears to be the stronger predictor. (2) When the two motives differ in their correlates, intimacy appears to capture a "being" orientation to interpersonal relations whereas affiliation emphasizes a "doing" orientation.

Correlations between intimacy motivation and the need for affiliation (n Aff) have generally proven to be moderate and positive, ranging from around +.25 to +.55. With respect to peer ratings, information processing, and psychosocial adaptation in adulthood, however, the intimacy motive has consistently proved a valid predictor of theoretically related individual differences, whereas the need for affiliation has proved almost totally ineffective. Subjects scoring high in n Aff were rated by their peers in the fraternity and the sorority as no different on the twenty-four adjectives than were subjects scoring low in affiliation (McAdams, 1980b). High affiliation motivaton did *not* significantly predict perceptual sensitivity to schematic faces (McAdams, 1979), intimacy themes in story memory (McAdams, 1979), or intimacy themes in autobiographical recollections (McAdams, in press). And the need for affiliation was not associated with higher levels of psychosocial adaptation in middle-aged men (McAdams and Vaillant, submitted for publication).

Surprisingly, the arousal conditions employed in McAdams's (1980b) original derivation studies did not generally appear to increase affiliation imagery in subjects' TAT stories. Although a nonsignificant but positive trend was noted for the fraternity-sorority-initiation arousal (Experiment 1), in which affiliation scores of aroused subjects were higher than those of controls, the psychodrama arousal (Experiment 4) showed a surprising negative relationship: Stories written under intimacy arousal conditions were significantly *lower* in affiliation imagery than stories written under control conditions.

On the other hand, McAdams and Powers (1981) have presented a fair amount of evidence that affiliation motivation energizes, directs, and selects some forms of behavior aimed at establishing and maintaining warm interpersonal relationships in a psychodrama setting. As you will recall, subjects scoring high in affiliation motivation made fewer references to self in their scenarios, elicited many outbursts of laughter among their peers, and positioned themselves in relatively close proximity to others in structuring their own dramas. Their scenarios were also coded significantly higher on positive affect and reciprocal dialogue than those of subjects low in affiliation motivation, although the correlations were not nearly as robust as those for the intimacy motive. And subjects high in affiliation motivation in the psychodrama study were seen by their peers as relatively more "likeable," "natural," "sincere," "expressive," and "enthusiastic," than subjects scoring lower in affiliation.

What was consistently lacking in these results, however, was evidence for the general theme of "surrender of control in the process of relating." Various indices of this behavioral theme consistently failed to differentiate high-affiliation from low-affiliation individuals. Rather, a theme of agency, control, or doing appeared to characterize the behavior of subjects especially high in affiliation motivation (and not high in intimacy), a theme whose antithesis—communion, the surrender of control, and emphasis on being over doing—appears to be a hallmark of intimacy motivation. Some evidence suggested that psychodrama subjects high in affiliation were perceived by their peers as "doers": They were rated as significantly more "enthusiastic" and "expressive" than subjects scoring lower in the motive, and a factor of "enthusiastic energy" in the adjective ratings accounted for a moderately significant amount of the variance in n Aff scores.

The pervasiveness of the theme of acting as an agent, or doing, is revealed clearly in an examination of the original theoretical formulations and arousal experiments employed in deriving the affiliation motive coding system (Atkinson, Heyns, and Veroff, 1954; Shipley and Veroff, 1952). Working from a drive-reduction theory of motivation, the pioneers in affiliation motivation research modeled their approach after earlier work on the need for achievement. The motive "state" of affiliation was aroused by depriving subjects of the security and comfort inherent in close relationships (through sociometric rating tasks or by choosing subjects recently rejected from fraternities). Stories written under these deprivation conditions were compared to stories written under neutral circumstances to derive the original scoring categories. As in achievement motivation, the emphasis in the scoring categories for n Aff is on the active striving to attain the desired goal, and the researcher is asked to code the act of "establishing, maintaining, or restoring a positive affective relationship with another person(s)" on the part of a character in the subject's story (Atkinson, Heyns, and Veroff, 1954, p. 406). Other action-oriented subcategories in the n Aff scoring system (Heyns,

Veroff, and Atkinson, 1958) include *Instrumental striving in service of* (I+): *Anticipating success in* (Ga+): *Encountering obstacles in the way of* (Bw and Bp): and *Feeling good about attaining the affiliation goal* (G+).

In a sense then, need for affiliation can be seen as a blend of intimacy and achievement, a striving to attain positive affective relationships. Since the emphasis in the *n* Aff coding scheme is upon the *act* of pursuing the goal state, the quality of the goal state itself is not well articulated. About all that can be said about it is that it is interpersonal and it concerns positive affect. In the intimacy motive system, on the other hand, the quality of the relationship is the focus of inquiry, the crux of the interpretive investigation. All ten coding themes address the quality of the characters' interactions. The act of pursuing the goal state, of attaining the desired quality of experience, on the other hand, is not addressed. Indeed, such striving theoretically attenuates the preferred experience, that is, striving undermines the striven-for goal state, rendering it less preferable, less intimate. As Buber so eloquently put it, "The Thou encounters me by grace—it cannot be found by seeking" (1970, p. 62).

Sex Differences. No consistent results concerning sex differences have yet been discovered in intimacy motivation research. Although females have generally scored slightly higher on the motive in more traditional settings, such as the two private midwestern colleges where much of the research has been undertaken, results from an eastern university have generally produced higher scores for males, perhaps reflecting a greater repudiation of traditional sex-role stereotypes concerning the communal nature of women and the agentic nature of men in this setting. In any case these differences have not reached statistical significance in any studies, and generalizations to larger populations are unwarranted. Thus far the only postcollege sample to be studied is the cohort of middle-aged men in the adaptation study (McAdams and Vaillant, submitted for publication).

Relationships between intimacy motive scores and other behavioral phenomena—peer ratings, psychodrama behavior, information processing, and the like—have generally been consistent across the sexes. With a few minor exceptions, significant correlations between motive scores and other variables for women have also been found in male samples. Again, generalizations are premature given the limited number and scope of empirical research projects to date.

The Future

In the final paragraphs of a review, it is usual to point out the need for more research. In keeping with precedent, this review focuses on two distinct research areas that appear particularly promising: (1) development of alternative methods for assessing intimacy motivation and (2) studies of intimacy motivation and mother-infant attachment.

From the time of David McClelland's and John Atkinson's landmark studies on thematic measurement of achievement motivation (McClelland, Clark, Roby, and Atkinson, 1949) to the most recent studies on the intimacy and power motives (McAdams, 1980b; Winter and Stewart, 1978), the tradition of assessing individual differences in human motivation has been criticized by some and eschewed by others because of perceived methodological shortcomings (Entwisle, 1972; Klinger, 1966). Critics have argued that the TAT methodology is inherently unreliable; empirical data have yielded low to moderate correlations speaking to test-retest reliability and to indices of internal consistency among scoring themes for the most commonly studied motive systems (Brody, 1980). Formidable rebuttals have put in doubt the relevance of classical test theory, with its canons of stable test scores and internal consistency, to thought-sampling techniques like the TAT (Atkinson, 1981; McClelland, 1980). Nevertheless, personality constructs such as power and intimacy motivation continue to suffer, in a scientific sense, by being tied to only one method of measurement—the thematic coding of fantasy. The psychometric problem of inadequate convergent validation remains a thorny one.

Self-report inventories purporting to measure social motives (see Jackson, 1967) do not appear to converge on the constructs tapped thematically in the TAT (McClelland, 1980). McClelland (1980, 1981) locates the problem in the disparate response formats of self-report questionnaires, which are "respondent" measures, and open-ended thought-sampling, which serves as an "operant" measure. According to McClelland, respondents tend to predict other respondents well, but to the extent that behavior becomes more spontaneous, that is, less bounded by environmental constraints, operant devices become the methods of choice in motivational assessment. Committed to the use of operant, open-ended measures of social motives for reasons akin to those presented in McClelland (1980, 1981), the author and colleagues at Loyola University of Chicago have recently initiated work on deriving and validating alternative operant techniques for assessing intimacy motivation, power, and achievement. So far, the research has focused on thematic coding of (a) significant life experiences as described in the subjects' own words and (b) sentence-completion protocols. The former approach, which draws upon McAdams's (in press) report of autobiographical recollections of peak experiences, appears especially promising at present. The goal of the project is to delineate and standardize a battery of operant procedures that are easily coded and, when used in conjunction with the TAT, will converge on the constructs of intimacy, power, and achievement motivation from multiple operant perspectives. An ancillary aim is to promote the study of motivational profiles (combinations of motives) by streamlining existing coding schemes for the TAT and applying them in other operant arenas.

Leaving behind psychometric concerns, research on intimacy motivation is moving forward on a number of different fronts. Projects in progress are investigating the influence of the intimacy motive upon (a) undergraduates' friendship patterns, (b) students' use of free time, (c) midlife identity decisions among men and women age forty to forty-five, (d) political behavior of radical and traditional adults, and (e) patterns of mother-infant attachment. The last of these warrants more elaboration.

Object-relations theorists such as Fairbairn (1952), Guntrip (1973), and Winnicott (1965) have argued that the psychologically healthy adult of our time embraces the position of "mature dependency." Both Winnicott and Guntrip point to the mature mother who facilitates the secure attachment relationship with her infant as the prototype of mature dependency. Guntrip (1973, p. 24) writes: "This perhaps is the peak of maturity (unfortunately easily neurotically counterfeited), to be able to give oneself to the utmost in love, for convincing reasons, without loss of ego-integrity. The model for this is the mature mother with her baby, which, as Winnicott says, may look like illness but is in fact the supreme mark of health; that is, not infatuation but genuine self-giving. This must also be the mature way of falling in love, which need not therefore be, as Freud seems to have thought, a neurotic infatuation. It must also be the hallmark of mature friendship of every degree, and finally of the psychotherapeutic relationship."

A reading of the theoretical and empirical literature on mother-infant attachment and early object relations reveals striking thematic parallels between the emerging construct of intimacy motivation and the parent-infant bond. It is tentatively suggested that the sensitive and receptive caregiver in the secure attachment relationship experiences the goal state of the intimacy motive in what may be its purest form. In her landmark study of infants and mothers in Uganda, Ainsworth (1967) remarks that subtle underlying variables in the mother's behavior may have a marked effect on the quality of the attachment relationship, the most prominent index of quality being the "felt security" (Sroufe and Waters, 1977) of the attachment bond for the infant. These variables are the sensitivity of the mother in responding to the infant's needs, distress, and social signals; the "amount of pleasure" both partners derive from the attachment exchange; the extent to which the mother's responses and interactions "come at the baby's timing rather than her own"; the extent to which the mother is free of distracting preoccupations; and how well the mother can satisfy the needs of the baby, including nutritional needs (Ainsworth, 1967, pp. 399-400). The first of Ainsworth's five suggested variables corresponds closely to the themes of Reciprocal dialogue (Dlg) and Harmony (H) in the intimacy motive system. The second corresponds to Mutual delight (+A). The third is very close to the theme Surrender of control (Sr) or blurring of self-boundaries that makes the intimacy motive system so characteristically reactive and self-effacing. The fourth connotes an interpersonal exchange that completely absorbs the consciousness of both partners and is captured in the thematic categories Time-space transcendence (TS) and Escape to intimacy (Esc).

Brazelton, Koslowski, and Main (1974) and Stern (1979) have sought to chart the degree of reciprocity and harmony in early mother-infant interaction while arguing that differences in reciprocity largely determine later differential qualities of attachment bonds. From observing mother-infant dyads at play, Brazelton and others conclude that "the most important rule for maintaining an interaction seemed to be that a mother develop a sensitivity to her infant's capacity for attention and his need for withdrawal—partial or complete—after a period of attention to her" (1974, p. 73). In developing such a sensitivity the mother learns to surrender some control of the relationship and to time her interactions according to cues from the infant. This same style of interaction, it will be recalled, characterizes the psychodramatic scenarios constructed by subjects high in intimacy motivation, as reported in McAdams and Powers (1981).

An hypothesis is beginning to take form: The secure mother-infant attachment relationship is the prototype of a particular quality of interpersonal experience that, throughout the life cycle, assumes great salience for a person with a particular motive profile. The key component in the profile is the relative strength of intimacy motivation for a given individual. If maternal behavior shapes the quality of attachment to the extent that some believe (for example, Ainsworth, 1967; Blehar, Lieberman, and Ainsworth, 1977; Bowlby, 1969; Brazelton, Koslowski, and Main, 1974; Mahler, Pine, and Bergmann, 1975; Sroufe and Waters, 1977; Spitz, 1965), then one might expect that caregivers generally high in intimacy motivation would engage in attachment relationships subsequently classified as more secure for the infant. Of course, the hypothesis disregards temperamental differences in the infant, but one might argue that the maternal behavior associated with high intimacy motivation— readiness for reciprocal exchange, surrender of control, delight, immersion in the experience of relating—would facilitate the development of felt security or "basic trust" (Erikson, 1950) in almost any baby.

One might further speculate that the secure attachment relationship characterized by mutual delight and reciprocal harmonious dialogue (generally nonverbal) provides a set of experiences for both partners that beckons to be found again in interpersonal relationships throughout life. In this light the intimacy motive system introduces a tool for assessing the quality of interpersonal relationships as manifested in thought samples or imaginative productions. As such, it invites the researcher to undertake a concerted and systematic inquiry into the nature of interpersonal relationships, from infancy to death. At present the study of the quality of interpersonal relationships over the life span remains a virtually uncharted sea. If the present review launches but a few inquisitive mariners, its undertaking will be considered a success.

References

Ainsworth, M.D.S. *Infancy in Uganda: Infant Care and the Growth of Love.* Baltimore: Johns Hopkins University Press, 1967.

Argyle, M., and Cook, M. *Gaze and Mutual Gaze.* Cambridge, Mass.: Cambridge University Press, 1976.

Atkinson, J. W. (Ed.). *Motives in Fantasy, Action, and Society.* New York: Van Nostrand, 1958.

Atkinson, J. W. "Studying Personality in the Context of an Advanced Motivational Psychology." *American Psychologist,* 1981, *36,* 117-128.

Atkinson, J. W., Heyns, R. W., and Veroff, J. "The Effect of Experimental Arousal of Affiliation Motive on Thematic Apperception." *Journal of Abnormal and Social Psychology,* 1954, *49,* 405-410.

Auden, W. H. *Selected Poetry of W. H. Auden.* (2nd ed.) New York: Vintage, 1971.

Bakan, D. *The Duality of Human Existence.* Boston: Beacon Press, 1966.

Blehar, M. C., Lieberman, A. F., and Ainsworth, M.D.S. "Early Face-to-Face Interaction and Its Relationship to Later Mother-Infant Attachment." *Child Development,* 1977, *48,* 182-194.

Bousfield, W. A. "The Occurrence of Clustering in the Recall of Randomly Arranged Associates." *Journal of General Psychology,* 1953, *49,* 229-240.

Bowlby, J. *Attachment.* New York: Basic Books, 1969.

Boyatzis, R. E. "Affiliation Motivation." In D. C. McClelland and R. S. Steele (Eds.), *Human Motivation: A Book of Readings.* Morristown, N.J.: General Learning Press, 1973.

Brazelton, T. B., Koslowski, B., and Main, M. "The Origins of Reciprocity: The Early Mother-Infant Interaction." In M. Lewis and L.A. Rosenblum (Eds.), *The Effect of the Infant on the Caregiver*. New York: Wiley, 1974.

Brody, N. "Social Motivation." In M. R. Rosenzweig and L. W. Porter (Eds.), *Annual Review of Psychology, 1980*. Palo Alto, Calif.: Annual Reviews, 1980.

Brunswik, E., and Reiter, L. "Eindruckscharaktere schematisierte Gesichter" ["Types of Impressions of Schematic Faces"]. *Zeitschrift für Psychologie* [*Journal of Psychology*], 1938, *142*, 67-134.

Buber, M. *Between Man and Man*. New York: Macmillan, 1965.

Buber, M. *I and Thou*. New York: Scribner's, 1970.

Ebel, A. L. *Measuring Educational Achievement*. Englewood Cliffs, N.J.: Prentice-Hall, 1965.

Entwisle, D. R. "To Dispel Fantasies About Fantasy-Based Measures of Achievement Motivation." *Psychological Bulletin*, 1972, *77*, 377-391.

Erikson, E. H. *Childhood and Society*. New York: Norton, 1950.

Erikson, E. H. *Identity: Youth and Crisis*. New York: Norton, 1968.

Exline, R. V., and Winters, L. C. "Affective Relations and Mutual Glances in Dyads." In S. S. Tomkins and C. Izard (Eds.), *Affect, Cognition, and Reality*. London: Tavistock, 1966.

Fairbairn, W.R.D. *Psychoanalytic Studies of the Personality*. London: Routledge & Kegan Paul, 1952.

Forster, E. M. *Howard's End*. London: Edward Arnold, 1910.

Guntrip, H. *Psychoanalytic Theory, Therapy, and the Self*. New York: Basic Books, 1973.

Hall, E. T. *The Silent Language*. New York: Doubleday, 1959.

Hastie, R., and Kumar, P. A. "Person Memory: Personality Traits as Organizing Principles in Memory for Behaviors." *Journal of Personality and Social Psychology*, 1979, *37*, 25-38.

Hauser, S. T. "Loevinger's Model and Measure of Ego Development: A Critical Review." *Psychological Bulletin*, 1976, *80*, 928-955.

Heyns, R. W., Veroff, J., and Atkinson, J. W. "A Scoring Manual for the Affiliation Motive." In J. W. Atkinson (Ed.), *Motives in Fantasy, Action, and Society*. New York: Van Nostrand, 1958.

Jackson, D. N. *Personality Research Form Manual*. Goshen, N.Y.: Research Psychologists Press, 1967.

James, W. *The Varieties of Religious Experience.* New York: New American Library, 1958. (Originally published in 1902.)

Klinger, E. "Fantasy Need Achievement as a Motivational Construct. *Psychological Bulletin,* 1966, *66*, 291-308.

Levinson, D. J., and others. *The Seasons of a Man's Live.* New York: Ballantine, 1978.

Loevinger, J. *Ego Development.* San Francisco: Jossey-Bass, 1976.

Lundy, A. "The Validity and Reliability of the Thematic Measures of the Intimacy Motive and Need for Affiliation." Unpublished manuscript, Harvard University, 1980.

McAdams, D. P. "Validation of a Thematic Coding System for the Intimacy Motive." Unpublished doctoral dissertation, Harvard University, 1979.

McAdams, D. P. "Scoring Manual for the Intimacy Motive." Unpublished manuscript, Loyola University of Chicago, 1980a.

McAdams, D. P. "A Thematic Coding System for the Intimacy Motive." *Journal of Research in Personality,* 1980b, *14*, 413-432.

McAdams, D. P. "Experiences of Intimacy and Power: Relationships Between Social Motives and Autobiographical Memories." *Journal of Personality and Social Psychology,* 1982, *42*, 292–302.

McAdams, D. P., Booth, L., and Selvik, R. "Social motives, ego stage, and the development of religious identity among young adults at a private college." Submitted for publication, 1980.

McAdams, D. P., and McClelland, D. C. "Social Motives and Memory." Submitted for publication, 1980.

McAdams, D. P., and Powers, J. "Themes of Intimacy in Behavior and Thought." *Journal of Personality and Social Psychology,* 1981, *40*, 573-587.

McAdams, D. P., and Vaillant, G. E. "Intimacy Motivation and Psychosocial Adaptation: A Longitudinal Study." Unpublished manuscript, Loyola University of Chicago,1980.

McClelland, D. C. *Assessing Human Motivation.* Morristown, N.J.: General Learning Press, 1971.

McClelland, D. C. *Power: The Inner Experience.* New York: Irvington, 1975.

McClelland, D. C. "Motive Dispositions: The Merits of Operant and Respondent Measures." In L. Wheeler (Ed.), *Review of Personality and Social Psychology.* Vol. 1. Beverly Hills, Calif.: Sage, 1980.

McClelland, D. C. "Is Personality Consistent?" In A. I. Rabin, J. Aronoff, A. M. Barclay, and R. A. Zucker (Eds.), *Further Explorations in Personality*. New York: Wiley, 1981.

McClelland, D. C., Atkinson, J. W., Clark, R. A., and Lowell, E. L. *The Achievement Motive*. New York: Appleton-Century-Crofts, 1953.

McClelland, D. C., Clark, R. A., Roby, T. B., and Atkinson, J. W. "The Projective Expression of Needs. IV: The Effect of Need for Achievement on Thematic Apperception." *Journal of Experimental Psychology*, 1949, *39*, 242-255.

McClelland, D. C., and Steele, R. S. *Motivation Workshops*. Morristown, N.J.: General Learning Press, 1972.

Maddi, S. *Personality Theories: A Comparative Approach.* (3rd ed.) Homewood, Ill.: Dorsey Press, 1976.

Mahler, M., Pine, F., and Bergmann, A. *The Psychological Birth of the Human Infant*. New York: Basic Books, 1975.

Mandler, G. *Mind and Emotion*. New York: Wiley, 1975.

Marcel, G. *Creative Fidelity*. New York: Farrar, Straus & Giroux, 1964.

Marcia, J. E. "Development and Validation of Ego-Identity Status." *Journal of Personality and Social Psychology*, 1966, *3*, 551-558.

Marcia, J. E. "Identity in Adolescence." In J. Adelson (Ed.), *Handbook of Adolescent Psychology*. New York: Wiley, 1980.

Markus, H. "Self-Schemata and Processing of Information about the Self." *Journal of Personality and Social Psychology*, 1977, *35*, 63-78.

Maslow, A. *Motivation and Personality*. New York: Harper & Row, 1954.

Maslow, A. *Toward a Psychology of Being*. New York: Van Nostrand, 1968.

Mehrabian, A. *Nonverbal Communication*. Hawthorne, N.Y.: Aldine, 1972.

Moreno, J. L. *Psychodrama*. Vol. 1. Beacon, New York: Beacon House, 1946.

Murray, H. A. *The Thematic Apperception Test: Manual*. Cambridge, Mass.: Harvard University Press, 1943.

Neisser, U. *Cognition and Reality*. San Francisco: W. H. Freeman, 1976.

Orlofsky, J. L., Marcia, J. E., and Lesser, I. M. "Ego Identity Status and the Intimacy Versus Isolation Crisis of Young Adulthood." *Journal of Personality and Social Psychology*, 1973, *27*, 211-219.

Patterson, M. L. An Arousal Model of Interpersonal Intimacy. *Psychological Review*, 1976, *83*, 235-245.

Peplau, L. A., Rubin, Z., and Hill, C. "The Sexual Balance of Power." *Psychology Today*, November 1976, pp. 142-151.

Rheingold, H. L. "The Effect of Environmental Stimulation on Social and Exploratory Behavior in the Human Infant." In B. M. Foss (Ed.), *Determinants of Infant Behavior*. Vol. 1. London: Methuen, 1961.

Robinson, J. A. "Sampling Autobiographical Memory." *Cognitive Psychology*, 1976, *8*, 578-595.

Rubin, Z. *Liking and Loving*. New York: Holt, Rinehart and Winston, 1973.

Shipley, T. E., and Veroff, J. "A Projective Measure of Need for Affiliation." *Journal of Experimental Psychology*, 1952, *43*, 349-365.

Spitz, R. A. *The First Year of Life*. New York: International Universities Press, 1965.

Sroufe, L. A., and Waters, E. "Attachment as an Organizational Construct." *Child Development*, 1977, *48*, 1184-1199.

Stern, D. *The First Relationship*. Cambridge, Mass.: Harvard University Press, 1979.

Sullivan, H. S. *The Interpersonal Theory of Psychiatry*. New York: Norton, 1953.

Vaillant, G. E. *Adaptation to Life*. Boston: Little, Brown, 1977.

Winnicott, D. W. *The Family and Individual Development*. New York: Basic Books, 1965.

Winter, D. G. *The Power Motive*. New York: Free Press, 1973.

Winter, D. G., and Stewart, A. J. "Power Motive Reliability as a Function of Retest Instructions. *Journal of Consulting and Clinical Psychology*, 1977, *45*, 436-440.

Winter, D. G., and Stewart, A. J. "The Power Motive." In H. London and J. Exner, Jr. (Eds.), *Dimensions of Personality*. New York: Wiley, 1978.

Sex Differences in Human Social Motives

Achievement, Affiliation, and Power

Abigail J. Stewart
Nia Lane Chester

Three human social motives—achievement, affiliation, and power—have been extensively studied, using the theoretical formulations and research techniques originally developed by David McClelland and his colleagues and students over thirty years ago. The purpose of this chapter is both to examine the evidence about sex differences in these three motives and, wherever we can, to examine how and when research questions in this area were posed and how evidence was interpreted and reinterpreted over time. It is in this sense that we intend to discuss not only the evidence about sex differences but also to some extent the way in which such sex differences have been explored.

We have attempted to be comprehensive without pretending to be exhaustive. Because we do aim to understand a large field of study over many years, we have defined our focus broadly but explicitly and have not tried to include everything. We have only surveyed studies conducted with white American subjects. We originally hoped to include a review of studies with black subjects. Unfortunately, there were too few to allow us to discuss any general issues on a secure empirical footing. Interested researchers might begin by examining Fleming (1978); Cowan and Goldberg (1967); Littig (1966, 1979); Mingione (1965, 1968); Moore (1977); Mednick and Puryear (1976).

We have included only those studies that used the three empirically based Thematic Apperception Test (TAT) scoring systems developed within the McClelland research tradition, which employed standard verbal and picture stimuli and which explicitly reported information suggesting that appropriate scientific procedures (blind coding, adequate interrater reliability, and so on) were followed. We included both published studies and unpublished dissertations of this type. Finally, we have been especially concerned to review studies that included both male and female subjects or that specifically tested the degree to which standard research findings with men also held for women. It should be noted that some studies apparently included both men and women but did not report analyses of sex differences. Others used male and female subjects and reported separate analyses, but used different cues for the two sexes and therefore did not allow direct comparisons; in these cases, we can compare the correlates of achievement motivation in men and women, but not the level of imagery itself.

The study of sex differences has never been the central focus of David McClelland's work, but he has addressed the question of sex differences in motivation repeatedly in the course of his career (for instance, McClelland, 1964; 1965; 1975, Ch. 3; McClelland, Atkinson, Clark, and Lowell, 1953, pp. 173-181), never leaving the impression that he had settled the question in his own mind. Thus we hope this essay reflects both one of the consistent themes in McClelland's work and the values he has modeled and taught—breadth of interest, confidence in the possibility of imposing conceptual order on a confusing welter of information, and a willingness to risk going too far in an attempt to be sure to go far enough in extricating meaning and implication from silent and neutral data.

Asking Questions About Sex Differences

There has been no systematic or programmatic study of sex differences in the three motives. This stems in part from the fact that neither gender nor sex role was originally conceptualized as a relevant or irrelevant variable in theoretical writing about motives. For that reason, researchers have lacked a clear theoretical direction in developing questions about the existence or meaning of hypothetical or discovered sex differences. The lack of programmatic research in this area may also stem from the fact that male researchers tended not to think of questions about sex differences or the psychology of women until the 1960s, when much of the initial construct validational work had already been done. The regrettable consequence is that most of the research on motives in women has taken findings with male subjects as the norm and compared findings with female subjects to them.

Given this theoretical vacuum, questions about sex differences, or motives in women, have been generated ad hoc. In the course of the past thirty years, researchers have tended to focus on four major issues: sex differences in *motivational imagery,* in responses to *eliciting stimuli,* in responses to *arousal conditions,* and in *behavioral correlates.* We began this project by reviewing the available evidence in each of these areas, under the assumption that consistent sex differences would indicate a need to incorporate the concepts of gender or sex role into our theory of motivation. After reviewing the evidence on the first two issues—sex differences in motivational imagery and responses to eliciting stimuli—we have concluded that there are no consistent differences between the sexes in either of these areas for any of the motives. In terms of motivational imagery, we considered two possibilities: that men and women write about achievement, affiliation, and power using different themes or images; and that men and women differ in the degree to which they write about achievement, affiliation, and power. In the first case, we find evidence that some apparently relevant themes are not covered by the standard scoring systems for achievement, affiliation, and power. However, these themes generally occur equally often in the imagery of males and females (see, for example, Depner and Veroff, 1979, on achievement; McAdams, 1979, on affiliation and intimacy; and Stewart, 1975b, on power).

In the case of motive strength, we reviewed twenty-three studies reporting need for achievement scores for both sexes; seventeen of these reported no difference. With regard to affiliation motive strength, eleven studies were reviewed and only three reported a significant sex difference. In the studies of power motivation that were reviewed, there was even less evidence for consistent differences between the sexes. Similarly, in our review of sex differences in responses to eliciting stimuli (that is, picture cues or verbal leads), we found that very few studies systematically examined the separate effects of sex of stimulus figure and motive cue value. Thus, some studies have shown that male figures elicit more achievement motivation and female pictures more affiliation motivation (although even this finding is not consistent). The very few studies that attempted to control for the potentially confounding effects of motive cue value have shown that most of the variance in motive scores in both sexes is attributable to cue value rather than to sex of stimulus figure (see, for example, Morrison, 1954; Dunbar, 1959; Stewart and Winter, 1976). Thus more careful research is needed to confirm our general impression that differences previously identified as due to gender are more likely the result of little understood aspects of eliciting stimuli. However, overall we found no reason to believe that there are important sex differences either in motivational imagery or in responses to eliciting stimuli.

The two remaining areas proved to be much more complex, both in terms of the findings themselves and the relevance of the findings for theory. Therefore, in the next three sections, we will review the evidence we found that was related to the two remaining questions for each motive in some detail. At the same time we will sometimes comment on how the evidence was generated. Our major goal is to understand the answers to our four major questions by reviewing the work that has been done. Our secondary goal is to understand how and why some questions have been fully and adequately explored and others have not.

The Achievement Motive in Women

Arousal Conditions. A total of fourteen *n* Achievement arousal experiments met our criteria for review and are summarized in Table 1. (An arousal study conducted by Orso (1969) is not included because the procedures were not described in sufficient detail.) The discovery of this large number of studies surprised us because the literature has been dominated by references to only a few of them. Moreover, important methodological aspects of the experiments have rarely been noted in secondary references to studies. The arousal studies most widely cited have generally been taken to demonstrate either that the achievement motive is difficult to arouse in women (see, for example, French and Lesser, 1964, p. 120; Alper, 1974, p. 194), or that it can be aroused best by reference to sex-role-relevant achievement (see, for example, Gralewski and Rodgon, 1980, p. 303; Field, 1951; Alper, 1974, p. 202; McClelland, Atkinson, Clark, and Lowell, 1953, p. 181). Since we believe that neither statement best summarizes what we have learned, we will review the fourteen studies in some detail, and then consider how the evidence has been interpreted.

The experimental arousal of n Achievement in women has been examined using two quite different research paradigms, as is reflected in the major divisions of our summary table. The first approach (reflected in the upper half of the table) is the same as that used to arouse the motive in men: it involves presenting an achievement task to subjects followed by administration of the TAT using instructions that stress its relevance to assessment of intelligence or leadership or administrative competence. Studies have varied in whether they included male and female subjects or only female ones and in whether they were conducted by male or female experimenters. Some used a within-subjects pre-post design, others a between-subjects comparison group design. All the studies used picture cues depicting both males and females and at least two conditions—one the above-described experimental condition, the other or others a form of control condition. Finally, all studies involved an experimental situation in a classroom setting. These eight studies conducted over nearly thirty years using the standard arousal procedures are presented in chronological order in Table 1.

As may be seen in the table, of these eight studies, five yielded no main effect for experimental condition and no interaction of condition with sex of picture for the women. Some of these did find other main effects: for sex (Field, 1951) and for pictures (the Veroff and the Wilcox thesis studies in Veroff, Wilcox, and Atkinson, 1953;

Author(s) and Date	Sex of Experimenter	Sex of Subjects	Type and Sex of Stimuli	Timing of TAT Before or After Achievement Task	Design	Key Finding(s)*
I. Studies Employing Standard "Male" Arousal Procedures (in chronological order)						
Field, 1951	male	males and females	male and female pictures	after	group comparison	main effect for conditions for men but not for women
Veroff thesis in Veroff, Wilcox and Atkinson, 1953	male	males and females	male and female pictures	after	group comparison	no main effect for conditions for either sex; for females main effect for pictures; increase in n Ach for males on male pictures only
Wilcox thesis in Veroff, Wilcox and Atkinson, 1953	female	females	male and female pictures	after	group comparison	main effect for pictures, but not conditions
Morrison, 1954	male	females	male and female pictures	after	group comparison	main effect for pictures, but not conditions
Lesser, Krawitz and Packard, 1963	female	females	male and female pictures	after	pretest posttest	main effects for group and pictures, not condition; interaction of group x picture x conditions
Lipinski, 1965	male	females	male and female pictures	after	pretest posttest	*main effects for condition and pictures*
Fontana, 1970 (conducted in 1963)	female	females	male and female pictures	after	group comparison	main effect for pictures, but not condition
Jacobson, 1977	female	females	male or female pictures	after	pretest posttest	*main effect for condition and condition by picture interaction*
II. Studies Employing Sex-Role-Relevant Arousal Procedures (in chronological order)						
Field, 1951	male	males and females	male and female pictures	after	group comparison	*main effect of conditions for women, not men*
Morrison, 1954	male	female	male and female pictures	after	group comparison	*main effect of conditions for women, not men*
French and Lesser, 1964	female	females	male and female verbal leads	before	pretest posttest	*main effect for type of condition; interactions of condition with pictures, etc.*
Friedrich, 1976	female	females	all female verbal leads	before	group comparison	no main effect; no interactions
Jacobson, 1977	female	females	pictures	after	pretest posttest	*main effect for conditions and interactions with pictures*
Gralewski and Rodgon, 1980**	female	females	male and female verbal leads	before	group comparison	*no test of main effect for condition; interactions between condition and role orientation*

*Italicized findings indicate successful arousal of achievement motive scores in women either as a main effect or as part of a predicted interaction.

**Used Alper's thema method of scoring achievement imagery.

Morrison, 1954; Fontana, 1970). One of the two studies that included men found that the arousal conditions affected male scores but not female ones (Field, 1951), but Field suggested that the problem was that the female scores in the relaxed condition were too high (rather than that the aroused-condition scores were low). Veroff's thesis data showed that male n Achievement scores were higher only when based on male pictures in the aroused condition. Female scores did not vary by condition at all; they were higher in response to male pictures, regardless of condition.

Three studies (Lesser, Krawitz, and Packard, 1963; Lipinski, 1965; Jacobson, 1977) did obtain either experimental condition main effects or predicted interactions with stimuli and achievement group. A total of three successful experimental arousals out of eight attempts is hardly an impressive showing. Such a record would seem to suggest that the achievement motive is not aroused in women under the same conditions as in men; many previous researchers have drawn precisely that conclusion. In our view, however, that conclusion is not warranted, for several reasons.

First, of the five studies that failed to show an arousal effect, three did not include male subjects. Thus, we cannot be sure those three experimental conditions would have had any effect on male n Achievement scores. Of the remaining two studies that did include male subjects only one (Field) showed a simple main effect for males. In short, for four out of five of the experiments that failed, we have no compelling reason to have confidence in the validity of the arousal condition.

Second, the important problem, at least in some cases, may be not the validity of the arousal condition, but the validity of the control condition. Four of the eight studies used "neutral" control conditions, two used "relaxed" control conditions, one used a "color preference task" control condition, and one used a specially designed control condition involving asking girls to "help" the experimenter with her thesis in a dormitory—not a classroom—setting (intended to be a relaxed condition). The importance of an adequately relaxed control condition has been underscored a number of times in the literature on arousing n Achievement in men. Even in the earliest studies, a number of researchers reported that neutral conditions did not yield significantly different scores from aroused conditions (see, for example, Atkinson, 1953; Birney, 1958; see also Klinger's 1966 review). Although an exhaustive review of efforts to arouse achievement motivation in men is well beyond the scope of this essay, it may be worth noting that in a quick review we discovered six successful arousal studies (Lowell, 1950, 1952; Ricciuti and Clark, 1954; Anderson, 1962; Martire, 1956; and Klinger, 1967) and nine unsuccessful ones (Atkinson, 1953; Haber, 1957; Peak, 1960; Murstein and Collier, 1962; Tedeschi and Kian, 1962; Turek and Howell, 1959; Murstein, 1963; Scott, 1956; Steele, 1973). Clearly, the arousal of achievement motivation in men has not been consistently successful. Indeed, in his review of the circumstances under which arousal has been successful, Birney (1968, p. 859) specifically suggests that the neutral condition is ordinarily problematic because it is "moderately achievement-cued." He points out that successful experiments have relied instead on a *relaxed* condition, in which the experimenter "dresses as a casual student, implies ignorance of the measures, and has no official connection with the institution of which the Ss are a part." It may be worth noting that *none* of the control conditions used in the studies cited in Table 1 meets those criteria, and that several of the "failures" (Field, 1951; women in Veroff, in Veroff, Wilcox, and Atkinson, 1953; Fontana, 1970) reported very high scores in the control condition.

There is a third issue that may be the most important of all. The successful attempts to arouse the achievement motive in women *all* share an important but unrecognized design characteristic. Moreover, *none* of the unsuccessful attempts have that characteristic. Lesser, Krawitz, and Packard (1963), Lipinski (1965), and Jacobson (1977), who were successful, all employed some kind of pretest-posttest design. Thus, the test of the hypothesis involved analysis of change scores. All the unsuccessful attempts compared scores across groups. In the case of some of these studies (Field and Fontana, for example), we have reason to believe that control group scores may actually have been "aroused." It may be that pretest-posttest designs, which make possible the more precise use of subjects as their own controls, provide an important increment to the power of any given analysis, at least in the case of experiments on the arousal of *n* Achievement in women.

With this notion in mind, we reviewed the data presented by McClelland, Atkinson, Clark, and Lowell (1953) in the original monograph on the achievement motive. Five experiments are reported (two by Lowell; one by McClelland, Clark, Roby and Atkinson; one by Field; and one by Veroff). Two (Lowell's) employ a pretest-posttest design; the others use the group comparison design. Lowell's two studies produce effects significant beyond the .01 level. The comparison of neutral and arousal conditions by McClelland, Clark, Roby, and Atkinson is not significant (though the relaxed and arousal conditions are different). Finally, Field does show a significant overall difference for males in comparing relaxed with arousal conditions, but Veroff does not, on overall scores (though he does on stories written to male pictures). In short, even in the original research with men, the pretest-posttest design produced stronger, more unequivocal results than the group comparison design.

To summarize, we believe that reasonable grounds exist for questioning the validity of the aroused conditions and/or the validity of the control conditions in several of the unsuccessful attempts to arouse the achievement motive in women. We believe that these validity problems have also plagued research on men, but that few researchers have recognized it. Thus, the arousal of the achievement motive in men has been described as consistent, straightforward, and simple (Alper, 1974, p. 194; Gralewski and Rodgon, 1980, p. 301; French and Lesser, 1964, p. 119, among many others) in contrast with its arousal in women. We believe that the literature on men is oversimplified and distorted by this characterization and that at the same time the complexities of the literature on women are exaggerated. Birney's (1968) very clearly spelled-out observations on both arousal and control conditions have not yet been successfully integrated into researchers' designs.

In addition, we believe that the group comparison designs may be particularly weak when researchers are attempting to minimize achievement cues. The context of university research, especially with college students, includes so many achievement cues that it may be quite difficult to control them, even if researchers are attentive to Birney's advice. The increased power of pretest-posttest designs may be critical to the success of experimental arousal of the achievement motive using the standard experimental paradigm for both men and women.

Finally, the exaggerated depiction of the difficulties encountered in attempts to arouse the achievement motive in women needs some explanation. Failures to arouse the motive have been readily and consistently interpreted as reflecting a real phenomenon in women, rather than as reflecting aspects of the research design or procedure, even though the great importance of procedural details in research with men had been pointed out (Birney, 1968; Klinger, 1966). It is hard to resist the interpretation that researchers were eager to see the arousal of the achievement motive in women as especially problematic. As we shall see, the concept of the sex-role relevance of achievement was, from a very early point, introduced as an important moderator of the arousal of achievement motivation in women, but not in men. Thus it was generally assumed that "achievement," even broadly defined as "a concern for excellence," was consonant only with the male sex role.

Beginning in 1951, researchers entertained the hypothesis that arousal of the achievement motive in women would be accomplished only under special conditions. Since that time, six studies (summarized in the second half of Table 1) have been designed, all building more or less directly on Field's (1951) original design. Only Field included male subjects. Three of the studies employed verbal cues, the other three pictures. In half, the projective test was administered before any achievement task, in the other half, after the task; thus, half the studies differed from the classic paradigm in the timing of the administration of the measure to be scored for achievement motivation (French and Lesser, 1964; Friedrich, 1976; Gralewski and Rodgon, 1980). All six studies involved a different experimental induction before administration of the TAT or Test of Insight. Most of them were variants on Field's original procedure.

Field had initially designed a special experimental condition described as arousing *n* Social, a condition that "stressed the importance of social acceptance within the classroom group as a predictor of acceptance in other social situations" (1951, p. 33). Subjects were given no feedback (relaxed) or were told that they had been socially accepted (*n* Social Success) or not accepted (*n* Social Failure). Field predicted that the achievement motive would be aroused in women, but not in men, under conditions of *n* Social Success and Failure, but not in the relaxed condition. His results confirmed this hypothesis. It is worth pointing out that the experimental induction preceding the TAT and described as stressing "social acceptance" refers to this quality as "more important than intelligence or education." It points out that "You must pass the test of other people's judgment of you. It may well be that your final satisfaction or success in life can best be predicted on the basis of your acceptance by college social groups" (p. 36). Clearly, these instructions strongly emphasize excellence and achievement; it is perhaps a measure of the rigidity of the male role in 1951 that college men did *not* respond to this induction with increased *n* Achievement scores, rather than a comment on the women that they did. Indeed, the women in Field's study responded to every experimental induction with achievement imagery *except* the one relaxed condition in which they received neither an achievement induction, nor any pencil and paper tasks. In all other conditions (taking place in a classroom and involving paper-and-pencil tasks and sometimes various inductions for social or intellectual achievements), they responded with higher *n* Achievement scores. Thus, this first study could well have been construed as suggesting that women have a broader, more flexible orientation to excellence than do men, for whom it is confined to the narrow arena of intelligence and leadership!

Needless to say, the study was not interpreted in that way. The five studies that followed Field's all assumed that the "problem" was to find some experimental condition, relevant to the female sex role, in which traditional female subjects would respond with achievement imagery. Morrison (1954) explored three conditions: neutral, achievement, and sociometric (like Field's *n* Social). There were no differences by condition, but these results are hard to interpret, since in the neutral condition subjects received male, traditional female, and career female cues; in the achievement condition they received only male and career female cues; and in the sociometric condition they received only male and traditional female cues. Morrison found that there was a strong overall picture effect, with the traditional female cues eliciting lower *n* Achievement scores than either the male or the career female cues. He did not find any overall condition differences, but of course his design, given the overall picture effects, does not allow us to draw any firm conclusions about the effect of experimental conditions.

In 1964, French and Lesser built on Field's and Morrison's studies and designed an elaborate pretest-posttest study simultaneously assessing the effects of two arousal conditions (traditional women's role—not precisely social acceptance—and intellectual), sex of stimulus, and subjects' values (traditional or intellectual). Their most important hypothesis was that women would show arousal of achievement motivation if and only if the arousal conditions were congruent with their own values (for example, traditional women with the women's role arousal condition). A highly significant interaction effect supported this hypothesis. Two other main effects were, however, not interpreted. First, there was no main effect for sex of stimulus (though there were a number of interpretable interactions); second, there was a significant main effect for arousal condition. The latter finding indicated that, *regardless of personal values*, the (standard) intellectual arousal condition increased achievement motivation more than the women's role arousal.

These results were not interpreted by French and Lesser or by later commentators, who no doubt viewed them as trivial, given the larger interaction effect. However, the confirmation of the complex interactive hypotheses was taken as evidence that the arousal of achievement motivation in women is a complex and tricky matter. The existence of the main effect argues against such a view. Moreover, since men were not included in this or any later study, it was not possible to determine whether the arousal of *n* Achievement in men is greater if the arousal conditions are congruent with their personal values (for instance, sports for athletes, school for scholars). Of the three later studies, only one even reports a test for the main effect for conditions: Jacobson (1977) did find, as had French and Lesser, a main effect for condition and interactions with sex of stimulus. Friedrich (1976) and Gralewski and Rodgon (1980) report no tests of the main effect; although the latter authors find interactions consistent both with French and Lesser and with Jacobson, Friedrich does not.

Overall, the research conducted using the sex-role-relevant experimental arousal paradigm has tended to proceed on the assumption that the female sex role constrains achievement fantasy, but that the male sex role does not. To the extent that we have data relevant to this assumption, it appears that the opposite may be true. Men may be relatively constricted in the range of situations that elicits achievement motivation, while women may respond to cues for standards of excellence in many domains. It seems to us that an intellectual and cultural climate of unconscious sexism has led researchers to adopt untested assumptions, ignore evidence, and make interpretations that depend on attending to only some of the data. Most problematic of all, the adoption of certain assumptions has led a number of researchers to design studies and analyses that partly preclude disconfirmation of their hypotheses. The exclusion of male subjects from the test of hypotheses involving sex-role values prevents us from understanding the unique and shared effects of sex-role adherence or rejection for men and women. Similarly, the presentation of only those results that are directly relevant to the research hypothesis, without those relevant to rival hypotheses, can only leave us with a partial picture.

We cannot sensibly interpret the results of these six studies as having clear implications for understanding sex differences in the arousal of achievement motivation. Five of the studies did not include men, and to our knowledge no comparable studies have been conducted with male subjects. The studies do suggest, though, that appeals to standards of excellence, even outside traditional areas of male achievement, often arouse achievement motivation in women.

Overall, we view the results of the fourteen arousal studies as having the following implications. First, evidence has existed for thirty years that n Achievement is arousable in women under a rather broad array of experimental conditions. The need for achievement is not and never has been difficult to arouse in women. Second, that evidence has been ignored or differently interpreted for the same period. Many members of the research community seem to have been committed to the belief that the need for achievement could be aroused in women only under special conditions, even as they developed evidence that that was not true. Third, research on the arousal of n Achievement in women, *like research on its arousal in men,* suggests that specific details of procedure and design have important consequences for the validity of the experimental conditions and the power of the analysis. Finally (and most positively), this research indicates that the effects of experimental conditions are mediated by aspects of the test instrument (sex of stimulus) and aspects of the person (sex-role values). How personal characteristics augment or reduce the power of situations is an important question, and one that can be separated from the matrix of assumptions about gender and sex role that have dominated the use of the non-traditional sex-role-relevant arousal paradigm.

  Behavioral Correlates. The classic areas in which achievement motive scores have been found to predict behavior in men are experimental performance on timed tasks, risk taking and entrepreneurship, and school achievement. We will review the findings for women in these classic areas as well as in several areas viewed by researchers as relevant to achievement motivation only in women. Generally, the correlates of a motive are studied using neutral or dispositional *n* Achievement scores. This will be true here, except in the case of experimental performance.

  Only a few researchers have reported on the classic prediction from neutral *n* Achievement scores in women to performance on timed laboratory tasks. Exceptions include Sherwood's (1966) finding that *n* Achievement predicted scrambled word and arithmetic performance and Rapaport's (1977) finding that *n* Achievement alone did not predict anagram performance, but tended ($p < .10$) to predict arithmetic performance and entered into three-way interactions predicting performance. Similarly, Mannan (1967) found that, in a sample of male and female high school students, *n* Achievement did predict performance on a timed intelligence test (despite no correlation with baseline IQ). In another study involving both sexes, Groszko and Morgenstern (1974) found that *n* Achievement predicted performance decrements under competitive (versus autonomous) conditions for women, as for men. In extensions of the performance paradigm Sturgis (1977) found that *n* Achievement predicted females' performance on problem-solving tasks, and Kuhl and Blankenship (1979) showed that there were no important sex differences in the pattern of experimental behavior change over time of subjects high and low in *n* Achievement. On the other hand, Rapaport (1977) found that *n* Achievement predicted women's performance only in interaction with *n* Affiliation and treatment condition and Karabenick (1977) found that though *n* Achievement scores predicted men's performance they did not predict women's. Lipinski (1965) actually found that *low* scores on *n* Achievement were associated with good performance on anagrams. Finally, in a recent study of reaction time performance (O'Connell, 1980), n Achievement did not predict performance for males or females; Horner reported similar results with classic timed tasks in her (1968) dissertation study.

Interestingly, a number of studies (Wilcox in Veroff, Wilcox, and Atkinson, 1953; French and Lesser, 1964; Morrison, 1954) have reported that aroused n Achievement scores predicted performance. In a related finding, Lesser, Krawitz, and Packard (1963) found that aroused scores differentiated underachieving and overachieving high school girls (in the predicted direction). Only Friedrich (1976) and Fontana (1970) report that there was no relationship between aroused scores and performance.

Overall, then, there is some evidence that women's n Achievement scores do predict laboratory performance. There are, however, few studies using standard tasks and neutral scores and it is hard to see any pattern responsible for the presence or absence of results. Finally, it does seem clear that women's aroused n Achievement scores generally *do* predict performance. We are not sure what this means. Perhaps the same women who are responsive to the experimental arousal are also responsive to the incentives provided by the contiguous performance task; and those not responsive to induction are also impervious to demands for task achievement. In any case, the meaning of the different strength of the results for neutral and aroused n Achievement scores needs clarification.

We have been unable to find any studies that both use female subjects and report results separately by sex that explore the moderate risk taking traditionally associated with n Achievement in men. We found one study that could be construed as relevant to the concept of entrepreneurship. Sée (1977) showed that in a sample of sixteen single women managers employed by New York City banks, n Achievement was associated with higher salary and position, being an officer in the corporate structure, and wanting to own one's own business. These correlates did *not* hold for the married female employees or for the men.

The somewhat related variable that has been studied fairly extensively in women is career achievement (despite the fact that Veroff (this volume) has found that women's achievement motive scores are not related to any *work-satisfaction* variables in a national sample, but instead to other kinds of life satisfactions). Thus, Baruch (1967) showed that high n Achievement in women was associated with paid employment, and that n Achievement predicted a strong career pattern among married women twenty years out of college. In a related study, Stewart (1975a) showed that freshmen n Achievement scores predicted a strong career pattern ten years after graduation, at least among women who assumed family responsibilities relatively late or who attended graduate school right after college. Similarly, Bloom (1971) showed that adolescent girls aiming to combine career and family were higher in n Achievement than those who were not. In a related study, Littig (1979) showed that women high in achievement motivation were less discrepant in their real and ideal occupational aspirations than women low in achievement motivation.

Shelton (1967), however, found that a sample of housewives scored lower than comparable professional women only when n Achievement was scored on the Test of Insight and not when it was scored on stories written to picture cures. Tangri (1969, 1972) found that n Achievement did not predict pursuit of nontraditional career paths in a heterogeneous sample of female college graduates.

Overall, then, though there is little direct evidence about the relationships between n Achievement and risk taking and entrepreneurship, there is evidence that at least under some conditions, women high in n Achievement also achieve career success. Stewart's and Bloom's findings indirectly suggest that sex-role values may indeed make a difference, not only in the arousal of the motive but in its expression in behavior. It may be that sex-role orientation, or education (as for Baruch and Stewart's elite samples), or other direct and indirect indicators of personal values are important moderators of the achievement motivation–work behavior relationship for both sexes. If Veroff's argument (this volume) about achievement motivation is right, the need for Achievement should predict work or career performance variables in those men and women who value work, but other kinds of performance in those who value other activities highly. The inconsistent pattern of findings about n Achievement and women's career activities may therefore result from examining the same variables in samples that vary in the meaning and value of those variables.

A number of investigators have examined the relationship between *n* Achievement and intellectual or school achievement. Several studies (Raynor, 1970; Kagan and Moss, 1958; Kagan, Sontag, Baker and Nelson, 1958; Skolnick, 1966; and Veroff, Atkinson, Feld and Gurin, 1960) have found that *n* Achievement was correlated with the choice of scientific and/or relatively difficult fields of study, at least for some subgroups of women. However, several others (for example, Littig and Yericaris, 1963; Crandall, Katkovsky, and Preston, 1962; McKeachie, Isaacson, Milholland, and Lin, 1968; Ratliff, 1980; Shaw, 1961; Stivers, 1958) found no relationship between *n* Achievement and these variables in female subjects. In two of these studies there was no relationship for male subjects either; in three (Littig and Yericaris; Shaw; and Stivers) there were significant relationships for male subjects. In the Ratliff study, the relationships seemed to hold for all men, but for only one of the two birth cohorts of women. Finally, *within* a rather large-scale study of high school students, Pierce (1960, 1961) found mixed results. The need-for-achievement scores of twelfth-grade girls were correlated with school achievement, but those of tenth-grade girls were not.

Apart from the study of these classic areas, researchers have explored the relationship between *n* Achievement and learning environment preferences, field dependence, and other personality traits. Thus, for example, O'Conner, Atkinson, and Horner (1966) found that both males and females high in the need for achievement perform better and express more interest in homogeneous classes than in heterogeneous classes; and McKeachie (1961) showed that both males and females high in *n* Achievement prefer classes with low achievement cues. However, McKeachie also showed that high *n* Achievement males do poorly in those classes, while high *n* Achievement females do well (consistent with our earlier interpretation that *n* Achievement in girls, but not in boys, may reflect a heightened sensitivity to achievement cues, regardless of context).

Several researchers have explored the connection between *n* Achievement and field dependence in girls. Wertheim and Mednick (1958) found that in a pooled sample of males and females, in which females predominated, *n* Achievement was correlated with field dependence scores based on the Embedded Figures Test (EFT). Similarly, Honigfeld and Spigel (1960) reported that *n* Achievement scores were significantly correlated with EFT scores for females, but not males. However, Thornton and Barrett (1967) pointed out that while *n* Achievement often correlates with EFT scores, women's EFT scores do not generally correlate well with their (more valid) Rod and Frame Test scores.

A number of researchers have found that women's *n* Achievement scores were correlated with attitudes or traits. Winter and Wiecking (1971) found, for example, that female political "radicals" in the late 1960s were higher in the need for achievement than matched controls (as were male "radicals"). Sundheim (1962) found that *n* Achievement was correlated with traditional sex-role ideology; Bickman (1975) found it was correlated with a "self-oriented" (versus "other-oriented") ideology; and Gilbert (1977) found that it was correlated with androgyny and masculinity in both adult men and adult women.

It is hard to draw coherent conclusions from research on such disparate topics. In a longitudinal study, Skolnick (1966) found that *n* Achievement was associated in men and women with a similarly bewildering variety of traits and outcomes. Perhaps it is simplest to note that McClelland (1966), in commenting on Skolnick's findings, shows that 33 percent of the theoretically relevant correlations Skolnick examined were significant for the males, while 43 percent were significant for the females. Many of these results were the same for both sexes. The literature on the behavioral correlates of the need for achievement in women does not generally provide such clearly comparable data. The correlates examined extensively in men or women have generally not been equally adequately examined in the opposite sex. It is not clear whether attempts to establish motive-behavior relationships have fared as well, better, or worse in women than in men. The record is mixed, but so are the hypotheses, samples, designs, and controls. It does not appear to us that there have been fewer, or different, correlates of *n* Achievement in women than in men. Only research designed to produce more directly comparable data, however, can finally settle this question.

The Affiliation Motive in Women

Arousal Conditions. The first arousal procedure used in research on the affiliation motive involved asking male fraternity members to stand in front of their "brothers" and be rated on a series of adjectives (Shipley and Veroff, 1952). An additional group of male freshmen who had been rejected by a fraternity and who had been identified as feeling particularly bad about the rejection was also included. TAT stories written by these two groups of men were then compared to stories written by men in a control group; the former group demonstrated higher scores for n Affiliation.

A second arousal study (Atkinson, Heyns and Veroff, 1954) essentially replicated Shipley and Veroff's results. Since then, few studies have been specifically designed to arouse the affiliation motive, but those that include women subjects suggest that the measure of affiliation is as valid for women as it is for men, at least with regard to the arousal of affiliation imagery.

In an early study, for example, Morrison (1954) asked female college students to rate each of their classmates on her degree of social acceptability, as well as to write down the names of three classmates they would most like to be friends with and three classmates they would most dislike having as close personal friends. Other groups were either given an achievement arousal orientation that stressed the importance of intellectual achievement on a test of verbal ability, or a neutral orientation (participation in a task involving statements of color preference), before writing projective stories. Morrison found that subjects in the sociometrically aroused groups had higher n Affiliation scores than the subjects in the achievement-aroused or neutral groups, at least on the female pictures. This study thus suggests that affiliation is aroused in both men and women by placing them in a situation in which they are concerned about acceptance by their same-sex peers, at least when same-sex picture cues are used.

A decade later Rosenfeld and Franklin (1966) designed a similar sociometric study with a hundred female college students to test the validity of the affiliation measure for women and to determine whether affiliation aroused in a sociometric arousal condition reflected hope of affiliation (the approach component) or fear of rejection (the avoidance component). However, before writing stories to TAT pictures (all of which showed females only) subjects were either given negative feedback about how well they were liked, positive feedback, or no feedback.

Rosenfeld and Franklin found that the affiliation scores of the groups that were given negative or no feedback were significantly higher than the affiliation scores of the control group. It thus appears that sociometric arousal is effective for arousing affiliation needs in women as well as in men, although it should be kept in mind that only same-sex peers and same-sex picture cues have been used in these arousal experiments. Additionally, a study by Dodds (1960) suggests that affiliation needs in children may not be as responsive to sociometric arousal as appears to be the case for college students. At least in his study, neither boys nor girls showed significant increases in affiliation imagery after being in situations where they were ignored by unfamiliar peers.

Behavioral Correlates. For the most part, previous research using all-male subjects (see Boyatzis, 1973, for a review) has confirmed that individuals high in *n* Affiliation are concerned about establishing and maintaining relationships with others. For example, they phone and visit friends more often (Lansing and Heyns, 1959), are more likely to choose an incompetent friend than a competent stranger to work on a task (French, 1956), and communicate more often with work associates (Lansing and Heyns, 1959). Laboratory task performance in men is affected by affiliation needs as well. For example, several studies note that men with strong affiliation needs performed better when the task at hand was related to or designed to satisfy an affiliative goal (French, 1955; Atkinson and Raphelson, 1956; deCharms, 1957).

Studies involving male and female subjects suggest that the correlates of affiliation tend to be similar for the sexes. For example, McAdams (1979) found that both males and females high in *n* Affiliation tended to remain physically closer to others, to laugh more, and to engage in more reciprocal dialogue in interpersonal exercises than individuals with weaker affiliative needs. In a study in which males and females were analyzed together, subjects high in *n* Affiliation also became more anxious than subjects with low affiliative needs when peers were rating how likeable they were (Byrne, 1961). In studies analyzing males and females separately, both sexes were more likely to avoid making potentially divisive comments to others working on the same group task (Exline, 1962); and they were more likely to say they wanted to work with the same group they worked with before, after performing a task with others of equal affiliative orientation (Exline, 1960). Additionally, Exline found that both male and female subjects high in n Affiliation who worked in groups described to them as concerned about group members' feelings perceived interpersonal preferences less accurately than those in groups that had not been given such a description. This result was interpreted as deriving from anxiety or overzealousness of the highly affiliative individuals, who may have sent out "too many cues for easy and accurate perception" (1960, p. 408).

A number of studies involving only female subjects demonstrated expected relationships between affiliation motivation and behavior. For example, college women who had strong affiliative needs were more likely to be emotionally involved with a man (Morrison, 1954), to express a desire for more dates per week (Morrison, 1954), and to plan to marry right after college (Bickman, 1975) than classmates with weaker affiliative needs. They engaged in more positive affiliative acts, fewer negative or antisocial acts in small group work with their peers (Fishman, 1966), and spent less time alone (Constantian, 1981) than their less affiliatively motivated classmates. In addition, a study of female musicians found that women with strong affiliative needs were more likely to be positive about their ability to perform in front of an audience (Mueller, 1975).

Overall, then, it seems clear that at least among college students, both males and females with high affiliative needs are concerned with establishing and maintaining relationships with others. It is not the case, however, that people motivated by affiliative needs necessarily accomplish their goals. Early studies of affiliation involving only male students found a negative relationship between popularity and strength of affiliation motive (Shipley and Veroff, 1952; Atkinson, Heyns, and Veroff, 1954). On the other hand, McAdams (1979) found that males and females high in affiliative needs were described as likable, natural, and enthusiastic by peers working with them. Similarly, Fishman's study, although involving only college women, produced a significant correlation between the strength of n Affiliation and how much one was liked by one's groupmates after an experiment-related task (Fishman, 1965). Nevertheless, a recent study found no relationship between popularity and affiliation motivation in boys, and a negative relationship between the two variables among girls (Ratliff, 1980). Thus, research to date has not provided definitive evidence with regard to the relationship between popularity and the affiliation motive in the two sexes.

Affiliation motivation appears to be consistently related to performance on achievement tasks. Studies involving only men suggest that persons high in affiliation need are more likely to achieve than those low in the motive only when the required behavior satisfies affiliative goals (French, 1955; Atkinson and Raphelson, 1956; deCharms, 1957). Studies involving females have tended to confirm these findings. For example, while there appears to be no relationship between n Affiliation and overall academic achievement for either males or females (Sundheim, 1962), the motive did predict better grades among male and female psychology majors in classrooms high in affiliative cues (McKeachie, Lin, Milholland, and Isaacson, 1966). This finding was replicated in mathematics classes for males but not for females; it may be that females' well-documented math anxiety is more relevant in determining their response in math classrooms than the level of affiliative cues in those classrooms. There also appears to be a tendency for both males and females high in n Affiliation to concentrate in more "people-oriented" majors, such as education, psychology, and sociology (see, for example, Sundheim, 1962; Exline, 1960).

One would expect that individuals high in n Affiliation would be concerned about not offending others. One arena in which this concern appears to affect performance is that of competitive situations. For example, Walker and Heyns (1962) found that women high in n Affiliation and low in n Achievement were more likely to be responsive to a friend's request to lower their performance in order to improve the friend's performance. In a study investigating the effects of different components of the affiliation motive (specifically, negative affiliation imagery, emphasizing fear of separation and rejection, versus positive affiliation imagery, emphasizing desires for maintaining relationships and positive affect regarding relationships), Karabenick (1977) found that women with high scores for negative affiliation imagery performed less well in competitive tasks than in tasks performed alone. This effect was particularly strong if the tasks were defined in advance as female sex-typed (that is, defined to the subject as being related to feminine abilities). Such a finding did not hold for the males in the sample. Presumably among women high in fear of rejection, the possibility of beating an opponent (and thereby incurring negative affect or rejection from the opponent) inhibited performance. Why this effect does not hold for men is not clear. It may be that since men are more socialized toward viewing competitive activity as a normal way of relating to others, they are less anxious about its social or relational consequences. On the other hand, it should be noted that the confederate subject against whom both the males and females competed in the competitive task was always male. Thus, it may be that men with strong fears of rejection would also inhibit their performance if they were competing with a female.

Results from another study looking at the effects of the affiliation motive on performance in competitive activities did not find a sex difference, however; and they support our view that the sex of the experimenter may have influenced the results in Karabenick's study. Sorrentino and Sheppard (1978) compared swimmers' times in group competitive events and individual competitive events; they found that males and females who were both high in affiliation and low in fear of social rejection (as measured by a separate instrument) did better in the group competitive situation (one group competing against another group) than in the individual situation. On the other hand, individuals with high n Affiliation and high fear of social rejection produced faster times in the individual competition than in the group competition. The authors interpret these results as suggesting that high-affiliation, approval-oriented individuals perform better in group competition because they want to win the approval of their group and can do so by swimming as fast as possible. The high-affiliation, rejection-oriented group, on the other hand, appear to be more motivated by fear of disapproval from their group if they lose than by the approval of their group if they win. The authors argue that increased anxiety over possibly letting their group down, and thus earning rejection, impaired their ability to perform in the group situation. Interestingly, both of these results were significantly stronger for males than for females. While it was also true that the males overall were faster swimmers than the females, part of the increased strength of the effect for the men may have been because successful athletic competition is more stereotypically appropriate for males than for females. Such an interpretation is supported by Rapaport (1977), who noted that females who were high in affiliation motivation *and* in achievement motivation performed better in competitive situations with same-sex peers than females high in both motives competing with opposite-sex peers. Parallel analyses were not conducted with male subjects, but the findings cited above suggest that the effects would be similar.

Overall, then, it would appear that affiliation affects performance similarly for males and females. That is, men and women with strong affiliative needs are motivated to perform better if they are not afraid of disappointing others, and if by doing well they can achieve positive affiliative goals (pleasing others, maintaining a relationship, etc.). Nevertheless, in trying to understand the relationship between behavior and affiliation in both men and women, it is important to keep in mind that the referent group—the "others" one wants to maintain a relationship with—may vary. In a group of high school students, for example, affiliation in both sexes was correlated positively with leadership and prestige, suggesting a relationship for adolescents between affiliation and responsiveness to their peer culture (Skolnick, 1966). In a group of women managers (Sée, 1977), affiliative motivation was correlated negatively with interpersonal sources of life satisfaction that one might assume would be positively related (that is, marriage and friends). Among the single women in this group, however, *n* Affiliation was correlated positively with the importance given to encouragement from one's co-workers and friends relating to career goals. Thus, while it may be normative in the larger society for women to express their affiliative needs through intimate relationships with friends and family, for businesswomen it may be normative to play down the importance of intimate personal relationships, and instead seek affiliative gratification in collegial relationships. This interpretation is congruent with the observations of Veroff and Feld (1970) and Veroff (this volume): They noted in their summary of relationships between motives and sources of satisfaction in national samples of men and women in 1957 and in 1976 that individuals with strong affiliative needs did not rate their marriages as particularly important sources of satisfaction. Similarily, Sée (1977) found that single men and women had significantly higher affiliation needs than married men and women. She inteprets this finding as evidence that marriage is a source of affiliative satisfaction; it is, however, more consistent with the findings cited above to view this difference as further evidence for the argument that affiliative needs and intimacy needs tend to be satisfied by different relationships.

The notion that individuals high in n Affiliation may violate larger group norms as long as they are adhering to a different set of (possibly more satisfying) smaller group norms finds support in two seemingly unrelated studies, one comparing radical and nonradical students (Winter and Wiecking, 1971) and one comparing delinquent and nondelinquent girls (Katkin, 1978). Winter and Wiecking found female radicals had stronger affiliative needs than female nonradicals, a difference not found in the male sample. It can be argued that it is more deviant from peer group norms for females to be active politically, especially in radical politics, than it is for males. These females' membership in a radical political group may thus reflect in part their need to be part of a small unit, the cohesiveness of which is emphasized not only by its deviance from general political norms but by its deviance from sex-role norms as well. An interesting parallel may be seen in Katkin's study (1978) showing that delinquent girls were higher in affiliation motivation than matched nondelinquent girls. While this difference may be related to the fact that the delinquent girls were in institutions (and thus perhaps particularly needy in terms of personal relationships), it is also true that they, like the female radicals, had violated both social-legal norms, and sex-role norms. Their delinquent behavior may thus have been in some sense a reflection of their adherence to a particular peer group's alternative norms.

In general, affiliation motivation appears to be a valid measure for both men and women. It is aroused in similar ways and expressed in fantasy by similar imagery. For both sexes, the motive appears to be related to behavior that is meant to establish and maintain relationships, particularly among one's peers. Those sex differences in behavioral correlates that have been found appear to be more a function of differing peer group norms than of gender differences.

The Power Motive in Women

The desire for power has often been characterized as a male concern; it is only recently that research on power motivation has included female subjects. A review of the resulting li.erature suggests, however, that men and women are equally interested in power, although they may express their interest in somewhat different ways.

Several scoring systems have been developed for the coding of power motivation. The first followed the model established for n Achievement and seemed to reflect the desire to have control or influence over others (Veroff, 1957). Later Veroff and Veroff (1972) argued that it stressed the negative side of power motivation and might be better thought of as measuring fear of weakness. Uleman (1966, 1972) developed an alternative coding system reflecting the desire for power or influence for its own sake. These two systems were not correlated with each other, even though each seemed to reflect aspects of power motivation. Winter (1973), therefore, developed a new system that incorporated both of the above as well as his own early system, and successfully differentiated between aroused and nonaroused groups in the Veroff, the Uleman, and the Winter arousal studies. Since 1957, studies including female subjects have been done using both the Veroff and the Winter coding systems. Although the two systems probably should be discriminated for some purposes (see Veroff, this volume), they are positively correlated and seem to emphasize different aspects of the same general construct—therefore, we have included studies that used either measure. We shall use the term "n Power" to denote Winter's system and "Veroff n Power" or "fear of weakness" to denote Veroff's measure.

Arousal Conditions. Most of the evidence suggests that similar experiences arouse power motivation in men and women. Stewart and Winter (1976) analyzed data from two studies designed to determine whether this is true. In the first study, data were analyzed that had originally been collected by Uleman (1966). Winter initially analyzed only the male stories, and found that the revised scoring system for n Power differentiated the two groups; in a subsequent analysis it appeared that the revised scoring system also differentiated the female aroused and non-aroused subjects as well

(Stewart and Winter, 1976). Thus, power motivation was aroused in both males and females by witnessing a situation in which one individual was able to control another (that is, through hypnosis).

In the second study, Stewart and Winter (1976) replicated an arousal experiment with female subjects that Steele (1973) had conducted with male subjects. This study involved an arousal condition in which subjects listened to taped "inspirational speeches" read by a male actor and then wrote stories to TAT-type picture cues. The control group listened to a travelogue by the same actor. The results were the same in both studies: that is, both females and males in the aroused groups showed higher *n* Power scores than females and males in the non-aroused groups.

On the other hand, although McClelland found that the consumption of alcohol increases the expression of power needs among men, other studies (Wilsnack, 1974; Durand, 1975) were not able to replicate this finding in samples of females. If anything, the female drinkers' power fantasies appeared to *decrease* after drinking alcohol. Wilsnack interprets these findings as the result of sex differences in the interpretation of physiological sensations due to differences in socialization experiences. That is, men may associate the physical effects of alcohol (increased autonomic arousal level, burning sensation in the mouth and throat, and so on) with feelings experienced during active, aggressive behavior; women, by contrast, may associate these same sensations with feelings experienced in affectionate interactions with others. "These 'womanly' feelings," Wilsnack argues, "are inconsistent with thoughts of personal power (in which one character disregards the needs of others in the interest of self-aggrandizement) and assertiveness" (Wilsnack, 1974, p. 259).

Overall, it appears that power motivation is aroused in men and women under similar conditions, at least when arousal techniques are used that are explicitly about power. As we shall see, the one area in which results for the sexes clearly diverge (the effect of drinking) foreshadows differences in behavior in the two sexes. In any case, the evidence seems to suggest that it is the meaning of drinking alcohol that differs for the two sexes, more than the meaning of power.

Behavioral Correlates. While women may not differ from men in the level of their concern with power, it is of course quite possible that they could manifest that concern differently, particularly in a society where men are more likely than women to have positions that allow them to exercise power in a legitimate public arena. In one important study of power motivation, McClelland (1975) demonstrated that for both men and women there are important interactions between power motivation and maturity in predicting behavior. He also found a number of sex differences in the behavioral correlates of power motivation, regardless of maturity level. Men high in power motivation, for example, were more likely than men with weaker power needs to recall dreams, to have trouble sleeping, to check on home security, and to believe that "good will is more important than reason." They also tended to share more information with others about their sex lives. Overall, they tended to be more disturbed by their emotional lives.

The findings for the women in his sample were somewhat different. Women high in n Power were more likely to be concerned with diet, appearance, and clothes, and to have more credit cards. They drank more fluids, were more willing to donate body parts after death, and had more unpleasant dreams than women with weaker power needs. These women thus appeared to be more interested in taking care of their bodies and more likely to see themselves as a valuable resource. McClelland concludes (1975, p. 51), "The male high in n Power has an emotionally assertive approach to life, whereas the female high in n Power focuses on building up the self which may be the object of that assertiveness. He finds strength in action, she in being a strong resource."

McClelland's findings highlight the negative affective experiences of power-motivated people, which were also outlined in Veroff and Veroff's (1972) analysis of "Veroff n Power" as reflecting a fear of weakness. In his recent analyses of the correlates of the power motive in national sample age and sex groups, Veroff (this volume) has found further evidence that both men and women high in power motivation tend to experience global negative emotions and to seek relief from those feelings in drugs and alcohol. In related findings, Sutherland (1978) showed that fear of weakness was positively correlated with fear of success, at least in women, and McClelland and his colleagues (see, for example, McClelland, Floor, Davidson, and Saron, 1980; McClelland and Jemmott, 1980) have found positive relationships between the power motive, stress, and susceptibility to illness. (McClelland has recently indicated in a personal communication that these effects may be moderated by sex, with women showing the stronger relationships between the variables. It is too early fully to assess these developments.)

Overall, then, power-motivated men and women seem to be similar in their vulnerability to negative emotional experience, though there is some evidence that the ways in which they cope with that experience may differ somewhat. There is, in addition, quite a bit of evidence that power-motivated men and women express their needs in very similar behaviors. Thus, for example, Winter (1973) found that in men the motive predicted holding or seeking to hold office in an organization, having prestigious possessions, and being in or seeking to enter professions that facilitate the experience of influencing others (psychology, teaching, business management, journalism, and so on). Studies conducted with women show a similar pattern. That is, women high in n Power are also more likely to seek and obtain positions of prestige and leadership than women low in power motivation (see, for example, Skolnick, 1966; Winter and Stewart, 1978; Winter, 1979). Similarly, McClelland (1975) noted that, regardless of gender, individuals high in n Power and low in affiliative needs (as well as high in what McClelland refers to as activity inhibition) are more likely to be involved in organizations, to like to work, to respect institutional authority, and to be concerned with discipline and self-respect than those not characterized by this motive pattern (called the leadership motive pattern). Women high in power motivation are also likely to enter the same professions with a potential for influence as men high in n Power, with the exception of college professor (Stewart, 1975a). Among female musicians, performers are likely to be higher in power motivation than teachers (Mueller, 1975), suggesting that influencing a large number of people even for a short period of time (as in a concert hall) is perhaps more attractive to a woman high in power motivation than influencing a smaller number of people over a longer period of time (as in a classroom over a semester). Since only women were included in this sample, however, we do not know whether this would be true for male musicians as well. Finally, Winter (1979) reports that both men and women high in the avoidance component of power motivation (that is, fear of power) tend to be independent, suspicious of power, and poor performers under stress.

Nevertheless, there is some literature to suggest that a particular set of behavioral correlates of power do differ among men and women. Winter (1979), for example, argued that while males and females high in *n* Power are similar to each other in terms of seeking and wielding formal social power, they are dissimilar in the degree to which their behavior is characterized by aggression in both public settings and private relationships. For example, power-motivated women are not as likely to demonstrate what Winter calls the "expansive, profligate" behavior characteristic of power-motivated men, such as participation in competitive sports, verbal aggression, gambling, reading "vicarious" magazines such as *Playboy*, and liquor consumption. This may help account for McKeachie's (1961) finding that in classrooms where public volunteering is encouraged, power-motivated females tend to do less well than power-motivated males, suggesting that public competitive performance may cause greater anxiety in females high in power motivation, inhibiting their performance. Different average experiences in the socialization of aggression in the two sexes may well account for these differences. In a comparison of delinquent girls and matched controls, Katkin (1978) found that the more "anti-social" delinquent girls were higher in power motivation. Thus in females who are not "successfully" socialized, we do see the relationship between power motivation and aggressive action that has been found for men.

In the areas of aggression and impulsiveness, female sex-role socialization may create inhibitions that affect the expression of power motives. Similarly, female sex-role socialization in the area of intimacy and relationships may so enhance girls' skills and create such uniformly positive valuing of relationships that even power-motivated women are relatively successful in their relationships (especially when compared to power-motivated men).

Several researchers have found that power motivation predicts difficulties in relationships with the opposite sex, break-up of relationships, and divorce in *men only* (Stewart and Rubin, 1974; Veroff and Feld, 1970; Winter, Stewart, and McClelland, 1977). This

finding may be related to an important difference in the way the
sexes select targets for the satisfaction of their power needs. While
both men and women high in n Power may find formal social power
satisfying, men appear to be *more* likely than women to use intimate
relationships as an arena for achieving power. Winter, Stewart, and
McClelland (1977) showed that well-educated men high in power
motivation were likely to be married to women without professional
careers (over whom, presumably, they could exercise considerable
influence and control). In contrast, women high in power motivation tend, if anything, to marry successful men (Winter, McClelland,
and Stewart, 1981) and to find marriage rather gratifying (Veroff,
this volume). Thus, power-motivated men seem to differ from
power-motivated women in defining intimate relationships as
power relationships. That definition may create opportunities for
the expression of power needs, but it is ultimately destructive of the
intimate relationship itself.

It seems clear, then, that at least some sex differences in the
behavioral correlates of power motivation are due to differences in
sex-role socialization experiences rather than gender per se. Within-
sex differences between groups with different socialization backgrounds support this notion. Winter and Stewart (1973) found that
power motivation predicted behavior in non-traditional self-
defining women that was similar to that predicted by power motivation in men. In more traditional socially defined women, however,
power motivation predicted behaviors congruent with the female
sex-role (commitment to home and family, endorsement of traditional sex-role definitions, and so on).

Other aspects of individuals' life situation have also been
shown to moderate the expression of power motivation in both sexes.
Thus, Winter, McClelland, and Stewart (1981) found that whether
or not one has children importantly interacts with the effects of the
leadership motive pattern (high power motivation, high activity
inhibition, and low affiliative motivation) similarly for both men and
women. The leadership motive pattern predicted the usual variables
(officeholding, organizational involvement, and political activity)
among women with children, but *not* among women without
children. Indeed, among women without children, the motive was
negatively correlated with these behaviors and positively related to

having an executive husband and spending time on hobbies and self-improvement activities (building up of inner resources). A similar pattern held for men. That is, the leadership motive pattern predicted organizational involvement and officeholding only among men with children. It also predicted number of publications and early career success for this group. Among men without children, the motive pattern was negatively correlated with early career success, and positively with career frustration. It is as if, for both sexes, having children tends to direct power motivation in positive, socially responsible directions. Not having children appears to encourage the expression of power motivation in more self-indulgent and perhaps professionally destructive ways. Winter (1981) has pursued this research finding and argues that sex differences in the socialization of "responsibility" (a concerned caring orientation toward weaker others) may help account for within-sex and between-sex differences in the correlates of the power motive. Thus, there is increasing evidence that the promising line of research on the correlates of n Power is less in gender differences and more in different dimensions of socialization (of aggression, of self-control, of responsibility for others).

Clearly the similarities between the sexes in overall level of power motivation, as well as many of the correlates of the motive, far outweigh the differences. Where there are fairly consistent sex differences, researchers have made considerable advances in pinpointing the specific socialization processes that may moderate the expression of the motive in behavior. These advances have also allowed researchers to demonstrate that results of within-sex analyses of groups differing only in socialization experience replicate apparent sex differences. In the area of research on the power motive, then, we see the beginning of an attempt to go beyond documenting the existence of sex differences to understanding how those differences arise.

Drawing Some Conclusions

Our goal in this review was to organize the relevant research on women and motivation in such a way as to make the findings and implications of an enormously complex set of studies more intelligible. We feel that it is now possible to draw some very general conclusions, both about specific motives and about research on women and motivation. A summary of the main points to be made regarding the answers to all four of the research questions reviewed for all three motives is presented in Table 2. (Results for the first two questions, not discussed in detail in this paper, are listed in Table 2 to complete the overview of our conclusions.) The table is intended only as a very general summary of findings as they relate to the questions, and certainly not as a definitive outline of all findings.

Question 3. Are the motives aroused under the same conditions for women as for men? Generally speaking, it appears that all three motives are aroused by similar stimulus situations for both sexes. It should be noted, however, that the arousal of n Affiliation has been successful in both sexes only when using same-sex stimulus cues. In addition, while it appears that the standard arousal situation is about as effective in arousing n Achievement for both sexes, too few studies have included both sexes or paid careful attention to details of design and procedure. Moreover, the effects of sex-role-relevant conditions and various aspects of eliciting stimuli on the arousal of achievement motivation in men are unknown (that is, the sex-role relevance of arousal conditions and various aspects of eliciting stimuli have been studied far more extensively with women than with men).

Question 4. Are the behavioral correlates of the motives similar for men and women? The data relevant to answering this question present a rather complicated picture. Nevertheless, although there are some differences in the form that the expression of the motives may take in men and women, the similarities are far more compelling than one might expect, given a literature that has assumed the reverse. Affiliation motivation appears to be expressed similarly in men's and women's relationships with others, for example, although it may be that females high in the affiliation motive are more popular than their male counterparts. N Affiliation appears to have a similar effect on performance for both sexes, however, and also elicits adherence to specific group norms for both men and women (although of course these groups, and hence the specific norms, may vary considerably for various within-sex and cross-sex group comparisons).

Table 2. A Summary of the Evidence Bearing on the Four Issues for the Three Motives

Question	n Achievement	n Affiliation	n Power
1. Are there differences in imagery?			
a) Are protocols scorable?	a) Yes	a) Yes	a) Yes
b) Are there differences in the amount of imagery found by sex?	b) No differences	b) Women may be higher, but confounded by sex of stimuli	b) No consistent differences
c) Are there missing themes?	c) Not themes not already covered by scoring system	c) Yes, but not sex-linked ones	c) Yes, but not sex-linked ones
2. Are the same eliciting stimuli valid in both sexes?	Relevant research mostly not available. Achievement cue value probably important for both sexes, and more important than sex of stimulus figure.	Sex of stimulus may affect both men and women in the same way. More research needed.	No differences found for sex of stimulus in either sex.
3. Are the motives aroused under the same conditions for women as for men?	Yes, when both arousal and control conditions are adequate, and pretest-posttest design is used. Some additional evidence for main and interactive effects of pictures, and relevance of sex-role-appropriate inductions. No comparable data on men.	Yes, though only with same-sex picture cues in both sexes.	Yes, except perhaps in terms of the effect of alcohol.
4. Are the behavioral correlates of the motives similar for men and women?	1) In the area of *performance*, neutral scores may predict less consistently for women than for men; aroused scores do predict quite consistently. No comparable data on men. 2. In the area of *risk-taking and entrepreneurship*, almost no comparable data for women. 3) In the area of *career achievement*, generally predicts for women; no comparable data for men. 4) In the area of *educational and intellectual attainment*, results similar for both. 5) In the area of other *personality correlates*, results similar where comparable data exist.	1) In the area of *relationships with others*, results similar. 2) In the area of *popularity*, relationships may be positive for women and negative for men. 3) In the area of *achievement and performance*, results similar. 4) In the area of *adherence to peer group norms*, results similar.	1) In the area of *negative emotional experience*, results similar (though some differences in details). 2) In the area of *organizational leadership*, results similar. 3) In the area of *career preferences and pursuit*, results similar. 4) In the areas of *aggressiveness and impulsiveness*, results differ: power motivation correlates with these in men but not in most women. 5) In the area of *intimacy*, results differ. Power motivation correlates with problems in maintaining intimate relationships for men, but not for women.

Similarly, achievement motivation appears, in general, to predict similar behaviors in men and women (although considerably more research testing both sexes in the same study is necessary to confirm this impression). For example, while n Achievement may not predict females' laboratory performance when using neutral scores, aroused n Achievement scores do seem to predict quite consistently for women. Comparable data for men and women really do not exist in the area of risk taking and entrepreneurship. In possibly related research, the achievement motive has fairly reliably predicted career success among women for whom career activity is both possible and reasonably consistent with personal values. The relationship (if any) between this research and the work on entrepreneurship and risk taking in men has not been conceptualized. Comparable data have been generated with respect to the role of n Achievement in predicting educational or intellectual attainment, and the results seem comparable for both sexes. Finally, a number of personality variables have been correlated with n Achievement in females, but not in males. It is difficult to draw any conclusions from data that are so frequently not comparable.

Finally, the correlates of power motivation appear to be similar for both men and women in all but two areas. That is, power-motivated men and women have similar negative internal emotional lives; they seek and hold leadership positions in organizations; and gravitate toward career areas in which they can influence others. However, men with strong power needs are more likely than power-motivated women to express these needs in aggressive, self-indulgent behavior and are more likely to have problems in establishing and maintaining intimate relationships with others.

Looking at the four research questions as a whole, it seems legitimate to argue—although a number of areas need more careful research—that all three motives can be aroused and measured similarly in men and women. The way the motives are expressed in behavior does vary somewhat, but this variation seems related less to gender differences than to differences in social norms and expectations.

Directions for Future Research

It seems clear that in the case of the achievement motive, the work on women has simply not been comparable to the work done with men, although there has been no paucity of research or lack of significant findings. Thus, we feel that systematic research examining the effect of various aspects of stimulus cues (including at least sex of stimulus cue and achievement cue value) and arousal conditions (both classic and value-linked) with both men and women remains an important research priority. This research should be designed with careful attention to the details of method and procedure identified both here and in Birney (1968) as important to successful arousal of the achievement motive. Similarly, comparable data on some of the key correlates of the achievement motive, especially risk taking and entrepreneurship in women, need to be gathered.

Affiliation motivation appears to be similarly aroused in males and females, but the evidence is still inconclusive with regard to the question of sex differences in the strength of the motive. Additional research should explore the effect of sex of picture cue on affiliation imagery in the stories of both men and women. In addition, it should be noted that no research to date has examined the issue of affiliation cue value. It may be that pictures of women depict interactions with affiliative significance more often than pictures of men. An effort should thus be made to control for affiliative cue value, as well as for sex of stimulus. With regard to behavioral and interpersonal correlates, it appears that social skills, socialization experience, and reference groups are potentially important moderators of the effect of *n* Affiliation.

Research on power motivation appears to be the most adequately conducted with regard to sex differences. However, it appears that including overall sex-role orientation is not the most productive approach to understanding differences in power motivation in men and women. Sex-role orientation is simply too global and general a construct to provide clarification of differences researchers have identified. Instead, specific aspects of sex-role orientation, such as socialization of aggression, or social skill training, appear to be more important, both in explaining between-sex and within-sex differences.

In fact, it seems to us that although it is still desirable for researchers to examine motive-behavior relationships in the two sexes separately, gender and sex-role orientation are not particularly useful constructs for understanding apparent sex differences in any of the three motives. Instead, particular dimensions of socialization may better account for those differences. Thus, socialization of aggression may influence responses to competition with others (relevant to the achievement motive), exploitative hostile behavior (relevant to the power motive), and even reactions to others' evaluations (relevant to the affiliation motive). Equally, social skill learning may affect the links between n Affiliation and popularity, n Power and intimacy, and n Achievement and competitive striving. Other dimensions of socialization, such as responsibility training and experience, may have more specific or limited consequences for a single motive.

Similarly, although researchers have assumed for many years that the incentive value of various goals may importantly moderate the prediction of behavior from motives, this assumption has very rarely been reflected in the literature on motives in women or men. (Instead, it has sometimes been assumed that women do not have the motive itself!) In addition, though it is well known that reference groups are an important source of norms and sanctions about behavior and expectations about goals, researchers have rarely incorporated that knowledge into predictions about motive-behavior relationships in women or men.

We feel that there is real hope for significant progress in research on motives in women if researchers can be persuaded to abandon the assumptions that lead them both to search for sex differences and to search for explanations of them. Instead, adequate conceptualization of the roles of values, reference groups, and socialization experience in moderating the manifestation of needs in behavior could guide productive research and the elaboration of a more complete theory of human social motivation.

References

Alper, T. G. "Achievement Motivation in College Women: A Now-You-See-It-Now-You-Don't Phenomenon." *American Psychologist*, 1974, *29*, 194–203.

Anderson, R. C. "Failure Imagery in the Fantasy of Eighth Graders as a Function of Three Conditions of Induced Arousal. *Journal of Educational Psychology*, 1962, *53*, 293–298.

Atkinson, J. W. "The Achievement Motive and Recall of Interrupted and Completed Tasks." *Journal of Experimental Psychology*, 1953, *46*, 381-390.

Atkinson, J. W., Heyns, R. W., and Veroff, J. "The Effects of Experimental Arousal of the Affiliation Motive on Thematic Apperception." *Journal of Abnormal and Social Psychology*, 1954, *49*, 405-410.

Atkinson, J. W., and Raphelson, A. C. "Individual Differences in Motivation and Behavior in Particular Situations." *Journal of Personality*, 1956, *24*, 349-363.

Baruch, R. "The Achievement Motive in Women: Implications for Career Development." *Journal of Personality and Social Psychology*, 1967, *5*, 260-267.

Bickman, L. D. "Personality Constructs of Senior Women Planning to Marry or to Live Independently Soon After College." Unpublished doctoral dissertation, University of Pennsylvania, 1975.

Birney, R. C. "The Achievement Motive and Task Performance: A Replication." *Journal of Abnormal and Social Psychology*, 1958, *56*, 133-135.

Birney, R. C. "Research on the Achievement Motive." In E. Borgatta and W. Lambert (Eds.), *Handbook of Personality Theory and Research*. Chicago: Rand McNally, 1968.

Bloom, A. R. "Achievement Motivation and Occupational Choice: A Study of Adolescent Girls." Unpublished doctoral dissertation, Bryn Mawr College, 1971.

Boyatzis, R. "Affiliation Motivation." In D. C. McClelland and R. S. Steele (Eds.), *Human Motivation: A Book of Readings*. Morristown, N.J.: General Learning Press, 1973.

Byrne, D. "Anxiety and the Experimental Arousal of Affiliation Need." *Journal of Abnormal and Social Psychology*, 1961, *63*, 660-662.

Constantian, C. "Solitude, Attitudes, Beliefs, and Behavior in Regard to Spending Time Alone." Unpublished doctoral dissertation, Harvard University, 1981.

Cowan, G., and Goldberg, F. "Need Achievement as a Function of the Race and Sex of Figures of Selected TAT Cards." *Journal of Personality and Social Psychology*, 1967, *5*, 245-249.

Crandall, V. J., Katkovsky, W., and Preston, A. "Motivational and Ability Determinants of Young Children's Intellectual Achievement Behaviors." *Child Development*, 1962, *33*, 643–661.

deCharms, R. "Affiliation Motivation and Productivity in Small Groups." *Journal of Abnormal and Social Psychology*, 1957, *55*, 222–226.

Depner, C. E., and Veroff, J. "Varieties of Achievement Motivation." *Journal of Social Psychology*, 1979, *107*, 283–284.

Dodds, J. B. "An Experimental Study of the Determinants of Affiliation Imagery in Thematic Apperception Stories." Unpublished doctoral dissertation, Cornell University, 1960.

Dunbar, D. S. "Sex-Role Identification and Achievement Motivation in College Women." Unpublished doctoral dissertation, Ohio State University, 1959.

Durand, D. E. "Effects of Drinking on the Power and Affiliation Needs of Middle-Aged Females." *Journal of Clinical Psychology*, 1975, *31*, 549–553.

Exline, R. "Effects of Sex, Norms, and Affiliation Motivation upon Accuracy of Perception of Interpersonal Preference." *Journal of Personality*, 1960, *28*, 397–412.

Exline, R. "Need Affiliation and Initial Communication Behavior in Problem-Solving Groups Characterized by Low Interpersonal Visibility." *Psychological Reports*, 1962, *10*, 79–89.

Field, W. F. "The Effects on Thematic Apperception on Certain Experimentally Aroused Needs." Unpublished doctoral dissertation, University of Maryland, 1951.

Fishman, D. B. "Affiliation: Need, Expectancy, and Small Group Interaction." Unpublished doctoral dissertation, Harvard University, 1965.

Fishman, D. B. "Need and Expectancy as Determinants of Affiliative Behavior in Small Groups." *Journal of Personality and Social Psychology*, 1966, *4*, 155–164.

Fleming, J. "Fear of Success, Achievement-Related Motives and Behavior in Black College Women." *Journal of Personality*, 1978, *46*, 694–716.

Fontana, G. J. "An Investigation into the Dynamics of Achievement Motivation in Women." Unpublished doctoral dissertation, University of Michigan, 1970.

French, E. G. "Some Correlates of Achievement Motivation." *Journal of Experimental Psychology*, 1955, *50*, 232–236.

French, E. G. "Motivation as a Variable in Work Partner Selection." *Journal of Abnormal and Social Psychology*, 1956, *53*, 96–99.

French, E. G., and Lesser, G. S. "Some Characteristics of the Achievement Motive in Women." *Journal of Abnormal and Social Psychology*. 1964, *68*, 119–128.

Friedrich, L. K. "Achievement Motivation in College Women Revisited: Implications for Women, Men, and the Gathering of Coconuts." *Sex Roles*, 1976, *2*, 47–61.

Gilbert, L. R. "Internal Attribution for Success and High Achievement Motivation for Men and Women." Unpublished doctoral dissertation, Catholic University, 1977.

Gralewski, C., and Rodgon, M. M. "Effects of Social and Intellectual Instruction on Achievement Motivation as a Function of Role Orientation." *Sex Roles*, 1980, *6*, 301–309.

Groszko, M., and Morgenstern, R. "Institutional Discrimination: The Case of Achievement-Oriented Women in Higher Education." *International Journal of Group Tensions*, 1974, *4*, 82–92.

Haber, R. N. "The Prediction of Achievement Behavior by an Interaction of Achievement Motivation and Achievement Stress." Unpublished doctoral dissertation, Stanford University, 1957.

Honigfeld, G., and Spigel, I. M. "Achievement Motivation and Field Independence." *Journal of Consulting Psychology*, 1960, *24*, 550–551.

Horner, M. S. "Sex Differences in Achievement Motivation and Performance in Competitive and Non-Competitive Situations." Unpublished doctoral dissertation, University of Michigan, 1968.

Jacobson, S. F. "Sex-Role Identity and Sex-Role Attitudes as Related to Achievement Motivation in Women." Unpublished doctoral dissertation, New York University, 1977.

Kagan, J., and Moss, H. A. "Stability and Validity of Achievement Fantasy." *Journal of Abnormal and Social Psychology*, 1958, *56*, 357–363.

Kagan, J., Sontag, L. W., Baker, C. T., and Nelson, V. L. "Personality and IQ Change." *Journal of Abnormal and Social Psychology*, 1958, *56*, 261–266.

Karabenick, S. A. "Fear of Success, Achievement and Affiliation

Dispositions, and the Performance of Men and Women Under Individual and Competitive Conditions." *Journal of Personality,* 1977, *45,* 117–149.

Katkin, F. S. "Personality and Motivation in Female Delinquents." Unpublished honors thesis, Harvard University, 1978.

Klinger, E. "Fantasy Need Achievement as a Motivational Construct." *Psychological Bulletin,* 1966, *66,* 291–308.

Klinger, E. "Modeling Effects on Achievement Imagery." *Journal of Personality and Social Psychology,* 1967, 7, 49–62.

Kuhl, J., and Blankenship, V. "Behavioral Change in a Constant Environment: Shift to More Difficult Tasks with Constant Probability of Success." *Journal of Personality and Social Psychology,* 1979, *37,* 551–563.

Lansing, J. B., and Heyns, R. W. "Need Affiliation and Frequency of Four Types of Communication." *Journal of Abnormal and Social Psychology,* 1959, *58,* 365–372.

Lesser, G. S., Krawitz, R. N., and Packard, R. "Experimental Arousal of Achievement Motivation in Adolescent Girls." *Journal of Abnormal and Social Psychology,* 1963, *66,* 59–66.

Lipinski, G. "Role Conflict and Achievement Motivation in College Women." Unpublished doctoral dissertation, University of Cincinnati, 1965.

Littig, L. W. *Personality Factors Related to Occupational Aspirations of Negro College Students.* Technical Report, U.S. Office of Education, Contract No. OE-6-85-0039. Washington, D.C.: U.S. Office of Education, 1966.

Littig, L. W. "Motivational Correlates of Real to Ideal Occupational Shifts Among Black and White Men and Women." *Bulletin of the Psychonomic Society,* 1979, *13,* 227–229.

Littig, L. W., and Yeracaris, C. "Academic Achievement Correlates of Achievement Affiliation Motivations." *Journal of Psychology,* 1963, *55,* 115–119.

Lowell, E. L. "A Methodological Study of Projectively Measured Achievement Motivation." Unpublished master's thesis, Wesleyan University, 1950.

Lowell, E. L. "The Effect of Need for Achievement on Learning and Speed of Performance." *Journal of Psychology,* 1952, *33,* 31–40.

McAdams, D. "Validation of a Thematic Coding System for the

Intimacy Motive." Unpublished doctoral dissertation, Harvard University, 1979.

McClelland, D. C. "The Harlequin Complex." In D. C. McClelland (Ed.), *The Roots of Consciousness.* New York: Van Nostrand, 1964.

McClelland, D. C. "Wanted: A New Self-Image for Women." In R. J. Lifton (Ed.), *The Woman in America.* Boston: Houghton Mifflin, 1965.

McClelland, D. C. "Longitudinal Trends in the Relation of Thought to Action." *Journal of Consulting Psychology,* 1966, *30,* 479–483.

McClelland, D. C. *Power: The Inner Experience.* New York: Irvington, 1975.

McClelland, D. C., Atkinson, J. W., Clark, R. A., and Lowell, E. L. *The Achievement Motive.* New York: Appleton-Century-Crofts, 1953.

McClelland, D. C., Clark, R. A., Roby, T., and Atkinson, J. W. "The Projective Expression of Needs. IV: The Effect of the Need for Achievement on Thematic Apperception." *Journal of Experimental Psychology,* 1949, *39,* 242–255.

McClelland, D. C., Floor, E., Davidson, R. J., and Saron, C. "Stressed Power Motivation, Sympathetic Activation, Immune Function, and Illness." *Journal of Human Stress,* 1980, *6* (2), 11–19.

McClelland, D. C., and Jemmott, J. B. "Power Motivation, Stress, and Physical Illness." *Journal of Human Stress,* 1980, *6,* 6–15.

McKeachie, W. J. "Motivation. Teaching Methods, and College Learning," *Nebraska Symposium on Motivation.* Lincoln: University of Nebraska Press, 1961.

McKeachie, W. J., Isaacson, R. L., Milholland, J. E., and Lin, Y. "Student Achievement Motives, Achievement Cues, and Academic Achievement." *Journal of Consulting and Clinical Psychology,* 1968, *32,* 26–29.

McKeachie, W. J., Lin, Y., Milholland, J., and Isaacson, R. "Student Affiliation Motives, Teacher Warmth, and Academic Achievement." *Journal of Personality and Social Psychology,* 1966, *4,* 457–461.

Mannan, G. "The Effects of Achievement Motive, Instructional Set, and Sex on the Performance of an Intelligence Test." Unpublished doctoral dissertation, Indiana University, 1967.

Martire, J. G. "Relationships Between the Self-Concept and Differences in the Strength and Generality of Achievement Motivation." *Journal of Personality*, 1956, *24*, 364–375.

Mednick, M., and Puryear, G. "Race and Fear of Success in College Women: 1968 and 1971." *Journal of Consulting and Clinical Psychology*, 1976, *44*, 787–789.

Mingione, A. D. "Need for Achievement in Negro and White Children." *Journal of Consulting and Clinical Psychology*, 1965, *29*, 108–111.

Mingione, A. D. "Need for Achievement in Negro, White, and Puerto Rican Children." *Journal of Consulting and Clinical Psychology*, 1968, *32*, 94–95.

Moore, H. B. "Race and Social Class: Socio-Cultural Factors in the Development of the Achievement Motive in College Women." Unpublished doctoral dissertation, Boston College, 1977.

Morrison, H. W. "The Validity and Behavioral Manifestations of Female Need for Achievement." Unpublished master's thesis, Wesleyan University, 1954.

Mueller, S. C. "Motivation and Reactions to the Work Role Among Female Performers and Music Teachers." Unpublished doctoral dissertation, University of Michigan, 1975.

Murstein, B. I. "The Relationship of Expectancy of Reward to Achievement Performance on an Arithmetic and Thematic Test." *Journal of Consulting Psychology*, 1963, *27*, 394–399.

Murstein, B. I., and Collier, H. L. "The Role of the TAT in the Measurement of Achievement as a Function of Expectancy." *Journal of Projective Techniques*, 1962, *26*, 96–101.

O'Connell, A. N. "Effects of Manipulated Status on Performance, Goal-Setting, Achievement Motivation, Anxiety, and Fear of Success." *Journal of Social Psychology*, 1980, *112*, 75–89.

O'Conner, P., Atkinson, J. W., and Horner, M. "Motivational Implications of Ability Grouping in Schools." In J. W. Atkinson and N. T. Feather (Eds.), *A Theory of Achievement Motivation*. New York: Wiley, 1966.

Orso, D. P. "Comparison of Achievement and Affiliation Arousal on *n* Achievement." *Journal of Projective Techniques and Personality Assessment*, 1969, *33*, 230–233.

Peak, H. "The Effects of Aroused Motivation on Attitudes." *Journal of Abnormal and Social Psychology*, 1960, *60*, 463–468.

Pierce, J. V. "Non-Intellectual Factors Related to Achievement in Above Average Ability High School Students." Unpublished doctoral dissertation, University of Chicago, 1960.

Pierce, J. V. *Sex Differences in Achievement Motivation.* Report on Cooperative Research Project No. 1097. Chicago: University of Chicago, 1961.

Rapaport, I. "An Investigation of the Interactive Effects of Need Achievement and Need Affiliation and Task Cues as An Interpretation of Horner's Motive to Aviod Success Construct." Unpublished doctoral dissertation, Ohio University, 1977.

Ratliff, E. S. "A Follow-Up Study of Achievement-Related Motivation and Behavior." Unpublished doctoral dissertation, University of Michigan, 1980.

Raynor, J. O. "Relationships Between Achievement Related Motives, Future Orientation, and Academic Performance." *Journal of Personality and Social Psychology,* 1970, *15,* 28–33.

Ricciuti, H. N., and Clark, R. A. *A Comparison of Need Achievement Stories Written by Experimentally "Relaxed" and "Achievement-Oriented" Subjects: Effects Obtained with New Pictures and Revised Scoring Categories.* Princeton, N.J.: Educational Testing Service, 1954.

Rosenfeld, H. M., and Franklin, S. S. "Arousal of Need for Affiliation in Women." *Journal of Personality and Social Psychology,* 1966, *3,* 245–248.

Scott, W. A. "The Avoidance of Threatening Material in Imaginative Behavior." *Journal of Abnormal and Social Psychology,* 1956, *52,* 338–346.

Sée, S. B. "Aspects of Career Achievement and Affiliation in Business Men and Women." Unpublished doctoral dissertation, Yeshiva University, 1977.

Shaw, M. C. "Need Achievement Scales as Predictors of Academic Success." *Journal of Educational Psychology,* 1961, *52,* 282–285.

Shelton, P. B. "Achievement Motivation in Professional Women." Unpublished doctoral dissertation, University of California, Berkeley, 1967.

Sherwood, J. "Self-Report and Projective Measures of Achievement and Affiliation." *Journal of Consulting Psychology,* 1966, *30,* 329–337.

Shipley, T. E., and Veroff, J. A. "A Projective Measure of Need for Affiliation." *Journal of Experimental Psychology*, 1952, *43*, 349–356.

Skolnick, A. "Motivational Imagery and Behavior over Twenty Years." *Journal of Consulting Psychology*, 1966, *30*, 463–478.

Sorrentino, R. M., and Sheppard, B. H. "Effects of Affiliation-Related Motives on Swimmers in Individual Versus Group Competition: A Field Experiment." *Journal of Personality and Social Psychology*, 1978, *36*, 704–714.

Steele, R. S. "The Physiological Concomitants of Psychogenic Motive Arousal in College Males." Unpublished doctoral dissertation, Harvard University, 1973.

Stewart, A. J. "Longitudinal Prediction from Personality to Life Outcomes Among College-Educated Women." Unpublished doctoral dissertation, Harvard University, 1975a.

Stewart, A. J. "Power Arousal and Thematic Apperception in Women." Paper presented at the 83rd annual meeting of the American Psychological Association, Chicago, 1975b.

Stewart, A. J., and Rubin, Z. "The Power Motive in the Dating Couple." *Journal of Personality and Social Psychology*, 1974, *34*, 305–309.

Stewart, A. J., and Winter, D. G. "Arousal of the Power Motive in Women." *Journal of Consulting and Clinical Psychology*, 1976, *44*, 495–496.

Stivers, E. H. "A Study of the Development of an Achievement Motive Motivation for a College Education." Unpublished doctoral dissertation, University of Chicago, 1958.

Sturgis, B. J. "Correlates of Problem Solving in Women." Unpublished doctoral dissertation, University of Missouri, Columbia, 1977.

Sundheim, B.J.M. "The Relationships Among *n* Achievement, *n* Affiliation, Sex-Role Concepts, Academic Grades, and Curricular Choice." Unpublished doctoral dissertation, Columbia University, 1962.

Sutherland, E. "Fear of Success and the Need for Power." *Psychological Report*, 1978, *43*, 763–766.

Tangri, S. S. "Role Innovation in Occupational Choice." Unpublished doctoral dissertation, University of Michigan, 1969.

Tangri, S. S. "Determinants of Occupational Role Innovation Among College Women." *Journal of Social Issues,* 1972, *28,* 177–199.

Tedeschi, J. W., and Kian, M. "Cross-Cultural Study of the TAT Assessment for Achievement Motivation: Americans and Persians." *Journal of Social Psychology,* 1962, *58,* 227–234.

Thornton, C. L., and Barrett, G. V. "Methodological Note on *n* Achievement and Field Independence Comparisons." *Journal of Consulting Psychology,* 1967, *31,* 631–632.

Turek, E. C., and Howell, R. J. "The Effect of Variable Success and Failure Situations on the Intensity of Need for Achievement." *Journal of Social Psychology,* 1959, *49,* 267–273.

Uleman, J. S. "A New TAT Measure of the Need for Power." Unpublished doctoral dissertation, Harvard University, 1966.

Uleman, J. S. "The Need for Influence: Development and Validation of a Measure, and Comparison with the Need for Power." *Genetic Psychology Monographs,* 1972, *85,* 157–214.

Veroff, J. "Development and Validation of a Projective Measure of Power Motivation." *Journal of Abnormal and Social Psychology,* 1957, *54,* 1–8.

Veroff, J., Atkinson, J. W., Feld, S., and Gurin, G. "The Use of Thematic Apperception to Assess Motivation in a Nationwide Interview Study," *Psychological Monographs,* 1960, *74,* Whole No. 499.

Veroff, J., Depner, C., Kulka, R., and Douvan, E. "Comparison of American Motives: 1957 versus 1976." *Journal of Personality and Social Psychology,* 1980, *39,* 1249–1262.

Veroff, J., and Feld, S. *Marriage and Work in America: A Study of Motives and Roles.* New York: Van Nostrand Reinhold, 1970.

Veroff, J., and Veroff, J. B. "Reconsideration of a Measure of Power Motivation." *Psychological Bulletin,* 1972, *78,* 279–291.

Veroff, J., Wilcox, S., and Atkinson, J. W. "The Achievement Motive in High School and College Age Women." *Journal of Abnormal and Social Psychology,* 1953, *48,* 108–119.

Walker, E. L., and Heyns, R. W. *An Anatomy for Conformity,* Englewood Cliffs, N.J.: Prentice-Hall, 1962.

Wertheim, J., and Mednick, S. A. "The Achievement Motive and Field Independence." *Journal of Consulting Psychology,* 1958, *22,* 38.

Wilsnack, S. "The Effects of Social Drinking on Women's Fantasy." *Journal of Personality*, 1974, *42*, 243–261.

Winter, D. G. *The Power Motive*. New York: Free Press, 1973.

Winter, D. G. "Research on the Power Motive and Power Behavior in Women." Paper presented at conference on women and power, Washington, D.C., March 1979.

Winter, D. G. "The Power Motive in Women." Paper presented at International Interdisciplinary Congress on Women, Haifa, Israel, 1981.

Winter, D. G., McClelland, D. C., and Stewart, A. J. *A New Case for the Liberal Arts: Assessing Institutional Goals and Student Development*. San Francisco: Jossey-Bass, 1981.

Winter, D. G., and Stewart, A. J. "The Power Motives and Self-Definition in Women." Unpublished manuscript, Wesleyan University, 1973.

Winter, D. G., and Stewart, A. J. "The Power Motive." In H. London and J. Exner (Eds.), *Dimensions of Personality*. New York: Wiley, 1978.

Winter, D. G., Stewart, A. J., and McClelland, D. C. "Husband's Motives and Wife's Career Level." *Journal of Personality and Social Psychology*, 1977, *35*, 159–166.

Winter, D. G., and Wiecking, F. A. "The New Puritans: Achievement and Power Motives of New Left Radicals." *Behavioral Science*, 1971, *16*, 523–530.

Part III

Examining
Motives
in Society

From an early point, McClelland concerned himself with applying laboratory-based technology and knowledge to real-world problems. The chapters presented in this part reflect this commitment and concern. Boyatzis discusses the role of motivation in work settings, while Winter explores its role in the political arena. Both chapters are concerned with the behavioral consequences of social motives in important contexts and among significant actors. Heckhausen and Krug review studies attempting to change the motives of individuals, and Aronson describes studies aimed at changing individuals by changing social environments. Both these chapters reflect McClelland's commitment to use psychology to make a better world. All four chapters reflect his commitment to avoid a simple, sterile laboratory science and to build a complex psychology adequate to studying—even changing—real people in the real world.

Competence at Work

7

Richard E. Boyatzis

Why do people work? How do they perform those activities called work? Why are some people effective in certain jobs while others are not? What can be done to make people and organizations more effective? Few aspects of human behavior have received as much scrutiny and have as much practical significance as the answers to these questions. In this century approaches have varied from Frederick W. Taylor's theory of "scientific management," which attempted to discover how to operate the human machine efficiently, to "humanism," in which attempts were made to stimulate human potential and self-actualization. The approaches abound but coherent answers are few. Recent developments have suggested a paradigm that integrates the investigations, explanations, predictions, and answers to the above questions.

The three main sections of this chapter expand upon three themes in the work of David C. McClelland and offer the basis for such a paradigm. At the core of it is the concept of competence. The first theme involves the links between human characteristics, human behavior, and work performance originally explored by McClelland and his colleagues in terms of the need for Achievement. In later publications, McClelland developed a theory of motivation and attempted to explain why people act the way they do both on and off

221

the job (McClelland, Baldwin, Bronfenbrenner, and Strodtbeck, 1958; McClelland, 1971, 1973, 1975). The second theme involves nonmotivational human characteristics related to work performance. Although McClelland was primarily interested in motivation, he periodically investigated other aspects of the human organism and their relationship to work performance (McClelland, 1951, 1981; McClelland, Baldwin, Bronfenbrenner, and Strodtbeck, 1958). The third theme involves applying the information, hypotheses, and implications drawn from studying job performance and models of competence. To date, models have been developed and applied to many aspects of human behavior, beginning with Achievement Motivation Training.

Effective Job Performance

A Model. Effective performance of a job may be assessed by looking at results (do they or don't they meet the objectives of the job) or at the way procedures are executed. Some jobs are easy to assess because there are established measures and goals, such as sales per month for a salesperson, completion of an income statement by the tenth of the month for a controller, or the redesign of a machine to reduce waste by 20 percent for a manufacturing engineer. Management or administrative jobs are assessed according to the performance of an organizational unit. For example, monthly production of a particular item may be a measure of the plant manager's performance because it summarizes the performance of the entire plant operation. For other jobs, such as manager of research and development, employee relations specialist, product design engineer, or scientist, there is no easy measure of performance. In these types of jobs it may be more appropriate to assess whether a person in the job is following certain procedures or processes that are important to the organization. Unfortunately, it is often easier to tell when a person's performance is *not* accomplishing its purpose or facilitating desired processes or results. For example, if a product manager is responsible for managing the interactions among the manufacturing, research and development, and marketing divisions within a company, corporate executives will be more likely to notice when three divisions are in conflict than to recognize when things are going smoothly because of effective management.

The problem in assessing job performance and determining what constitutes effective and ineffective performance is that it requires measuring several factors at the same time. Some evaluation programs try to simplify this assessment by stating that a person's effective performance is reflected in the degree to which specific objectives are attained. Unfortunately, these objectives are often short-sighted (Levinson, 1970) and do not incorporate a full appreciation of what performance of the particular job means. For example, a sales manager may have a goal of generating $10 million in sales in a particular quarter. If the sales unit produces that amount of sales but experiences 50 percent turnover of staff in the same quarter, has the sales manager performed the job effectively? It is not clear.

Effective performance in a job can be defined as demonstrating a system and sequence of behaviors that produce the specific results required by the job while maintaining or being consistent with policies, procedures, and conditions of the organizational environment. The individual's competencies, the demands of the job, and the organizational environment must intersect, as illustrated in Figure 1 (see Boyatzis, 1982, for a detailed account).

Every individual has certain characteristics that can be called competencies. When individuals are asked to perform specific jobs within the context of an organization, they demonstrate some behavior in response. If individuals' competencies lead to behavior that would satisfy or respond to the requirements and responsibilities of the job and be consistent with the policies, procedures, and conditions of the organizational environment, that behavior will be effective. Effective behavior of the individual occurs when all three critical components in the model are consistent, or "fit." If any two are inconsistent with each other, ineffective behavior or inaction will result.

Organizational Environment. Every organization creates and exists in an environment. Whether the environment is a suitable one in which to accomplish organizational objectives, whether all aspects of the environment are understood by members of the organization, and whether these aspects of the environment are explicitly stated, are all issues that determine how the organizational environment affects individuals' performance in their jobs.

The organizational environment can be described in terms of a number of factors. "Organizational climate" has been used to

Figure 1. A Model of Effective Job Performance

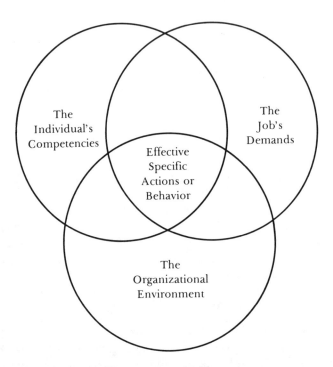

describe the impact of the organization's structure, policies, and procedures on its members (Litwin and Stringer, 1968; Klemp, 1975; Spencer, Klemp, and Cullen, 1978). Whether it is used as an intermediate indicator variable or whether the actual policies, procedures, and structure of an organization are used directly, the atmosphere or environment that the organization creates and transmits to its members affects their performance. For example, McClelland and Burnham (1976) reported that sales divisions within a consumer products company whose clarity about objectives and team spirit were high achieved higher sales volume than divisions with relatively less of these variables in their climate. Dalziel (1979) showed that manufacturing plants which had greater clarity and concern about performance standards showed greater cost savings due to waste reduction than did plants with less of these variables in their climate. Kinkaid and Becklean (1968), Lawrence and Lorsch (1967), and many others have also demonstrated the importance of climate, structure, policies, and procedures in regard to organizational performance and individuals' contribution to that performance.

Other factors, such as the strategic position of the company's products in its industry, the maturity of the industry, and the economic, political, social, and religious conditions of the culture in which the organization functions are also important aspects of the organizational environment.

Demands of the Job. A job is usually described by a title, a list of responsibilities, the decisions that job occupants are expected to make, and the results they are expected to produce. Every job can be said to have a set of functional requirements, that is, tasks that a person in the job should fulfill. Ideally, these functional requirements and the associated output are designed to contribute to the output of people in other jobs. Taken as a whole, the output of the integrated performance of the jobs by all members of an organization yields the performance of the organization with respect to its mission and objectives.

Any job can be described in terms of general functional requirements. For example, a synthesis of the work of Drucker (1954) and Appley (1969) would produce a description of a manager's job in terms of five basic functions: planning, organizing, controlling, motivating, and coordinating. These functions can, of course, be specified. For example, it may be expected that a marketing manager will plan, design, and coordinate a new campaign for one of the company's major products at least once a year. Or, even more specifically, such a manager may be expected to identify, in conjunction with the corporate strategic planning staff and financial analysts, which product is most in need of a new marketing campaign. The campaign must be designed on the basis of market research conducted by the staff, but the budget for the campaign must be presented by the manager to the vice-president of marketing by August of the calendar year preceding the campaign, and so forth.

Job requirements may also be stated in terms of output. For example, a plant manager is supposed to produce 250,000 units of product A and 75,000 units of product B during the year. This may be further qualified by conditions regarding the quality of the products, the seasonal nature of production, and so forth.

If the job demands conflict with aspects of the organizational environment, effective performance either will not be forthcoming or will be costly and highly inefficient. Consider, for example, a research and development division of a $150-million-a-year industrial products company that changed to a matrix structure in an attempt to increase the number of new products designed. A senior scientist or engineer was appointed as project leader for each project. The project leader was given a budget by the vice-president of the division and a statement of objectives. When five of the seven project teams failed to meet their first-half objectives and most were over budget, the vice-president concluded that he had named the wrong people as project leaders. Several questions asked of the project leaders quickly revealed that the company, and in particular the research and development division, had failed to change two critical procedures. First, the company's procedure regarding development of objectives had not been modified to include the newly appointed project leaders and/or the designated project staff. Second, the management information system had not been converted to allow for the various scientists, engineers, and technicians to charge their time to more than one project when in fact many were asked to work on several projects. Project leaders were given budgets based on the number of person days needed to perform various phases of the work, but their quarterly statements of labor and other costs reflected the full labor cost of staff who were not exclusively assigned to their projects.

In this case, either the demands on the project leader had to be changed, or aspects of the division's procedures (that is, of the organizational environment) had to be changed. They were clearly inconsistent. Without these changes, the vice-president of the research and development division could not know whether he had made sound decisions in assigning particular senior scientists or engineers as project leaders.

Competency of Individuals

What Is Competency? As illustrated in Figure 1, an individual's competencies are necessary but not sufficient for effective performance in a job. A job competency is a characteristic (of a person) that results in consistently effective performance in a job (adapted from Klemp, 1980). It may be a motive, trait, aspect of self-image or social role, or a skill or body of knowledge that a person uses. The existence and possession of these characteristics may or may not be known to the person. In this sense, the characteristic may be an unconscious aspect of the person.

Because job competencies are *underlying characteristics*, they can be said to be generic. A generic characteristic may be apparent in many forms of behavior, or a wide variety of different actions. Baldwin (1958) explained that when people perform an act that has a result, or several results, they also express one or more of these characteristics.

Actions, their results, and the characteristics being expressed do not necessarily have a one-to-one correspondence. The reason for the lack of direct correspondence is evident in Figure 1: The action, or specific behavior, is the manifestation of a competency in the context of the requirements of a specific job and a particular organizational environment. Given a different job or different organizational environment, the competency may be revealed through other specific actions. In the same manner, the effect of the action is related to the requirements and setting in which it occurs. If, for example, someone were to describe you in terms of the clothes you wore last Tuesday afternoon, would this be an accurate description of your style of dress, your variations in dress, or your wardrobe? It would probably not be an accurate description of how you dress on Saturday mornings, at a dinner party, or while mowing the lawn. Would inferences about your values, skills, or style be accurate if they were based on the knowledge of what you were wearing last Tuesday afternoon? Making these kinds of inferences about your style of dress or other aspects of your behavioral style would be assuming that a specific action was directly related to an underlying characteristic.

A great deal of the inaccuracy in models and frameworks as to what constitutes "competence" in various jobs emerges from confusion between the generic and the particular. It has been complicated by methodological problems in what is actually being assessed or measured. It has been further complicated by the use of the term "competency" by many professionals who are referring to different concepts.

Let us take the example of a manager giving a subordinate information about the effectiveness of something the subordinate did. The manager's actions might be described in terms such as "communicating with subordinates" or "providing subordinates with feedback with respect to a performance goal." In either case, we are describing an interaction in which the manager is telling the subordinate how well he did according to the manager's view. The result or effect of this interaction can vary: The subordinate may walk away feeling rewarded, recognized, helped, punished, disciplined, or criticized.

Aspects of the interaction may contribute to which effect occurs. If managers ask subordinates to assess their own performance before providing their view, the subordinates may feel that they are being given a chance to explain what happened. If the performance was not up to par and subordinates know it, this action on the part of the manager allows the subordinates to show that they know when something has not gone well. If the manager provides this information along with a discussion of the performance goal, how the goal was established, and why the goal is important to the job and to the organization, his subordinates may feel condemned as persons but may recognize how some aspect of their performance was ineffective. By this behavior, managers allow subordinates to feel that only this one incident is in question, not their entire performance of the job.

If you try to define the managerial competency in this incident in terms of the manager's actions alone, you are back to the problem of "what were you wearing Tuesday afternoon." If you define the manager's competency in terms of the results alone, you may have committed a serious error. Suppose a particular subordinate walked away from the interaction feeling that he had not done part of his job adequately. It could be true; or the interaction could be another instance in a long history of inadequate performance suggesting that the subordinate's job is in danger; it could mean that the manager or the subordinate was having a bad day; it could mean that the manager's own performance is inadequate and to cover himself the manager is looking for ways to blame others.

Even if you define the manager's competency, expressed in this situation, in terms of his actions *and* the results, you may not know *why* the manager acted in this manner, nor would you know whether he could act in the same manner and produce the same result if the situation were somewhat different. Therefore, to define a competency, we must determine what the actions were, their place in a system and sequence of behavior, what the results or effects were, *and* what their meaning was to the manager.

It is through such a definition that the concept of a job competency represents an ability. A person's set of competencies reflects his capability. It describes what he *can do*, not necessarily what he does, or does all the time, regardless of the situation and setting. To understand the individual's competencies, we would like to know what capability the individual has brought to the job. Without knowing, it will be hard to predict, describe, or interpret specific actions or to say why they were effective.

Types of Competencies. Earlier it was mentioned that the type of characteristic that is a competency may be a motive, trait, aspect of the person's self-image or social role, or a skill that he/she uses. Recognizing the distinctions is important not only for understanding competence but also for understanding methodological issues in measuring and assessing competence. To explore this topic, let us examine the competencies of two people, one a neurosurgeon who specializes in brain surgery, and the other a computer technician who specializes in repair and maintenance of computer circuitry. Let us assume that each is effective in his job. For the sake of the illustration, let us assume that their jobs differ in that the computer technician works primarily alone and the neurosurgeon works in conjunction with other surgeons, nurses, an anesthesiologist, and attendants.

There are a number of competencies each person must have. Each must be able to diagnose functional problems, think logically and have a "systems" orientation in order to make the diagnosis, have fine-muscle control to operate in delicate arenas requiring precise movements, be able to take initiative to identify necessary additional information, and accurately understand his talents and limitations to know when to call on others for help or to transfer the patient to another practitioner. In short, the neurosurgeon and the computer technician each must have several traits (fine-muscle control and a disposition to take initative) and skills (thinking in terms of systems, diagnostic ability, and accurate self-assessment).

To be effective in carrying out their respective responsibilities, each must have some competencies that the other does not need. While both desire positive results from their actions, the computer technician must be interested in efficiency and must fix the computer as quickly as possible. The repairs should involve a minimum of lost computer functioning time, a minimum of time spent, and a minimum of replacement parts to satisfy the needs of the computer user and the computer manufacturer or service agency he represents. The technician can take moderate risks in attempting solutions, maximizing effort at the repair and the result to the user and the user's organization. The neurosurgeon, on the other hand, must take a minimum amount of time during the surgery, but cannot take moderate risks and seek shortcuts that *might work* as a means to the desired results. Neither the neurosurgeon nor the patient can afford experimentation. Although the neurosurgeon has some concern about efficiency, it does not emerge from a similar disposition nor can it involve a level of risk similar to that of the computer technician. Each specialist also uses a different body of knowledge to perform his functions. Given one of our assumptions, we can also add that the neurosurgeon must be able to work effectively with others in order to orchestrate their efforts during an operation. Beyond the interpersonal skills needed to communicate with the users of the computer, these skills are not necessary for the technician who works alone.

In examining those competencies that differ for the effective neurosurgeon and the effective computer technician, we find some of the types of competencies mentioned earlier: traits (for example, risk orientation), skills (interpersonal ability to manage or orchestrate the work of others), and specialized knowledge (facts about and understanding of the systems on which they are operating).

We must be able to conceptually distinguish among these types of competencies, because the distinctions have implications for selection systems and training programs, and for how each type of competency is measured or assessed. They may also help to explain why findings from various investigators that appear to disagree should, with proper definition and measurement, support each other.

Motives and Traits. A motive, according to McClelland (1971), is "recurrent concern for a goal state, or condition, appearing in fantasy, which drives, directs, and selects behavior of the individual," whereas trait is the dispositional or characteristic way in which the person responds to equivalent stimuli (McClelland, 1951). (See Table 1.) Motives and traits exist at both unconscious and conscious levels within people.

A motive includes thoughts related to a particular goal state or theme. For example, people who think (consciously or unconsciously) about improving and competing against a standard of excellence are said to have an achievement motive (McClelland, 1961; Atkinson, 1958; McClelland, Atkinson, Clark, and Lowell, 1953). When people with a high achievement motive encounter a

Table 1. Comparison of Motives and Traits

PATTERN	*MOTIVES*	*TRAITS*
Orientation of thoughts	Concern for a theme or goal state	Generalized response to events
Stimulus (that is, what arouses the thoughts)	Perception of situational cues as related to the particular theme or goal state (that is, the person perceives an opportunity for attainment of the goal state)	Any of a number of related situational cues
Observed resultant behavior	Varied behavior related to attainment of the goal state	Stylized behavior (that is, behavior typical of the person) in a variety of related situations which have no apparent theme
Overall probability that any event will arouse the thought pattern	Moderate	High
Examples	Need for achievement, Need for power	Taking initiative, walking fast

situation in which their performance can be measured and a goal can be stated, their achievement motive is aroused. Once aroused, the motivated thought directs and selects their behavior; that is, they will choose to do things that will get them feedback on their performance and will engage in activities that may improve their performance.

Traits, on the other hand, include thoughts and psychomotor activity related to a general category of events. For example, people who believe they can control their future and fate are said to have the trait of efficacy (deCharms, 1968; White, 1963; Rotter, 1966; Boyatzis, 1969; Stewart and Winter, 1974). When people with this trait encounter a problem or issue in any aspect of life, they take initiative to resolve the problem or understand the issue. They do not wait for someone else to do it, or expect that luck or fate will take care of it. The thought pattern and resultant behavior occur in response to any general set of events that allows the trait to be expressed. Traits are easier to arouse than are motives if the cues related to the traits are present.

In our example, the computer technician would probably perform the job more effectively if he had a high need for achievement rather than a low need for achievement. Although the neurosurgeon would be expected to have a moderate degree of need of achievement, we would not expect it to be as strong as the computer technician's. If it were, an undesirable level of risk taking might occur. As mentioned, both would be expected to have traits of fine-muscle control and an orientation to take initiative in collecting information and solving problems.

Self-Image and Social Roles. Self-image refers to a person's self-perception and the evaluation of that perception. This definition incorporates the constructs self-concept and self-esteem. People's evaluation of their self-concept results from comparing themselves to others in their environment (Pettigrew, 1967) and assessing where they stand in terms of values held by themselves and others in their environment. Self-image is therefore not only a concept of the self but an interpretation and labeling of the concept in terms of values. These values and the resulting judgments may be rooted in the individual's past beliefs, current beliefs, or beliefs held and espoused by people in the environment within which the individual lives and works.

For example, a person may have a self-concept that is described in part by statements such as, "I am creative and innovative, I am expressive, and I care about others." If this person's job requires routine performance of tasks in an organization that expects him to be highly self-disciplined, his evaluation of this self-concept may emerge in statements such as, "I am creative and innovative, I am too expressive, I care about others, and I lack sufficient self-discipline."

Social role refers to a person's perception of a set of social norms for behaviors that are acceptable and appropriate in the social groups or organizations to which he belongs. The various social roles people adopt help them determine how they should behave as members of an organization, business, social group, family, community, church, or nation. A social role, therefore, represents an individual's view of how he fits the expectations of others. The particular social role an individual adopts is a function of his view of his own characteristics and the way others expect him to act.

Self-image and social role aspects of competencies mediate motives and traits in determining behavior. That is, where motive or trait levels of a competency exist, self-image and social role levels of the competency help in the selection of actions to be taken by defining which actions are appropriate. They integrate the person's other characteristics (for example, motives, traits, and skills) and the environment's expectations and values regarding the appropriateness of these characteristics to the job.

The neurosurgeon might have an image of himself as precise, careful, expert in the field, and one of the few who could perform such operations. With such a self-image, he may adopt the social role of the star or prima donna. While this self-image and social role might not cause any problems at the country club, it could lead to conflicts in the operating room. Interactions with the other professionals assisting in an operation could be filled with resentment, arguments, or differences of opinion as to procedures, all of which decrease the surgeon's ability to effectively orchestrate the medical team during the operation. A similar self-image and social role would not necessarily lead to any problems for the computer technician. Assuming that he works alone, the technician would not run the risk of arousing such interpersonal difficulties.

Like any of the types of competencies, self-image and social
role competencies must be appropriate to the job and organizational
setting for the individual to be most effective. Unlike other types of
competencies, the appropriateness of self-image and social role
competencies involves others' perceptions. Others' views become
part of the person's organizational environment.

Skills. Skill is the ability to demonstrate a system and
sequence of behaviors that are functionally related to attaining a
performance goal. Using a skill is not a single action. The relationship among specific actions is such that each contributes directly to
the capability to function effectively or ineffectively in a situation.
Since a skill is the ability to *demonstrate* a system and a sequence of
behavior, it must result in something observable. For example,
planning ability is a skill. People who have it can identify a particular sequence of actions to be taken to accomplish a specific objective.
They can identify potential obstacles and potential sources of help
in avoiding or overcoming them. None of these separate actions
constitutes a skill, but the system of behavior does. Together these
behaviors are called skill in planning, and they enable individuals to
reach objectives or perform aspects of jobs.

It is also important to distinguish skills from tasks or functions that are required in the job. People who have a skill can apply
it in any number of situations or contexts. Completing a weekly
activity sheet for subordinates does not necessarily constitute demonstration of a planning skill; it may merely indicate the ability to
complete that specific form. A function such as organizing resources
requires a person to use multiple skills to perform it effectively.
Performing an organizing function would use analytic and planning skills. In communicating a particular organization of resources
to others, additional interpersonal skills would be needed, such as
persuasion. Therefore, selecting staff, making decisions, delegating
responsibility, and repairing a machine are tasks or functions, not
skills. They are aspects of the job, not aspects of the individual's
capability or competencies.

Implications for Human Resource Development Systems

Organizations need integrated human resource development
(HRD) systems to address many aspects of personnel, industrial rela-

tions, and human resource management as a result of three major trends in society: the growth of the service sector of our economy; increased demands on people's productivity, efficiency, and creativity; and the steadily increasing expectations of the work force. Although some companies, government institutions, and other organizations are making advances toward an integrated HRD system, most have not achieved it, and the search for a paradigm that would guide the development of such a system has been hindered by the lack of integrating principles. The concept of competence, specifically job competency, can be used as the core of an integrated HRD system.

For the sake of brevity, I will not explain or describe *how* to apply the concept of competence and validated competency models to components of an HRD system, but I will briefly explain *why* these concepts would be useful and why they could become the core of an HRD system.

Development of Competency Models. Prior to application within an HRD system, competencies must be identified and empirically determined. Because they are related to performing particular jobs within specific organizational environments, competency models must be developed and tested on many, and eventually all, of the jobs and job families in an organization. McClelland (1976), Klemp (1979), Boyatzis (1982), and Klemp and Spencer (in preparation) have presented a research design for validating the competencies of persons in a particular job or job family.

These research designs must and do incorporate methods that allow for inductively identifying competencies, not merely testing a priori models. The methods must include a number of operant techniques to avoid method-bound or culturally specific results. To conform to legal and ethical guidelines covering selection, promotion, or performance appraisal systems, the results must be cross-validated. To be most useful, the validated competencies in a model must also be related to the functonal and task demands of jobs and to specific aspects of the organizational environment. Research based on the concept of competence and validated competency models can provide empirically based answers to questions related to the following systems.

Selection and Promotion Systems

- What characteristics should I look for in a candidate?
- Am I discriminating according to performance-related characteristics and not according to non-performance-related characteristics?
- How do I collect such information on individuals?
- How effective are the procedures I currently use to assess capability?

Planning Career Paths and Succession

- Is there a sequence of jobs that would prepare someone to have the capability to perform each job effectively?
- How do I know when a person is ready for the next job in the sequence?

Career Planning

- For what types of jobs am I currently most suited?
- What capability should I develop to be prepared for the job or jobs that I wish to have?
- Is there a sequence of particular jobs that will prepare me most effectively for a job, or jobs, I want to have?

Training Programs

- What should be the objectives of my training programs?
- What capabilities can be taught?
- When should a person receive the training?
- How can I evaluate the effectiveness of the training?

Of all the applications of the concept of competence and validated competency models, training has received the most attention from professionals working with these concepts as explained in this chapter. From the experimentation with training methods that began with achievement motivation training (McClelland, 1965a, 1965b; McClelland and Winter, 1969; Miron and McClelland, 1979) to application to management training (McClelland and Burnham, 1976) and even therapeutic treatment programs (Boyatzis, 1976), aspects of adult education (Knowles, 1970), experiential learning (Kolb and Fry, 1975; Kolb, 1976), and self-directed change (Kolb and

Boyatzis, 1970) have been incorporated into a competency acquisition process (Spencer, 1979). This process can provide answers to the following additional questions about training programs:

- How should my training program be designed?
- What types of activities (for example, lectures, role plays, simulations, exercises, case studies and analyses, self-study) should be incorporated into the training program?
- How should these activities be integrated within the program to maximize effectiveness?

Developmental Assessment

- What characteristics of personnel should I assess?
- What is the most accurate and efficient method of assessing personnel on these characteristics?
- How do I know when to recognize or reward meaningful development?

Mentoring

- On what topics should mentoring focus?
- What characteristics should I look for in candidates to be mentors?

Performance Appraisal Systems

- What besides output or results should I include in a performance analysis?
- How can I appraise a person's ability to improve his performance
- or maintain effective performance in the future?
- What criteria do I use if results expected from job performance are difficult to measure?

Benefits and Perquisites

- How do I know whether benefits and perquisites are appropriate incentives?
- For what characteristics should my benefits and perquisites be incentives?
- What types of nonmonetary rewards will be meaningful to various persons in the organization?

Organizational Climate

(The concept of competency and validated competency models will not by themselves answer many of the questions related to organizational climate, but they can help by providing answers to the following question.)

- What policies and procedures, either stated or assumed, will produce an environment in which people can use their capabilities most effectively?

Job and Organization Design

(Again, the concept of competency or models alone will not answer some questions related to job and organization design, but they can be helpful in answering these questions.)

- Can the jobs and overall structure of the organization produce jobs with requirements and responsibilities that enable people to use their capabilities most effectively?
- Are the jobs designed, in terms of tasks and functions, in such a manner that certain competencies will be utilized in a number of ways, thereby maximizing the use of my human resources?
- Do the demands of various jobs and the conditions of the organizational environment support each other, are they in conflict, or do they reflect divergent demands on the individual?

Other HRD Systems. A number of components of integrated HRD systems are not directly affected by the concept of competence or validated competency models: personnel planning, job evaluation, and grievance procedures, for example. The operation of the personnel planning system, essential in determining how many people are needed in various jobs, is not directly affected by the concept of competence; nevertheless, an organization's ability to identify, hire, and keep personnel with the desired competencies will result in more efficient use of human resources and may reduce the number of people needed. A job evaluation system, used to determine appropriate salary and benefit levels for various jobs, is another important component of an HRD system. Ideally this system would be based on two factors: (1) the relative importance of the effective performance of the job to the organization's performance and (2) comparability to wages for similar work in other organizations. As part of a job evaluation system, the concept of competence and validated competency models can provide useful information about the construction of benefits, perquisites, and merit increase programs.

The concept of competence and validated competency models also do not appear to aid in the development of an efficient and meaningful grievance procedure, but they do help in managing the grievance process because they provide information about which characteristics are desirable in personnel responsible for conducting and managing grievance processes for maximum organizational effectiveness and personal benefit.

Conclusion

If you are part of the scientific management tradition, you may view competencies as the specifications for the human machinery desired to provide maximum organizational efficiency and effectiveness. If you are part of the humanistic tradition, you may view competencies as the key that unlocks the door to maximizing individuals' growth and developing ethical organizational systems that facilitate human development. If you work in organizations or study, think about, and help organizations use their human resources effectively, the concept of competence should offer needed relief from the exaggerated cynicism or optimism that most of us have developed. Regardless of orientation, the concept of competence is fertile ground for research, development, and testing of integrated human resource development systems and seeking answers to the important questions posed at the beginning of this chapter.

References

Appley, L.A. *A Management Concept*. New York: American Management Associates, 1969.

Atkinson, J. W. (Ed.). *Motives in Fantasy, Action, and Society*. New York: Van Nostrand, 1958.

Atkinson, J. W., and Feather, N. T. (Eds.). *A Theory of Achievement Motivation*. New York: Wiley, 1966.

Baldwin, A. L. "The Role of an Ability Construct in a Theory of Behavior." In D. C. McClelland and others (Eds.), *Talent and Society*. New York: Van Nostrand, 1958.

Boyatzis, R. E. "Building Efficacy: The Effective Use of Managerial Power." *Industrial Management Review*, 1969, *11* (1), 65–76.

Boyatzis, R. E. "Power Motivation Training: A New Treatment Modality." In F. Seixas and S. Eggleston (Eds.), *Work in Progress on Alcoholism: Annals of the New York Academy of Sciences*, 1976, *273*, 525–532.

Boyatzis, R. E. "Managing Motivation for Maximum Productivity." Paper presented at the 87th Annual meeting of the American Psychological Association, New York, Sept. 1979.

Boyatzis, R. E. *The Competent Manager: A Model for Effective Performance*. New York: Wiley, 1982.

Boyatzis, R. E., and Williamson, S. A. "Designing, Selecting, and Using Assessment Methods in Human Resource Development." Paper presented at meeting of the National American Society of Training and Development, Anaheim, Calif., April 1980.

Dalziel, M. *Confidential Report to an Industrial Organization*. Boston: McBer, 1979.

deCharms, R. *Personal Causation*. New York: Academic Press, 1968.

Drucker, P. *The Practice of Management*. New York: Harper & Row, 1954.

Flanagan, J. C. "The Critical Incident Technique." *Psychological Bulletin*, 1954, *51* (4), 327–358.

Hackman, J. R., and Oldham, G. R. *Work Redesign*. Reading, Mass.: Addison-Wesley, in press.

Heckhausen, H. *The Anatomy of Achievement Motivation*. New York: Academic Press, 1967.

Kincaid, M., and Becklean, K. *The Organizational Audit*. Cambridge, Mass.: Entretech, Inc., 1968.

Klemp, G. O., Jr. *Technical Manual for the Organization Climate Survey Questionnaire*. Boston: McBer, 1975.

Klemp, G. O., Jr. "Three Factors of Success." In D. W. Vermilye (Ed.), *Relating Work and Education: Current Issues in Higher Education 1977*. San Francisco: Jossey-Bass, 1977.

Klemp, G. O., Jr. "On the Identification, Measurement, and Integration of Competence." In P. S. Pottinger and J. Goldsmith

(Eds.), *New Directions for Experiential Learning: Defining and Measuring Competence*, no. 3. San Francisco: Jossey-Bass, 1979.

Klemp, G. O., Jr. (Ed.). *The Assessment of Occupational Competence*. Report to the National Institute of Education, Washington, D.C., 1980.

Klemp, G. O., Jr., and Spencer, L. M., Jr. *Job Competence Assessment*. Reading, Mass.: Addison-Wesley, in preparation.

Knowles, M. S. *The Modern Practice of Adult Education: Androgogy Versus Pedagogy*. New York: Association Press, 1970.

Kolb, D. A. *Learning Style Inventory*. (Technical Manual.) Boston: McBer, 1976.

Kolb, D. A., and Boyatzis, R. E. "Goal-Setting and Self-Directed Behavior Change." *Human Relations*, 1970, *23* (5), 439–457.

Kolb, D. A., and Fry, R. "Toward an Applied Theory of Experimental Learning." In C. Cooper (Ed.), *Theories of Group Processes*. London: Wiley, 1975.

Lawrence, P., and Lorsch, J. *Organization and Environment*. Boston: Harvard Business School, 1967.

Levinson, H., "Management by Whose Objectives?" *Harvard Business Review*, 1970, *48* (4).

Litwin, G. H., and Stringer, R. A., Jr. *Motivation and Organization Climate*. Cambridge, Mass.: Harvard Univerity Press, 1968.

McClelland, D. C. *Personality*. New York: William Sloane, 1951.

McClelland, D. C. "Methods of Measuring Human Motivation." In J. W. Atkinson (Ed.), *Motives in Fantasy, Action, and Society*. New York: Van Nostrand, 1958.

McClelland, D. C. *The Achieving Society*. New York: Van Nostrand, 1961.

McClelland, D. C. "Achievement Motivation Can Be Developed." *Harvard Business Review*, Nov.-Dec., 1965a, pp. 6–25.

McClelland, D. C. "Toward a Theory of Motive Acquisition." *American Psychologist*, 1965b, *20* (2), 321–333.

McClelland, D. C. *Assessing Human Motivation*. Morristown, N.J.: General Learning Press, 1971.

McClelland, D. C. "Testing for Competence Rather than for 'Intelligence.'" *American Psychologist*, 1973, *28* (1), 1–14.

McClelland, D. C. *Power: The Inner Experience*. New York: Irvington, 1975.

McClelland, D. C. *A Guide to Job Competency Assessment.* Boston: McBer, 1976.

McClelland, D. C. "Managing Motivation to Expand Human Freedom." *American Psychologist,* 1978, *33* (3), 201–210.

McClelland, D. C. "Is Personality Consistent?" In A. I. Rubin, J. Aronoff, A. M. Barclay, and R. A. Zucker (Eds.), *Further Explorations in Personality.* New York: Wiley, 1981.

McClelland, D. C., Atkinson, J. W., Clark, R. A., and Lowell, E. L. *The Achievement Motive.* New York: Appleton-Century-Crofts, 1953.

McClelland, D. C., Baldwin, A. L., Bronfenbrenner, U., and Strodtbeck, F. L. *Talent and Society.* New York: Van Nostrand, 1958.

McClelland, D. C., and Boyatzis, R. E. "Opportunities for Counselors from the Competency Assessment Movement." *Personnel and Guidance Journal,* 1980, *58,* 368–372.

McClelland, D. C., and Burnham, D. H. "Power Is the Great Motivator." *Harvard Business Review,* 1976, *54* (2), 100–111.

McClelland, D. C., Davis, W. N., Kalin, R., and Wanner, E. *The Drinking Man: Alcohol and Human Motivation.* New York: Free Press, 1972.

McClelland, D. C., and Winter, D. G. *Motivating Economic Achievement.* New York: Free Press, 1969.

Miron, D., and McClelland, D. C., "The Impact of Achievement Motivation Training on Small Business." *California Management Review,* 1979, *21* (4), 13–28.

Murray, H. *Explorations in Personality.* New York: Wiley, 1938.

Pettigrew, T. F. "Social Evaluation Theory: Convergences and Applications." In D. Levine (Ed.), *Nebraska Symposium on Motivation: 1967.* Lincoln: University of Nebraska Press, 1967.

Rotter, J. B. "Generalized Expectancies for Internal Versus External Control of Reinforcement." *Psychological Monographs,* 1966, *80* (Whole No. 609).

Spencer, L. M., Jr. "Identifying, Measuring, and Training Soft Skill Competencies Which Predict Performance in Professional, Managerial, and Human Service Jobs." Paper presented at Soft Skill Analysis Symposium, Department of the Army Training Development Institute, Fort Monroe, Va., Aug. 1979.

Spencer, L. M., Jr., Klemp, G. O., Jr., and Cullen, B. J. *Work Envir-*

*onment Questionnaires and Army Unit Effectiveness and Satis-
faction Measures.* Report to the Army Research Institute,
Washington, D.C., 1978.

Stewart, A. J. "Scoring Manual for Stages of Psychological Adaptation to the Environment." Unpublished manuscript, Department
of Psychology, Boston University, 1977.

Stewart, A. J., and Winter, D. G. "Self-Definition and Social Definition in Women." *Journal of Personality,* 1974, *42* (2), 238-259.

White, R. W. "Sense of Interpersonal Competence: Two Case Stu-
dies and Some Reflections on Origins." In R. W. White (Ed.),
The Study of Lives: Essays in Honor of Henry A. Murray. New
York: Atherton Press, 1963.

Williamson, S. A., and Schaalman, M. L. "Assessment Centers:
Theory, Practice, and Implications for Education." In G. O.
Klemp (Ed.), *The Assessment of Occupational Competence.*
Report to the National Institute of Education, Washington, D.C.,
1980.

Winter, D. G. *The Power Motive.* New York: Free Press, 1973.

Winter, D. G. "Business Leadership and the Liberal Arts." *New
Jersey Bell Journal,* 1978/1979, *1* (3), 41-48.

Winter, D. G. *An Introduction to LMET Theory and Research.*
Unpublished report to the U.S. Department of the Navy, Bureau
of Personnel, Aug. 1979.

Winter, D. G., and McClelland, D. C. "Thematic Analysis: An
Empirically Derived Measure of the Effects of Liberal Arts Education." *Journal of Educational Psychology,* 1978, *70* (1), 8-16.

Winter, D. G., McClelland, D. C., and Stewart, A. J. *A New Case for
the Liberal Arts: Assessing Institutional Goals and Student
Development.* San Francisco: Jossey-Bass, 1981.

Motivation and Performance in Presidential Candidates

8

 *David G. Winter*

For over two thousand years, philosophers have speculated about the motives of political leaders. Why do they seek office? How will they act when they assume power? Are their own expressed reasons, policies, and values a useful guide to their actions? Are most political leaders fundamentally alike, or are there different types of leaders, perhaps with different motives? In the *Republic*, Plato classified the motives of political leaders according to the kind of society in which they flourished: wisdom and justice in aristocracy; power and ambition in timocracy (rule according to property); avarice in oligarchy; aggressive protest in democracy; and caprice in tyranny.

In twentieth-century America, both political scientists and ordinary citizens alike estimate presidential candidates' motives

I would like to acknowledge the advice of Abigail J. Stewart in the design, execution, and analysis of this research, and the John and Mary R. Markle Foundation for financial support during the writing of the manuscript.

every four years and make predictions about their likely performance in office. The interesting thing is that these estimates and
predictions, whether based on campaign pledges, party platforms,
or prior records, are very often wrong. Thus Richard Nixon capped
a career of hunting down domestic Communists by toasting Mao
Zedong in Beijing's Great Hall of the People. Lyndon Johnson ran
as the peace candidate in 1964 and then drew the United States
deeper into its longest and bitterest war. The presidential performances of Harry Truman and Chester Arthur, among others, also
confounded the forecasters. It seems that in real political life, as well
as in the psychological laboratory, people's declared opinions and
previous responses do not always predict their "operant" or open-
ended behaviors in new situations that involve novel stimuli and
contingencies. Such a conclusion will scarcely be surprising to those
familiar with David McClelland's (1972, 1980) emphasis on the sur-
passing importance of the distinction between self-report or
"respondent" measures and operant behaviors.

Measuring Motivation in Politics

Since historical, ideological, and structural factors do not
offer a complete guide to people's political goals and performances,
there is ample scope for a good theory and measure of human motivation to increase our understanding and prediction of political life.
Over twenty years ago, McClelland (1961) first demonstrated how
objective and systematic measures of human motivation could help
to explain individual and national economic performance. Following his lead, we now turn to studying the relationship of the
achievement, affiliation, and power motives to political life.

Since politics is the ongoing story of how people get and use
power, it seems obvious that political life will easily arouse and
engage the power motive—both in the participants and, vicariously,
in the citizenry as audience and voters. Yet not every political leader
wants power. According to legend, the farmer Cincinnatus (519-439
B.C.) was given absolute power in order to defeat the enemies of
Rome; but after the victories he resigned his dictatorship and went
home to his farm. Others look to politics as the means of achieving
personal and national excellence. Not a few people find affiliation

fulfillment in the bonds of political association. For them, national or group identity brings personal identity; inclusion and unity validate the sense of being loved and wanted. At all levels, then—individual and collective, actor and observer—politics can engage the whole range of human motives. In Lasswell's (1930, Ch. 5) classic formulation, politics is thus private motives displaced onto public objects, rationalized in terms of public interest.

The specific focus of this chapter is the relationship between motivation and performance among the major candidates in the 1976 American presidential campaign, using motive imagery scores originally reported elsewhere (Winter, 1976). The present research is, however, only one of a wider series of studies of motive imagery in political leaders (see Donley and Winter, 1970, and Winter and Stewart, 1977a, on American presidents; Winter, 1980, on political leaders in southern Africa; and Hermann, 1980a, on members of the Soviet Politburo). These studies of political leaders who are already in power show a good deal of continuity with laboratory studies of human motivation. Power-motivated leaders, for example, are rated as strong, active, and prestigious. They like the power of office— perhaps too much, since they are also aggressive and warlike. Achievement-motivated American presidents choose expert advisers and are active, but also feel restless and are not especially happy in the job. Presidents who score high in the affiliation motive surround themselves with advisers like themselves (whose influence they are vulnerable to), and seek peace through accommodation and interdependence. Thus the achievement, affiliation, and power motives appear to affect the ways in which political leaders exercise power. Do they also predict the ways in which people seek power? In reporting the present research, I will suggest some preliminary answers to this question and also raise some broader issues of political motivation and political psychology.

While the 1976 presidential campaign was interesting from the perspective of American political history, it was also in many ways ideally suited for studying the relationships between the candidates' individual psychological characteristics and their behavior and performance in the campaign. Both major nominations were vigorously contested, especially in the Democratic party. Incumbent president Gerald Ford did not have the full legitimacy and presumptive campaign advantage that come from already having been elected president. There were no great, clearcut issues to divide the candidates (Bicker, 1979, p. 108). Changes in campaign financing laws and intraparty procedural rules (especially among the Democrats) made the 1976 campaign more "open" than previous ones— that is, more dependent on the actions and qualities of the individual candidates as persons and less dependent on negotiations and bargaining among party bosses. (Jimmy Carter's surprising success is the most obvious illustration of the effects of these changes. For example, he entered twenty-six out of twenty-seven presidential preference primaries, whereas in 1960 John F. Kennedy contested only seven out of sixteen primaries.) Compared to previous campaigns, then, the performance and outcomes of the 1976 campaign were probably more a function of individual characteristics and less a function of structural and other nonpsychological variables. Although there is already a good deal of expert political "lore" (Moore and Fraser, 1977; Barber, 1979) and some excellent narrative studies of the 1976 campaign (Barber, 1980; Witcover, 1977), apart from the usual public opinion polls there has been little systematic and quantitative study of the campaign. Yet the reports of the Federal Election Commission (FEC) and the information and numbers reported in the *Congressional Quarterly* are an excellent resource for deriving and defining systematic, quantitative variables that reflect the candidates' behavior.

Measuring Candidates' Motives. The motives of presidential candidates cannot, of course, be measured in the usual way—a group-administered modification of the Thematic Apperception Test (TAT) developed by McClelland and his colleagues over thirty-five years ago. Kaltenbach and McClelland (1958) and Browning and Jacob (1964) have tested influential local leaders and officials; Grupp (1975) has tested state bureaucrats; Rothman and Lichter (1980) have tested nationally prominent radical leaders; and other researchers have administered other psychological tests to state legislators and members of national parliaments. But it is probably impossible to give a TAT to any presidential candidate. Even if it were possible, to report and interpret the results would raise awkward ethical problems. Like all major political leaders, presidential candidates have a vested interest in maintaining an image and controlling information, especially "personal" information, about themselves. To overcome these problems of access and privacy in political psychology research, while at the same time maintaining scientific standards of objectivity and rigor, many researchers have measured personality "at a distance," using content analysis of publicly available verbal and written material, such as press conference transcripts and speeches (see Winter and Stewart, 1977a).

What material should be scored for presidential candidates? They come from different backgrounds, with varying prior opportunities and occasions for giving speeches and press conferences. To comply with various laws and procedures, however, all serious candidates for president must at some point officially declare their candidacy. Almost all candidates use this occasion to give a speech—articulating their fundamental concerns and aspirations as well as setting the tone and atmosphere for their campaign. (In 1976, California governor Jerry Brown was an exception. He casually declared his candidacy in the course of a rambling, informal conversation with reporters; hence he is not included in the present study.) Since the formal properties and situational contexts for these announcement speeches are fairly similar across all candidates, they are appropriate material for scoring motive imagery content. At present we do not know how comparable "set" speeches of this kind are to other speeches (such as ordinary campaign speeches) or to more spontaneous verbal imagery, nor do we know which kind of material gives the most valid predictions. As a start on answering this question, evidence of some empirical convergence between announcement speeches and inaugural addresses is presented below. Meanwhile, we can at least be certain that all candidates were measured in the "same" situation, and predictions will be made only to campaign behavior and not to other aspects of their political careers. These two considerations should maximize the validity of the measure of motive imagery by minimizing the effects of extraneous situational variables.

We consider here the fourteen major candidates in 1976—those (except Brown) who had qualified for matching funds from the Federal Election Commission. Once copies of the official announcement speeches had been secured from the national campaign headquarters of each candidate, they were then scored for achievement, affiliation, and power motive imagery using an adapted and simplified version of the traditional TAT scoring systems. (See Winter, 1981, and Winter and Healy, 1981, for a full discussion of the modified motive imagery scoring system. In brief, it drops the subcategories and scores only imagery. The sentence is the unit of scoring motive imagery, but contiguous sentences cannot be scored for the same motive except under certain special circumstances. A few further scoring conventions have been added to cover topics and issues not dealt with in the existing scoring manuals, and a few complexities of scoring definitions have been simplified.) To correct for varying speech lengths, the scores were expressed in terms of motive images per 1000 words and then transformed to standardized form. The average announcement speech was about 1350 words long. These standardized scores are shown in Table 1. Although they never embarked on a formal campaign, Hubert Humphrey and (to a lesser extent) Nelson Rockefeller were considered by some people to be possible candidates, and so are represented in the table by announcement speeches from earlier campaigns. The candidacy of Ellen McCormack raises some additional problems. Unlike most single-issue fringe candidates, she did enter eighteen out of the twenty-seven preference primaries and did qualify for matching federal funds; yet her candidacy was explicitly intended to dramatize opposition to abortion, and was not at all a traditionally organized effort. Her announcement speech is included in the standardization sample and in Table 1, but it would have been misleading to include her in any of the subsequent analyses.

    Portraits of the Candidates. What can the motive scores tell us about the candidates? Jimmy Carter, the ultimate winner in 1976, showed a relatively high achievement motive score, which is certainly consistent with his background in high technology engineering and small business. But was he an achievement-motivated president? While at the time of writing it is too early to make a definitive evaluation of his administration, as president he did act in ways consistent with his score: a cooperative negotiating style, in which he took moderate rather than extreme risks (the Camp David accords and the hostage negotiations with Iran); a desire for personal responsibility (to the point of excessive concern with details, many observers said); and a restless concern for excellence (moments after

Table 1. Standardized Motive Scores for the 1976 Candidates

Candidate	Achievement Imagery	Affiliation Imagery	Power Imagery
Democrats			
Birch Bayh	49	47	44
Lloyd Bentsen	59	57	39
Jimmy Carter	57	51	50
Frank Church	50	40	46
Fred Harris	33	58	71
Hubert Humphrey (1972)[a]	56	55	44
Ellen McCormack[a]	37	38	56
Henry Jackson	45	38	53
Terry Sanford	52	46	51
Milton Shapp	65	49	55
Sargent Shriver	44	66	49
Morris Udall	42	50	54
George Wallace	37	38	59
Republicans			
Gerald Ford	68	63	24
Ronald Reagan	56	38	53
Nelson Rockefeller (1968)[a]	52	65	52
Raw Scores: mean	5.31	2.58	8.41
standard deviation	3.13	2.13	2.18

Note: Scores expressed in terms of motive images per 1,000 words and then standardized with mean = 50 and standard deviaition = 10.
[a] Used for standardization purposes only; not included in subsequent analyses.

conceding defeat on November 4, 1980, he vowed to lead the "best transition" in history).

His predecessor in office, Gerald Ford, showed a high affiliation imagery score, which was also true of his inaugural and nomination acceptance speeches. (The high achievement imagery score was apparently unique to Ford's announcement speech.) While this profile fits with his image as a friendly, compliant person, it is also consistent with one of his most important political acts as president—the pardoning of Richard Nixon. This was done, we are told, out of sympathy for a man "who had suffered enough," and in compliance with the counsel of close advisors (high affiliation); at the same time, however, the pardoning seemed to display an almost reckless disregard for the political and judicial consequences (low power motive score).

In 1976, Ronald Reagan showed a pattern of high achievement and power motive scores, strikingly like that of Franklin D. Roosevelt's first inaugural address. At the time, I wrote as follows (Winter, 1976): "Although motives do not predict ideology or political beliefs, FDR and Reagan are alike in style. In their rhetoric, both emphasize that the nation's great heritage is threatened by crisis. Both emphasize that specific programs aren't enough; both call for a new philosophy of government . . . [preferring] to enunciate a new course in Olympian terms. It is not unreasonable to suppose that the first hundred days of a Reagan presidency would involve a New Deal of the Right." In his 1980-81 nomination acceptance and inaugural addresses, Reagan showed the same pattern, only more sharply defined. At this writing, it is too early to say whether the Roosevelt parallels will hold as Reagan tries to rally the United States to a new political "revelation"; still, in 1980-81 explicit comparisons to FDR were made by many observers and even by Reagan himself.

Finally, many 1976 candidates who scored high in power motive imagery and low to moderate in everything else were great crusaders in the mold of Woodrow Wilson, who showed the same motive pattern: Fred Harris, who crusaded against wealth and corporate economic power; Ellen McCormack, whose opposition to abortion apparently had little to do with babies as the object of an affiliation motive; George Wallace, who opposed the "establishment" in general and school integration via busing in particular; Henry Jackson, who echoed the more traditional crusades of the Cold War; and Morris Udall, whose crusades on behalf of traditional liberal causes were more muted and even nurturant, consistent with an affiliation motive only a little less strong than his power motive.

A Methodological Excursion: Do the Speeches Reflect Candidates' Enduring Personality? Many readers will wonder whether an announcement speech (or any other kind of political speech) really expresses the speaker's personality. In most cases, these speeches are written by speechwriters in a calculated attempt to emphasize salient cultural values and create the broadest possible appeal. Nevertheless, political leaders select their writers carefully, and writers know how to adapt to the personality and style of their clients. (See Crown, 1968, pp. 34-38, on the close relationship between John F. Kennedy and Theodore Sorenson; and Safire, 1975, pp. 316-326, on how writers adapt to different clients.) Before giving a really important speech, most political leaders review successive drafts, modifying the imagery until it feels appropriate and comfortable. (While working closely with Sorenson to prepare his inaugural address, for example, John F. Kennedy wrote out a late draft in his own handwriting, and actually inserted some scorable motive images into the penultimate typed draft.) Thus it is reasonable to assume that the verbal content of major speeches, at least, reflects what the speaker wants it to reflect. While factors such as audience, campaign issues, cultural values, and political stereotypes do affect speech content, they do not by themselves wholly determine motive imagery scores (see Hermann, 1980a, p. 344; Winter and Stewart, 1977a, p. 51). That is, it is possible to talk about topics such as the economy, the nation's heritage, even war and peace, from almost any policy perspective and either use or not use achievement, affiliation, or power images. The motive imagery scoring system seems to pick up the subtle shades of image or emphasis that reflect personal factors, rather than merely the common currency of cultural symbols or ideological stances.

Do the motive imagery scores derived from announcement speeches reflect stable attributes of the candidate? The original TAT motive measures have a reputation for low temporal reliability, although this is largely undeserved (McClelland, 1980), partly because it is due to artifacts induced by retesting (Winter and Stewart, 1977b). In any case, split-half reliability figures for motive imagery scores derived from press conferences reported by Hermann (1980a, 1980b) and Winter (1980) are in the highly respectable .70 range. From the present research, moreover, three separate estimates of the achievement, affiliation, and power motive imagery scores are available for Carter, Ford, and Reagan—from their 1976 announcement-of-candidacy speeches, their nomination acceptance speeches, and their inaugural addresses. The coefficient of concordance, or W, for these three estimates of nine scores (three motives each for three leaders) is .74, a magnitude that together with the other evidence suggests that the motive imagery scoring technique has quite satisfactory reliability credentials when applied at a distance to the verbal material of political leaders.

Motives and Campaign Behavior in 1976

In the psychological laboratory, motives are traditionally thought of as hypothetical constructs that have two kinds of effect: (1) They *guide* or *steer* behavior, selecting particular responses from an array of choices and directing the flow of action around obstacles toward the final goal of the motive. (2) They *energize* behavior, keeping subjects moving toward the goal, so that they usually persist longer after difficulty and failure, and generating emotional responses in anticipation of the goal and again after attaining it. In the laboratory these effects of motivated behavior are easy to define, observe, and measure; but in the excitement, complexity, and confusion of a presidential campaign, they may be much harder to isolate and study. While campaign journalists do an excellent job of reporting the "whole momentous story in all its human richness," in the words of one book advertisement, their accounts do lack the precision of operational definitions and quantitative measurements that are important to systematic research. Consider, for example, the notion of "persistence." Morris Udall stayed in the 1976 campaign until the Democratic convention, whereas Milton Shapp (and several other candidates) withdrew after the first few primaries. One could therefore say that Udall was more persistent than Shapp and the others. On the other hand, since Udall had done much better than Shapp in the early primaries, wouldn't we have expected him to stay in the race for a longer time anyway, regardless of whether he is a more "persistent" person? And since Jimmy Carter actually began his presidential quest in September 1972 (Witcover, 1977, pp. 117-118) wasn't he the most persistent of all?

To study the relationship of motive imagery to political behavior in the 1976 presidential campaign, then, it will be necessary to go beyond the usual terms of political journalism and political history. We must create a whole series of operationally defined, precisely measured variables to describe the candidates' behavior, so that we can then use the usual analytical and statistical methods of psychological research. In this task lies much of the fun of doing research in a new field like political psychology; and it is certainly an appropriate part of an essay honoring David McClelland, who has developed so many innovative nonreactive measures for studying the role of motivation in society and history. Data collection for this research thus ranged far and wide: from scrutiny of the *New York Times Index,* a close reading of fourteen months of a New Hampshire newspaper, and calculations with Federal Election Commission figures, to content analysis of biographical sketches. Still, some very important topics have *not* been measured adequately, especially many aspects of the organizational structure and style of a campaign, such as the following: media strategy and the use of media consultants, mobilization of volunteers, the use of telephone "banks" and voter canvassing, relations between headquarters and field staff, logistics and scheduling of the candidate, and so forth.

We are also inevitably faced with a small sample. In one sense, we are studying not a sample but rather the total population of major candidates for the presidency in 1976 (except Brown), although most readers will wish to generalize to the larger population of past and future candidates for political office. I will report many significant relationships, but because of the small sample size, I will also report some relationships that are only marginally significant or not significant at all. This seems appropriate in an exploratory venture, because I hope to arouse interest and suggest relationships that can be checked in future research as well as to demonstrate some striking convergence of results between laboratory and societal studies of motivation.

Popular Impressions of the Candidates. We begin with the everyday validity of these motive imagery scores. Do they also fit the more traditional impressions of the candidates in the minds of experienced observers and the general public? Because most of the major candidates were in fact unknown to most voters before the campaign, we did not use opinion poll responses, but rather turned to the brief standardized sketches written by the experienced and knowledgeable staff writers of the *Congressional Quarterly,* published before the campaign as *Candidates '76 (Congressional Quarterly,* 1976). All adjectives or phrases that suggested personality or behavioral traits were extracted from each sketch, placed in alphabetical order, and then judged for possible motive-related content by two judges familiar with the human motivation literature. Adjectives and phrases were assigned to one of the three motive clusters only when both judges, working independently, assigned them thus. The following three clusters resulted:

Achievement: able, effective, efficient, good judgment, hard-working, initiative, innovative, managerial, persistent, problem-solving, well-organized

Affiliation: charming, garrulous, loyal, well-liked

Power: aggressive, hard-hitting, hawkish, impressive, inspiring, moral fervor, strident, verbal baiting, verbal overkill

The judges also suggested a fourth cluster of words and phrases that seem to suggest "energy" or "surgency," but not necessarily any of the three motives:

Energy: energetic, exuberant, optimistic, upbeat, vitality, zest

A cluster was considered to describe a candidate if at least one of the words or phrases from that cluster was used in the *Congressional Quarterly* sketch of the candidate.

Table 2 presents the relationships between cluster descriptions and motive imagery scores. While the relationships are not very strong, each of the motive imagery scores is positively correlated with its corresponding cluster of descriptive words and, except in the case of achievement, negatively correlated with the descriptive clusters for the other motives. Achievement-motivated candidates are seen as affiliative, or friendly, as well as achieving. Perhaps this is an artifact of the small number of candidates who were seen as affiliative, or perhaps it is the result of the cooperative negotiating style associated with the achievement motive (Terhune, 1968). Power-motivated candidates are seen as energetic as well as aggressive and impressive. Seeking political office clearly involves power, so that it should be an especially attractive activity to power-motivated persons, leading them to more energetic and enthusiastic performance. Studies of American presidents, (Winter and Stewart, 1977a) and of

Table 2. Correlation of Motive Imagery with Adjective Descriptions
in Biographical Sketches (N = 13)

Adjective Cluster	Achievement Imagery	Affiliation Imagery	Power Imagery
Achievement	.38	−.25	−.07
Affiliation	.51⁺	.36	−.52⁺
Power	−.48⁺	−.37	.45
Energy	−.41	−.34	.43

$^+p < .10$

political leaders in southern Africa (Winter, 1980) also show relationships between power motives and judges' ratings of "activity." Perhaps, then, there is a deep, intrinsic, symbolic relationship between *social power* and *energy or physical power*, as Canetti (1962) suggests. Further evidence comes from Steele (1977), who found relationships between power motivation and adrenaline secretion.

Overall, these results suggest at least modest convergence between motive imagery scores and personality descriptions given by experienced observers. On the other hand, the correlations are low enough to suggest that judges' ratings do not measure exactly the same thing as does coding of operant verbal behavior, and that the two kinds of measures are therefore not interchangeable (see McClelland, 1958). Further illustration of this point comes from a study of southern Africa political leaders (Winter, 1980) in which motive imagery scores were not related to judges' ratings of the motives themselves, but were highly related to judges' ratings of the actions characteristic of the motives (much more highly, in fact, than were the judges' ratings of the motives). Judges' ratings and motive imagery scored at a distance certainly have discriminant validity; and the motive imagery scoring technique may thus have superior construct validity.

Persistence. Presidential candidates come and go throughout a campaign. In 1976, 617 days elapsed from the first formal announcement of candidacy (by Morris Udall, on November 23, 1974) to the nomination of Gerald Ford at the Republican convention (on August 19, 1976). With a chance for the presidency at stake, we would certainly expect power-motivated candidates to show persistence toward the power goal of the nomination. On the other hand, as I suggested at the beginning of this chapter, political life contains incentives for many motives. No doubt each motive will show its characteristic relationship to persistence in the quest for the presidency. From the extensive research on achievement motivation and risk taking (see Atkinson and Feather, 1966), we would expect candidates high in achievement motivation to persist only when the chances of success were moderate. When the probability of success is low, in contrast, they should be more likely to quit. Finally, affiliation-motivated candidates should react to primary defeats with a quick retreat because of their sensitivity to rejection (Boyatzis, 1973).

Table 3 presents the relationship of various measures of campaign persistence to the three motive imagery scores. For each candidate the dates of announcement and official withdrawal (taken from the *New York Times Index*) are counted from November 23, 1974, as Day 1; the length of the campaign is simply the difference between the two numbers. (Excluded from the withdrawal and length of campaign figures are nomination winners Carter and Ford, as well as Terry Sanford, who withdrew in large part for medical reasons.)

These three measures take no account of how well the candidates were doing or what their changing probability of success was—factors that should interact with some of the motives. How can the chances of success be calculated for any candidate at a particular time? In constructing the two measures used in Table 3, I proceeded as follows: Candidates' initial probability-of-success figures, before the first primary, were set at the proportion of choices they received in the most recent public opinion poll (the Gallup Poll reported on January 22-23, 1976). Calculations were done separately for Republicans and Democrats because of the different number of candidates; only active candidates were included; and .03 was arbitrarily set as a minimum probability-of-success figure. Every week during the primaries, these prior probability-of-success figures were moved toward the proportion of delegates that the candidates won during the week, with the distance moved equal to the discrepancy between

Table 3. Correlation of Motive Imagery with Campaign Timing
and Persistence

Variable	Achievement Imagery	Affiliation Imagery	Power Imagery
Beginning and End of Campaign			
Date of announcement[a] (N = 13)	.14	-.32	-.17
Date of withdrawal[a] (N = 10)	-.30	-.66*	.30
Length of campaign[b] (N = 10)	-.39	.16	.37
Persistence and Probability of Success			
Persistence at low probability of success[c] (N = 10)	-.80**	.08	.49
Average probability of success during active campaign (N = 10)	.55+	-.14	-.55+

[a] Counting November 23, 1974, as Day 1; Carter, Ford, and Sanford are not included in withdrawal or campaign length calculations.
[b] Date of withdrawal minus date of announcement.
[c] Proportion of weeks during active campaign where probability of success (as defined in text) was ≤ .10. The three candidates who withdrew before the first primary are not included.
+$p < .10$ *$p < .05$ **$p < .01$

the two figures multiplied by the proportion of delegates still to be selected. In other words, the results of each week's elections affect a candidate's chances, but this effect diminishes as the number of delegates chosen increases and the number still to be chosen declines. Thus, for example, Frank Church's successes in Nebraska, Oregon, and Rhode Island came so late in the campaign that they had little effect on his chances of overcoming Carter's strong early showing. (According to Barber, 1980, p. 185, Hamilton Jordan used "sequence points" in a similar way to allocate time and money among the primaries.)

From these constantly changing figures for each candidate, two measures were then created: (1) the proportion of weeks in a candidate's formal campaign (after the first primary up to withdrawal) in which the probability of success was below .10—a measure of persistence when chances of success are quite low—and (2) the average probability of success during the weeks of formal campaigning.

While only some of the relationships reported in Table 3 are significant at usual levels, the overall pattern of relationships is quite consistent with what we would expect on the basis of laboratory research on the three motives. Candidates high in achievement motivation tend to persist only under conditions of moderate risk— in this case, where the probability of success is .10 or greater. As soon as they win less than ten percent of the delegates for a week or two, they get out of the campaign. In other words they pay attention to feedback from the electorate. As a result their campaigns tend to be relatively short overall. Power-motivated candidates, by contrast, tend to stay in the race until the bitter end, and are apparently not much affected by information about how well they are doing or how slim their chances of success may be. This is consistent with the results of McClelland and Watson (1973) and McClelland and Teague (1975), who found that power-motivated men actually prefer high-risk situations, even though they may lose. Perhaps there is some impact or intrinsic sense of power even in losing an important contest, or perhaps the power motive is simply less affected by information about results than is the achievement motive. Finally, candidates who score high in affiliation motive imagery show a curious pattern: they tend to enter the race early, but are even more likely to quit early. Perhaps they are too much influenced by the opinions of their close friends and supporters, which they initially interpret as evidence of broad popular support for their candidacy. When a primary defeat or two demonstrates that they do not have widespread popular support and admiration, they quickly withdraw, perhaps as a defensive retreat from a threatening situation (see Winter and Stewart, 1977a, pp. 46-47).

Ideology and Money. Once a person decides to run for president, the next steps are to build a campaign organization and to build popular appeal by developing and articulating a position on the important issues. However ambiguous and contradictory that position may be, the candidate must still be perceived as saying something about the issues. Are candidates' motive imagery scores related to their ideological stances? Since it is often hard to pin down a candidate's exact position on the issues, an estimate can be made by identifying committed supporters of each candidate and asking them about their own positions. This technique assumes that most citizens consider candidates' issue positions important in deciding whom they will support (an assumption that receives some support from Nie, Verba, and Petrocik, 1976, and that seems especially true of primary campaigns), and that they can somehow determine or intuit the approximate positions of each candidate. During the 1976 campaign the New York Times-CBS Poll conducted such a survey (published February 13, 1976), placing each of the major candidates along a liberal-conservative dimension according to the average position of self-identified supporters of that candidate on six issues. I took the absolute score (distance from a neutral zero point in either a liberal or conservative direction) as a measure of extremism versus moderation. As shown in Table 4, achievement-motivated candidates tend to occupy a relatively moderate ideological position, which is consistent with laboratory findings connecting the achievement motive with a preference for moderate, calculated risks and an unobtrusive, sober personal style (McClelland, 1961, Ch. 8). Also as expected on the basis of studies cited above, the candidates scoring high in power motivation occupy the more extreme positions at both ends of the liberal-conservative spectrum.

Presidential campaign organizations are complex, evanescent, secretive, and often chaotic operations; thus they are not easily accessible for research. Because of election reforms enacted after the Watergate scandals, however, the 1976 candidates were required to make financial reports to the newly created Federal Election Commission (FEC). The Commission's published report on receipts and expenditures (Federal Election Commission, 1977) gives information sufficient to reconstruct at least the major financial outlines of each candidate's organization. Thus Table 4 also reports the relationships between motive imagery scores and several variables reflecting campaign finances.

Raising money is the first and most important aspect of campaign financing. How do the different candidates go about it? The FEC report breaks down receipts by size of contribution. Although there are no relationships between motives and the total amount raised, Table 4 shows that the motive imagery scores do predict the ways in which candidates raise money. Achievement-motivated candidates raise a relatively large proportion of their total funds from big contributions ($500 or more), and a relatively small proportion

Table 4. Correlation of Motive Imagery with Ideology and Fund-Raising

Variable	Achievement Imagery	Affiliation Imagery	Power Imagery
Moderate[a] ideological position (N = 10)	.49	–.20	–.53[+]
Fund-raising (N = 13):			
Percent funds raised in contributions ⩽ $100	–.70**	–.26	.58*
Percent funds raised in contributions ⩾ $500	.70**	.38	–.72**
Use of own funds	.08	.59*	.22
Deficit size at end of campaign	–.29	.36	.03
More than one authorized campaign committee (N = 13)	–.21	.18	.53[+]

[a]Absolute distance from neutral zero point on liberal-conservative scale. New York Times-CBS Poll reported February 13, 1976.

[+]$p < .10$ *$p < .05$ **$p < .01$

from small contributions ($100 or less). Since it is probably more efficient to raise campaign funds from a few large contributors rather than many small contributors, this pattern may reflect an efficiency orientation characteristic of the achievement motive. It may also reflect the application of market principles in the political arena. That is, individuals and corporations generally give large contributions in the implicit anticipation of a later quid pro quo; perhaps achievement-motivated candidates respond like the successful entrepreneurs they are at heart, soliciting present support in anticipation of future political services in order to accumulate the capital necessary to finance a successful political campaign. Taking an entrepreneurial perspective, this probably appears as a rational, cooperative bargain struck in the mutual self-interest of both parties (see Terhune, 1968; Winter and Stewart, 1977a, pp. 46-47). Politics, in other words, is just another business. From the "civic" perspective of American political life, however, the pattern may appear as corrupt or at least indecent—as in the 1972 campaign of highly achievement-motivated Richard Nixon or the nineteenth-century campaigns of achievement-motivated Ulysses S. Grant.

Power-motivated candidates emphasize smaller contributions. These are more likely to be a demonstration of support or an expression of emotional arousal than a gift in anticipation of future services. In a strictly business sense, the small-contribution strategy is not as efficient, but from the political point of view, it recognizes that fund-raising can be an integral part of gathering and mobilizing voter support. An appeal for a vote is probably more likely to "stick" if it also involves an appeal for at least a small contribution. According to well-known principles of cognitive dissonance, moreover, people who have made a contribution should also be likely to proselytize on behalf of "their" candidate. Thus the power-motivated strategy expands and mobilizes support, both by increasing the number of "campaign workers" and by bringing out the committed voters. Under the laws in force for the 1976 campaign, finally, individual contributions were matched with federal funds only up to the amount of $250. By concentrating on these smaller contributions, the power-motivated candidates thus generated the maximum possible additional support from the government, while at the same time keeping themselves relatively independent of the demands of large contributors for later political services. Thus their campaign financial strategy is, overall, effective from a *political* perspective, even if it is not as fiscally efficient as the large contribution strategy of the achievement-motivated candidates.

The preference of power-motivated candidates for alliance with institutions (such as the government, via FEC matching funds) is also reflected in their tendency to have more than one authorized campaign committee—for one candidate, as many as thirty-eight separate regional committees. Perhaps the major differences between one central organization and many regional committees are that in the latter case the total effort seems larger and more impressive, while at the same time more workers feel deeply involved. These themes of direct influence, autonomy from powerful others, and institutional connection and proliferation are also characteristic of laboratory studies of the power motive (see Winter, 1973; Winter and Stewart, 1977a; McClelland, 1975).

Affiliation-motivated candidates tend to use their own funds to finance at least part of their campaign. Are they trying, literally, to "buy" influence and perhaps also self-esteem? This would be consistent with the defensive, threat-oriented profile of the affiliation motive sketched by Boyatzis (1973). Although personal funds may be useful as "seed money" at the beginning of a campaign, they are obviously not enough to pay for more than a tiny fraction of the total cost. Relying on personal funds may therefore reflect some lack of realism about political finances—a possibility that is further strengthened by the tendency for affiliation-motivated candidates to end their primary campaigns with relatively large deficits. (To pay off these deficits, in turn, they may later have to accept money from special interest groups, perhaps leading to the kinds of political scandal characteristic of affiliation-motivated presidents, as Winter and Stewart, 1977a, p. 57, reported.) Thus although the relationships between the affiliation motive and campaign financing are not strong, they are at least consistent with other research on affiliation motivation.

Effort in New Hampshire. The New Hampshire presidential primary, traditionally the first in the nation, is certainly the first milestone (and perhaps the most important one) of the long primary campaign (see Matthews, 1979, pp. 64–66; Witcover, 1977, Ch. 16). For all the "special characteristics" of New Hampshire voters, and for all of the media "overkill" surrounding the New Hampshire primary, it is the first actual test of candidates' relative strength. (Matthews, 1979, p. 65, points out that in 1976 the New Hampshire primary drew 2.63 network television stories per delegate selected, whereas the later New York primary drew .07 stories per delegate.) Although the earlier Iowa party caucuses stole some of the spotlight in 1976, and more in 1980, New Hampshire is still the beginning of the winnowing process: The candidate who wins (or who does unexpectedly well) gains considerable momentum and important media coverage, while candidates who have not done well begin to drop out of the race. In recent decades, several successful campaigns were really launched in New Hampshire (Eisenhower in 1952, McGovern in 1972), while more than one fast-sailing effort has foundered there (Johnson in 1968, Muskie in 1972). Henry Jackson later decided that his staying out of the New Hampshire primary in order to concentrate on the large industrial states whose primaries were later put him at a disadvantage that he was never able to make up (Witcover, 1977, pp. 203–204).

What does it take to do well in New Hampshire? Money, obviously; and time. Witcover (p. 246) estimated that New Hampshire "is ideal for the candidate who is trying to launch a campaign on a shoestring, because it is a place where time and energy can effectively overcome lack of money. [However,] it was imperative for any candidate serious about New Hampshire . . . not simply to go there but to go there often, and to work the voters as if they were constituents in a precinct or neighborhood election." Two simple indexes of the effort that candidates devoted to the New Hampshire primary campaign are used in Table 5. First, based on the FEC report, how much money did the candidate spend in New Hampshire? (These figures greatly underestimate the New Hampshire media expenses, however, because most New Hampshire television comes from Boston, so that for most candidates, television expenses were allocated to the later and larger Massachusetts primary totals.) Second, how much time did the candidate spend in New Hampshire? This was measured by the number of days (whole or part) that the candidate spent in New Hampshire from January 1, 1975, through the day before the primary (February 23, 1976), based on close study of the state edition of the *Manchester Union-Leader,* the principal newspaper of the state. (Although the *Union-Leader* has pronounced extreme editorial views, it seems to report the physical presence of all candidates objectively.)

Table 5 presents the relationships of the motive imagery scores to these measures. The numbers are especially small here because not all major candidates entered the New Hampshire primary; those who did not were naturally excluded from these analyses. The financial measures require some additional comment. In general, the candidates who spent the most money in New Hampshire were those who had the most money to spend during that time, the FEC limit of $218,200 for the state notwithstanding. (For the nine major candidates on the ballot, the correlation between New Hampshire expenditure and national receipts through February 29, 1976, is .89, $p = .001$). Thus although it initially appears that achievement motivation tends to predict spending a lot of money, and affiliation motivation predicts spending little money in New Hampshire, the former relationship tends to wash out when New Hampshire expenditures are corrected (by regression on total receipts) for total

Table 5. Correlation of Motive Imagery with New Hampshire
Campaign Strategy (N = 7)

Variable	Achievement Imagery	Affiliation Imagery	Power Imagery
Total expenditures in New Hampshire campaign	.62	-.59	-.33
Allocation of available funds to New Hampshire campaign[a]	.12	-.67[+]	.04
Time spent in New Hampshire, 1/1/75 through 2/23/76	-.52	-.30	.71[+]
Partial Correlations			
Allocation of funds, given time spent in New Hampshire	.76[+]	-.67	-.86*
Time spent in New Hampshire, given allocation of funds	-.89*	.29	.93**

[a]Funds spent in New Hampshire campaign, corrected for regression on total
receipts available through February 29, 1976.
[+]$p < .10$ *$p < .05$ **$p < .01$

funds available. Power motivation is significantly related to the
number of days the candidate actually spends in New Hampshire,
while the other two motives show nonsignificant but negative
correlations.

Studies of the New Hampshire primary are further complicated by the high correlation between allocation of available funds
(that is, money spent given the total receipts available) and time
spent in the state ($r = .68$). Regardless of Witcover's comments
above, the use of time and (available) money go together rather
closely in New Hampshire. Still, by the use of partial correlations, it
is possible to determine the *relative* emphasis on time versus money
and to relate these two relative emphases to motive imagery scores.
When this is done, as shown at the bottom of Table 5, a much clearer
and symmetrical pattern of relationships emerges. Achievement-
motivated candidates, as we might expect from their entrepreneurial
efficiency orientation, tend to spend money rather than time in New
Hampshire. Power-motivated candidates, consistent with their preferences for direct interpersonal influence and organization-building,

tend to spend time rather than money. Affiliation-motivated candidates spend relatively little money, but there is no relationship to spending time.

Which works better, time or money? Both the adjusted and unadjusted measures of money spent in New Hampshire correlate above .80 ($p < .05$ in each case) with actual performance in the election, as measured by number of votes received minus the number expected on the basis of the total party vote and the number of party candidates. (These corrections were necessary because of the larger number of Republican voters and the larger number of Democratic candidates.) Time spent in New Hampshire correlates only .47 with performance in the primary. Was Witcover wrong, then, when he said that time and energy can overcome lack of money in New Hampshire? Perhaps not, for time spent up through August 31, 1975—almost six months before the primary—does correlate significantly with performance ($r = .77$, $p < .05$). Apparently the time that is wisely spent in New Hampshire is *early* time, recruiting and building an effective organization, rather than time spent in personal appearances and a media blitz just before the election. As always, money seems to be important. (Ralph Nader's Public Citizens Congress Watch reported after the 1980 elections, for example, that the candidate who spent the greater amount of money won in thirty-five out of forty-two Congressional elections in which no incumbent ran. Chi-square for this proportion is 18.67, $p < .001$.)

Motives and American Political Life

Our findings up to this point suggest a clear pattern of political behavior associated with each of the three major motives. Achievement-motivated candidates seem to approach politics with the brisk efficiency, moderation, and calculation of an effective business person or entrepreneur. Power-motivated candidates appear to enjoy the political process for its own sake, relishing direct interpersonal influence and organization-building, often in the service of more extreme ideological positions. Affiliation-motivated candidates emerge as impressionable and defensive. (Unfortunately we were not able to construct variables that might reflect the more gregarious, outgoing components of the affiliation motive, behaviors which in the laboratory emerge at least under "safe" conditions of perceived agreement and liking from others.)

Who Gets Elected? We now raise some larger questions about the role of motivation in the American political system. The most obvious and, to many readers, the most interesting question is: Which motive pattern is the most successful? What motives win elections? Obviously election victories depend on many factors besides the candidates' motive profiles. Perhaps the New Hampshire results give the purest test of motive profile effects in 1976, because they were the first actual voting returns and were therefore less likely to be affected by other, nonmotivational influences such as media emphasis and the structural dynamics of the campaign process. (Yet even here, candidates can actively shape some of these forces. For example, we might expect that power-motivated candidates would be more adept at using the media to their own advantage, just as power-motivated presidents Franklin Roosevelt and John F. Kennedy surely were.)

In any case the New Hampshire results are straightforward: Only achievement motivation is significantly correlated ($r = .77$, $p < .05$) with electoral performance, using the adjusted measure described above. How general is such a relationship? Do achievement-oriented candidates always tend to do better in elections? Among the nine major Democratic candidates who stayed in the race for at least two primaries, a similar measure of performance aggregated across all primaries for which they actively campaigned shows a much lower correlation with achievement motivation ($r = .48$, p not significant), and no relationships to the other motives. Interestingly enough, the achievement motive/performance relationship is much stronger ($r = .89$) for small states, where personal effort and organization are presumably more important than "media presence" and charisma.

It seems as though 1976 was a year in which achievement-motivated candidates had a slight edge, but other elections, in other years, might favor other motives. Barber (1980) argues that there is a regular cycle in American presidential elections: from conscience (achievement?) to conciliation (affiliation?), then to conflict (power?), and finally back to conscience again. If these three social motives are coordinated with Barber's stages in the way I suggest, then we would expect the motivational advantage to proceed in a parallel cycle. Such a comprehensive theory could be tested by, say, scoring the nomination acceptance speeches of the major candidates for several past elections. The winning candidate should have been relatively more achievement-motivated in the "conscience" elections of 1916, 1940, and 1964, as well as in 1976. In the "conciliation" elections of 1920, 1932, 1956, and 1968 (also 1980?), the advantage should have rested with the more affiliative candidate. Finally, the candidate higher in power motive imagery should have won in the "conflict" elections, such as 1900, 1948, 1960, and 1972. (In the 1980 New Hampshire primary election, both affiliation and achievement imagery scores were correlated, r's = .49 and .67, respectively, with an adjusted measure of election performance, which provides some support for Barber's general notion of a cyclic alternation of campaign themes.)

Other theories can be constructed to specify the motivational factors that might be relevant to a particular election. Perhaps the advantage lies with the candidate whose overall motive profile is closest to that of the nation as a whole—as measured, for example, by the American motivational "time series" taken from cultural documents reported by McClelland (1975, Appendix 4). Yet even this hypothesis is too simple. At any one time, American culture does not show a single monolithic motivational profile. Rather, different subgroups—classes, ages, sexes, levels of education—are likely to have different motive profiles, as Inkeles and Levinson (1969) have persuasively argued. Thus, given a choice among several candidates, each subgroup might be drawn toward the candidate with the most similar (or perhaps the most complementary or even "opposite") motive profile. The actual election results would then depend upon the size and voter turnout of each subgroup, aggregated across all subgroups. Models incorporating these ideas could be tested for the late 1950s and the late 1970s, with data about motive profiles of different subgroups taken from the National Sample Surveys carried out during those eras (see Veroff, Depner, Kulka, and Douvan, 1980) and data on candidate preference of different subgroups from the compilation by Miller, Miller, and Schneider (1980). Adding other known influences on voting decisions, such as party identification and perceived competence of the candidates and parties (see Kinder and Kiewiet, 1979), should further improve the predictive power of the model.

The Best of Motives. Even though different motives and combinations of motives may be successful in different elections, many readers will still ask: What is the best combination or profile of motives for a political leader? It would be pleasant to suggest, for example, that high power motivation, or perhaps high scores on all three motives, would make the "best" president or political leader. McClelland (1975, Ch. 8 and 9) has suggested, along these lines, that the "imperial motive pattern"—high power motivation, which is both greater than affiliation motivation and also combined with self-control or "activity inhibition"—characterizes successful managers and other empire builders. At least for presidents, however, I think that the answer is more complex and even confusing. Previous research has suggested that each of three social motives is associated with actions and outcomes that are "good" *and* "bad." The power-motivated president may become a hero, highly rated by historians, but may also involve the country in imperial ventures, including war. From the administration of affiliation-motivated presidents come not only arms limitation agreements with other major powers, but also scandals that mark their places in history with disgrace. Finally, presidents scoring high in achievement motivation bring to the job a concern for technical competence, but in the end may be impatient, frustrated, and bitter, ineffective at articulating goals and mobilizing public opinion, and therefore unable to translate their concern for competence into effective political action.

In the end, our search for a single ideal motive or motive profile in political life may be not only an oversimplification but even a scientific illusion. The question of ideal political motives is really a question about our own values. Different motives tend toward different outcomes; the motives that make a "great" president or other leader, then, are the motives that lead to whatever outcomes we like and value. These change, both with time and with revisionist historical sophistication. Political performances that look important and heroic at the high noon of empire may appear different in an age of ambiguity, limits, and choices.

Why study the motives of political leaders, then? As scientists, of course, we wish to understand the motivational and other psychological factors that mediate their goal setting, choices, and responses to events. As citizens, however, we can use information about candidates' motives just as we use any other information about the candidates: that is, to "predict" their likely performance in office. Like most political leaders, American presidents are really chosen at a distance, "by a mass electorate which knows them only faintly at second hand" (Matthews, 1979, p. 77). Any reliable and valid method of studying their motives, necessarily also at a distance, could only improve the electorate's chances of making successful predictions and thereby intelligently and instrumentally maximizing their values through their political choices. Thus the study of motives in politics, as David McClelland (1978) has argued regarding the study of motives in other areas, can expand both human knowledge and also human freedom.

References

Atkinson, J. W., and Feather, N. T. (Eds.). *A Theory of Achievement Motivation.* New York: Wiley, 1966.
Barber, J. D. (Ed.). *Race for the Presidency: The Media and the Nominating Process.* Englewood Cliffs, N.J.: Prentice-Hall, 1979.
Barber, J. D. *The Pulse of Politics: Electing Presidents in the Media Age.* New York: Norton, 1980.
Bicker, W. E. "Network Television News and the 1976 Presidential Primaries: A Look from the Networks' Side of the Camera." In J. D. Barber (Ed.), *Race for the Presidency: The Media and the Nominating Process.* Englewood Cliffs, N.J.: Prentice-Hall, 1979.
Boyatzis, R. E. "Affiliation Motivation." In D. C. McClelland and R. S. Steele (Eds.), *Human Motivation: A Book of Readings.* Morristown, N.J.: General Learning Press, 1973.
Browning, R. P., and Jacob, H. "Power Motivation and the Political Personality." *Public Opinion Quarterly,* 1964, *28,* 75-90.
Canetti, E. *Crowds and Power.* New York: Viking, 1962.
Congressional Quarterly: Candidates: '76. Washington, D.C.: Congressional Quarterly, 1976.
Crown, J. T. *The Kennedy Literature: A Bibliographical Essay on John F. Kennedy.* New York: New York University Press, 1968.
Donley, R. E., and Winter, D. G. "Measuring the Motives of Public

Officials at a Distance: An Exploratory Study of American Presidents." *Behavioral Science,* 1970, *15,* 227-236.

Federal Election Commission. *1976 Presidential Campaign Receipts and Expenditures.* FEC Disclosure Series No. 7. Washington, D.C.: Federal Election Commission, 1977.

Grupp, F. "The Power Motive in the American State Bureaucracy." Unpublished manuscript, University of Connecticut, 1975.

Hermann, M. G. "Assessing the Personalities of Soviet Politburo Members." *Personality and Social Psychology Bulletin,* 1980a, *6,* 332-352.

Hermann, M. G. "Examining Foreign Policy Behavior Using the Personal Characteristics of Political Leaders." *International Studies Quarterly* 1980b, *24,* 7-46.

Inkeles, A., and Levinson, D. J. "National Character: The Study of Modal Personality and Sociocultural Systems." In G. Lindzey and E. Aronson (Eds.), *Handbook of Social Psychology.* Vol. 4. (Rev. ed.) Reading, Mass.: Addison-Wesley, 1969.

Kaltenbach, J. E., and McClelland, D. C. "Achievement and Social Status in Three Small Communities." In D.C. McClelland and others (Eds.), *Talent and Society.* New York: Van Nostrand, 1958.

Kinder, D. R., and Kiewiet, C. R. "Economic Discontent and Political Behavior: The Role of Personal Grievance and Collective Economic Judgments in Congressional Voting." *American Political Science Review,* 1979, *23,* 495-527.

Lasswell, H. *Psychopathology and Politics.* Chicago: University of Chicago Press, 1930.

McClelland, D. C. "Methods of Measuring Human Motivation." In J. W. Atkinson (Ed.), *Motives in Fantasy, Action, and Society.* New York: Van Nostrand, 1958.

McClelland, D. C. *The Achieving Society.* New York: Van Nostrand, 1961.

McClelland, D. C. "Opinions Predict Opinions: So What Else Is New?" *Journal of Consulting and Clinical Psychology,* 1972, *38,* 325-326.

McClelland, D. C. *Power: the Inner Experience.* New York: Irvington, 1975.

McClelland, D. C. "Managing Motivation to Expand Human Freedom." *American Psychologist,* 1978, *33,* 201-210.

McClelland, D. C. "Motive Dispositions: The Merits of Operant and Respondent Measures." In L. Wheeler (Ed.), *Review of Personality and Social Psychology.* Vol. 1. Beverly Hills, Calif.: Sage, 1980.

McClelland, D. C., and Teague, G. "Predicting Risk Preferences Among Power-Related Tasks." *Journal of Personality,* 1975, *43,* 266-285.

McClelland, D. C., and Watson, R. I., Jr. "Power Motivation and Risk-Taking Behavior." *Journal of Personality,* 1973, *41,* 121-139.

Matthews, D. R. "'Winnowing': The News Media and the 1976 Presidential Nominations." In J. D. Barber (Ed.), *Race for the Presidency: The Media and the Nominating Process.* Englewood Cliffs, N.J.: Prentice-Hall, 1979.

Miller, W. G., Miller, A. E., and Schneider, E. J. *American National Election Statistics Data Source Book 1952-1978.* Cambridge, Mass.: Harvard University Press, 1980.

Moore, J., and Fraser, J. (Eds.). *Campaign for President: The Managers Look at '76.* Cambridge, Mass.: Ballinger, 1977.

Nie, N. H., Verba, S., and Petrocik, J. R. *The Changing American Voter.* Cambridge, Mass.: Harvard University Press, 1976.

Rothman, A., and Lichter, S. R. "Personality Development and Political Dissent: A Reassessment of the New Left." *Journal of Political and Military Sociology,* 1980, *8,* 191-204.

Safire, W. *Before the Fall: An Inside View of the Pre-Watergate White House.* New York: Belmont Tower Books, 1975.

Steele, R. S. "Power Motivation, Activation, and Inspirational Speeches." *Journal of Personality,* 1977, *45,* 53-64.

Terhune, K. W. "Motives, Situation, and Interpersonal Conflict within Prisoner's Dilemma." *Journal of Personality and Social Psychology Monograph Supplement,* 1968, *8* (3), Part 2.

Veroff, J. Depner, C. Kulka, R., and Douvan, E. "Comparison of American Motives: 1957 Versus 1976." *Journal of Personality and Social Psychology,* 1980, *39,* 1249-1262.

Winter, D. G. *The Power Motive.* New York: Free Press, 1973.

Winter, D. G. "Why the Candidates Run." *Psychology Today,* 1976, *10* (2), 45-49, 92.

Winter, D. G. "Measuring the Motives of Southern Africa Political Leaders at a Distance." *Political Psychology,* 1980 *2* (2), 75-85.

Winter, D. G. *Revised Manual for Scoring Motive Imagery in Running Text.* Unpublished manuscript, Wesleyan University, 1981.

Winter, D. G., and Healy, J. M., Jr. "Scoring Human Motives in Running Text: Reliability, Validity, and Convergence." Paper presented at the 89th annual meeting of the American Psychological Association, Los Angeles, August 1981.

Winter, D. G., and Stewart, A. J. "Content Analysis as a Method of Studying Political Leaders." In M. G. Hermann (Ed.), *A Psychological Examination of Political Leaders.* New York: Free Press, 1977a.

Winter, D. G., and Stewart, A. J. "Power Motive Reliability as a Function of Retest Instructions." *Journal of Consulting and Clinical Psychology,* 1977b, *45,* 435–440.

Witcover, J. *Marathon: The Pursuit of the Presidency 1972–1976.* New York: New American Library, 1977.

Motive Modification

9

Heinz Heckhausen
Siegbert Krug

Students of motivation have not only been interested in describing and explaining behavioral phenomena but also in trying to find suitable applications for their findings. Early on, David McClelland pointed to the significant role played by the achievement motive in individual career choices and national economic growth. Therefore it seemed reasonable to try to apply his insight to other practical situations. Among the applied approaches, surely the most significant was the attempt to modify motives. Here too McClelland did the pioneer work and helped to take this approach further.

Programs for altering motives have passed through three distinct waves. In each case, more precise definition of theoretical constructs has also led to refinement and modification of the intervention techniques. The theoretical basis and methodology for the original training courses (given during the early and middle 1960s) were not systematically derived from the then current theory of achievement motivation. Rather they were based on heterogeneous principles that had proven useful in modifying many different types of behavior. The second wave began at the end of the 1960s. Although new programs incorporated some aspects of the earlier procedures, they introduced significant changes. They were more closely tied to the theory of achievement motivation of that day, particularly with respect to its elaboration in terms of causal attribution theory. The third wave began in the late 1970s. It incorporated all of these aspects into a unified approach. Beginning with Heckhausen's (1972, 1975) cognitive theory of motivation, reference norms for performance evaluation became the central focus of programs for altering the behavior of teachers and students as well as for classroom management.

Findings from these new training programs permitted a number of conclusions about specific program content and also identified the indispensable components of the programs. Beyond that they raised a number of new questions about the effects of social interventions, the personality and developmental aspects of the achievement motive, optimal intervention at various age levels and, last but not least, ethical justifications for intervention.

The First Wave: Eclecticism

Courses for Adults. In 1961 McClelland began to design and carry out motive-training programs. This fact is noteworthy not just because it represents a new departure in the discipline. Its more surprising aspect is that McClelland was willing to move in this direction despite his earlier claim that the achievement motive represented a stable personality disposition (McClelland, 1958). How could it possibly be changed in adults?

Fortunately McClelland did not rely on what he had said earlier about the dispositional stability of this motive. Apparently he felt a need to do something to help people achieve those motivational characteristics that he was convinced contributed to their economic improvement. This desire to help others was more important than theoretical consistency. The theoretical justification for carrying out the training courses came later, in 1965, long after the courses had been completed. As a matter of fact, in his justification McClelland relied more on the optimism of missionaries, therapists, idealists, and political leaders than on any theoretical assumptions about motivation. Beyond that, he examined all areas of psychology that had achieved behavioral change in one way or another. The outcome was a highly eclectic and general framework, hardly convincing theoretically but rather effective in its application.

Strengthening a motive (that is, moving its position up in the hierarchy) requires: (1) extending, strengthening, and improving the affective network, (2) clearly conceptualizing the network, (3) tying the network to everyday life, and (4) relating the new network to the superordinate associative clusters, like the self, reality, and cultural values. Under these four headings McClelland (1965) developed a total of twelve propositions for a training program encompassing the achievement syndrome, self-study, goal setting, and interpersonal supports.

A detailed description of the implementation in terms of specific program content is presented by McClelland and Winter (1969). The courses, which were held in Southern India, were designed to lay the basis for more effective entrepreneurial behavior through increased achievement motivation. With respect to the managerial activities the courses were an unquestioned success. What remained unclear was the effect on the motive. Did it really change as a function of the training as the theory postulated? Immediately after the course the n Achievement scores reached levels that were double the base level. However, since the course participants had been trained in writing achievement-related Thematic Apperception Test (TAT) stories and had familiarized themselves with the coding key, the increased n Ach scores are more likely to reflect the effects of learning, memory, and social desirability than genuine motive change. The training program had invalidated the TAT procedure as an assessment technique. These inflated TAT scores also failed to distinguish between active and inactive participants after the course. A few years later, after it had been shown that training courses for students were relatively unsuccessful—in contrast to those for businessmen—McClelland concluded that "it is parsimonious and more theoretically sound to conclude that achievement motivation training courses improve school learning by improving classroom and life management skills rather than by changing n Ach levels directly" (1972, p. 145).

A reinterpretation of the TAT protocols from the Indian training courses undertaken by Heckhausen (1971), using his scoring key for "hope for success" (HS) and "fear of failure" (FF), showed that McClelland may have been too hasty in his conclusion. Because the participants had no knowledge of this scoring key they could not have made their stories conform to it. Thus it was possible to establish the levels of these two opposing motive tendencies immediately before the course and two to three years later. (The TAT protocols obtained immediately after the course were unfortunately lost.) This new interpretation of the TAT material showed a difference in the motive between those participants who became active after the course and those who remained inactive. The greatest likelihood of success after the course was demonstrated by those who had previously shown some degree of fear of failure (FF > HS), particularly if they were also in a position that required them to make economic decisions. Two or three years later they had changed considerably and were dominant in the hope-of-success motive (HS > FF). On the other hand, those who started the course with some confidence of success as part of their achievement motive left some confidence of success as part of their achievement motive left it rather inactive and, if they also held a position requiring decision making, even with a failure motive that had become dominant (see Figure 1).

Varga (1977), who on behalf of the United Nations Industrial Development Organization (UNIDO) evaluated a number of training courses in Indonesia, Pakistan, Persia, and Poland, was able to confirm Heckhausen's findings, that is, to show relationships between the change in motive, a dominant failure motive prior to the course, and economic activity after the course.

Figure 1. Change of Net Hope Scores (HS-FF) Before and After *n*-Ach Training. (Participants were labeled "changers" or "inactives" after training; *a* is a reanalysis of data from courses in India (McClelland and Winter, 1969) by Heckhausen, 1971, p. 258; *b* shows results of the UNIDO courses in Indonesia, Pakistan, Iran, and Poland by Varga, 1977, p. 193.)

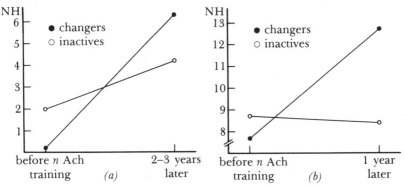

These positive reassessments cannot completely refute McClelland's assertion that the courses simply conveyed better life skills, because without knowing the participants' motive scores immediately after the course, it is impossible to say when the actual change in motive occurred. The possibilities are as follows: (1) The motive modification occurred during the course; under favorable job conditions the newly acquired motive manifested itself, resulting in increased economic activity and entrepreneurial success. (2) The course had no effect on the motive, but participants acquired managerial skills; under favorable job conditions these skills were applied and led to economic success, which in turn strengthened self-confidence, encouraged achievement-oriented thinking, and finally resulted in greater achievement motivation.

Courses for Students. It is not clear how the original training courses for businessmen achieved their effects. Originally McClelland (1965) wanted to eliminate the twelve input variables one by one in order to identify which ones were essential and which were not. This never happened. Finally it became clear that the importance of the achievement motive for effective entrepreneurial behavior had been overestimated. Greater attention was focused on other motives like power and affiliation and their influence on behavior (McClelland, 1975: McClelland and Burnham, 1976).

Nevertheless, the training programs for students continued their steady development. They included the program developed by Kolb (1965), who tried to modify the motives and academic performance of underachievers in accordance with McClelland's assumptions. The program was successful for some subgroups. Compared to a control group that had only participated in a special tutoring program, program participants coming from a higher socioeconomic level profited more from the motive-enhancing program than did participants from a lower socioeconomic level.

Various investigators in the McClelland camp have run courses for students. Such courses were geared to local needs and lasted from three to ten days, or at most from three to four weeks. They ran outside the normal school program on weekends or during vacation periods. These courses were similar to the training programs for managers in their structure and content. One course also included the training components related to achievement syndrome, self-study, goal setting, and interpersonal supports. Differences in the outcomes of the programs were attributed to the total available training time and the age of the participating students (see Alschuler, Tabor, and McIntyre, 1970; McClelland and Alschuler, 1971; McClelland, 1972; Alschuler, 1973).

But again these training programs did not identify the processes responsible for initiating motive modification or the aspects of the training that were particularly effective. How little is known about this is reflected in Smith and Troth (1975), who concluded after reviewing the relevant literature that successful training is (1) well structured, (2) at least one semester in length, (3) appropriate to the needs of the students, (4) focused on cognitive as well as affective processes, and (5) therapeutic, reflecting warmth and genuineness.

The Second Wave: Some Elaboration

Despite, or perhaps because of, the many unanswered questions raised by the student training, others took up McClelland's ideas and developed them further, tying the relevant training components more closely to theory development. At the theoretical level, specific cognitive (primarily attributional) processes were now thought to play a determining role. At the practical level, the training programs began to be incorporated in the ongoing school curricula.

Experimental Studies. Stamps (1973) tried to manipulate the behavior of fourth-, fifth-, and sixth-graders with a high fear of failure either through self-reinforcement following improvement in performance or through group therapy. In the self-reinforcement procedure the students attended half-hour sessions during a two-week period. At each session they were given ten math problems. They were asked to indicate how many problems they thought they would be able to solve and to indicate their so-called level of aspiration, above or below which they would be surprised by their success or failure. If they reached their level of aspiration they were allowed to take a token (the experimenter was not present) that could be exchanged for a prize at the end of the session. These procedures forced the students to measure themselves in terms of their own earlier performance (not in terms of other students), setting goals to

be achieved through their own efforts. The group therapy intervention involved the students in a number of competitive games. Each
subject's success or failure here depended on the performance of
others. The experimenter praised success and reacted neutrally to
failure. Extra effort was followed by special praise. The subjects'
reactions to success or failure were discussed and clarified in a non-
directive manner.

Following each of these interventions subjects' fear of failure (as measured by the "hostile press" scoring system) was reduced
but their n Ach scores did not increase. Only the self-reinforcement
procedures resulted in a more realistic and objective level of aspiration. The students did not simply reduce their level of aspiration in
order to get more tokens. Their performance also improved considerably. Just the opportunity for self-reinforcement, based on individual reference norms, appears to be sufficient for reducing fear of
failure without the external influence of group therapy. It can also
serve to establish a more realistic and more clearly defined level of
aspiration.

Andrews and Debus (1978) began their investigation by establishing a relationship between attributing failure to lack of effort
and perseverance and resistance of responses to extinction. Students
who were least likely to attribute failure to lack of effort were
assigned to a control group, to a social reinforcement group, or to a
token plus social reinforcement attribution retraining group. The
experiment employed an "attribution box" with two four-field pan-
els corresponding to Weiner's (1975) four causal factors of ability,
effort, task difficulty, and luck. Reinforcement (that is, the combination of reinforcers) was given whenever the subject registered
"effort" following success, and "lack of effort" following failure.
Immediately after this phase, and again four months later, subjects
were tested on the training tasks and on two transfer tasks. Both
reinforcement groups showed a significant increase in persistence
following failure and also an increase in "effort attribution."

In an experiment that was not directly related to the research
in achievement motivation, Dweck (1975) was able to demonstrate
impressively the effectiveness of altering the attribution of failure.
She selected eight- to thirteen-year-old school children who demonstrated extreme learned helplessness, and subjected them to two

intervention programs of twenty-five sessions each. In one of these (attribution retraining treatment) the children experienced occasional failures and were urged to take responsibility for them, attributing them to insufficient effort. The other program (success-only treatment) involved a strategy, commonly used in clinical psychology, by which the children experienced only success. This procedure brought no improvement in their later behavior or its outcomes. However, following "attribution therapy" (cf. Valins and Nisbett, 1971) the children did show improvement in performance when confronted with failure and were more likely to attribute their failure to insufficient effort than they had been before.

Curriculum-Integrated Programs. The studies cited so far all involved relatively isolated laboratory conditions. However, a number of studies were also able to demonstrate that training programs can be integrated with regular teaching programs. The first study of this kind was reported by Mehta (1968, 1969; Mehta and Kanade, 1969). His design was largely based on the original programs, designed for businessmen, and did not yet represent a theoretical expansion. There was a pretraining phase for teachers. The study involved two programs, one designed to increase achievement motivation and the other designed to boost aspirations for academic performance.

The pretraining for teachers involved ten days in the first program and two days in the second. During a four-month period both programs, either separately or in combination, were incorporated in the school curriculum for four hours a week. The program that involved setting more demanding goals incorporated an implicit attribution element. In order to convey to the students a more favorable picture of their performance capabilities, they were urged to set goals for their monthly tests of performance and received encouraging feedback. The two programs in combination brought about the clearest improvements in both motivational levels and academic performance (most pronounced in the natural sciences). The findings lacked consistency, however, and the improvement in academic performance did not persist in the long run.

DeCharms (1968, 1976) proceeded in a similar but far more precisely defined manner. His aim was to improve the academic

performance of disadvantaged ghetto children. Independent of
Heider's (1958) attribution theory, deCharms based his curriculum-
integrated, motive-modification program on the specific experiential phenomenon of being motivated, namely the "feeling of
origin." DeCharms described this phenomenon as follows: (1) setting demanding but realistic goals for one's self, (2) knowing one's
own strengths and weaknesses, (3) having confidence in the effectiveness of one's actions, (4) determining concrete behavioral strategies for reaching one's goals, (5) seeking feedback on whether the
goals have been reached, and (6) taking responsibility for one's
actions and their consequences, as well as taking responsibility for
others. DeCharms attempted to convey this feeling of origin through
a series of discrete steps.

In a one-week pretraining program teachers got personal
experience in viewing themselves as causal agents. In cooperation
with the psychologists they developed instructional units incorporating opportunities for students to make their own decisions, take
responsibility, and set binding goals, in short to perceive themselves
as "origins." The results showed not only that students increasingly
perceived themselves as origins and increased the appropriateness of
their causal attributions within the classroom setting but that they
became more realistic in setting goals and improved their academic
performance in relation to national norms. When compared to other
programs for improving academic performance that were developed
in the 1960s in the United States, deCharms's programs have proved
remarkably effective (cf. McClelland, 1978).

Again these second wave programs were effective in bringing
about the desired behavior changes. They were able to achieve
improvements in learning and performance and resulted in more
realistic goal setting and more appropriate attribution. However,
strictly speaking, neither Dweck (1975) nor deCharms (1968) had
developed their programs on the basis of achievement motivation
theory.

The Third Wave: Self-Evaluation

With the expansion of achievement motivation theory undertaken by our institute at Bochum (Heckhausen, 1972, 1975), new

training programs were developed and tested. They were focused on a few individual factors of motivational processes. Of primary interest were factors of self-evaluation, that is, the determinants of people's most important incentives for achievement-oriented behavior. The theoretical basis was a conceptualization of the achievement motive as a self-evaluative system (or a self-reinforcing system). At first the content of the intervention program was focused on individual determinants in the self-evaluation process. Later programs concentrated on so-called individual reference norms, which guided teachers in assessing student performance. These reference norms were to affect the student's self-evaluation. Both of these approaches will be described here in some detail.

Achievement Motive as a Self-Evaluation System. Achievement-oriented behavior is strongly motivated by the incentive of anticipated self-evaluation. Self-evaluation itself depends on the discrepancy between the established performance standard (level of aspiration) and the accomplished outcome, as well as its attributed cause. Success- and failure-oriented individuals (that is, those scoring high in hope of success or fear of failure, respectively) differ with respect to two of these three determinants, namely their preferred performance standards and their preferred patterns of attribution in response to success or failure (see Heckhausen, 1972, 1975, 1977).

Compared to people who are success-oriented, failure-oriented individuals are more likely to have unrealistic performance standards and a pattern of attribution for success and failure resulting in unfavorable self-assessments of ability. They will circumvent performance-oriented activities or, if that is impossible, choose levels of difficulty that are far above or below their capacities. Although this habit protects them from inferences that diminish their self-value, it also prevents them from learning about their actual capabilities and from increasing their self-confidence. This circular process is compounded by their preferred patterns of attribution. Success is devalued because they are more likely to attribute it to the ease of the task or to good luck than to their ability; whereas failure is more likely to be attributed to low ability than to the difficulty of the task or bad luck. Both of these biases—the unrealistic setting of standards and the self-defeating patterns of attribution—result in a self-reinforcing motive system that, because it is immune to unexpected experiences of success, maintains itself.

This conceptualization would predict that changes in motivation should occur whenever this circular process is interrupted. Accordingly, failure-motivated individuals must learn to set more realistic goals and to attribute success and failure to less self-defeating causes, in order to experience a more positive pattern of self-reinforcement, ultimately increasing the incentive value of the achievement behavior.

Extracurricular Programs. These considerations formed the basis for the first training program involving failure-motivated, low-achieving fourth-graders (Krug and Hanel, 1976). In sixteen training sessions lasting one to two hours outside the normal school hours, the children learned to set more realistic goals and to develop causal attributions that enhanced their self-value and promoted a positive self-image.

Participants in the program were first introduced to non-academic tasks in order to capture their interest and to circumvent established avoidance behavior vis-à-vis academic tasks. Step by step the tasks became more school-relevant, thus ensuring transfer of training to the classroom situation. All tasks were selected or redesigned so that success and failure depended solely on the students' own proficiency, permitting them to set concrete goals before each session and enabling them to get immediate feedback.

The first session included games of skill, such as dart-throwing and labyrinth games; in the last session preparation of school assignments was planned and discussed.

The program used the following techniques to achieve its training goals: (1) behavior training through repeated practice, (2) reinforcement in the form of praise and recognition by the instructor, (3) imitational learning through observing the instructor and other participants, and (4) self-observation and self-control by means of recorded verbalizations of all motive-relevant behaviors and cognitions.

Specifically, the training sessions proceeded as follows:

1. The instructor reviewed the exercise of the previous session and introduced a new task.

2. Participants talked to the instructor about the critical aspects of the new task, how it could be solved most successfully, how difficult tasks of this nature are, and so on.

3. The instructor reviewed the task once more, taking into consideration the points raised in the discussion. He verbalized all motive-relevant cognitions (expectations, intentions, affects, solution strategies, and causal attributions) before, during, and after the task. ("What have I accomplished so far? What do I want to accomplish on the next trial? How much effort do I have to expend? What brought about my success? How much do I enjoy my performance? How happy will I be if I succeed the next time?") The instructor did not present himself as infallible, but intentionally planned for failures. In this way, more favorable goal setting, causal attribution, and self-reinforcement were conveyed for both success and failure (Meichenbaum, Turk, and Burnstein, 1974, call this "coping behavior.")

4. Subsequently each participant tried to solve the task independently, while others observed. The instructor watched carefully for errors in carrying out the tasks and made sure that each child verbalized appropriately. In this manner each child, as well as the instructor, served as a model for the others.

5. This was followed by a short discussion of the behaviors common to all participants. Once again the instructor pointed to the salient features of the task, and, if necessary, demonstrated it once more.

6. The participants now worked through the exercises by themselves. Depending on the instructions, they either verbalized the relevant cognitions quietly or "silently" (internal speech, see Meichenbaum and Goodman, 1971). Both before and after completing the exercises the instructor recorded the student's level of aspiration, anticipated affect, causal attribution, and actual performance.

Appropriate behavior during the exercises was praised, and suggestions for correction were made through individual counseling. Such counseling included a detailed explanation of the relationship between level of aspiration, causal attribution, and self-reinforcement, encouraging the students to set more realistic goals, make more appropriate attributions, and develop positive self-reinforcing cognitions.

The outcome of the training was revealing. Compared to a control group and an expectation control group, the training group not only showed the expected changes in the performance standard, attribution, and self-reinforcement but showed a clear modification of motive (net hope, NH), which, as is shown in Figure 2, resulted from a reduction in fear of failure as well as an increase in hope of success.

But like McClelland's training programs, these procedures did not result in improved school performance, despite the fact that the students in the training program performed better than the comparison groups not only on the test of motivation but on an intelligence test as well. It is not yet clear why there was no improvement in school performance. It could be that the time span of the study was too short to permit the change in motivation to manifest itself. It is also possible that the change in motivation did not result in improved performance because the required instructional conditions were not present. Clearly there must be regular opportunities for manifesting the improved achievement motive or it can hardly become stabilized in the long run. This was shown by McClelland and Winter (1969) in their courses for Indian businessmen.

Figure 2. Changes in Motive Scores from Pretest to Posttest as a Result of Training (from Krug and Hanel, 1976, p. 283).

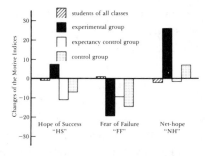

A follow-up study by Krug, Peters, and Quinkert (1977) showed that, given particular learning conditions, a change in motive can result in improved school performance and can in fact be maintained over time (see Figure 3). Their subjects were fifth- and sixth-graders who were learning-disabled and in a special class. Krug and Hanel's program was adapted to this group of students. Six months later it was still possible to demonstrate improvements of motivation, self-concept of ability, test anxiety, manifest anxiety, and school performance, and a reduction of the general dislike of school, all of which had been achieved through the training.

Postulated Negative Effects of Motive Modification. Motive-enhancement programs are geared to change the motive as well as the behavior. If we examine the various programs from this perspective, we will see that changes in motive have rarely been demonstrated. The American studies include the analysis of TAT stories in the training program, which means that posttest results have little meaning. The programs developed in our institute did produce changes in motive, but the changes turned out to be stable only in one study (Krug, Rheinberg, and Peters, 1977). We still do not know how long-term improved performance comes about. All present

Figure 3. Average Motive Scores of Pupils with Learning Disabilities: *a* shows fear of failure scores and *b* shows net hope scores (from Krug, Peters, and Quinkert, 1977, p. 673).

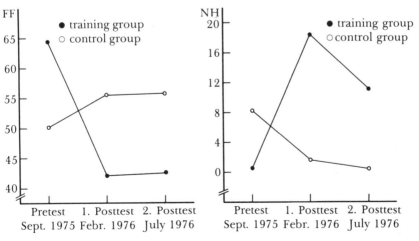

programs have had one of three kinds of results. (1) No change in behavior (Krug and Hanel, 1976; most of the programs of McClelland and Alschuler, 1971; Smith and Troth, 1975). (2) Changes only for subgroups (McClelland and Winter, 1969; Kolb, 1965). (3) Consistent improvement in performance (Mehta, 1968; Ryals, 1969, as cited in McClelland, 1972; deCharms, 1972; Krug, Rheinberg, and Peters, 1977).

Perhaps it should not be surprising that the extracurricular training programs were ineffective. Most of them were designed to change the achievement motivation of students characterized by low achievement, fear of failure, or low motivation. They were supposed to foster a readiness to work more intensively and more effectively in order to improve performance in line with the individual's abilities. But one can expect an enduring improvement of performance based solely on motive manipulation only under the premise that there is a direct relationship between the strength and the intensity of a motive as measured by persistence of the achievement-oriented behavior. Atkinson (1957), however, has already shown that such a linear relationship is not the rule. No matter how success-oriented the achievement motive may be, it will determine the behavior only if it is elicited by the necessary situational conditions, such as feedback of results, self-responsibility, and intermediate task difficulty. Such motive-inducing conditions were generally part of the training phase but not part of everyday life after the training.

The training increases the desire to achieve and develops a sense of the relevant situational factors. One learns when effort pays off, under what conditions results can be attributed to one's effort, and when one can be pleased with or even proud of one's performance. Although the children are more achievement motivated after the training program, they are still academic low achievers. They would like to be successful, but they now find that the school situation does not lend itself to satisfying their need to achieve. It may be possible to assume self-responsibility, but setting one's own goals is hardly feasible. Furthermore, assignments are too difficult compared to one's performance standard. Success, if any, is therefore still more likely to be attributed to chance than to effort, and there are few opportunities for self-reinforcement or for anticipating positive affects.

Paradoxically, a successful enhancement of motivation should therefore result in a further reduction in the motivation of low-achieving students, if there is no change in the curriculum. This conclusion is also consistent with Atkinson's (1957) risk-preference model: If the difficulty level of a task is too high, it will "demotivate" the success-motivated individual, but it will demotivate the failure-oriented individual less than will tasks of appropriate difficulty. Seen in this light one might wonder why there are no reports of negative effects from successful motive modifications. Perhaps some aspects of the training muted such negative aftereffects, or the motive modification was fortunately not as effective as intended. But there are conditions under which the negative effect cannot occur or can be avoided. For example, it may not occur in a motive-enhancement program for good-to-average students. Here the modification of motive should result in better performance. In the case of low-achieving students a negative effect can be avoided if the students receive additional tutoring, raising their level of performance to at least average. (This appears to be the basis of Kolb's positive findings.) Similarly, motive modification ought not to be harmful for low-achieving students if the principles of the extracurricular training programs are integrated into the normal school program, as Mehta (1968) and deCharms (1976) have reported.

Curriculum-Integrated Programs. The negative modification effects that are likely to occur in low-achieving students can be averted by means of supportive tutoring, and there are theoretical as well as economical reasons for suggesting improvements in the motivating conditions in real-life situations. Such a training program would have to be focused on two goals: (1) developing motive-enhancing performance situations and (2) facilitating new cognitive modes that permit a more appropriate perception of the restructured situation and result in more effective responses.

Since Mehta and deCharms had already shown that such procedures could be successful, we were faced with the question "How could such programs be carried out with a minimum expense?" and at the same time we were led by theory as closely as possible. Our guidelines derived from the assumptions of cognitive motivation theory (Heckhausen, 1972, 1975) and from the prototype ideal teacher, who elicits maximal motivation from the students.

The training program designed by Krug and others (Krug and Hanel, 1976; Krug, Peters, and Quinkert, 1977) had already shown that motive-related goal setting and self-reinforcement are sufficient to produce at least short-term modification of the achievement motive. What was not clear was the way in which one would have to manipulate these motivational components within the classroom in order to achieve more long-term behavioral effects.

Scherer (1972) had already taken the first step in this direction. From twelve groups of fourth-graders he selected students who were more likely to attribute their failures to a lack of ability than to a lack of effort and who, on the basis of their IQ scores, should have been capable of getting better grades. Both of these facts were shared with the classroom teacher along with a short explanation of the Pygmalion effect (Rosenthal and Jacobsen, 1968). They were asked to suggest to the students, on appropriate occasions, that with greater effort they were capable of better performance. Four months before and after these expectations were suggested, the experimental and control groups were scored on achievement motive (TAT), causal attribution for success and failure, intelligence, anxiety, performance in mathematics, and school grades. The posttests showed an effect of the facilitating causal attribution through the teachers. Such effects were observed not only among the target pupils, but also, unexpectedly, among most of the rest of the class. However, compared to the control group, the students in the experimental group now attributed their failures more to their inadequate effort and were less likely to lower their level of aspiration; they also achieved higher scores on individual intelligence tasks and were less anxious.

Kraeft and Krug (1979) expanded this approach. Nine fourth-grade teachers were given a short introduction to attribution and motivation theory. The teachers were then asked to adapt their task demands to the individual student's performance level, to reinforce students in light of their individual performance standards, and to attribute failure to a lack of effort. The most important element appeared to be the individualization of the nature of the task and its difficulty level.

It was assumed that if teachers were to make an effort to adapt the task to the performance level of the students, they would soon perceive a more differentiated picture of the child's learning capacity, and improvements in performance would become more easily recognized, which should automatically lead to more appropriate reinforcement and attribution. The subsequent training phase was carried out over eight weeks. During this time the frequency with which the desired target behaviors occurred was recorded several times a week and reported back to the individual teachers. To avoid excessive demands on either the observers or the teachers the latter were asked to make a particular effort to attain the target behavior for six students who manifested fear of failure, who were underachievers, but whose ability would be at least average. It was expected that the teachers would generalize their behavior in dealing with the other pupils as soon as they had mastered the desired behavior patterns, which would bring about a positive effect for all students.

Posttests ten weeks later showed the expected findings for the target pupils. Their fear of failure had been significantly reduced. Still there remained three problems: (1) The target pupils did not improve their classroom performance, (2) the remaining students did not manifest a change in the achievement motive; instead there was some indication that these pupils became *more* afraid of failure, (3) not all teachers changed their target behaviors in the desired direction. The less the teacher's behavior changed, the less the students profited from the teacher training and the more significant were the decrements in the motives of the remaining pupils.

Reference Norms for Self-Evaluation of Achievement. Apparently Kraeft and Krug had actually been "successful" in demonstrating (for a subgroup of students) the predicted negative effects of a motive-enhancing program. In order to avoid further negative effects it was decided to refine the approach. It appeared to make more sense to analyze in advance behaviors of a teacher who optimally motivates his or her students. Despite the fact that educational psychologists have not been very successful in identifying the personality traits of a successful teacher, there are salient differences in teaching. Why shouldn't there be teachers who, without knowing motivational psychology, can teach in a motivating manner, facilitating a more favorable motive development without necessarily intending to do so?

The first indication of this was provided by a study by Krug, Rheinberg, and Peters (1977). They were examining the effects on the personality development of pupils who, after four or five years in a regular school, were transferred to a special school for learning-disabled pupils. Stigmatization theory would predict a negative effect, primarily a decrement in self-image. But no such effects were observed after the change in schools. On the contrary, the newly transferred special students showed an improvement in their level of motivation and self-concept, and their test anxiety was reduced. A motive-enhancement program involving some of these students proved to be superfluous, because the positive effects of the change of schools were so pervasive that they could not be improved.

This indicated that a positive motivational effect could be achieved simply on the basis of a change in the school environment. Under the given circumstances that was hardly surprising. In their old school these students were among the lowest achievers and were accustomed to failures. Now that they had transferred to the special school they suddenly became the best in the class, experienced considerable success, and perceived themselves as high achievers in comparison with their new classmates.

Of course, such a favorable reference group effect can hardly serve as a model for inducing motive changes. The required procedures would have a profound impact, would be uneconomical, and would undoubtedly be accompanied by many undesirable side effects. Instead the question is, are there not teaching methods that not only enable high achieving students to perceive themselves as diligent, efficient, and successful but that produce the same perception in all pupils?

Reference Norms and Their Effects. In the case of reference norms, it was again a theoretical conception rather than practical experience that brought about progress. Behavioral consequences can be perceived and evaluated in terms of success or failure only if there are performance measures with which the outcomes can be compared (Heckhausen, 1963). Performance measures can be based on different reference systems (Heckhausen, 1974). For instance, performance can be measured in terms of objective, criterion-oriented norms (objective reference norms) or in terms of the performance of others (social reference norms), or it can be measured in terms of an individual's earlier achievements, that is, individual reference norms.

From the perspective of educational psychology and the psychology of motivation it should make a difference which of these measures is used to evaluate a student, because each evaluation should be accompanied by certain behaviors and attitudes. A teacher who evaluates performance in terms of *social reference norms* prefers a cross sectional perspective, that is, a comparison of students at a particular test period. From this perspective, differences in performance appear to be static, suggesting fixed and enduring explanations for individual performance. Valid social comparisons generally require the selection of tasks that result in the greatest level of discrimination—that is, tasks that are of intermediate difficulty for a given group. In accordance with the social comparison standard, those who do not attain it should be blamed. This standard should produce rather positive conditions for one half of the performance group and rather negative conditions for the other half.

The *individual perspective* focuses more on improvement in the individual's performance than on his position in the group. But an individual's progress in performance can be judged reliably only if he is assigned tasks that are of intermediate difficulty given his *present* level of performance. Because under this condition success and failure are more or less equally distributed, it makes sense to posit the variable factors as causal explanations. Similarly, praise and rebuke based on individual criteria should result in more positive learning conditions for the entire group.

Rheinberg (1977) developed a method of differentiating teachers whose orientation favors individual or social reference norms, so that it was possible to test the assumptions stated above. A variety of studies (reviewed by Rheinberg, 1980) have shown that teachers do, in fact, view performance from one of two perspectives. There are teachers who perceive their students' performance in line with their individual history of performance. They employ a longitudinal perspective, assessing the achievements of an individual student in terms of past performance (*individual reference norm orientation*). Because these teachers are keenly aware of an individual's learning progress they are likely to employ the "principle of the match"; that is, they will make an effort to find an appropriate task for a student, one that is neither too easy nor too hard. In the ideal case success and failure become equally likely for each student independent of ability. This variability in performance is likely to suggest that success and failure are a function of momentary causes, especially the immediate level of motivation and interest in the subject matter at hand. Teachers who are more likely to view classroom performance as a function of momentary circumstances are less inclined to form stable expectations concerning the future learning progress of their students. They suspend their judgment and at best expect more or less rapid progress longitudinally.

Those teachers who favor social reference norms tend to perceive an individual student's performance in terms of the class average. They employ a cross sectional perspective, comparing the student's performance to that of the rest of the class at a particular point. They strive for equality in assigning tasks; that is, they frequently assign equally difficult tasks to all students. Although that practice permits them to compare the performance of all students directly, it results in tasks that are too easy for the good students and too hard for the bad ones. This means that one part of the class is usually successful while the other usually fails. Success and failure are now attributed to stable causes, particularly work ability, work habits, and home environment. These biased explanations in turn influence the teacher's expectations of each student's performance. Endowing the student with such enduring attributes can hardly lead to an expectation of change in future performance, unless it is that the good students will improve while the bad students will get worse. These teachers also employ praise and rebuke according to socially derived scales. Performance is praised if it is above average and rebuked if it is below (Rheinberg, 1977).

The expected relationships between behavior and reference norm orientation (summarized in Table 1), were found not only in the data from various questionnaires but also in observed classroom behavior. Questioning the students revealed that they could perceive their teachers' different reference norms. Hence one can make the assumption that teachers' reference-norm-specific behaviors correlate with students' attitudes and motivations. This assumption is strengthened by a comparison of the training components of motive-enhancement programs and instructional approaches that incorporate individual reference norms. As Rheinberg (1980) has shown (Table 2), there is a great deal of similarity between individualized instruction and programs for motive enhancement. In the long run, individualized instruction ought to produce the same motive-specific effects as a short-term motive-enhancement program. This assumption was proven correct. A number of investigations (see, for example, Rheinberg, 1980) have shown that students of teachers with individual reference norm orientation show less fear of failure, have less test anxiety, and are generally less anxious. They are also less likely to attribute failure to lack of ability or task difficulty, and are more likely to feel that they have improved academically during the past year. All of these differences were observed for the class as a whole, but were particularly apparent among the low achievers.

Table 1. Prototypical Differences in Reference Norm Orientation

	Reference Norm Orientation	
Variables	*Social*	*Individual*
Primary Difference		
Performance comparisons	Between students cross sectionally	Within a student longitudinally
Secondary Differences		
Causal attribution	Absolute rather than relative attributions, particularly with respect to enduring factors contributing to individual differences in performance	Ambivalence with regard to attribution. Relative preference for attributing to instructional factors
Expectations	More enduring and oriented toward general levels of performance	Oriented toward individual performance development
Individualization	Equality of assigned tasks	Principle of adapting tasks to the individual

Source: Based on Rheinberg, 1980, p. 123.

Table 2. Comparisons of the Elements of Individualized Instruction
Programs and Programs Designed to Modify Motives

Element	Motive Modification Programs	Individualized Instruction Programs
Goal setting and task assignment	Training the individual to set realistic levels of aspiration (goals/tasks that are appropriate to the individual's ability, neither too hard nor too easy)	A tendency toward individually tailored assignments of tasks (considering the student's current level of knowledge they are neither too easy nor too difficult)
Affective tone in the face of success and failure	Emphasis on positive affects (more joy and satisfaction in the case of success than anger and shame in the case of failure)	Assessment strategies result more frequently in recognition or praise than disapproval or rebuke (insofar as the instructional program results in increased learning)
Causal attribution	Emphasis on more favorable predisposition (success, own ability and effort; failure, lack of effort or bad luck). Particular emphasis on reducing ability/talent attributions following failure	Causal explanations rarely involve factors like ability; more frequently involve current level of interest, effort, motivation program content, and teaching method
Assessment of performance	Encouraging assessment of performance in terms of the individual's improvement	Performance assessed in terms of an individual reference norm (trend orientation)
Personal effectiveness	Strengthening of the view that factors like one's present knowledge are not fixed but can be altered through one's own actions	Assumption that school performance is relatively flexible over time, and therefore hard to predict; causal explanations of academic performance in terms of transitory causal factors

Source: Based on Rheinberg, 1980, p. 126.

Modification Studies Based on Individual Reference Norms.
If it is true that individual reference norms have such a favorable
effect, then one should ask to what extent one can induce teachers to
incorporate them in their instruction. At the same time it would be

important to determine whether teachers who are persuaded to adopt them would be as successful as those who use them "naturally."

A number of studies were designed to answer these questions. One of the first was a study by Rheinberg, Krug, Lübbermann and Landscheidt, 1980). It was designed to persuade teachers to perceive and evaluate their students' performance in terms of individual reference norms. The intervention techniques required that changes in performance be continuously observable. This was important for the teacher and especially for the experimenter. The simplest method for accomplishing this was to instruct the teacher to verbalize intra-individual performance comparisons as often as possible. Getting the teachers to make such observable verbalizations also ensured that they would pay greater attention to intra-individual changes, thereby adopting the perspective of a teacher employing an individually oriented reference norm. Observational and questionnaire data were obtained before the experiment. The teachers were then told that an analysis of these data had revealed a need for telling each student that his performance today was better or worse than yesterday's and for avoiding inter-individual comparisons. It was agreed that the teachers would make every effort to modify their relevant evaluative behavior and that the observers would facilitate the modification by recording and giving them feedback on behavior that was inappropriate.

Observations were made in every second session of a mathematics class. After each session the teacher was truthfully informed about the frequency of his intra-individual performance evaluations. This was accomplished by encouraging commentary, but at the same time he was urged to increase the relevant behaviors. Particularly at the beginning of the intervention there was also discussion of how one can verbalize such performance comparisons. Other than that, there were no intrusions. It was decided not to introduce the teachers to concepts of motivation theory so as to see whether such a modification of primary behavior (evaluation) would also produce changes in secondary behavior patterns: attribution of causes, expectations of future performance, and individualization of tasks.

The results showed that such focused intervention does not produce generalized changes in the teaching behavior. Although the teacher did give the students more frequent feedback related to their own prior performance, there was little change in the frequency of the secondary variables. Moreover, for those teachers who manifested individually oriented reference norms before training, there was little opportunity to increase the frequency of the secondary variables. In contrast, teachers who "naturally" used social reference norms had difficulty giving individually oriented feedback appropriately. They were not convinced that the procedure was appropriate and just. For them, only those students who did better than the rest were worthy of praise. Those whose performance was below average were "bad" and deserved to be reprimanded.

It was surprising, then, that despite this largely forced change in the teachers' behaviors, there were positive effects observed among the students: they made more frequent contributions to the class, caused fewer disturbances, engaged in fewer behaviors irrelevant to the classroom situation, and became less passive. On the posttest questionnaire, both exam anxiety and attributions of own performance to ease or difficulty of the task were reduced.

Overall, these findings were surprisingly positive. They probably would have been even more significant if the authors had introduced the teachers to the concept of reference norm orientation and given them the rationale for it.

A methodologically different approach was employed by Rheinberg, Kühmel and Duscha (1979), who used the role-playing technique first reported by Lewin, Lippitt, and White (1939). To different classes, the same teacher acted in ways reflecting either social or individual reference norms.

The study was carried out in two parallel classes of tenth-graders. The role-playing teacher had not previously taught either of the classes. For six weeks he employed in each of the classes one or the other reference norm orientation. According to Rheinberg, Kühmel, and Duscha (1979, p. 5) the following behaviors were manifested: (1) feedback on performance within the classroom ("Willy, your answer was much better than the one given by Frank and John," versus "Willy, your answers today were much better than those you gave yesterday"), (2) feedback of results from informal performance tests (results reported in rank order and extensive class discussion of the rank ordering versus a comparison of results with each student's earlier grades, reinforced by individualized comments on the student's progress), (3) difficulty level of task and test (directing questions to the entire class, calling on another student if the first cannot answer, versus gearing the difficulty of a question to the individual student, varying it in accordance with the student's response), (4) sanctions (praise or reprimand) based on a comparison with class average versus sanctions based on improvement or decrement in individual performance. No systematic communications concerning attribution or expectations were employed, because in the case of social reference norms the teacher would have had to make ethically unjustifiable comments on poor performance.

The teacher's behavior was continually observed. It became apparent that it was easier for this teacher to emit individualized rather than social reactions (the ratio was 4:3). By contrast, the reverse was easier for the students. Instructions based on social reference norms did not result in any significant student reactions, presumably because it was no different from what the students were used to. But the individualized instruction tended to confuse the students. They weren't sure whether the teacher was being facetious when he praised the mediocre contribution of a weak student as good performance. A few students protested when they found that their excellent work on the first test resulted in the teacher's comment that they had only maintained their performance level, while more mediocre papers elicited praise because they were clearly above the student's previous level.

Despite this slight confusion, the expected changes were observed. Influenced by their teacher's example, students who received individualized instruction showed a significant decrease in their tendency to make social comparisons (see Figure 4). While the class based on social reference norms showed an increase in test anxiety and manifest anxiety, these were decreased for those who were exposed to individual reference norms.

An informal performance test at the end of the course resulted in better performance for students exposed to individual reference norms; furthermore, two thirds of these students viewed their performance as successful. As expected, only half of the students

Figure 4. Average Reference Norm Orientation Scores of Students Exposed
to Individual Reference Norms (iRN) or Social Reference Norms (sRN)
for Six Weeks (*a* shows individual reference norm orientation; *b* shows
social reference norm orientation).

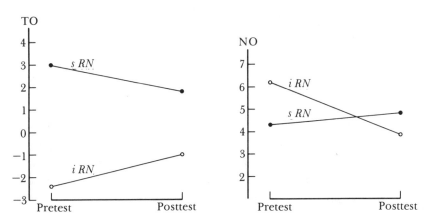

exposed to the social reference norms experienced their test results as
successes, and the other half viewed them as failures.

Students in the individualized reference norm group were
more likely to attribute their test performance to variable causes and
were less likely to explain their failures in terms of stable causes than
were students in the group with the social reference norms.

With this it has been demonstrated that teachers can bring
about desirable motivational effects by means of teaching behaviors
based on principles derived from motivation theory. Most remarkable is the slight expenditure of effort required to achieve such effects.
It dispenses with the long pretraining for teachers as well as the need
for developing specialized course content for students (deCharms,
1976). Although students feel somewhat insecure at the beginning,
the positive changes remain convincing. Furthermore, teachers
experience instruction based on individual reference norms as more
satisfying than that based on social reference norms. Presumably
they recognize for the first time that a longitudinal perspective
results in increasing the student's motivation to learn and also
improves his performance. Surely that is also a reason for the teacher
to take pride in his own proficiency. This is rarely the case with the
social perspective. Here an improvement in learning is ignored so

long as the relative standings of the students are maintained, and that stability is typical when social norms are applied.

Yet another approach to influencing student performance was chosen by Krug, Mrazek, and Schmidt (1980). In the context of physical education classes they conveyed to the students an individualized performance orientation by encouraging them to set realistic goals as well as by giving them individualized feedback. These authors were interested solely in the effect on motives, since motives had not been examined in the previous reference-norm-oriented intervention studies.

The training group consisted of thirty-two fifth-grade boys selected from two classes. The training began shortly after the physical education instructor had taken over the group. The course into which the training program was incorporated encompassed five single and five double periods as well as a one-hour "introduction to the basic principles of achievement-oriented behavior." The motive-strengthening element of the single periods consisted of circuit training (see below), while the double periods focused on gymnastics.

The circuit training was designed to make students aware of goal setting and of improvements in their performance. The circuit consisted of eight stations involving sprinting, throwing a medicine ball, and so on, and the course was to be repeated as often as possible. Students worked in pairs. While one student performed at one of the stations the other recorded the desired goal and the number of repetitions. Each student performed for thirty seconds at each station; during the next thirty seconds his performance was recorded and the partners changed roles or moved to the next station.

The gymnastics exercises gave groups of five students an opportunity to practice activities that varied in difficulty. The group was told that the purpose of the exercises was to improve each individual's fitness and that by keeping a record each student would clearly see whether his performance had improved or not. It was made clear that these records would not be used for assigning grades. The teacher remained in the background as much as possible. He avoided excessive praise or encouragement, restricting his comments to questioning inappropriately set levels of aspiration or to briefly commenting on the possible causes of successes and failures.

The "introduction to the basic principles of achievement-oriented behavior" took place in the middle of the course and was given to each class separately. The students were taught the relationship between performance, proficiency, goal setting, affects, and causal explanation.

As was the case in the study by Rheinberg, Kühmel, and Duscha (1979), the students were perplexed at the beginning of the program. They were not sure the teacher was serious when he praised the progress made by the weaker students. Furthermore, there was a conflict between the new system of assessment and the students' expectations. All of them wanted to know what criteria would now be used for assigning grades. The high performers and the very weak students in particular reacted negatively. The very good students were unhappy because they would lose their "star" positions if it was not the absolute but the relative level of performance that was assessed. It is not yet clear whether these initial reactions can easily be surmounted.

What *was* clear in each case was the change in motive. Compared with the control groups, which did not participate in the training, there were significant changes in the motives of the training group. The same difference was observed vis-à-vis the students who were given the "introduction to the basic principles of achievement-oriented behavior" but did not participate in the training. This shows that knowing about theoretical relationships does not, by itself, bring about a change in attitude or in motive.

Questions Arising from Motive Modification Research

Role of Training Inputs. These last studies clearly show the changes that have occurred in programs for improving motives since the pioneering work was undertaken by McClelland. Significant changes have occurred only in the theoretical assumptions on which the programs were based. They became more precise, simpler, and more parsimonious, as did the programs arising from them. But one central element was always retained, one that McClelland, Atkinson, Clark, and Lowell (1953) defined at the very beginning of the research on achievement motivation: the concern with a standard of excellence.

This is not really surprising. All of the hitherto existing theories of motivation attribute to this central element not only definitional but also functional meaning. The setting of realistic goals is a prerequisite for changes in the remaining components of the achievement motive. If the goals are set at an intermediate level of difficulty, then the achieved results are most directly experienced as depending on one's own efforts. Exerting enough effort will lead to success; too little will lead to failure.

In this light it would appear that realistic goal setting and its corresponding principle of individualized instruction could serve as sufficient conditions for optimizing the learning and achievement motives. However, this conclusion has limited validity. Other situational variables (related to the teacher) and personal factors (related to the student) must also be considered, as is shown in the following examples.

As we pointed out earlier, when task difficulty levels are adjusted to performance, the outcome is not necessarily positive. It may even have negative effects on individuals who demonstrate high fear of failure or who are extreme underachievers. An achievement motive characterized by being confident of success is induced by performance on tasks of intermediate difficulty. However, this is precisely the situation in which failure-motivated students become fearful and try to avoid task-related behavior (Atkinson, 1964). Without the other components of the achievement motive, namely appropriate causal attribution, increased confidence in one's ability, and more favorable self-reinforcement, an improvement in learning and performance can hardly be expected. A student who demonstrates fear of failure is not likely to evolve these processes on his own. Thus, at least at the beginning, the teacher must intervene by suggesting specific causal attribution and by providing external reinforcement whenever students are confronted by tasks of appropriate difficulty as part of a program of more individualized instruction. Otherwise there is the possibility that failure-motivated students will experience a program incorporating tasks of intermediate difficulty as more threatening than before (O'Conner, Atkinson, and Horner, 1966).

Similar problems can be observed with extreme underachievers. Here too it is almost impossible to accomplish the desired positive changes in motive and performance, despite the appropriate difficulty level of the task, if causal attribution, performance feedback, and reinforcement continue to be based on social norms. The principle of adjusting the difficulty of tasks to the individual student can have negative effects if the student gets no feedback about his own proficiency, but is instead made aware of how incompetent he is compared to others (as indicated by the objectively easy task). For example: "Here we have a few particularly hard problems for the really clever ones, and two that are very easy for Mike and Peter."

The need for considering a variety of factors together also applies to the other components of the achievement motive. There would be no assurance of success if the modification attempt were solely concerned with causal attribution. Admittedly it is generally rather favorable to attribute failure to a lack of effort rather than a lack of ability (Weiner, 1975). Lack of effort implies that it is in one's own hands to accomplish short-term changes (Heider, 1958; Rheinberg, 1975). But here too there can be undesirable effects. If the failures of underachieving students are constantly explained in terms of lack of effort, and if increased effort does not lead to success, then for these students the situation becomes even more depressing and hopeless. If despite their heightened effort they are not able to accomplish anything, then their ability must appear to be even lower than they had assumed. Starting at about age ten students are able to draw such inferences based on amount of effort and lack of ability. This is when they cognitively master compensatory explanations of causality (Heckhausen, in press; Kelley, 1972). Obviously, such inferences are detrimental to the student's self-image.

Finally, comparison of performance and reinforcement also cannot be viewed in isolation. Again a generally favorable effect can be achieved by evaluating students in terms of individual rather than social reference norms. But even here there can be too much of a good thing. If performance is *always* assessed intra-individually and longitudinally, and if this is combined with setting tasks that are predominantly too easy, then the student will eventually consider effort to be superfluous (Kukla, 1972; Meyer, 1973). That is particularly the case if the series of successes is explained in terms of the student's high ability. This would result in an unrealistic self-concept that can be maintained only under the sheltered conditions of an artificial classroom. In everyday situations, both inside and outside the classroom, this self-concept could not survive peer comparisons and would soon collapse.

Thus despite the desirability of individualizing task difficulty and evaluation, there are two reasons why social reference norms should not be completely eliminated from the classroom. First, it will always serve to determine the relative difficulty of tasks based on the performance outcomes within a class. Second, only social comparisons lead to a realistic self-concept that will facilitate appropriate career choices and success and satisfaction throughout life.

Importance of Teacher Differences. Kraeft and Krug's (1979) previously mentioned study shows how important it is to the success of an intervention that individual components be applied in combination. They had trained teachers to assign tasks geared to the individual student and to adopt more favorable causal attributions and student assessments. Observing the teachers' actual classroom behavior showed that they differed in their ability to change their teaching in the desired direction. Changes in students' achievement motives could be interpreted only if one considered the extent to which the individual teacher was able to modify all aspects of his classroom behavior. There was a significant correlation between the combined score of the classroom observations and the average increase in success orientation in one class (pretest-posttest differences in the hope-of-success score from Schmalt, 1976, $r = .74$, $p < .05$). There was an even stronger relationship with the questionnaire for teachers, which separately measured all three aspects of classroom behavior that are important to motivation: attribution, expectations, and individualization (from Rheinberg, 1977). The extent to which a teacher's score on the questionnaire was changed in the desired direction as a result of the intervention was highly correlated with an increase in the hope-of-success motive of the students ($r = .90$, $p < .05$). But if instead of such combined scores only the increased individualization in assignments was considered, there tended to be a negative correlation with improvement of motivation and performance among the students. The more the ratio of right to wrong solutions approached 50:50 (that is, intermediate task difficulty) the more the students in this class were motivated to avoid failure ($r = .59$, $p < .10$).

Newer training programs have been expanded to incorporate reference norm orientations in order to avoid the possibility that teachers, after their training, will try to influence only selected components of the achievement motive. We have already said that reference-norm-evaluation appears to be a primary variable that can bring about changes in related secondary variables (assignment of tasks, attribution, sanctions). This assumption has now been tested in a study by Rheinberg, Krug, Lübbermann and Landscheidt (1980). According to their findings, teachers who already tend toward individual reference norms were easily persuaded to adopt the behaviors stressed in the training program. Right from the beginning of the intervention program they accepted the challenge for more intraindividual comparisons. They even apologized, somewhat self-critically, for not having paid more attention to individual levels of ability before. In contrast, teachers who strongly tended toward social reference norms were willing to give individualized feedback only because the project leaders insisted on it. These teachers' attitudes were not changed by the training; their scores for reference norm orientation remained unchanged at the end of the training program.

We suspect that the resistance to longitudinal evaluation by teachers with a social-reference-norm orientation is reinforced by a particular view of the goals of education. Brophy and Good (1974) pointed out that teachers differed on whether they were oriented more toward the person or the subject matter and whether they were more interested in improving or assessing their students' performance. If this is the case, then the individualized comparison of performance (after Rheinberg, 1980) does not represent a primary variable for teacher training, because it arises from the basic values and attitudes of the teacher (see Table 3) and mediates between these values and attitudes and such classroom behavior as adjusting difficulty level, making attributions, and stating expectations.

At this point, we encounter several important issues. Each deserves to be explored in its own right. Taken together, they may ensure that the search for more efficient motive-modification procedures is not too narrowly focused on particular processes and personality variables or limited to unique settings like the classroom.

Social Intervention. Let us begin with the question whether an enduring modification of a student's motive can be achieved

Table 3. Fundamental Attitudes and Value Orientations of Teachers

Individual Reference Norm	Social Reference Norm
• variable attribution	• stable attribution pattern
• short-term expectations	• long-term expectations
• individualized assignment of tasks	• equality of assignments
• reinforcement based on individual standards	• reinforcement based on social standards

without changes in the values and attitudes of the classroom teacher who assigns a higher value to assessing performance than to improving it. According to the above-mentioned findings by Rheinberg, Krug, Lübbermann, and Landscheidt (1980), one would suspect that this orientation is a necessary but not sufficient condition. One must also have at one's disposal a repertoire of behaviors that translate one's convictions into actions in the classroom. At least this appeared to be the case for the teachers with an individual reference norm orientation. On the other hand, teachers characterized by a social reference norm orientation finally did change their assessment of students in terms of greater individualization (probably only until the end of the investigation), but they did not change their attitude. That does not necessarily mean that one would first of all need to change the basic values. It could also be true that teachers remained unaware of the effects of their behavior on the students because of their prevailing attitude and that nothing in the training program would have sensitized them to such effects.

This possibility needs to be investigated. But beyond that it points to the need for viewing modification programs as systems of social interaction in an even broader sense. It is not just the student but the teacher whose experiences must be modified to show that the new behavior pattern results in useful and rewarding outcomes. In other words, we must not view the teacher simply as an opportunity structure for the students. We must also make the teacher aware of the new situation from the students' perspective. The teacher particularly needs help here, because a change in the student's situation is far less noticeable to the teacher—requiring a highly tuned sensitivity to subtle clues—than a change in the teacher's behavior is to the students. To the students it becomes immediately apparent that the

teacher's orientation has become individualized, but teachers who
are predominantly social-norm-oriented must first learn to recognize the factors that signal improvements in their students' motivation to learn. In fact, they probably must first learn to acknowledge
that individualized instruction is time consuming and that the aim
is not solely to achieve instructional goals as quickly as possible but
also to get as many students as possible to reach these goals.

One index that more than any other might convince teachers
with social-reference-norm orientations to adopt a more individualized approach is one that reflects improvement in the average performance of all students. Of course it would be hard to measure this
directly. This would require a scale that incorporated both the individual and the social reference norms, that is, one that is both task-
referenced and criterion-referenced. It would go beyond realizing
that even the most mediocre student is making progress and reporting this global impression to him. Indications of the degree to which
previously set, intermediate goals of the teaching/learning system
have been reached provide a framework for assessing improvement
in the individual student's performance. Of course, not all academic
subjects are equally suitable for measuring improvement in performance in terms of a criterion-oriented reference norm. Perhaps
teachers could be made sufficiently aware of this by applying the
principle of mastery learning (Block, 1971) to just one of their academic subjects.

But aside from this increased awareness of improvement in
performance, there are other immediate effects of individualization
that might reinforce individualized instruction: for example,
improvement in classroom participation and increased attention
span. Teachers with social reference norms can also be made more
aware of these changes. One would need to investigate whether the
proposed procedures, which are quite economical, are in themselves
sufficient to result in the desired attitude changes which, once they
have been set in motion, will be followed by the teachers on their
own.

Cross-Situational Stability of the Achievement Motive. But
even a successful program for modifying a motive raises questions.
Does a change in the student's achievement motive really represent a
generalizable change of an evaluative disposition? Or are these

effects limited to school learning or even more specifically to the particular subjects taught by a teacher employing individualized instruction? In speaking of successful motive modifications we have probably overestimated the dispositional characteristics of our criterion variables, and stretched them to cover a variety of real-life attribution patterns that are largely learned in the classroom and were in fact derived from the school setting. Admittedly there are neither theoretical nor empirical reasons for attributing to the individual a separate achievement motive for each sphere of activity (school, work place, sports, hobbies, and so on). But we also do not know to what extent the achievement motive represents a homogeneous dimension, applying equally to all of an individual's activities. The global conceptualization of this motive has undoubtedly contributed to a lack of study of this dimension. Again it was McClelland (1972) who expanded the horizon. He reported that, although the original programs did not have any effect on academic performance, they did affect extracurricular activities; follow-up telephone conversations revealed that students had become more venturesome in organizing their spare time and vacation periods.

School as a Developmental Environment. In recent years, motive modification has been increasingly focused on students. Surely, this is not just because students are easily accessible subjects. Probably the school setting also generates more motive-related problems than any other. This means that motive enhancement for an entire class can be viewed in two ways. One, it represents a compensation for the institutional weakness of the school, including the traditional teaching systems and the training of teachers. Two, it represents an improvement in the achievement motive of the individual student, that is, a remedy for an unfavorable motive state, however acquired.

Both of these views are questionable, because they restrict the possibilities for interventions a priori. In terms of the school, motive modification becomes a remedial adjunct to poor teaching in particular classes without bringing about any changes in the school system. More sweeping effects can only be achieved by totally incorporating the essence of the training programs in the education of teachers, the organization of the curriculum, the development of text materials (McClelland, 1969), and the teaching methods. With the other perspective, the one focused on the individual student, motive modification inadvertently becomes a form of therapeutic intervention, analogous to psychotherapy. This is questionable for three reasons. First, the effectiveness of a therapeutic intervention focused on the individual is rather insignificant when compared to a preventative intervention focused on a system. Second, there is the danger of ignoring or misperceiving those aspects of the system that generate the need for a motive enhancement. Third, it ignores the fact that motives are not yet fully developed during the school years, but that they are subject to a long—perhaps life-long— development.

Let us briefly examine the last two points. We must recognize that the dominant teaching models in our school systems (at least in industrialized societies with highly developed educational systems) restrict the development of the achievement motive by favoring social comparisons of proficiency. That in turn leads to a trait-like perception of one's ability. Self-evaluation is centered on success and failure. Compared to this ego-involved achievement behavior there is relatively little opportunity for task-involved behavior. Motivation that is intrinsic to the task itself is not likely to develop in the face of the variety of ego-involved primary and secondary effects of academic achievement (Heckhausen and Rheinberg, 1980; Nicholls, 1980). This characterization applies particularly to students who, for whatever reasons, remain below the average performance of their class. For them the school establishes conditions for an unfavorable development of their achievement motive, leading to failure, avoidance of performance demands, an unrealistic level of aspiration, and self-deprecating patterns of attribution.

Admittedly these are speculations and simplifications. To date there has not been an empirical analysis of the development of motives during the school years. What is remarkable is that its absence has not been noticed. McClelland and Winter (1969) did investigate the conditions for motive development among young and middle-aged businessmen. But in the case of our schools, apparently no one has come up with the same idea. Schools represent something that is "normal."

The Developmental Perspective. One needs to account not only for age-dependent changes in the surrounding environment, with all of their possible influences, but also for age-dependent changes in the cognitive prerequisites for the modal or typical development of motives. There is an interaction between these environmental and cognitive factors. The same environmental factors may not have the same effects at all stages of life, if indeed they have any. Thus, a particular level of motive development must exist before certain school-related influences can become effective and bring about developmental divergences. For example it is only during the early school years (around ages eight to ten) that the child develops the cognitive prerequisites for realistic goal setting, facilitating the formation of individual differences in personal standards. At this stage the child is able to understand the relationship between task difficulty and incentive and to develop a stable concept of ability based on social comparisons. Somewhat later, presumably about age eleven, the child acquires the cognitive prerequisites for individual differences in patterns of attribution, resulting in a differentiated self-evaluation that is crucial to the development of the achievement motive (see Heckhausen, in press).

The identification of such age-related factors is crucial for the development and employment of motive-training programs. They facilitate the move from therapeutic or vaguely defined interventions to preventive programs, particularly if they can inoculate against later negative developmental influences.

A developmental view of this kind also opens up new avenues for motive training after the school years. Examples would be the various phases of career development in professions, changes in occupation for men, the change from the mother role to paid occupation for women, and changes brought about by retirement. The goals for motive training programs would by no means have to be the same for all cases, nor would they necessarily have to correspond to the previously established programs.

Ethics. Finally, there are ethical questions to be raised. It should go without saying that interventions designed to modify motives must be justified to the individuals involved. McClelland and Winter (1969) were able to defuse ethical objections to their program for businessmen by asserting that (1) the intent to influence was presented without deception from the very beginning, (2) participation was completely voluntary, and (3) the intended goals were seen to be desirable for the development of the individual's personality and for the economic development of the country. Later McClelland (1978) pointed out that successful programs serve to "expand human freedom." In the case of students and curriculum-integrated programs, ethical questions are not answered so easily. Much depends on how one conceptualizes the processes leading to the actual changes in behavior. For example, if one assumes that one has increased the determining role of the achievement motive in the sense of an enduring evaluative disposition, then one would have to justify sacrificing the importance of another motive, such as affiliation, which might previously have played the determining role in the individual's life. This could not be justified scientifically. At best one could point to its usefulness and desirability for certain stages in life or career.

If one assumes (and this appears to be closer to the truth) that one is not simply increasing the strength of the motive but is also providing a more favorable restructuring, then the ethical problems become less distressing. We can argue that the student can now achieve more demanding goals with greater efficiency, more autonomy, and fewer negative emotions. But this argument immediately leads to another question. Once the student has achieved the goals of the training program, he may perceive the traditional school setting as totally nonmotivating and may try to escape from it as soon as possible, restricting his job choices later on. Such ethical problems can best be minimized if motive training is viewed as an aid to ensuring that future developments are not precluded through premature solidification of the self and to facilitating developmental tasks that are optimally appropriate to the particular stage of life.

But what is it that motive-training programs really accomplish? How changeable is a motive's course of development across the various stages of life, and how modifiable is it? How different are the motive-specific demands that must be met at each life stage and in each life sphere in order to maximize the individual's development while promoting the welfare of others.

All these questions remain unanswered, if indeed they are reasonable and answerable at all. The search for fundamental answers will require the kind of intellectual and interventionist courage that characterized David McClelland's introduction of motive-training programs for research as well as for humanitarian goals.

References

Alschuler, A. S. *Developing Achievement Motivation in Adolescents.* Englewood Cliffs, N.J.: Educational Technology Publications, 1973.

Alschuler, A. S., Tabor, D., and McIntyre, J. *Teaching Achievement Motivation.* Middletown, Conn.: Educational Ventures, 1970.

Andrews, G. R., and Debus, R. L. "Persistence and the Causal Perception of Failure: Modifying Cognitive Attributions." *Journal of Educational Psychology*, 1978, *70*, 155–166.

Atkinson, J. W. "Motivational Determinants of Risk Taking Behavior." *Psychological Review*, 1957, *64*, 359–372.

Atkinson, J. W. *An Introduction to Motivation.* New York: Van Nostrand, 1964.

Binney, R. C., Burdick, H., and Teevan, R. *Fear of Failure.* New York: Van Nostrand, 1969.

Block, J. H. (Ed.) *Mastery Learning.* New York: Holt, Rinehart and Winston, 1971.

Brophy, J. E., and Good, T. L. *Teacher-Student Relationships: Causes and Consequences.* New York: Holt, Rinehart and Winston, 1974.

deCharms, R. *Personal Causation.* New York: Academic Press, 1968.

deCharms, R. "Personal Causation: Training in the Schools." *Journal of Applied Social Psychology*, 1972, *2*, 95–113.

deCharms, R. *Enhancing Motivation: Change in the Classroom.* New York: Irvington, 1976.

Diener, C.I., and Dweck, C.S. "An Analysis of Learned Helplessness: Continuous Changes in Performance, Strategy, and Achievement Cognitions Following Failure." *Journal of Personality and Social Psychology*, 1978, *36*, 451–462.

Dweck, C. S. "The Role of Expectations and Attributions in the Alleviation of Learned Helplessness."*Journal of Personality and Social Psychology*, 1975, *31*, 674–685.

Heckhausen, H. *Hoffnung und Furcht in der Leistungsmotivation,* [*Hope and Fear in Achievement Motivation*]. Meisenheim: Hain, 1963.

Heckhausen, H. "Trainingskurse zur Erhöhung der Leistungsmotivation und der unternehmerischen Aktivität in einem Entwicklungsland: Eine nachträgliche Analyse des erzielten Motivwandels" ["Training Courses to Increase Achievement Motivation and Enterpreneurial Activity in a Developing Country: A Further Analysis of the Obtained Motive Changes"]. *Zeitschrift für Entwicklungspsychologie und Pädagogische Psychologie* [*Journal of Developmental and Pedagogical Psychology*], 1971, *3*, 253–268.

Heckhausen, H. "Die Interaktion der Sozialisationsvariablen in der Genese des Leistungsmotivs" ["The Interaction of Socialization Variables in the Origin of the Achievement Motive"]. In C. F. Graumann (Ed.), *Handbuch der Psychologie* [*Handbook of Psychology*]. Vol. 7, Part 2. Göttingen: Hogrefe, 1972.

Heckhausen, H. *Leistungsmotivation und Chancengleichheit* [*Achievement Motivation and Equality of Opportunity*]. Göttingen: Hogrefe, 1974.

Heckhausen, H. "Fear of Failure as a Self-Reinforcing Motive System." In J. G. Sarason and C. Spielberger (Eds.), *Stress and Anxiety*. Vol. 2. Washington, D.C.: Hemisphere Press, 1975.

Heckhausen, H. "Motivation: Kognitionspsychologische Aufspaltung eines summarischen Konstrukts" ["Motivation: A Cognitive Psychological Differentiation of a Summary Construct"]. *Psychologische Rundschau* [*Psychological Review*], 1977, *28*, 175–189.

Heckhausen, H. *Motivation und Handeln* [*Motivation and Action*]. Berlin, Heidelberg, New York: Springer, 1980.

Heckhausen, H. "The Development of Achievement Motivation." In W. W. Hartup (ed.), *Review of Child Development Research*. Vol. 6. Chicago: University of Chicago Press, forthcoming.

Heckhausen, H., and Rheinberg, F. "Lernmotivation im Unterricht, erneut betrachet" ["Instruction and Motivation to Learn Reconsidered"]. *Unterrichtswissenschaft* [*Instructional Science*], 1980, *8*, 7–47.

Heider, F. *The Psychology of Interpersonal Relations*. New York: Wiley, 1958.

Kelley, H. H. *Causal Schemata and the Attribution Process*. Morristown, N.J.: General Learning Press, 1972.

Kolb, D. A. "Achievement Motivation Training for Under-Achieving High-School Boys." *Journal of Personality and Social Psychology*, 1965, *2*, 783–792.

Kraeft, U., and Krug, S. "Ursachenzuschreibung in schulischen

Lernsituationen" ["Causal Attribution in a School Learning Situation"]. In L. Eckensberger (Ed.), *Bericht* über den 31. Kongreb der Deutschen Gesellschaft für Psychologie, Mannheim, 1978 [*Proceedings* of the 31st Congress of the German Psychological Psychology]. Göttingen: Hogrefe, 1979.

Krug, S. "Förderung und Änderung des Leistungsmotivs: Theoretische Grundlagen und deren Anwendung" ["Encouraging and Changing the Achievement Motive: Theoretical Basis and Its Application"]. In H. D. Schmalt and W. U. Meyer (Eds.), *Leistungsmotivation und Verhalten* [*Achievement Motivation and Behavior*]. Stuttgart: Klett, 1976.

Krug, S., and Hanel, J. "Motivänderung: Erprobung eines theoriegeleiteten Trainingsprogramms" ["Motive Change: Test of a Theoretically Based Training Program"]. *Zeitschrift für Entwicklungspsychologie und Pädagogische Psychologie* [*Journal of Developmental and Pedagogical Psychology*], 1976, *8*, 274–287.

Krug, S., Mrazek, J., and Schmidt, C. "Motivationsförderung im Sportunterricht durch Leistungsbewertung unter individueller Bezugsnorm" ["Encouraging Motivation in Sports Instruction Through Evaluation of Achievement by Individually Referenced Norms"]. *Psychologie in Erziehung und Unterricht* [*Psychology in Learning and Instruction*], 1980, *27*, 278–284.

Krug, S., Peters, J., and Quinkert, H. "Motivförderungsprogramm für lernbehinderte Sonderschüler" ["Programs for Encouraging Motivation among Learning Disabled Students"]. *Zeitschrift für Heilpädagogik* [*Journal for Health Psychology*], 1977, *28*, 667–674.

Krug, S., Rheinberg, F., and Peters, J. "Einflüsse der Sonderbeschulung und eines zusätzlichen Motivänderungsprogramms auf die Persönlichkeitsentwicklung von Sonderschülern" ["Influence of Special Education and an Additional Motive Change Program on the Personality Development of Special Students"]. *Zeitschrift für Heilpädagogik* [*Journal for Health Psychology*], 1977, *28*, 431–439.

Kukla, A. "Foundations of an Attributional Theory of Performance." *Psychological Review*, 1972, *79*, 454–470.

Lewin, K., Lippitt, R., and White, R. K. "Patterns of Aggressive

Behavior in Experimentally Created 'Social Climates.'" *Journal of Social Psychology*, 1939, *10*, 271–299.

McClelland, D. C. "The Importance of Early Learning in the Formation of Motives." In J. W. Atkinson (Ed.), *Motives in Fantasy, Action, and Society*. New York: Van Nostrand, 1958.

McClelland, D. C. *The Achieving Society*. New York: Van Nostrand, 1961.

McClelland, D. C. "Toward a Theory of Motive Acquisition." *American Psychologist*, 1965, *20*, 321–333.

McClelland, D. C. "The Role of an Educational Technology in Developing Achievement Motivation." *Educational Technology*, 1969, *9* (10), 7–16.

McClelland, D.C. "What Is the Effect of Achievement Motivation Training in the Schools?" *Teachers College Record*, 1972, *74*, 129–145.

McClelland, D. C. "Testing for Competence Rather Than for 'Intelligence.'" *American Psychologist*, 1973, *28*, 1–14.

McClelland, D. C. *Power: The Inner Experience*. New York: Irvington, 1975.

McClelland, D. C. "Managing Motivation to Expand Human Freedom." *American Psychologist*, 1978, *33*, 201–210.

McClelland, D. C., and Alschuler, A. S. "Achievement Motivation Development Project." Unpublished manuscript, Harvard University, 1971.

McClelland, D. C., Atkinson, J. W., Clark, R. A., and Lowell, E. L. *The Achievement Motive*. New York: Appleton-Century-Crofts, 1953.

McClelland, D.C., and Burnham, D. H. "Power Is the Great Motivator." *Harvard Business Review*, 1976, *54*, 100–110.

McClelland, D. C., and Winter, D. G. *Motivating Economic Achievement*. New York: Free Press, 1969.

Mehta, P. "Achievement Motivation Training for Educational Development." *Indian Educational Review*, 1968, *3*, 1–29.

Mehta, P. *The Achievement Motive in High School Boys*. New Delhi: National Council of Educational Research and Training, 1969.

Mehta, P., and Kanade, H. M. "Motivation Development for Educational Growth: A Follow-Up Study." *Indian Journal of Psychology*, 1969, *46*, 1–20.

Meichenbaum, D. H., and Goodman, J. "Training Impulsive Children to Talk to Themselves: A Means of Developing Self-Control." *Journal of Abnormal Psychology*, 1971, *77*, 115–126.

Meichenbaum, D., Turk, D., and Burnstein, S. "The Nature of Coping with Stress." Paper presented at the NATO conference on stress held at Athens, Greece, 1974.

Meyer, W. U. *Leistungsmotiv und Ursachenerklärung von Erfolg und Misserfolg [Achievement Motive and Causal Attribution of Success and Failure]*. Stuttgart: Klett, 1973.

Nicholls, J. G. "The Development of the Concepts of Effort and Ability, Perception of Academic Attainment and the Understanding That Difficult Tasks Require More Ability." *Child Development*, 1978, *49*, 800–814.

Nicholls, J. G. "Striving to Demonstrate and Develop Ability: A Theory of Achievement Motivation." Unpublished manuscript, Department of Educational Psychology, Purdue University, 1980.

O'Conner, P., Atkinson, J. W., and Horner, M. S. "Motivational Implications of Ability Grouping in Schools." In J. W. Atkinson and N. T. Feather (Eds.), *A Theory of Achievement Motivation*. New York: Wiley, 1966.

Rheinberg, F. "Zeitstabilität und Steuerbarkeit von Ursachen schulischer Leistung in der Sicht des Lehrers" ["Temporal Stability and Measurability of the Causes of School Achievement in the View of the Teacher"]. *Zeitschrift für Entwicklungspsychologie und Pädagogische Psychologie [Journal of Developmental and Pedagogical Psychology]*, 1975, *7*, 180–194.

Rheinberg, F. "Soziale und individuelle Bezugsnorm" ["Social and Individual Reference Norms"]. Unpublished doctoral dissertation, Ruhr-Universität Bochum, 1977.

Rheinberg, F. *Leistungsbewertung und Lernmotivation [Evaluation of Achievement and Motivation to Learn]*. Göttingen: Hogrefe, 1980.

Rheinberg, F., Krug, J., Lübbermann, E., and Laudscheidt, K. "Beeinflussung der Leistungsbewertung im Unterricht: Motivationale Auswirkungen eines Interventionsversuchs" ["Influence of Evaluation of Achievement in Instruction: Motivational Effects of an Intervention Attempt"]. *Unterrichtswissenschaft [Instructional Science]*, 1980, *1*, 48–60.

Rheinberg, F., Kühmel, B., and Duscha, R. "Experimentell variierte Schulleistungsbewertung und ihre motivationalen Folgen"

["Motivational Effects of Experimental Variations in Evaluation of School Achievement"]. *Zeitschrift für empirische Pädagogik* [*Journal of Empirical Pedagogy*], 1979, *3*, 1-12.

Rosenthal, R., and Jacobsen, L. J. *Pygmalion in the Classroom.* New York: Holt, Rinehart and Winston, 1968.

Ryals, R. K. "An Experimental Study of Achievement Motivation Training as a Function of the Moral Maturity of Trainees." Unpublished doctoral dissertation, Washington University, St. Louis, 1969.

Scherer, J. "Änderung von Lehrerattribuierung und deren Auswirkungen auf Leistungsverhalten und Persönlichkeitsmerkmale von Schülern" ["The Effects of Changing Teacher's Attributions on the Achievement Behavior and Personality Characteristics of Students"]. Unpublished diploma thesis, Psychologisches Institut der Ruhr-Universität Bochum, 1972.

Schmalt, H. D. *Die Messung des Leistungsmotivs* [*Measuring the Achievement Motive*]. Göttingen: Hogrefe, 1976.

Smith, R. L., and Troth, W. A. "Achievement Motivation: A Rational Approach to Psychological Education." *Journal of Counseling Psychology*, 1975, *22*, 500-504.

Stamps, L. "The Effects of Intervention Techniques on Children's Failure Behavior." *Journal of Genetic Psychology*, 1973, *123*, 85-95.

Valins, S., and Nisbett, R. E. *Some Implications of Attribution Processes for the Development and Treatment of Emotional Disorders.* Morristown, N.J.: General Learning Press, 1971.

Varga, K. "Who Gains from Achievement Motivation Training?" *Vikalpa "The Journal for Decision Makers"*, [Indian Institute of Management, Ahmedabad], 1977, *2*, 187-200.

Varga, K. "Who Gains from Achievement Motivation Training?" *Vikalpa: The Journal for Decision Makers* [Indian Institute of Management, Ahmedabad], 1977, *2*, 187-200.

Weiner, B. *Die Wirkung von Erfolg und Misserfolg auf die Leistung* [*The Effects of Success and Failure on Achievement*]. Stuttgart: Klett, 1975.

Modifying   10
the Environment
of the Desegregated
Classroom

Elliot Aronson

One of the most exciting aspects of David McClelland's work is his earnest attempt to apply basic research findings to the betterment of society. It is in this context that I would like to present some of my own recent research, inspired in part by the example of McClelland's enduring optimism about the practical value of psychological research. In a sense my research is the mirror image of McClelland's: While he attempted to affect society and social institutions primarily by changing the motivations of its individual members, I have tried to influence the behavior and attitudes of individuals by changing the structure of one of the basic institutions of society: its schools. Specifically, my colleagues and I have tried to increase self-esteem, reduce prejudice, and improve academic performance by changing the classroom structure of elementary and secondary schools. The research program described here drew on a rich blend of casual observation, systematic observation, evaluation research, change agentry, group dynamics, and experimentation.

As is well known, in 1954, in the case of *Brown* v. *Board of Education*, the Supreme Court overruled an earlier decision (*Plessy* v. *Ferguson*, 1896) which had determined that a railroad could segregate its passengers racially as long as it provided equal facilities for both races. The impact of that 1896 decision extended far beyond railways, most seriously affecting black children who were being educated in segregated schools. In the *Brown* case, the court held that "separate but equal" was psychologically impossible because the mere fact of segregation implied to a segregated minority group that its members were inferior to the majority. Such an implication, the court said, could be damaging to the spirit of racial minorities.

This case may be the first instance in which the young science of social psychology significantly influenced the decision of a supreme court. Several social psychologists filed an amicus curiae brief testifying to the harms of segregation. The brief read in part: "Segregation, prejudices, and discriminations, and their social concomitants potentially damage the personality of all children. . . . Minority group children learn the inferior status to which they are assigned. . . . They often react with feelings of inferiority and a sense of personal humiliation. . . . Under these conditions the minority group child is thrown into a conflict with regard to his feelings about himself and his group. He wonders whether his group and himself are worthy of no more respect than they receive. This conflict and confusion leads to self-hatred " (quoted in Stephan, 1978, p. 220).

The degree of influence of social psychology can be best appreciated by noting the similarity between the thrust of the amicus brief and that of the actual ruling, which read in part: "To separate [Negro children] from others of similar age and qualifications solely because of their race generates a feeling of inferiority as to their status in the community that may affect their hearts and minds in a way unlikely ever to be undone. . . . We conclude that in the field of public education the doctrine 'separate but equal' has no place. Separate educational facilities are inherently unequal" (quoted in Stephan, 1978, p. 217).

The *Brown* decision was not only a humane interpretation of the Constitution, it was also the beginning of a profound social experiment. The testimony of social psychologists, in the Brown case, as well as in previous similar cases in state supreme courts, strongly suggested that desegregation would not only increase the self-esteem of minority groups, but that it would also improve their academic performance and lead to better understanding between the races. Of course the social psychologists who testified never meant to imply that such benefits would accrue automatically. Certain preconditions had to be met. These preconditions were most articulately stated by Gordon Allport in his classic study, *The Nature of Prejudice* (1954, p. 281), published the same year as the Supreme Court decision: "Prejudice . . . may be reduced by equal status contact between majority and minority groups in the pursuit of common goals. The effect is greatly enhanced if this contact is sanctioned by institutional supports (i.e., by law, custom, or local atmosphere), and provided it is of a sort that leads to the perception of common interests and common humanity between members of the two groups."

Let us look at the results of this social experiment. By and large, they are not encouraging. One of the better longitudinal studies of desegregation, conducted by Gerard and Miller (1975) in Riverside, California, found that long after the schools were desegregated, black, white, and Mexican-American children tended not to integrate but to hang together in their own ethnic clusters. Moreover, anxiety increased and remained high long after desegregation occurred. These trends can be seen in several other studies. Indeed, the most careful, scholarly reviews of the research show few, if any, benefits (see St. John, 1975; Stephan, 1978). According to Stephan's review, there is no single study that shows a significant increase in the self-esteem of minority children following desegregation; in fact, in fully 25 percent of the studies, desegregation is followed by a significant *decrease* in the self-esteem of young minority children. Moreover, Stephan reports that desegregation reduced the prejudice of whites toward blacks in only 13 percent of the school systems studied. The prejudice of blacks toward whites *increased* in about as many cases as it decreased. Similarly, studies of the effects of desegregation on the academic performance of minority children present a mixed and highly variable picture.

Observations in the Classroom

What went wrong? In the early 1970s, a research team at the University of Texas at Austin had been doing laboratory research on the antecedents of interpersonal attraction. We were speculating about the effects of desegregation on interpersonal attraction across racial and ethnic boundaries when the outbreak of racial tensions and hostility following the desegregation of Austin schools made the question particularly compelling. Moreover, the fact that the schools were in a state of crisis encouraged school administrators (who are usually not prone to encourage long-range research in their schools) to open their doors wide to our research team, allowing us the opportunity to do systematic research in the classrooms.

We began with the casual observation of scores of elementary school classrooms. The typical situation we observed was something like this: The teacher stands in front of the class and asks a question. Six to ten eager students strain in their seats and frantically wave their hands, anxious to be called on. Several others slink low in their seats, eyes averted, as if trying to make themselves invisible. When the teacher calls on one student, usually one of those with raised hands, looks of disappointment and dismay appear on the faces of the other eager students. If the fortunate student comes up with the right answer the teacher nods and smiles approvingly, a great reward for the child. Simultaneously an audible groan can be heard from classroom rivals, who apparently have been rooting for the child to fail so that they themselves might have the opportunity to demonstrate how smart (or how much smarter) they are.

On a few occasions the teacher bypasses the volunteers and calls on one of the students who is trying to avoid being called on. This child may not know the answer, may be nervous speaking in front of the class, or may have trouble with English. It is an uncomfortable moment. The student feels put on the spot. His classmates get impatient waiting for his response and want to show off their own superiority. They may snicker or even verbally insult the intelligence or the accent of the respondent. The teacher is also uncomfortable, wanting to give attention to the child, but to avoid causing further ridicule or embarrassment. Therefore these occasions *are* few and far between. The teacher and student forge an unwritten agreement. The child becomes anonymous; the teacher doesn't call on him. By ignoring him, however, the teacher has, in effect, written him off. The message that the other students get, and that the child in question almost certainly comes to believe, is that he is stupid and not worth bothering with.

Our observations made it crystal clear that this classroom game is fiercely competitive and that the stakes are high. The kids are competing for the attention and approval of a most important person in their world, as well as for status and grades. The process does not encourage friendliness and understanding among any of the children, who are led to view one another as foes to be heckled and vanquished. This state of affairs exists in most classrooms—even segregated ones. Desegregation adds racial tensions and exacerbates prejudices in this already volatile atmosphere of one-upmanship and resentment.

How might this situation be remedied? One doesn't need to look far. Let us return to Allport's prediction: Equal status contact in pursuit of common goals sanctioned by authority will produce beneficial effects. Has each of these preconditions been met? Let us look at each of them separately.

Sanction by authority. In some school districts there was clear acceptance and enforcement of desegregation by the responsible authority. In others the acceptance was not as clear. In still others (especially in the early years) local authorities openly defied the law. Pettigrew (1961) has shown that desegregation proceeded more smoothly and with less violence in localities where local authorities sanctioned integration. But such variables as self-esteem and the reduction of prejudice do not necessarily change for the better even where authority clearly sanctions desegregation. While sanction by authority may be necessary, it is clearly not a sufficient condition.

Equal status contact. The definition of equal status is slippery. In the case of desegregated schools we could claim that there is equal status on the grounds that all the children in the fifth grade (for example) have the same "occupational" status—that is, they are all fifth-grade students. On the other hand, if the teacher is prejudiced against blacks, blacks may be treated less fairly than whites; thus their perceived status in the classroom is lowered (see Gerard and Miller, 1975). Moreover, if black or Mexican-American students perform poorly in the classroom because of an inferior education prior to desegregation or because of language difficulties, their status among their peers may be low. An interesting complication was introduced by Cohen (1975). Whereas Allport (1954) predicted that positive interactions would result if a cooperative equal status were devised, expectation theory, as developed by Cohen, holds that even in such an environment biased expectations by both whites and blacks may lead to sustained white dominance. Cohen reasoned that both of these groups accept the premise that the majority group's competence results in dominance and superior achievement. She suggested that alternatives be created to reverse these often unconscious expectations, specifically at least a temporary exchange of majority and minority roles. In one study, for example (Cohen and Roper, 1972), black children were taught both how to build radios and how to teach this skill to others. Then a group of white children and the newly trained black children viewed a film of the black children building the radios. This was followed by some of the black children teaching the whites how to construct radios while others taught a black administrator. Then all the children came together in small groups. Equal status interactions were found in the groups where black children had taught whites how to build the radios. The other group, however, demonstrated the usual white dominance. We will return to this point in a moment.

In pursuit of common goals. As we mentioned earlier, in the typical American classroom, children are almost never engaged in the pursuit of common goals. The process of education is highly competitive. Children vie with one another for good grades, the respect of the teacher, and so on. In a newly desegregated school, all other things being equal, this atmosphere can exacerbate whatever prejudice existed prior to desegregation. A dramatic example of dysfunctional competition was demonstrated by Sherif and others (1961) in their classic "Robber's Cave" experiment. In this field experiment, the investigators encouraged intergroup competition between two teams of boys at a summer camp; this created fertile ground for anger and hostility even in previously benign, noncompetitive circumstances such as watching a movie. Positive relations between the groups were ultimately achieved only after both groups were required to work cooperatively to solve a common problem.

Interdependent Learning: The Jigsaw Technique

It is our contention that the competitive process interacts with "equal status contact." That is to say, whatever differences in ability existed between minority children and white children prior to desegregation are emphasized by the competitive structure of the learning environment, and since segregated school facilities are rarely equal, minority children frequently enter the newly desegregated school at a distinct disadvantage made more salient by the competitive atmosphere.

It was this reasoning that led my colleagues and me (1975, 1978) to develop the hypothesis that interdependent learning environments would establish the conditions necessary for the increase in self-esteem and performance and the decrease in prejudice that were expected to occur as a function of desegregation. Toward this end we developed a highly structured method of interdependent learning and systematically tested its effects in a number of elementary school classrooms. The aim of this research program was not merely to compare the effects of cooperation and competition in a classroom setting. This has been ably demonstated by other investigators dating as early as Deutsch's (1949) experiment. Rather, the intent was to devise a cooperative classroom structure that could be used easily by classroom teachers over the long term and to evaluate the effects of this intervention via a well-controlled series of field experiments. In short, this project was an action research program aimed at developing and evaluating a classroom atmosphere that could be sustained by classroom teachers long after the researchers have packed up their questionnaires and returned to the laboratory.

Basically, we designed a method of instruction that incorporated the beneficial features of cooperation and peer teaching into the highly structured atmosphere of the traditional classroom. We dubbed the process the "jigsaw" method, for reasons that will soon become obvious. In this technique the students are placed in small learning groups consisting of five or six participants. They might meet in these jigsaw groups for about an hour a day to learn one subject and follow their usual routine the rest of the time. Each student in the group is assigned one portion of the day's lesson and is responsible for teaching that segment to the other members of the group. Since the other members have no other access to this information, without which they can't put together the entire lesson, interdependence is essential to completing the assignment.

For example, suppose the students are to learn about the life of Eleanor Roosevelt as part of a unit in social studies. The teacher might arrange the biography so that it consisted of six paragraphs of approximately the same length. Each child would be given one paragraph. The first paragraph would be about Eleanor Roosevelt's early childhood; the second, her young adulthood; the third, her years as a wife and young mother; the fourth, her husband's paralysis and her role in his quest for the presidency; the fifth, her years in the White House; the sixth, her coming into her own as a world political figure, her work for the United Nations, and so on. Thus each group would have within it the entire biography, but each child would have no more than one-sixth of it. To learn "Eleanor Roosevelt," the students would have to master their own paragraphs, teach them to the others in their group, and listen closely to each other.

Each student would first read one paragraph over a few times and then join with counterparts from the other groups. For instance, if Julie is given Eleanor Roosevelt's White House years, she would consult in a counterpart group with Ted, Pam, and Juan, each of whom is a member of a different jigsaw group but has been given the same paragraph of the biography. The students could use each other as sounding boards to be sure they understood the important aspects of that phase of Eleanor Roosevelt's life and to rehearse their presentations to their jigsaw group. This procedure enables the poorer readers to get assistance in learning their section of the material, and it encourages the more advanced children to assume a teaching role.

A short time later, the children would return to their six-person jigsaw groups to teach their parts of the biography to one another. The teacher would tell them that they had a certain amount of time for the task and that they would be tested on the whole life of Eleanor Roosevelt later on. Though each student will be evaluated individually, they will clearly have to depend on one another to learn all the material.

As you can see, in the jigsaw structure children must work together and teach each other, and they are reinforced for doing so. In addition, the structure demands that the students use one another as resources rather than depend on the teacher as the sole provider of information, the more usual state of affairs in schools. In this situation, the only way a child can be a good learner is to begin to be a good listener and interviewer. The students also reward each other instead of allowing the teacher to be the major source of reinforcement in the classroom.

When left on their own in such a situation, the children eventually learn to teach and to listen to each other. They come to two important realizations: First, none of them could do well without the aid of every other person in the group; second, each member has a unique contribution to make.

The jigsaw technique is highly structured and very demanding. The structure not only induces children to imitate and model skills of group dynamics and social interaction, such as listening carefully and asking good questions, but also requires them to integrate these skills cognitively in their interactions with fellow group members. Indeed, group members spend the last few minutes of their meeting reviewing how their group proceeded and suggesting improvements.

What is the role of the teacher in this cooperative process? Instead of being primarily a lecturer and provider of substantive information, the teacher assumes the role of facilitator of group process. Teachers observe the groups and intervene on occasion to enhance constructive group interactions. They also retain the task of planning the curriculum and adapting the material to the jigsaw format (for specific details and examples, see Aronson and others, 1978).

It should be noted that problems may arise when the jigsaw technique is introduced. Cooperation does not occur smoothly or all at once; old competitive habits die hard. Moreover, not all students easily adapt to a cooperative classroom. For example, some students, because they are extremely poor readers, have trouble holding their own. Others, because they are extraordinarily shy or antisocial, *prefer* to work alone. With some ingenuity, however, the teacher can often turn some of these difficulties into strengths.

The experience of a Mexican-American child in one of our groups serves as a useful illustration. We will call him Carlos. Carlos was not very articulate in English, his second language. Because he had been ridiculed when he spoke up in the past, he had learned to keep quiet in class. He was one of those students we discussed earlier who had entered into a contract of silence with his teacher, opting for anonymity and being called on rarely.

While Carlos hated school and was learning very little in the traditional classroom, at least he was left alone. Accordingly, he was quite uncomfortable when the jigsaw system was introduced because it required him to talk to his groupmates. He had a great deal of trouble presenting his paragraph, stammering and hesitating. The other children reacted out of old habits, resorting to insults and teasing. "Aw, you don't know it," Susan accused. "You're dumb, you're stupid. You don't know what you're doing."

One of the researchers, assigned to observe the group process, intervened with a bit of advice when she overheard such comments: "OK, you can tease him if you want to. It might be fun for you, but it's *not* going to help you learn about Eleanor Roosevelt's young adulthood. And let me remind you, the exam will take place in less than an hour." Note how this statement brings home the fact that the reinforcement contingencies have shifted considerably. Now Susan doesn't gain much from humiliating Carlos. And she stands to lose a great deal, not just from the teacher singling her out for criticism but because she needs Carlos's information.

Gradually, but inexorably, it began to dawn on the students that they could *only* learn about Carlos's segment by paying attention to what he had to say. If they ignored him or continued to ridicule him, his segment would be unavailable to them and the most they could hope for would be an 80 percent score on the exam—an unattractive prospect to most of the children. And with that realization, the kids began to become pretty good interviewers, learning to pay attention to Carlos, to draw him out, and to ask probing questions. Carlos, in turn, began to relax and found it easier to explain out loud what was in his head. What the children came to learn about Carlos is even more important than the information about the lesson that they got from him. After a couple of days, they began to see that Carlos wasn't nearly as dumb as they had thought he was. After a few weeks they noticed talents in him they hadn't seen before. They began to like Carlos, and he began to enjoy school more and to think of his Anglo classmates as helpful friends and partners rather than tormentors.

In sum, working with the jigsaw technique, children gradually learn that the old competitive behaviors are no longer appropriate. In order to learn all of the material (and thus perform well on a quiz), each child must begin to listen to the others, ask appropriate questions, and so on. Furthermore, each child spends some time in the role of expert. Thus, the method incorporates Cohen's findings within the context of an equal status contact situation. The process opens the possibility for children to pay attention to one another and begin to appreciate one another as potentially valuable resources. It is important to emphasize that the children's motivation is not altruism; it is self-interest which, in this case, happens to benefit everyone.

Evaluating the Jigsaw Technique

Over the course of several experiments, we have evaluated the effects of participating in jigsaw learning groups on students like Carlos and Susan. We began on a small scale, carrying out pilot studies in individual classrooms. Finding that the method seemed to be successful, we conducted more systematic and comprehensive experiments in many classes in several schools. Then we brought the research back into the social psychological laboratory to investigate some of the mechanisms we hypothesized to underlie the beneficial changes we measured.

Taken together, the results of our project show a strong positive pattern of feelings, behaviors, and abilities that are clearly the result of the interdependence brought on by the jigsaw structure. We will provide a brief summary of our major findings.

Systematic research in the classroom has produced consistently positive results. The first experiment to investigate the effects of the jigsaw technique was conducted by Blaney and others (1977). As mentioned previously, the schools in Austin, Texas, had recently been desegregated, producing a great deal of tension and even some interracial skirmishes throughout the school system. In this tense atmosphere, the jigsaw technique was introduced in ten fifth-grade classrooms in seven elementary schools. Three classes from among the same schools were used as controls. The control classes were taught by teachers whose traditional techniques were rated very highly by their peers. The experimental classes met in jigsaw groups for about forty-five minutes a day, three days a week for six weeks. The curriculum was basically the same for the experimental and control classes. Students in the jigsaw groups showed significant increases in their liking for their groupmates both within and across ethnic boundaries. Moreover, they showed a significantly greater increase in self-esteem than children in the control classrooms. This was true for Anglo children as well as ethnic minorities. Anglos and blacks showed greater liking for school in the jigsaw classrooms than in traditional classrooms. (The Mexican-American students showed a tendency to like school *less* in the jigsaw classes, though obviously Carlos did not; this will be discussed in a moment.)

These results were essentially replicated by Geffner (1978) in Watsonville, California, a community about half Anglo and half Mexican-American. As a control for the possibility of a Hawthorne effect, Geffner compared the behavior of children in classrooms using cooperative learning with that of children in two other situations: highly innovative but not interdependent classrooms and traditional classrooms. Geffner found consistent and significant gains within classrooms using cooperative learning techniques. Specifically, children in these classes showed increases in self-esteem as well as increases in liking for school. Negative ethnic stereotypes were also diminished; children increased their positive general attitudes toward their own ethnic group and toward members of other ethnic groups to a far greater extent than children in the control classrooms.

Gonzalez (1979) extended the range of inquiry (also in Watsonville, California) by showing that high school students significantly increased their perception of an internal locus of control after six weeks of "jigsawing." This was significantly different from students in traditional classes, who tended to attribute the locus of control to external causes.

Changes in academic performance were assessed in an experiment by Lucker, Rosenfield, Sikes and Aronson (1977). The subjects were 303 fifth- and sixth-grade students from five Austin, Texas, elementary schools. Six classrooms were taught in the jigsaw manner; five were taught traditionally by highly competent teachers. For two weeks children were taught a unit on colonial

America taken from a fifth-grade textbook. All children were then given the same standardized test. The results showed that Anglo students' performance was roughly the same in jigsaw classes and traditional classes, $\bar{x}$ = 66.6 and 67.3 respectively. (The mean scores have been converted to percentage of correct answers.) Minority children performed significantly better in jigsaw classes than in traditional classes ($\bar{x}$ = 56.6 and 49.7, respectively). The difference in performance for minority students in the two types of classrooms was highly significant. Only two weeks of jigsaw activity succeeded in narrowing the performance gap between Anglos and minorities from more than 17 percentage points to about 10 percentage points. Interestingly enough, the jigsaw method apparently does *not* work a hardship on students with high ability: Students in the highest quartile in reading ability benefited from the jigsaw structure just as much as students in the lowest quartile.

Underlying Mechanisms

Increased Participation. We have seen that learning in a small interdependent group leads to greater interpersonal attraction, self-esteem, and liking for school; more positive inter-ethnic and intra-ethnic perceptions; and, for ethnic minorities, improvement in academic performance. We think that some of our findings result from the more active participation in the learning process, under conditions of reduced anxiety, that the jigsaw structure requires. This increase in participation should enhance interest, which would result in better performance as well as greater liking for school, other things being equal. But other things are sometimes not equal. For example, in the study by Blaney and others (1977) there was some indication from our observation of the groups that many of the Mexican-American children were made anxious by being required to participate more actively. They seemed embarrassed by their difficulty with English in a group dominated by Anglos. This observation was confirmed by the data on liking for school. Blaney and others found that Anglos and blacks in the jigsaw classrooms liked school better than those in the traditional classrooms, while for Mexican-Americans the reverse was true. It seemed clear that this anxiety could be reduced if Mexican-American children were in a situation where it was not embarrassing to be more articulate in Spanish than in English. Thus, Geffner (1978), working in a situation where both the residential and school population was approximately 50 percent Spanish-speaking, found that Mexican-American children (like Anglos and blacks) increased their liking for school to a greater extent in the cooperative groups than in traditional classrooms.

Increases in Empathic Role Taking. Evidently people working together in an interdependent fashion increase their ability to take one another's perspectives. To return to our earlier example, suppose that Susan and Carlos are in a jigsaw group. Carlos is reporting and Susan is having trouble following him. She doesn't quite understand the material because his style of presentation is different from what she is accustomed to. Not only must she pay close attention but she must find a way to ask questions that Carlos will understand and that will elicit the information she needs. To accomplish this she must get to know Carlos, put herself in his shoes, empathize.

Bridgeman (1977) tested the notion that the ability to take another's perspective is required, practiced, and rewarded in jigsaw learning. The more experience students have with the jigsaw process, she believed, the greater their role-taking abilities would become. She administered a revised version of Chandler's (1973) role-taking cartoon series to 120 fifth-grade students. Roughly half the students spent eight weeks in a jigsaw learning environment while the other half were taught either in traditional classrooms or in innovative small group classrooms. Each of the cartoons in the Chandler test depicts a central character caught up in a chain of psychological cause and effect such that the character's subsequent behavior is shaped by and fully comprehensible only in terms of the events preceding it. In one sequence, for example, a boy who has been saddened by seeing his father off at the airport begins to cry when he receives a gift of a toy airplane similar to the one that carried his father away. Midway into the sequence, a second character is introduced in the role of a late-arriving bystander who witnesses the central character's behavior, but is not privy to its cause. Thus, the subject is in a privileged position relative to the bystander in the story, whose role the subject is later asked to assume. The cartoon series measures the degree to which the subject can set aside facts known only to himself and adopt a perspective measurably different from his own. For example, while the subject knows why the child in the above sequence cries when he receives the toy airplane, the mailman who delivers the toy does not. What happens when the subject is asked to take the mailman's perspective?

After eight weeks, students in the jigsaw classrooms could put themselves in the bystander's place more successfully than students in the control classrooms. For example, when the mailman delivers the toy airplane to the little boy, students in the control classrooms tend to assume that the mailman knows the boy will cry; that is, they behave as if they believe the mailman knows that the boy's father recently left town on an airplane simply because they (the subjects) have this information. On the other hand, students who had participated in a jigsaw group were much more successful at taking the mailman's role—realizing that the mailman could not possibly understand why the boy would cry upon receiving a toy airplane.

Attributions for Success and Failure. Working together in the pursuit of common goals changes the "observer's" attributional patterns. There is some evidence to support the notion that cooperation increases the tendency for individuals to make the same kind of attributions for success and failure to their partners as they do for themselves. In one of our laboratory experiments (Stephan, Presser, Kennedy and Aronson, 1978) it was found that when an individual succeeds at a task he tends to attribute his success dispositionally (for example, to skill), but when he fails he tends to make a situational attribution (for example, to luck). This finding is consistent with a host of findings in the attribution theory literature. But we went further: In our experiment we demonstrated that individuals engaged in an *interdependent* task make the same kinds of attributions for their partner's performance as they do for their own. This was not the case in competitive interactions.

Effects of Dependent Variables on One Another. It is reasonable to assume that the various consequences of interdependent learning become antecedents for one another. Just as low self-esteem can interfere with a child's performing well, anything that increases self-esteem is likely to improve the performance of the underachiever. Conversely, as Franks and Marolla (1976) have indicated, better performance should bring about higher self-esteem; similarly, being treated with more attention and respect by one's peers (as almost inevitably happens in jigsaw groups) is another important antecedent of self-esteem. There is ample evidence for a two-way causal connection between performance and self-esteem (see Covington and Beery, 1976; Purkey, 1970).

Summary and Conclusions

The results of our research are striking. They illustrate how the solution for a social problem might be suggested and advanced by using social psychological theory and research. First a problem arose. Observation led us to frame hypotheses derived from the psychological literature and to design a method of action research. A program was implemented and its effectiveness was evaluated in the field. Mechanisms assumed to be influencing the process were isolated and brought back into the laboratory to be investigated. Thus the theories were tested and the program was increasingly refined.

The first goal of our research strategy was to evaluate the effectiveness of the jigsaw method. We have shown that a wide variety of beneficial effects occurred as a result of structuring the social psychological aspects of classroom learning so that children spent at least part of their time pursuing common goals. These effects are in accord with predictions made by social scientists over twenty-five years ago in their testimony favoring desegregation, and they confirmed our hypotheses for the jigsaw technique as well.

Since our research was action research, we were also concerned to go beyond the measures and hypotheses involved in the evaluation process. Our further goal was to perfect the jigsaw technique, to design a simple procedure for teaching it to teachers, and to encourage its widespread adaptation in the schools. Thus we wanted to know whether its goals were adequately specified and whether the program met its goals in a workable and efficient manner. At this writing, the jigsaw technique seems to have passed all tests. It works, it is easily implemented, and there appear to be no serious unwanted side-effects. Research and implementation continue.

References

Allport, G. *The Nature of Prejudice.* Reading, Mass.: Addison-Wesley, 1954.

Aronson, E., Bridgeman, D.L., and Geffner, R. "The Effects of a Cooperative Classroom Structure on Students' Behavior and Attitudes." In D. Bar-Tal and L. Saxe (Eds.), *Social Psychology of Education: Theory and Research.* Washington, D.C.: Hemisphere Press, 1978.

Aronson, E., and others. "Busing and Racial Tension: The Jigsaw Route to Learning and Liking. *Psychology Today,* 1975, *8,* 43-59.

Aronson, E., and others. *The Jigsaw Classroom.* Beverly Hills, Calif.: Sage, 1978.

Blaney, N.T., and others. "Interdependence in the Classroom: A Field Study." *Journal of Educational Psychology,* 1977, *69,* 139-146.

Bridgeman, D.L. "The Influence of Cooperative, Interdependent Learning on Role Taking and Moral Reasoning: A Theoretical and Empirical Field Study with Fifth-Grade Students." Unpublished doctoral dissertation, University of California, Santa Cruz, 1977.

Chandler, M. J. "Egocentrism and Antisocial Behavior: The Assessment and Training of Social Perspective-Taking Skills." *Developmental Psychology,* 1973, *9,* 326-332.

Cohen, E.G. "The Effects of Desegregation on Race Relations." *Law and Contemporary Problems,* 1975, *39,* 271-299.

Cohen, E. G., and Roper, S. "Modification of Interracial Interaction Disability: An Application of Status Characteristics Theory." *American Sociological Review,* 1972, *6,* 643-657.

Covington, M. V., and Beery, R. G. *Self-Worth and School Learning.* New York: Holt, Rinehart and Winston, 1976.

Deutsch, M. "An Experimental Study of the Effects of Cooperation and Competition upon Group Process." *Human Relations,* 1949, *2,* 199-231.

Franks, D. D., and Marolla, J. "Efficacious Action and Social Approval as Interacting Dimensions of Self-Esteem: A Tentative

Formulation Through Construct Validation, *Sociometry*, 1976, *39*, 324–341.

Geffner, R.A. "The Effects of Interdependent Learning on Self-Esteem, Inter-Ethnic Relations, and Intra-Ethnic Attitudes of Elementary School Children: A Field Experiment." Unpublished doctoral dissertation, University of California, Santa Cruz, 1978.

Gerard, H., and Miller, N. *School Desegregation*. New York: Plenum, 1975.

Gonzalez, A. "Classroom Cooperation and Ethnic Balance." Unpublished doctoral dissertation, University of California, Santa Cruz, 1979.

Lucker, G. W., Rosenfield, D., Sikes, J., and Aronson, E. "Performance in the Interdependent Classroom: A Field Study." *American Educational Research Journal*, 1977, *13*, 115–123.

Pettigrew, T. "Social Psychology and Desegregation Research." *American Psychologist*, 1961, *15*, 61–71.

Purkey, W. W. *Self-Concept and School Achievement*. Englewood Cliffs, N.J.: Prentice-Hall, 1970.

St. John, N. *School Desegregation: Outcomes for Children*. New York: Wiley, 1975.

Sherif, M., and others. *Intergroup Conflict and Cooperation: The Robber's Cave Experiment*. Norman: Institute of Intergroup Relations, University of Oklahoma, 1961.

Stephan, C., Presser, N. R., Kennedy, J. C., and Aronson, E. "Attributions to Success and Failure in Cooperative, Competitive, and Interdependent Interactions." *European Journal of Social Psychology*, 1978, *8*, 269–274.

Stephan, W. G. "School Desegregation: An Evaluation of Predictions Made in *Brown* vs. *Board of Education*." *Psychological Bulletin*, 1978, *85*, 217–238.

Reflections

 *David C. McClelland*

As I look over the contributions to this volume, I am excited, pleased, and proud—excited by the many new directions in motivation research that they represent, pleased at the thought that I may have helped at some point in the development of the psychologists who have made the contributions, and proud of what they have accomplished. From my perspective, the progress that has been made in motivation research since the end of World War II is impressive. I remember thinking when I returned to teaching psychology at Wesleyan that what we needed was a good five-cent measure of human motivation. We set out to create one and "The rest, gentlemen, is history"—to revert to the standard cliché of a master of ceremonies. We did not succeed entirely, because first of all the measure did not turn out to be cheap. Most psychologists are still unwilling to spend the time or money necessary to code thought content, preferring self-report inventories despite their obvious limitations. Secondly, the measures did not have the psychometric properties that people thought they should have, which justified them in continuing to use less expensive questionnaires. In the end this has led to some rethinking of measurement issues, which is fully represented in the chapters by Atkinson and Fleming in the present volume. Still, there is a long way to go before traditional psychology fully accepts the innovations we introduced over 35 years ago.

I say "we" because it was always a collective enterprise. From the beginning I was driven by the desire to know more about human motivation through actual empirical studies rather than through armchair speculation or clinical observation, but I realized that there were limits to what one investigator could do by himself in a lifetime. So I consciously set out to develop a disciplined band of investigators who would catch some of my enthusiasm for this enterprise and go off and do research on their own. Perhaps this was just a post hoc rationalization for the fact that I like working with students. I have a hard time thinking things through entirely on my own. My ideas develop much better in the give and take of planning a research enterprise together.

Did I succeed in helping create an intrepid band of investigators or "inquisitive mariners," to use Dan McAdams's felicitous phrase? The answer is a clear "yes," to judge by the contents of this volume, although the "yes" has some qualifications that shed some light on the history of science and the nature of teacher-student relationships. The most obvious qualification is that I didn't do it. I feel a little like somebody who has started a snowball rolling down a hill and who stands amazed at how it grows bigger and bigger as it rolls down, then hits a rock and breaks into several snowballs that also accumulate size as they go off in various directions. I can't even keep up with much that is going on in the field of motivation research. That, of course, is just what I hoped would happen, but to claim that I had a major role in later developments is certainly questionable.

Secondly it has been sobering to review my influence on all my students throughout my career. Between 1946–1981, I have worked intensively with about 55 people who went on to become professional psychologists. Of that number, 15, or 27%, have turned out to be outstanding researchers in their own right, at a level defined by the contributors to this volume. Perhaps another ten, to make it 45% in all, have been at least moderately productive, having published at least one original book or at least half a dozen such papers. Is this a good record or not? In terms of my own goals, it represents a considerable shortfall, since the majority of those with whom I have worked did not continue to do research and publish. This is not to say, of course, that they have not made very important contributions to society as clinicians or teachers. I need only recall the career of my student Richard Alpert to remind myself that there are many ways other than through research that psychologists can contribute to improving the human condition. As Ram Dass, he has produced books and lectures that have touched and benefited the lives of millions of Americans.

Of the 15–25 students who have continued to be productive, only about half have stayed in the field of motivation research proper, employing techniques and points of view that I had attempted to convince them were all-important. So the ultimate yield of my efforts may seem small (20-40%), but it is very much larger than for the general run of Ph.D.'s. According to the data published by Kenneth E. Clark in *America's Psychologists* (American Psychological Association, 1957), 69% of Ph.D.'s do not publish much beyond their thesis (0-4 publications), as contrasted with only 55% of the students who have been closely associated with me, a difference which is statistically significant. Even greater is the difference for those who have been very productive, which runs around 27% for my students and 5-10% for Ph.D.'s in general. Furthermore the band of inquisitive mariners associated with me, though small in number, have with their students accomplished a tremendous amount, as the present volume indicates.

They have made contributions to general theory and to the understanding of how psychology should be conducted (see the chapters by Atkinson and by deCharms). They have challenged the assumptions of traditional psychometric theory and proposed new methods in this area (see the chapters by Atkinson and by Fleming). They have made contributions to economics and the world of work (see the chapter by Boyatzis), and to political science (see the chapter by Winter). They have explored motivational patterns in national sample surveys a generation ago and today, among the poor and the rich, among different occupational groups, and among men and women (see chapters by Veroff and by Stewart and Chester). They have investigated new motives and explored their relation to mental health (chapter by McAdams) and investigated improving performance in the schools through motivational principles (chapters by Heckhausen and Krug and by Aronson).

Most of the contributions represented here have been in the framework of the psychology of motivation, but I tend to agree with those who think that the more lasting contribution of our work to psychology as a whole is its emphasis on the importance of coding thought content that is spontaneous and not the product of introspection or reflection by the subject on what is going on. The picture-story test of imagination on which most of the motivation research is built is, after all, only one example of the way thought can be sampled. More recent work in the management area, in the study of politics, and in the study of memory has demonstrated that spontaneous thought content elicited in a variety of ways can be meaningfully coded for a number of psychological characteristics of importance that need not be considered motives in the narrow sense (see the chapters by Winter and by McAdams). For far too long psychology has been stuck in the self-reflective mode, in which what is going on in a person's head is passed through the filter of his or her own judgments before it gets to the observer. Obviously subjects edit what they report and are limited by the concepts they themselves use to understand their thought processes. It is far better to observe and code the thought stream directly without interference from this editing process. If there is one lesson that motivation research has to give to the rest of psychology, it is this one.

Can anything of general interest be gleaned from the history of this band of inquisitive mariners? As noted already, it very soon outgrew any influence that I might have had. Atkinson, after graduating from Wesleyan, went to the University of Michigan to get his Ph.D., where he trained a whole generation of motivation researchers and developed a theory of the dynamics of action that was far beyond anything that I had ever essayed. Similarly, Heckhausen trained a corps of motivation researchers in Germany, although my contact with him was at second-hand—another German, Hans-Werner Wendt, whom I had met at the Salzburg Seminar in 1951 came to study at Wesleyan, where he became thoroughly acquainted with the approach to measuring motivation that we were developing; he then took this back to Germany to his friend Heinz Heckhausen, who adopted the methodology and turned out dozens of dedicated motivation researchers. In the 1960s we worked with Manohar Nadkarni, an Indian psychologist, and developed achievement motivation training courses for Indian businessmen that led to the wide-scale adoption of our methods of measuring motivation by Indian psychologists like T. V. Rao and Prayag

Mehta. Often the ideas spread by diffusion and not by direct intervention on my part.

The early group of researchers at Wesleyan has been extraordinarily productive, as attested by the fact that four of the contributions to this volume are by members of that group (Atkinson, deCharms, Veroff, and Aronson). This is surprising, because at that time Wesleyan did not grant the Ph.D. degree, so that those doing research were either undergraduates working on senior honor theses or Masters' candidates. When I was originally offered a tenured position at Harvard in 1950, I turned it down because I felt that at Wesleyan I had all the exciting students I could handle in an environment where I would not be distracted by all kinds of other responsibilities. But by the mid-fifties I was beginning to worry that the students I had trained were sidetracked into other fields of endeavor when they got to their Ph.D. departments. So one of the main reasons I went to Harvard the second time I was offered a professorship there, in 1956, was because I thought I would have more opportunity to develop the kind of investigators I was trying to create. Looking back I would judge that I was wrong in this estimate. The null hypothesis cannot be disproved that going to Harvard made no difference. In the time that I was at Wesleyan from 1946-1956 I worked with 19 students who turned into professional psychologists, of whom five would be regarded as outstandingly productive and another four or five at least moderately productive. At Harvard in the 1960s I worked with 19 students of whom five could be regarded as outstandingly productive and another four moderately productive. In the 1970s I worked with 18 students of whom five could be regarded as outstandingly productive and another one or two moderately productive—although it is early to be sure in this case. In other words the yield of my efforts to train psychologists for research has been about the same in every decade and the same at Harvard as it was at Wesleyan, despite what might seem to be the much greater opportunities to get top students at Harvard. On the other hand, there were more distractions at Harvard: I was in a Social Relations department in the 1960s where we were also training sociologists and social anthropologists. And there were many more brilliant teachers and researchers in the Harvard environment to attract the attention of the best students.

Academic aptitude has not seemed to be strongly related to which of my students would turn out to be most productive. In the late 1940s at Wesleyan I worked with two students, one of whom had a Scholastic Aptitude Test score in the 800's and the other one in the 500's. Both went on for a Ph.D. The former so far as I know never contributed to psychological research and never published anything. The latter has had a brilliant career and made profound contributions to psychology. I had still another student at Wesleyan whom I accepted as a research assistant before he had taken his final examinations for honors in psychology—which he then proceeded not to pass at the honors level. That student has also turned out to make brilliant theoretical and empirical contributions to psychology. Neither he nor the previous student could have been admitted to Harvard or probably to any outstanding graduate school in psychology. What a loss to psychology if they had not been permitted to go on! Over and over again I have pleaded with my colleagues at Harvard not to use Scholastic Aptitude Test scores as the basis for admission, but year after year the final rank order of admission is almost perfectly correlated with the sum of the verbal and mathematical aptitude test scores. My skepticism about such scores was based on my experience—on facts—but I find that experience, no matter how factual, stands little chance of influencing those who believe that such tests are measuring some abstract general ability that must be related to excellence in research.

Sex of the student also does not seem to have made a difference in productivity. I have worked intensively with nine women, of whom three could be regarded as outstandingly productive—a 30% return rate, which is comparable to that for men.

Over the years there have been many surprises—students who were wonderfully exciting in graduate school, who stopped producing a few years beyond the Ph.D.—the morning glories—or other students who seemed hopeless and later turned out to be genuinely productive scholars—the late bloomers. I remember one in particular whom I frankly and somewhat brutally told would never make a successful research psychologist because he couldn't write a simple sentence that made sense. He later turned out to be the author of several very successful and important books. The morning glories I recall with great regret—the students who had such interesting ideas, who carried out exciting research and wrote such good reports of it, yet who later stopped producing research altogether. It obviously takes more than some influences in graduate school to turn out people who continue to be excited by the possibilities of pushing back the frontiers of knowledge throughout their lifetime.

As I reflect on these matters, I realize I am behaving like a person with high n Achievement. I am searching for feedback on how well I have been doing as a teacher of future researchers. But there is another deeper sense in which I realize the answer to the question is not all that important to me. For years there was a picture of a bird placed on the top of the bookcase behind my desk at Harvard. At the bottom of the picture was written: "A bird doesn't sing because it has a message. It sings because it has a song." That is the way I feel about the scientific enterprise. I do research because I enjoy it and I am still doing it because I still like it. And I work with students because I enjoy working with them on a project that may turn up something new. Some of them have clearly caught that enthusiasm, perhaps influenced a bit by me and certainly by many others. But even if I were to discover that none of my students had later been productive, I don't think it would modify my behavior in the least. For I always believe that the latest student of mine is the best and that he or she is going to make the breakthrough that will revolutionize what we know about something.

In this volume you have been introduced to some of the breakthroughs such students have made, and I think you will agree with me that psychology is much further along as a science because of their efforts.

Chronological
Bibliography of
David C. McClelland

1942

McClelland, D. C. "Functional Autonomy of Motives as an Extinction Phenomenon." *Psychological Review*, 1942, *49*, 272–283.

McClelland, D. C. "Habit Reversal in Serial Verbal Discrimination Learning." *Psychological Bulletin*, 1942, *39*, 496–497.

McClelland, D. C. "Studies in Serial Verbal Discrimination Learning. I: Reminiscence with Two Speeds of Pair Presentation." *Journal of Experimental Psychology*, 1942, *31*, 44–56.

McClelland, D. C. "Studies in Serial Verbal Discrimination Learning. II: Retention of Responses to Right and Wrong Words in a Transfer Situation." *Journal of Experimental Psychology*, 1942, *31*, 149–162.

1943

McClelland, D. C. "Factors Influencing the Time Error in Judgments of Visual Extent." *Journal of Experimental Psychology*, 1943, *33*, 81–95.

McClelland, D. C. "Studies in Serial Verbal Discrimination Learn-ing. III: The Influence of Difficulty on Reminiscence in Responses to Right and Wrong Words." *Journal of Experimental Psychology*, 1943, *32*, 235-246.

McClelland, D. C. "Studies in Serial Verbal Discrimination Learn-ing. IV: Habit Reversal After Two Degrees of Learning." *Journal of Experimental Psychology*, 1943, *33*, 457-470.

McClelland, D. C., and Heath, R. M. "Retroactive Inhibition as a Function of Degree of Association of Original and Interpolated Activities." *Journal of Experimental Psychology*, 1943, *33*, 420-430.

1944

McClelland, D. C. "Simplified Scoring of the Bernreuter Personality Inventory." *Journal of Applied Psychology*, 1944, *28*, 414-419.

1945

McClelland, D. C., and Apicella, F. S. "A Functional Classification of Verbal Reactions to Experimentally Induced Failure." *Journal of Abnormal and Social Psychology*, 1945, *40*, 376-390.

1947

Gory, A. E., and McClelland, D. C. "Characteristics of Conscien-tious Objectors in World War II." *Journal of Consulting Psy-chology*, 1947, *11*, 245-257.

McClelland, D. C. "Further Application of Simplified Scoring of the Bernreuter Personality Inventory." *Journal of Applied Psy-chology*, 1947, *31*, 182-188.

McClelland, D. C., and Apicella, F. S. "Reminiscence Following Experimentally Induced Failure." *Journal of Experimental Psy-chology*, 1947, *37*, 159-169.

1948

Atkinson, J. W., and McClelland, D. C. "The Projective Expression of Needs. II: The Effect of Different Intensities of the Hunger

Drive on Thematic Apperception." *Journal of Experimental Psychology*, 1948, *38*, 643–658.

McClelland, D. C. "Bernreuter Personality Inventory." In O. J. Kaplan (Ed.), *Encyclopedia of Vocational Guidance*. Vol. 2. New York: Philosophical Library, 1948.

McClelland, D. C., and Atkinson, J. W. "The Projective Expression of Needs. I: The Effect of Different Intensities of the Hunger Drive on Perception." *Journal of Psychology*, 1948, *25*, 205–222.

1949

McClelland, D. C., Atkinson, J. W., and Clark, R. A. "The Projective Expression of Needs. III: The Effect of Ego-Involvement, Success, and Failure on Perception." *Journal of Psychology*, 1949, *27*, 311–330.

McClelland, D. C., Clark, R. A., Roby, T. B., and Atkinson, J.W. "The Projective Expression of Needs. IV: The Effect of the Need for Achievement on Thematic Apperception." *Journal of Experimental Psychology*, 1949, *39*, 242–255.

McClelland, D. C., and Liberman, A. M. "The Effect of Need for Achievement on Recognition of Need-Related Words." *Journal of Personality*, 1949, *18*, 236–251.

1950

McClelland, D. C. Review of *Frustration: The Study of Behavior Without a Goal* by N.R.F. Maier. *Journal of Abnormal and Social Psychology*, 1950, *45*, 564–566.

1951

McClelland, D. C. "Measuring Motives in Phantasy: The Achievement Motive." In H. Guetzkow (Ed.), *Groups, Leadership, and Men*. Pittsburgh: Carnegie Press, 1951.

McClelland, D. C. *Personality*. New York: William Sloane, 1951.

1952

McClelland, D. C. Review of *Perception: An Approach to Personality*, R. R. Blake and G. V. Ramsey (Eds.). *Psychological Bulletin*, 1952, *49*, 72–75.

McClelland, D. C., and Friedman, G. A. "A Cross-Cultural Study of the Relationship Between Child-Training Practices and Achievement Motivation Appearing in Folk Tales." In G. E. Swanson, T. M. Newcomb, and E. L. Hartley (Eds.), *Readings in Social Psychology*. (Rev. ed.) New York: Holt, 1952.

1953

McClelland, D. C. "The Measurement of Human Motivation: An Experimental Approach." In *Proceedings of the 1952 Conference on Testing Problems*. Princeton, N.J.: Educational Testing Service, 1953.

McClelland, D. C., Atkinson, J. W., Clark, R. A., and Lowell, E. L. *The Achievement Motive*. New York: Appleton-Century-Crofts, 1953. (Reprinted by Irvington, New York, 1976).

McClelland, D. C., and McGown, D. R. "The Effect of Variable Food Reinforcement on the Strength of a Secondary Reward." *Journal of Comparative and Physiological Psychology*, 1953, *46*, 80–86.

1954

McClelland, D. C. "The Recruitment of Scientific Psychologists." *American Psychologist*, 1954, *9*, 811–813.

1955

deCharms, R., Morrison, H. W., Reitman, W., and McClelland, D. C. "Behavioral Correlates of Directly and Indirectly Measured Achievement Motivation." In D. C. McClelland (Ed.), *Studies in Motivation*. New York: Appleton-Century-Crofts, 1955.

McClelland, D. C. "The Psychology of Mental Content Reconsidered." *Psychological Review*, 1955, *62*, 297–302.

McClelland, D. C. Review of *Motivation and Personality* by A. H. Maslow, and of *Nebraska Symposium on Motivation 1954*, M. R. Jones (Ed.). *Psychological Bulletin*, 1955, *52*, 159–161.

McClelland, D. C. "Some Social Consequences of Achievement Motivation." In M. R. Jones (Ed.), *Nebraska Symposium on Motivation 1955*. Lincoln: University of Nebraska Press, 1955.

McClelland, D. C. (Ed.). *Studies in Motivation*. New York: Appleton-Century-Crofts, 1955.

McClelland, D. C., Rindlisbacher, A., and deCharms, R. "Religious and Other Sources of Parental Attitudes Toward Independence Training." In D. C. McClelland (Ed.), *Studies in Motivation*. New York: Appleton-Century-Crofts, 1955.

1956

McClelland, D. C. "The Calculated Risk: An Aspect of Creative Scientific Performance." In C. W. Taylor (Ed.), *Research Conference on the Identification of Creative Scientific Talent*. Salt Lake City: University of Utah Press, 1956.

McClelland, D. C. "Personality." In P. R. Farnsworth (Ed.), *Annual Review of Psychology*. Palo Alto, Calif.: Annual Reviews, 1956.

McClelland, D. C. "Personality: An Integrative View." In J. L. McCary (Ed.), *Psychology of Personality*. New York: Logos Press, 1956.

McClelland, D. C., and Clark, R. A. "A Factor Analytic Integration of Imaginative and Performance Measures of the Need for Achievement." *Journal of General Psychology*, 1956, *55*, 73–83.

1957

McClelland, D. C. "Conscience and the Will Rediscovered." Review of *Wille und Leistung* by K. Mierke. *Contemporary Psychology*, 1957, *2*, 177–179.

McClelland, D. C. "Die wiedergefundene Psychologie von den psychischen Inhalten" ["The Rediscovered Psychology of Mental Content"]. *Psychologische Beiträge* [*Psychological Contributions*], 1957, *3*, 21–33.

McClelland, D. C. "Freud and Hull: Pioneers in Scientific Psychology." *American Scientist*, 1957, *45*, 101–113.

McClelland, D. C. "Toward a Science of Personality Psychology." In H. P. David and H. von Bracken (Eds.), *Perspectives in Personality Theory*. New York: Basic Books, 1957.

1958

Kaltenbach, J. E., and McClelland, D. C. "Achievement and Social Status in Three Small Communities." In D. C. McClelland, A. L. Baldwin, U. Bronfenbrenner, and F. L. Strodtbeck, *Talent and Society*. New York: Van Nostrand, 1958.

McClelland, D. C. "Issues in the Identification of Talent." In D. C. McClelland, A. L. Baldwin, U. Bronfenbrenner, and F. L. Strodtbeck, *Talent and Society*. New York: Van Nostrand, 1958.

McClelland, D. C. "Methods of Measuring Human Motivation." In J. W. Atkinson (Ed.), *Motives in Fantasy, Action, and Society*. New York: Van Nostrand, 1958.

McClelland, D. C. "Review and Prospects." In D. C. McClelland, A. L. Baldwin, U. Bronfenbrenner, and F. L. Strodtbeck, *Talent and Society*. New York: Van Nostrand, 1958.

McClelland, D. C. "Risk-Taking in Children with High and Low Need for Achievement." In J. W. Atkinson (Ed.), *Motives in Fantasy, Action, and Society*. New York: Van Nostrand, 1958.

McClelland, D. C. "The Use of Measures of Human Motivation in the Study of Society." In J. W. Atkinson (Ed.), *Motives in Fantasy, Action, and Society*. New York: Van Nostrand, 1958.

McClelland, D. C., Baldwin, A. L., Bronfenbrenner, U., and Strodtbeck, F. L. *Talent and Society*. New York: Van Nostrand, 1958.

McClelland, D. C., Sturr, J., Knapp, R. H., and Wendt, H. W. "Obligation to Self and Society in the United States and Germany." *Journal of Abnormal and Social Psychology*, 1958, 56, 245-255.

1959

McClelland, D. C. "Religious Overtones in Psychoanalysis." *Theology Today*, 1959, 16, 40-64.

1961

McClelland, D. C. "The Achievement Motive in Economic Growth." In *Proceedings of the 14th International Congress of Applied Psychology.* Copenhagen: Munksgaard, 1961.

McClelland, D. C. "The Achievement Motive in History." *Mercurio* [Rome], 1961.

McClelland, D. C. *The Achieving Society.* New York: Van Nostrand, 1961. (Reprinted by Irvington, New York, 1976. German, Spanish, and Japanese translations. Abridged version, sponsored by the United States Information Agency, published in several languages.)

McClelland, D. C. "Encouraging Excellence." *Daedalus,* 1961, *90,* 711–724.

1962

McClelland, D. C. "Business Drive and National Achievement." *Harvard Business Review,* July-Aug., 1962, 99–112.

McClelland, D. C. "On the Psychodynamics of Creative Physical Scientists." In H. E. Gruber, G. Terrell, and M. Wertheimer (Eds.), *Contemporary Approaches to Creative Thinking.* New York: Atherton Press, 1962.

1963

McClelland, D. C. "Changing Values for Progress." In H. W. Burns (Ed.), *Education and the Development of Nations.* Syracuse, N.Y.: Syracuse University Press, 1963.

McClelland, D. C. "The Harlequin Complex." In R. W. White (Ed.), *The Study of Lives.* New York: Atherton Press, 1963.

McClelland, D. C. "Motivational Patterns in Southeast Asia with Special Reference to the Chinese Case." *Journal of Social Issues,* 1963, *19* (1), 6–19.

McClelland, D. C. "Motivation to Achieve: Some Clinical Approaches." In G. Watson (Ed.), *No Room at the Bottom: Automation and the Reluctant Learner.* Washington, D.C.: National Education Association, 1963.

McClelland, D. C. "National Character and Economic Growth in Turkey and Iran." In L. W. Pye (Ed.), *Communication and Political Development*. Princeton, N.J.: Princeton University Press, 1963.

McClelland, D. C. "Values in Popular Literature for Children." *Childhood Education*, 1963, *40*, 135-138.

McClelland, D. C. "Why Men and Nations Seek Success." Interview in *Nation's Business*, September, 1963, *51* (9), 32-33, 72-79.

Winter, D. G., Alpert, R. A., and McClelland, D. C. "The Classic Personal Style." *Journal of Abnormal and Social Psychology*, 1963, *67*, 254-265.

1964

McClelland, D. C. "A Psychological Approach to Economic Development." Review of *On the Theory of Social Change* by E. E. Hagen. *Economic Development and Cultural Change*, 1964, *12*, 320-324.

McClelland, D. C. *The Roots of Consciousness*. New York: Van Nostrand, 1964. (Also in German translation.)

1965

Kalin, R., Kahn, M., and McClelland, D. C. "The Effects of Male Social Drinking on Fantasy." *Journal of Personality and Social Psychology*, 1965, *1*, 441-452.

McClelland, D. C. "Achievement Motivation Can Be Developed." *Harvard Business Review*, Nov.-Dec., 1965, 6-25.

McClelland, D. C. "*N* Achievement and Entrepreneurship: A Longitudinal Study." *Journal of Personality and Social Psychology*, 1965, *1*, 389-392.

McClelland, D. C. "Reply." *Quarterly Journal of Economics*, 1965, *79*, 242-245.

McClelland, D. C. "Toward a Theory of Motive Acquisition." *American Psychologist*, 1965, *20*, 321-333.

McClelland, D. C. "Wanted: A New Self-Image for Women." In R. J. Lifton (Ed.), *The Woman in America*. Boston: Houghton Mifflin, 1965.

1966

Kalin, R., Davis, W. N., and McClelland, D. C. "The Relationship Between Use of Alcohol and Thematic Content of Folktales in Primitive Societies." In P. J. Stone, D. C. Dunphy, M. S. Smith, and D. M. Ogilvie (Eds.), *The General Inquirer: A Computer Approach to Content Analysis.* Cambridge, Mass.: M.I.T. Press, 1966.

McClelland, D. C. "Does Education Accelerate Economic Growth?" *Economic Development and Cultural Change,* 1966, *14,* 257–278.

McClelland, D. C. "The Impulse to Modernization." In M. Weiner (Ed.), *Modernization.* New York: Basic Books, 1966.

McClelland, D. C. "Longitudinal Trends in the Relation of Thought to Action." *Journal of Consulting Psychology,* 1966, *30,* 479–483.

McClelland, D. C. "That Urge to Achieve." *Think,* Nov.-Dec., 1966, 19–23.

McClelland, D. C., Davis, W. N., Wanner, E., and Kalin, R. "A Cross-Cultural Study of Folktale Content and Drinking." *Sociometry,* 1966, *29,* 308–333.

1967

McClelland, D. C. Introduction and (with K. F. Butler and R. C. Birney) translation of *The Anatomy of Achievement and Motivation* by H. Heckhausen. New York: Academic Press, 1967.

McClelland, D. C. "Money as a Motivator: Some Research Insights." *The McKinsey Quarterly,* 1967, *4,* 10–21.

McClelland, D. C. "Motivation." In *Encyclopaedia Britannica.* Vol. 15. Chicago: William Benton, 1967.

1968

McClelland, D. C. "Can Motivation Be Taught?" *Read,* 1968, *18,* 1–4.

McClelland, D. C. "Measuring Behavioral Objectives in the 1970s." In *Technology and Innovation in Education.* New York: Praeger, 1968.

McClelland, D. C. "A Psychological Path to Rapid Economic Development." *Mawazo* [Uganda], 1968, *1*, 9–15.

McClelland, D. C. "The Role of an Achievement Orientation in the Transfer of Technology." In W. H. Gruber and D. G. Marquis (Eds.), *The Human Factor in the Transfer of Technology*. Cambridge, Mass.: M.I.T. Press, 1968.

McClelland, D. C., and Watt, N. F. "Sex-Role Alienation in Schizophrenia." *Journal of Abnormal Psychology*, 1968, *73*, 226–239.

1969

McClelland, D. C. "As I See It." *Forbes*, June 1, 1969, 53–57.

McClelland, D. C. "Black Capitalism: Making It Work." *Think*, July-Aug., 1969, 6–11.

McClelland, D. C. Review of *Reports on Achievement Motivation, Barpali, India* by T. M. Frazer, Jr. *American Anthropologist*, 1969, *71*, 333–334.

McClelland, D. C. "The Role of an Educational Technology in Developing Achievement Motivation." *Educational Technology*, 1969, *9*, 7–16.

McClelland, D. C., and Winter, D. G. *Motivating Economic Achievement*. New York: Free Press, 1969. (Also in Spanish translation.)

1970

McClelland, D. C. "Formation of the Need to Achieve." In W. A. Sadler, Jr. (Ed.), *Personality and Religion*. New York: Harper & Row, 1970.

McClelland, D. C. "On Introducing Social Change to Study It." *Et Al.*, 1970, *2*, 49–54.

McClelland, D. C. "The Two Faces of Power." *Journal of International Affairs*, 1970, *24*, 29–47.

Watt, N. F., Stolorow, R. D., Lubensky, A. W., and McClelland, D. C. "School Adjustment and Behavior of Children Hospitalized for Schizophrenia as Adults." *American Journal of Orthopsychiatry*, 1970, *40*, 637–657.

1971

McClelland, D. C. *Assessing Human Motivation.* Morristown, N.J.: General Learning Press, 1971.

McClelland, D. C. "Factors Contributing Towards Modernization and Socio-Economic Performance. IV: Entrepreneurship and Achievement Motivation." In P. Lengyel (Ed.), *Approaches to the Science of Socio-Economic Development.* Paris: UNESCO, 1971.

McClelland, D. C. "Motivational Indicators of Economic and Social Trends." *Wall Street Transcript,* December 20, 1971.

McClelland, D. C. *Motivational Trends in Society.* Morristown, N.J.: General Learning Press, 1971.

McClelland, D. C. "The Power of Positive Drinking." *Psychology Today,* 1971, *4* (8), 40–41, 78–79.

McClelland, D. C. "To Know Why Men Do What They Do." A conversation with David C. McClelland and T. George Harris. *Psychology Today,* 1971, *4* (8), 35–39, 70–71, 74–75.

1972

McClelland, D. C. "Achievement and Administrative Action in Developing Countries." In K. J. Rothwell (Ed.), *Administrative Issues in Developing Countries.* Lexington, Mass.: Heath, 1972.

McClelland, D. C. "Alcohol and Human Motivation: Drinking as a Response to Power Needs in Men." In *Proceedings of the 2nd Annual Alcoholism Conference.* Washington, D.C.: National Institute on Alcohol Abuse and Alcoholism, 1972.

McClelland, D. C. "Comment." In M. H. Appley (Ed.), *Adaptation-Level Theory.* New York: Academic Press, 1972.

McClelland, D. C. "Conversation: An Interview with David McClelland." *Organizational Dynamics,* 1972, *1*, 56–72.

McClelland, D. C. "I.Q. Tests and Assessing Competence." *The Humanist,* 1972, *32* (1), 9–12.

McClelland, D. C. "Opinions Predict Opinions: So What Else Is New?" *Journal of Consulting and Clinical Psychology,* 1972, *38*, 325–326.

McClelland, D. C. "Some Themes in the Culture of India." In A. R. Desai (Ed.), *Essays on Modernization of Underdeveloped Societies.* Vol. 2. New York: Humanities Press, 1972.

McClelland, D. C. "What Is the Effect of Achievement Motivation Training in the Schools?" *Teachers College Record*, 1972, *74*, 129–145.

McClelland, D. C., Davis, W. N., Kalin, R., and Wanner, E. *The Drinking Man: Alcohol and Human Motivation*. New York: Free Press, 1972.

McClelland, D. C., and Steele, R. S. *Motivation Workshops*. Morristown, N.J.: General Learning Press, 1972.

1973

McClelland, D. C. "Erziehung zur Tuchtigkeit" ["Education for Competence"]. In W. Edelstein and D. Hopf (Eds.), *Bedingungen des Bildungsprozesses* [*Conditions of the Educational Process*]. Stuttgart: Klett Verlag, 1973.

McClelland, D. C. "Testing for Competence Rather Than for 'Intelligence.'" *American Psychologist*, 1973, *28*, 1–14.

McClelland, D. C., and Watson, R. I., Jr. "Power Motivation and Risk-Taking Behavior." *Journal of Personality*, 1973, *41*, 121–139.

1974

McClelland, D. C., and Dailey, C. *Improving Officer Selection for the Foreign Service*. Boston: McBer, 1974.

1975

McClelland, D. C. "Love and Power, the Psychological Signals of War." *Psychology Today*, 1975, *8* (8), 44–48.

McClelland, D. C. *Power: The Inner Experience*. New York: Irvington, 1975. (Also in German translation.)

McClelland, D. C. Review of *The Psychology of Motivation* by A. Korman. *Contemporary Psychology*, 1975, *20*, 876.

McClelland, D. C., and Burnham, D. H. "Power-Driven Managers: Good Guys Make Bum Bosses." *Psychology Today*, 1975, *9* (7), 69–70.

McClelland, D. C., Rhinesmith, S., and Kristensen, R. "The Effects of Power Training on Community Action Agencies." *Journal of Applied Behavioral Science*, 1975, *11*, 92-115.

McClelland, D. C., and Teague, G. "Predicting Risk Preferences Among Power-Related Tasks." *Journal of Personality*, 1975, *43*, 266-285.

1976

McClelland, D. C. Review of *Becoming Modern* by A. Inkeles and D. H. Smith. *Economic Development and Cultural Change*, 1976, *25*, 159-166.

McClelland, D. C. "Sources of Stress in the Drive for Power." In G. Serban (Ed.), *Psychopathology of Human Adaptation*. New York: Plenum, 1976.

McClelland, D. C., and Burnham, D. H. "Power Is the Great Motivator." *Harvard Business Review*, 1976, *54*, 100-111.

1977

McClelland, D. C. "The Impact of Power Motivation Training on Alcoholics." *Journal of Studies on Alcohol*, 1977, *38*, 142-144.

McClelland, D. C. "Power Motivation and Impossible Dreams." *The Wharton Magazine* [University of Pennsylvania], Summer 1977.

McClelland, D. C. "The Psychological Causes and Consequences of Modernization: An Ethiopian Case Study." *Economic Development and Cultural Change*, 1977, *25*, Supplement.

Winter, D. G., Stewart, A. J., and McClelland, D. C. "Husband's Motives and Wife's Career Level." *Journal of Personality and Social Psychology*, 1977, *35*, 159-166.

1978

McClelland, D. C. "Entrepreneurship and Management in the Years Ahead." In C. A. Bramlette and M. H. Mescon (Eds.), *The Individual and the Future of Organizations*. Vol. 7. Atlanta: Georgia State College of Business Administration, 1978.

McClelland, D. C. "Managing Motivation to Expand Human Freedom." *American Psychologist*, 1978, *33*, 201-210.

McClelland, D. C., Constantian, C. A., Regalado, D., and Stone, C. "Making It to Maturity." *Psychology Today*, 1978, *12* (1), 42-43, 114.

Winter, D. G., and McClelland, D. C. "Thematic Analysis: An Empirically Derived Measure of the Effects of Liberal Arts Education." *Journal of Educational Psychology*, 1978, *70*, 8-16.

1979

McClelland, D. C. "Inhibited Power Motivation and High Blood Pressure in Men." *Journal of Abnormal Psychology*, 1979, *88*, 182-190.

McClelland, D. C. "Stadien in der Entwicklung des Machmotivs" ["Stages in the Development of the Power Motive"]. In L. Montada (Ed.), *Brennpunkte der Entwicklungspsychologie* [*Focal Points of Developmental Psychology*]. Stuttgart: Verlag Kohlhammer, 1979.

McClelland, D. C., Colman, C., Finn, K., and Winter, D. G. "Motivation and Maturity Patterns in Marital Success." *Social Behavior and Personality*, 1979, *6*, 163-171.

Miron, D., and McClelland, D. C. "The Impact of Achievement Motivation Training on Small Businesses." *California Management Review*, 1979, *21* (4), 13-28.

1980

McClelland, D. C. "Motive Dispositions: The Merits of Operant and Respondent Measures." In L. Wheeler (Ed.), *Review of Personality and Social Psychology*. Vol. 1. Beverly Hills, Calif.: Sage, 1980.

McClelland, D. C., and Boyatzis, R. E. "Opportunities for Counselors from the Competency Assessment Movement." *Personnel and Guidance Journal*, 1980, *58*, 368-372.

McClelland, D. C., Davidson, R. J., and Saron, C. "Effects of Personality and Semantic Content of Stimuli on Augmenting and Reducing in the Event-Related Potential." *Biological Psychology*, 1980, *11*, 249-255.

McClelland, D. C., Davidson, R. J., Saron, C., and Floor, E. "The

Need for Power, Brain Norepinephrine Turnover, and Learning." *Biological Psychology*, 1980, *10*, 93-102.

McClelland, D. C., Floor, E., Davidson, R. J., and Saron, C. "Stressed Power Motivation, Sympathetic Activation, Immune Function, and Illness." *Journal of Human Stress*, 1980, *6* (2), 11-19.

McClelland, D. C., and Jemmott, J. B. III. "Power Motivation, Stress, and Physical Illness." *Journal of Human Stress*, 1980, *6* (4), 6-15.

1981

McClelland, D. C. "Child-Rearing vs. Ideology and Social Structure as Factors in Personality Development." In R. H. Munroe, R. L. Munroe, and B. B. Whiting (Eds.), *Handbook of Cross-Cultural Development*. New York: Garland STPM Press, 1981.

McClelland, D. C. "Is Personality Consistent?" In A. I. Rubin, J. Aronoff, A. M. Barclay, and R. A. Zucker (Eds.), *Further Explorations in Personality*. New York: Wiley, 1981.

Winter, D. G., McClelland, D. C., and Stewart, A. J. *A New Case for the Liberal Arts: Assessing Institutional Goals and Student Development*. San Francisco: Jossey-Bass, 1981.

Works in Press

McClelland, D. C. "Comment on Lord Vaizey's Paper." In H. Giersch (Ed.), *Proceedings of a Conference on "Toward Explaining Economic Growth."* Kiel, Germany: Institute of World Economics, in press.

McClelland, D. C. (Ed.). *How Character Develops*. Vol. 1: *The Development of Social Maturity*. Vol. 2: *Education for Values*. New York: Irvington, in press.

McClelland, D. C. *Motives in Thought, Action, and Adaptive Functioning: Selected Papers*. New York: Praeger, in press.

McClelland, D. C. "What Behavioral Scientists Have Learned About How Children Acquire Values." In D. C. McClelland (Ed.), *The Development of Social Maturity*. New York: Irvington, in press.

McClelland, D. C. "What Can We Do About Developing Character?" In D. C. McClelland (Ed.), *Education for Values*. New York: Irvington, in press.

McClelland, D. C., Alexander, C., and Marks, E. "The Need for Power, Stress, Immune Function, and Illnesses among Male Prisoners." *Journal of Abnormal Psychology*, in press.

McClelland, D. C., and Boyatzis, R. E. "The Leadership Motive Pattern and Long-Term Success in Management." *Journal of Applied Psychology*, in press.

McClelland, D. C., Constantian, C., Pilon, D., and Stone, C. "Effects of Child-Rearing Practices on Adult Maturity." In D. C. McClelland (Ed.), *The Development of Social Maturity*. New York: Irvington, in press.

McClelland, D. C., and Pilon, D. "Sources of Adult Motives in Patterns of Parent Behavior in Early Childhood." *Journal of Personality and Social Psychology*, in press.

Works in Preparation

Johnson, E. W., and McClelland, D. C. *Learning to Achieve: The Basic Basic*. (Three workbooks.) To be published by Scott, Foresman.

McClelland, D. C. *The Nature of Human Motivation*. To be published by Scott, Foresman.

Name Index

Subject Index

A

Achievement motivation: affiliation motivation related to, 22–23, 193; age effects on, 105; analyzed, 99–132; arousal conditions for, 175–185; and background, 114, 119; and behavior, 114, 117; behavioral correlates of, 185–189; cohort effects on, 109–110; and competency, 231–232; correlates of, 113–120; cross situational stability of, 308–309; decision theory of, 9; determinants of, 23–24; and economic development, 42, 52, 55–56; and education, 106–107; and field dependence, 188–189; as future-oriented, 106, 116, 129; and hierarchy of motives, 24; and housewife role, 115; and internalization of norms, 117, 120; and leisure, 114, 117; and marriage, 114, 116–117, 118; in men, 103–104, 105, 114–115, 118, 178, 179, 180, 182, 183, 185, 186, 188, 189; modification of, 274–318; and parenthood, 114, 116, 117, 118; peak of, 8; power motive distinct from, 100–101, 106, 108, 129; and presidential candidates, 245, 246, 249–250, 251, 255–256, 257–259, 260, 261, 265, 266, 267, 268; and pretest-posttest design, 179–180; research needed on, 206–207; and risk taking, 186–187; and school achievement, 188; as self-evaluation system, 283–284; sex differences in, 172–218; social conse-